GEORGE
ORWELL

A Literary and Biographical Study by

JOHN ATKINS

FREDERICK UNGAR PUBLISHING CO.

NEW YORK

New printing, 1965

Contents

Chapter I

Decency the Foundation

THE COMMON element in all George Orwell's writing was a sense of decency. Decency itself is one of the vaguest terms in the English language yet most of us have little hesitation in recognising 'decent' behaviour. It is behaviour which takes into account the feelings and personality of the other person. Although decency still exists it is felt to be a rather old-fashioned virtue and English people are prone to think they have perhaps more than their fair share of it. This is not so insular as it sounds because the special connotation of this English word is a complex of English living and English attitudes. I want to make this clear at the outset because the love of England was especially strong in Orwell and his vision of the true England tended to be a society that was on the point of disappearance— or at most, that was struggling to maintain itself against alien and hostile forces. Orwell's uniqueness lay in his having the mind of an intellectual and the feelings of a common man. In the conflict between intellect and sentiment the latter usually won. This is very rare in the present era though probably more common in Great Britain than in any other advanced country. In Orwell the conflict usually took the shape of realising that our civilisation is based on intellect but perceiving that intellect unrefined by sentiment (or decency) may well destroy the culture based on it and eventually itself. He waged a running battle with other intellectuals on this score alone. Towards the end the menace became an obsession and his last book, *1984*, was based on a sense of defeat. The intellectuals would not revert to a sense of decency.

Stephen Spender called Orwell 'an Innocent, a kind of English Candide of the twentieth century. The Innocent is ordinary because he accepts the value of ordinary human decency; he is not a mystic, nor a poet. Ordinary and yet extraordinary, because his faith in qualities of truth and decency drives like a drill through the facade of his generation. He is a drill made of steel driving through ordinary things. He happens to believe that two and two make four; and that what happens, happens. The consequences of *really* believing this are shattering. Christ was brought up as a carpenter in a carpenter's shop.' (Revaluation of *Homage to Catalonia* in *World Review*, June 1950.)

The world Orwell foresaw was one where two and two would make whatever its ruler desired it to make. It was the world of *1984*, the world of power-driven intellect triumphant. But he did not see himself in the role of Innocent, or Fool as he once called it. The Fool was a Chestertonian figure who really held out no hope for the world of decency. While he was making his runes and chanting his mystical prophecies the net would be closing in on him and he would be powerless to resist it. The innocent eye, however admirable, was not sufficient. It needed reinforcement from the cleansed intellect, the intellect purged of base motives which it prided itself on having jettisoned in an evil past.

Put in another way, the modern intellect has succumbed to a craving for power (it has discovered how easy it is to control the physical environment and, to a lesser extent, the human environment) while the sense of decency wants freedom above all things. The situation is made complex because both freedom and power employ the same weapons to achieve their ends. Orwell noticed that power-wanters could often and easily persuade others that they were really seeking freedom. But there was one medium in which they were quite incapable of blinding those with eyes to see, and that was in literary expression. A friend of Orwell, Paul Potts, claimed that the clarity of Orwell's literary style was the direct result of his genuine search for freedom. A man can hide many things but he cannot manipulate his literary style (or probably any other style) except in a blatantly artificial way.

'Orwell is not primarily an artist, which makes it all the more strange that he uses language so magnificently. His own explanation would be that the ability to think creatively contains within it the ability to express these thoughts clearly. That the end conditions the means, that if one really is concerned with freedom rather than with power, the language one uses to express that concern will bear some relationship to that which is being discussed. It is noticeable that those whose hunger for power drives them to use language, write in a manner reminiscent of a machine gun in action.' ('George Orwell', *London Forum*. 1949.)

Although I wish to reserve a consideration of Orwell's style to a later chapter, it is worth noting here that Orwell considered that the best writers, in the pure sense of style, among his contemporaries were for the most part reactionary in political tendency. There were not the new-style power-wanters, whether fascist, communist, pacifist or Marxian socialist, but those who harped back nostalgically to a past of inequality but also of relative decency in human relations. Briefly, your style will find you out, and if you believe in murder as a political weapon you will write like a concentration camp commandant. (If the reference to pacifists above is felt to be out of place, please understand that Orwell was extremely dubious about their actual motives as opposed to their apparent ones.)

Orwell's heart was in his own past and particularly in the literature of his past. His models were the novelists and story-tellers and popular ballad-writers of his boyhood. He felt that in their works, even in those of the imperialist Kipling, there was a human warmth that was lacking in most of the publications that followed the first World War. In the essays he wrote for *Tribune* under the general title 'As I Please', some of which were reprinted in the volume *Shooting an Elephant*, he constantly referred to half-forgotten books and songs, all of which contained the element of 'cosiness' that the modern world lacks so completely. (Chesterton once wrote that 'cosiness' was the true mark of English society.) There were many things wrong with that society—gross inequality contrasted with some of the grossest vulgarity that wealth has ever displayed in any epoch—but there was a gentleness that mitigated even the worst oppression. (These were the days when a distant people could become genuinely horrified by atrocities in Bulgaria.) In songs like 'Riding Down From Bangor' and books like *Helen's Babies* Orwell detected 'a sort of sweet innocence', a state in which people were slightly shocked at behaviour which is commonplace today and which forms the starting-point for literary situations rather than their culmination. We may

laugh at our 'narrow-minded' ancestors but the corollary is
that we suffer continually from our own immense tolerance.
Writing of nineteenth-century America Orwell said '. . . it
is hard not to feel that it was a better kind of society than that
which arose from the sudden industrialisation of the later part
of the century. The people in *Helen's Babies* or *Little Women* may
be mildly ridiculous but they are uncorrupted. They have
something that is perhaps best described as integrity, or good
morale, founded partly on an unthinking piety.' And the twin
modern nightmares were absent, whatever other ones existed.
'Nineteenth-century America was a rich, empty country which
lay outside the main stream of world events, and in which the
twin nightmares that beset nearly every modern man, the
nightmare of unemployment and the nightmare of State
interference, had hardly come into being.' ('Riding Down From
Bangor.') This fascination that the past held for Orwell sometimes found the most unexpected expression as when he deplored the declining quality of English murder! He had little
patience with the new style, the Cleft Chin and Bristol Bank
Manager affairs. They compared badly with 'the old domestic
poisoning dramas, product of a stable society where the all-
prevailing hypocrisy did at least ensure that crimes as serious
as murder should have strong emotions behind them'. ('Decline
of the English Murder.') The decency of the recent, remembered
past, the past of his own boyhood, even pervaded the under-
world with its charm.

It is very easy to get a false impression of Orwell from his
books. His literary personality often seemed to be divided from
his daily-routine personality by a wide gap. Reading his books
it was easy to imagine a man riddled with bitterness, one to
whom the virtues of everyday life were anathema. All those
who knew him discovered that this was a completely false
picture. When he wrote he was possessed. As a writer he
seemed to be driven by forces which were normally inhibited.
The soured and pessimistic man who speaks to us in the pages
of *The Road to Wigan Pier* and *1984* was actually sociable and
home-loving. He once surprised his friend Richard Rees by
saying, 'I hope you love your family!' He believed that every
normally healthy man should love his family, as he remembered

them doing before the first War. It was the constant pressure which modern conditions exerted against the possibility of this love that angered him. He was not angry because he liked being angry. He was angry because there was something to be angry about.

Orwell often said that the subject of most books could be summed up in a single word. This was particularly true of his own books. His craving for the old decency found its best expression in the novel *Coming Up For Air*. Decency is the key-word, though it should be qualified as remembered decency. It is the tale of a man who has a little spare money and decides to revisit the scenes of his boyhood. He asks himself why he wants to go back. 'I didn't mean to do anything. That was part of the point. I wanted peace and quiet. Peace! We had it once, in Lower Binfield. I've told you something about our old life there, before the war. I'm not pretending it was perfect. I dare say it was a dull, sluggish, vegetable kind of life.' But it was a world where you weren't continually scared of the future.

At first sight this is a very unpromising starting point for a modern writer. Some people are frightened of 'modern' literature because it seems to revel in the wretchedness of our own time. The popular writer usually avoids it, but the writers who are praised in high-class reviews insist on rubbing our noses in the dirt and sometimes seem to imply that it is good for us. Orwell also rubbed our noses in the dirt but he did not regard it as a healthy occupation. It was a kind of therapy. It is this quality that distinguished him from the popular writers on the one hand and the more conventional intellectuals on the other. It was never far from his mind that in the not very distant past serious writers actually regarded the simple human virtues of decent behaviour, tender feeling, sentiment and family love as being admirable. It is the basis of his excellent appreciation of Dickens (*Critical Essays*). 'His whole message is one that at first glance looks like an enormous platitude: If men would behave decently the world would be decent.' And again, 'All he can finally say is, "Behave decently", which, as I suggested earlier, is not necessarily so shallow as it sounds.' Left-wing political philosophers argued that no one could behave decently if they were not treated decently by their

environment. Orwell's reply was that one's environment
ultimately consists of other people, so that the whole question
is reduced to a matter of decent behaviour by everyone concerned. This used to infuriate his antagonists. Orwell never
pretended that this was a political or social programme. He
was not naive. But it was a fundamental principle that he
clung to. What he was really getting at was not that we must
expect a change of heart from those who already control us
but that unless the reformers and revolutionaries behave as
decently as they consider others ought their reforms and
revolutions will bring no improvement. This was something new
in Left-wing thought—at least, during his adult lifetime.

   1984 is the story of a society in which decency had been
destroyed. The terrifying thing is that this society had been
established by men who claimed that they were the champions
of the oppressed. Because they thought decency did not matter
they created a worse oppression than the world had ever known
before. Decency is based on respect for the other person, and
respect derives from love—not sexual passion, of course, but
the quieter passion, or conviction, that all men are brothers and
that unless we keep this in mind we will slip into a belief that
all men are enemies, with the inevitable results. Winston and
Julia believe that love has become increasingly difficult in a
society where all loyalty is owed to the State, but that it is not
yet impossible. They talk about their love affair and the like-
lihood of its being discovered and subjected to the fiercest
strains. One day they will take hold of us, says Winston, and we
will be powerless.

   'The one thing that matters is that we shouldn't betray one
another, although even that can't make the slightest difference.'
   'If you mean confessing', she said, 'we shall do that, right
enough. Everybody always confesses. You can't help it. They
torture you.'
   'I don't mean confessing. Confession is not betrayal. What you
say or do doesn't matter: only feelings matter. If they could
make me stop loving you—that would be the real betrayal.'
   She thought it over. 'They can't do that', she said finally.
'It's the one thing they can't do. They can make you say anything—*anything*—but they can't make you believe it. They can't
get inside you.'
   'No', he said a little more hopefully, 'no; that's quite true.

They can't get inside you. If you can *feel* that staying human is worth while, even when it can't have any result whatever, you've beaten them.'

The really horrifying thing is that they did get inside and they did destroy the love Julia and Winston felt for each other. They believed that only feelings mattered, so their new masters proceeded to destroy and cauterise their feelings.

Most of us feel at some time or other that it is monstrous that a servant should sacrifice his chances of a full life, including marriage, to the whims and enjoyment of his master. This is a familiar situation in some of the old novels, including those of Dickens. Sam Weller puts Mr Pickwick's interests before his own and those of the young 'ooman who was waiting to marry him. So far as Sam was concerned, she might never stop waiting. This is not an attractive type of loyalty. We feel it is not necessary that one person's fulfilment should be based on another's thwarting. Orwell certainly shared this view. 'Such loyalty, of course', he writes, 'is natural, human and likeable; but so was feudalism.' The loyalty is lovable if mistaken. The important thing is that it existed. The aim should be to give it a nobler outlet. But in the coming society it will have disappeared altogether. There is something poetic about such loyalty and the new society will declare war on poetry. The old-fashioned loyalty, based on love and respect, was unpredictable. The new loyalty must be scientific, completely manageable and directable. And Orwell takes the opportunity to contrast the old hated feudalism ('feudal' and 'mediaeval' are nearly always terms of reproach in modern literature) with the much more detestable totalitarianism that is coming. The irony is that most of us do not see the implications of the new society. It may be an evil dream of Orwell's but it is a dream evolved out of reality. The violence and brutality of the modern mass State is not a mere aberration. It is based on the destruction of sentiment that we see going on all around us.

Tubby Bowling in *Coming Up For Air* feels vaguely what is happening. It would be too much to say he understands. He simply knows that the old cosiness, the decency, warmth and friendliness of life have slowly been draining away. Why is it, he wonders, that we know what we like and refuse to go after

it? Why is it that the happiest days of our lives are spent in
rambling round the country, fishing, just looking at things,
pleasant things like flowers and trees, and yet we hardly ever
trouble to do it? Instead of which we are preparing for war,
rushing madly between home, office and restaurant, eating
disgusting food and getting worked up about things that don't
even interest us. Many people have presumably lost the old
glow that comes from feeling fully alive, but Bowling hadn't.

'Here's that feeling that I get inside me—not often, I admit,
but now and again. I know it's a good feeling to have. What's
more, so does everybody else, or nearly everybody. It's just round
the corner all the time, and we all know it's there. Stop firing that
machine-gun! Stop chasing whatever you're chasing! Calm
down, get your breath back, let a bit of peace seep into your
bones. No use. We won't do it. Just keep on with the same bloody
fooleries.'

And in the course of his worrying at this question he makes a
great discovery, although it is certain he never understood how
important it was. It was simply that most of the decent people
have stopped minds. A friend of his, Porteous, a retired schoolmaster, was one of them. He would never deliberately harm
anyone. He was the last person in the world who would want
to go around smashing people in the face simply because they
had a minor disagreement. But at the same time Porteous and
millions like him took no interest at all in what was happening
around them. It never entered their heads that the new men
who hated the old decency were determined to destroy it.
When they were compelled to notice the acts of the Hitlers and
the Stalins they usually dismissed them as fleeting phenomena.
'They can't defend themselves against what's coming to them,
because they can't see it, even when it's under their noses.'
They were as helpless as the North American Indians in the
face of the new challenge. They bathed in their decent feelings
and had forgotten or never learnt how to think.

The systematic destruction of decency was happening everywhere. Orwell returned to this theme in his essay on Boys'
Weeklies (*Critical Essays*). The old boys' papers of his childhood
were ridiculous and often snobbish but they were not depraved.
They had their villains but they were either gentlemen or
ineffectual hooligans. Their evil was mild and restrained and

always had a recognisable motive. There was no destructive lust. The moral code of these papers, Orwell said, was a decent one. Crime and dishonesty were never held up to admiration. But compare this with the influences, that were coming from across the Atlantic, the moral code that was being inculcated by the New World:

'The huge sale of the Yank mags in England shows that there is a demand for that kind of thing, but very few English writers seem able to produce it. When hatred of Hitler became a major emotion in America it was interesting to see how promptly "anti-Fascism" was adapted to pornographic purposes by the editors of the Yank mags. One magazine which I have in front of me is given up to a long complete story, "When Hell Came to America", in which the agents of a "blood-maddened European dictator" are trying to conquer the U.S.A. with death-rays and invisible areoplanes. There is the frankest appeal to sadism, scenes in which the Nazis tie bombs to women's backs and fling them off heights to watch them blown to pieces in mid-air, others in which they tie naked girls together by their hair and prod them with knives to make them dance, etc., etc. The editor comments solemnly on all this, and uses it as a plea for tightening up restrictions against immigrants. On another page of the same paper: "LIVES OF THE HOTCHA CHORUS GIRLS. Reveals all the intimate secrets and fascinating pastimes of the famous Broadway Hotcha girls. NOTHING IS OMITTED. Price 10c." "HOW TO LOVE. 10c." "FRENCH PHOTO RING. 25c." "NAUGHTY NUDIES TRANSFERS. From the outside of the glass you see a beautiful girl, innocently dressed. Turn it around and look through the glass and oh! what a difference! Set of 3 transfers 25c.", etc., etc., etc. There is nothing at all like this in any English paper likely to be read by boys. But the process of Americanisation is going on all the same. The American ideal, the "he-man", the "tough guy", the gorilla who puts everything right by socking everybody else on the jaw, now figures in probably a majority of boys' papers.'

The intrusion of sadism into modern literature is one of the things that distinguishes it most sharply from the literature of the recent past which Orwell had enjoyed so much. The popularity of the sex-crime thriller is recent and the taste for it is acquired at an early age. Moreover, this taste can be indulged in the service of apparently admirable causes. The atrocity-monger is on the whole a modern phenomenon. There is reference to atrocities galore in Gibbon and in Motley, but they are not gloated over. The first genuinely popular outcry in Britain against atrocities occurred at the time of the Bulgarian Massacres in 1875. They led to diplomatic and political action and naval demonstrations. Since then we have been liberally fed with atrocities, the first peak being reached in the first World War. The literary result was the emergence of a type of writer who did little else than collect and publish accounts of mass murders, rapes, brutality and violence of every kind. These accounts were always intended to rouse the nation, but the propagandist section was often half-hearted compared with the passion of the descriptive section. If the authors really wished to combat terror they were to be commended. But in too many cases we were given the impression that they merely enjoyed the psychological impact of sadistic horrors. While one part of the population acquired a taste for this kind of literature quite divorced from the intention of political or social action, another part recoiled in disgust and assumed that all the reports were untrue or grossly exaggerated. This Orwell was always careful not to do. But he was deeply impressed by the coexistence of atrocity-mongering on a large scale and the obvious decay of decency to which I have referred. He expressed his feelings on this point in an essay in the *New English Weekly* called 'The Lure of Atrocity' (23 June, 1938):

'There is no doubt that atrocities happen, though when a war is over it is generally impossible to establish more than a few isolated cases. In the first few weeks of war, especially in a civil war, there are bound to be massacres of non-combatants, arson, looting and probably raping. If these things happen it is right that they should be recorded and denounced, but I am not so sure about the motives of people who are so enthralled by the subject that they will compile whole books of atrocity-stories. They usually tell you that they are trying to stir up hatred "against Fascism" or "against Communism". But you notice that they seldom hate these things sufficiently to fight against them themselves; I believe no soldier has ever compiled a book of atrocity-stories. One is left with the suspicion that some of the atrocity-mongers rather like writing about rapes and summary executions.'

This accelerating harshness in human behaviour, the atrophy of the sense of pity, is the mark of the society which we feel to be peculiarly modern. Orwell was a socialist and a socialist must look to the future. The modern societies which seemed to give an indication of what the future might be like,

U.S.A., U.S.S.R. and Nazi Germany, were not very promising. These societies seemed to have made a disastrous mistake. Each claimed that it sought the welfare of its people but in each of them the quality of life was being debased. Nineteenth-century America and Edwardian England were unjust societies, yet Orwell knew from literature in the one case and personal experience in the other that people in those days lived under much less strain than they do today, when so much is supposedly being done to make conditions easier. But he found that it was not necessary to return to the past to find the social decency that meant so much to him. *Homage to Catalonia* is full of references to the unsuspicious friendliness of the Spanish people. He had never found it easy to make friends. Within a day or two of his arrival a score of militiamen were calling him by his first name and overwhelming him with hospitality. They were mostly Catalans and it was impossible not to be struck by their 'essential decency', their straightforwardness and generosity. Spanish generosity was at times embarrassing. If you asked a Spaniard for a cigarette he would force the whole packet on you. There is probably an element of romanticism in this (Orwell did at times tend to romanticise the people he liked) and there is normally an intensification of sociability during the early stages of a war in which the people believe. But however much this might detract from the accuracy of Orwell's observations, he himself was again impressed by the simple decency of people in a comparatively backward society. It is true, they were fighting for socialism but they had not attained it. Their lives had been conditioned by a capitalist, in some ways a feudal, society. So once again Orwell was faced with the question that nearly everyone else appeared to have missed: modern capitalism is bad and must be replaced by a juster society; but how can we ensure that the best qualities of the old society will be retained while destroying the worst? Any society is a delicately articulated organism and it is easier to destroy the whole of it than to change it selectively.

These Spaniards reinforced his belief in human decency. Orwell had seen through the Soviet tyranny earlier than most other Left-wing writers and for a time he was rather like a man who doesn't know in which direction to take the next step.

Spain gave him no political answer, but it did convince him
that his instinctive trust in the decency of human individuals
was more valid than a mere faith in political panacea. Various
little incidents occurred in Spain which did not belong to the
new world that was being hammered out of the ruins of the
old one. When Orwell's P.O.U.M. friends were being arrested
and imprisoned and he himself was in danger of apprehension
by the Communist police, he discovered that the latter still
retained their traditional decency under the harsh Ogpu-like
exterior. After moments of the utmost fear and tension on
Orwell's part, the officer to whom he had just confessed his
P.O.U.M. sympathies (technically, his criminality) stepped
across and shook hands with him. 'I do not know if I can bring
home to you how deeply that action touched me. It sounds a
small thing, but it was not. You have got to realise what was
the feeling of the time—the horrible atmosphere of suspicion
and hatred, the lies and rumours circulating everywhere, the
posters screaming from the hoardings that I and everyone like
me was a Fascist spy.' A few nights earlier the police had
searched his wife's room. They did it with typical totalitarian
efficiency. They sounded the walls, took up the mats, examined
the floor, felt the curtains, probed under the bath and the
radiator, emptied every drawer and suitcase, felt every gar-
ment and held it up to the light. But they never searched the
bed! Orwell's wife was lying in it at the time and, as he says,
there might have been half a dozen sub-machine-guns under
the mattress and a library of Totskyist documents under the
pillow. 'One must remember that the police were almost
entirely under Communist control, and these men were
probably Communist Party members themselves. But they
were also Spaniards, and to turn a woman out of bed was a
little too much for them.'

Orwell's general approach to Socialism should now be
fairly apparent. He was indeed what used to be called an
'English socialist' as opposed to the continental Marxist type.
He was in the tradition of Owen and William Morris. At first
sight it may not seem surprising that an Englishman should
be an 'English Socialist', yet the type is almost extinct today.
The continental criticism of this brand of Socialism is that it is

Utopian, it is based on mere aspirations and a faulty appreciation of history, economics and psychology. Orwell was one of
the few prominent Socialists of our time who stuck to this
conception of Socialism and threw the accusation back,
claiming that it was the Marxists and the scientific socialists
who were at fault because all their ideas were based on a view
of humanity which was quite unreal. One of the finest things
about people, he said in effect, is their capacity for loyalty and
sympathy towards each other. The new scientific socialist was
keenly interested in loyalty (it is the key to power) but he
wished it canalised in the service of the State. First of all he had
to *invent* the State (the State as a 'living organism' with a life
of its own scarcely existed before this century) and then he
found it necessary to change the people. Orwell stuck to the
simple and positive conception of Socialism based on general
ideas of brotherhood, fair play and honest dealing, and he
distrusted the involved metaphysics of Marxist thought. He
did not forget that Socialism once aimed at human happiness,
nor did he confuse the means once considered necessary to this
end (higher production, more consumer goods, international
prestige and power) with the final aim. He did not believe in
deliberately destroying a relatively happy society simply
because it was not organised in a particular way. [1]

This view of Socialist method is expressed in an article,
'Authentic Socialism', which appeared in the *New English
Weekly* (16 June, 1938). He is referring to the constant betrayal
of the working class by its leaders:

'It would seem that what you get over and over again is a
movement of the proletariat which is promptly canalised and
betrayed by astute people at the top, and then the growth of a
new governing class. The one thing that never arrives is equality.
The mass of the people never get the chance to bring their innate
decency into the control of affairs, so that one is almost driven to
the cynical thought that men are only decent when they are
powerless.'

Every large-scale modern Left-wing movement has forsaken
the ideal of equality, or at least the leaders have, though they

[1] Orwell's own sense of responsibility towards other people, including his readers,
is expressed in *Homage to Catalonia* when he apologises to those who had written
to him and had not received an answer. His papers had been confiscated by the
police, and they included many letters about his previous books.

may pay it lip-service for other reasons. Orwell, like Shaw, continued to believe that equality was the core of Socialism. The difference between him and Shaw was that he believed in this ideal passionately whereas it is very doubtful if Shaw did. There was for Orwell a close connection between equality and decency and he did not see how either could flourish in a society without the other.

Decent relationships are only possible among those who feel they are essentially equal. Decency is immediately destroyed by snobbery or any form of servility. It was possible in the past and to a lesser extent in the present in those parts of society where a general equality exists. For instance, Orwell always found friendliness and tolerance among the mass of working-class people providing you treated them as equals. Once you let it be known that you regarded them as an inferior kind of animal you invited their ill-feeling, and the possibility of a decent relationship no longer existed. But during the last century society has become much more complex. The old simple division into aristocrats, townsmen and countrymen, all living their own communal lives in comparative isolation, has disappeared. Modern capitalist society is characterised by a complicated class-structure, each division of which has its own totems and tabus. But these groups do not form geographical entities. They are dissipated into small units which accounts for the appalling loneliness of so many people today. They are people who cannot come to terms with their neighbours because they belong to a different sub-group. They feel a compulsion to behave in a rather artificial way to others, according to their position in the scale. What Orwell understands by decency is obviously impossible under such circumstances. That is why decency is more likely to be found still existing in rather old-fashioned areas, such as isolated villages or squalid urban areas which no one wants to live in or even visit.

The people who suffer most are the dispossessed, particularly those whose aesthetic senses have been trained to the extent where they begin to loathe their environment. There is a vast mass of people today who have been educated to admire and to want exactly those things which it is becoming increasingly difficult to obtain—beautiful houses, solitude, dignity, time to meditate. Sooner or later they become convinced that a decent life is no longer possible. The world has been conquered by advertising and noise. These are the people who look for 'escape' and hardly ever find it:

'Modern mechanised life becomes dreary if you let it. The awful thraldom of money is upon everyone and there are only three immediately obvious escapes. One is religion, another is unending work, the third is the kind of sluttish antinomianism—lying in bed till four in the afternoon, drinking Pernod—that Mr Connolly seems to admire. The third is certainly the worst, but in any case the essential evil is to think in terms of *escape*. The fact to which we have got to cling, as to a lifebelt, is that it is possible to be a normal decent person and yet to be fully alive. Mr Connolly seems to suggest that there are only two alternatives: lie in bed till four in the afternoon, drinking Pernod, or you will infallibly surrender to the Gods of Success and become a London social-cum-literary backstairs-crawler. The orthodox Christian tries to pitchfork you with a very similar dilemma. But both dilemmas are false and unnecessarily depressing.' (Review of *The Rock Pool*, *New English Weekly*, 23 July, 1936.)

These victims certainly feel the lack of decency in modern life, yet they cannot face a return to a simpler society. They believe it would be unutterably boring. Hence they grudgingly accept the change of quality inherent in the new tendencies and pin their hopes on some form of personal escape.

The politicians objected that decency is not and cannot be a foundation for a political programme, any more than free love or *esprit de corps*. But this was a mechanical method of thought that seemed dangerous to Orwell. Every political programme needed a structure and he himself was not fitted to supply it. (He was not happy with political detail.) But no structure could be raised without a principle and it was the lack of principle in modern political thought that appalled him. In the case of India, for instance, in which he was especially interested, it was usual to find Indians considering only what would be best for India and Englishmen only what would be best for England. To him it seemed obvious that a solution that did not benefit both sides was no solution at all. In 'Letter To An Indian' (*Tribune*, 19 March, 1943) he wrote:

'You and I both know that there can be no real solution of the Indian problem which does not also benefit Britain. Either we all

live in a decent world, or nobody does. It is obvious, is it not, that
the British worker as well as the Indian peasant stands to gain by
the ending of capitalist exploitation, and that Indian independence
is a lost cause if the Fascist nations are allowed to dominate the
world.'[1]

His criterion of every political act was not to ask whether it
would increase production or give one class advantage as
against another but whether it would make life a little easier
for all the people concerned. His outlook was co-operative, not
competitive. In this he remained true to his Socialist faith while
the majority of people who called themselves Socialists were
viewing political action in a competitive spirit, pitting one
regime against another, even a Socialist regime against another
Socialist regime. Their belief in co-operation only extended
to their own political friends. What happened when an intellectual threw decency overboard was demonstrated by the career
of Shaw. Writing of Thomas Mann, Orwell said: 'One has only
to compare his remarks on Hitler and Mussonlini with, say,
those of Bernard Shaw to see that respect for common decency
is not a bad guide, even in international politics'. ('The Faith
of Thomas Mann', *Tribune*, 10 September, 1943.)

Writers like Shaw, he felt, had made a mockery of Socialism.
They had accepted the structure and utterly forgotten the
spirit. It was futile to expect an inanimate political structure to
retain the spirit which originally inspired its authors. Politics
are conducted and society is controlled by men and there cannot
be a good society organised by evil men. All through his
writing runs this vein, asserting that decency between man and
man is the first essential of any political system. 'Either power
politics must yield to common decency, or the world must go
spiralling down into a nightmare of which we can already catch
some dim glimpses.'('Gandhi in Mayfair', *Horizon*, September,
1943.) And a few years later the nightmare materialised in his
own mind in the shape of *1984*, a world from which decency
had been ruthlessly and deliberately burnt out.

Orwell connected the decay of decency with the decay of
religion. To any Marxist this was, of course, heresy. Religion

[1] But elsewhere he said the British worker benefited from the exploitation of
India.

was such a bogey with them (except when it temporarily provided tactical advantages) that they regarded its destruction
as the *sine qua non* of social improvement. Orwell saw much
further into the situation left by the decay of religion. Whatever
abuses had been sheltered under the wing of the churches,
religion had provided men with a necessary code. Men must
live according to some view of the universe and themselves, and
religion provided it and along with it a morality. Orwell did
not join in the demand for a religious survival. He knew that
such revivals did not spring from demands made in newspapers.
He did not even think such a revival was desirable because it
would be like the warming up of a corpse. For the majority of
men religion had already died. There were millions who went
through the ancient ceremonies and called themselves Christians, but to most of them a real religious experience was
unknown. It had become impossible to believe the old religious
dogmas, although men still pretended to believe them out of
habit. The danger of the situation lay not in losing religion but
in putting something worse in its place, a glorification of much
too imperfect Man. In the same way decency had been thrown
on one side and personal loyalties had been replaced by the
one-way loyalty of man to State. There is certainly no obvious
connection between churchgoing and Orwell's conception of
decency, but there is a close one between it and Christian doctrine. But the important point was that the old Christian
society, although horribly cruel and unjust, had been a reasonably decent one. The new atheistic society had dismissed decency
and gave every sign of being much more cruel.

Modern man is in the position of having cut away his soul
and living for twenty years without noticing it. In his view
religious belief had become a lie, simply an attempt to persuade
the poor to accept their lot. After sawing off the branch in which
he sat man fell, not into a bed of roses but into a cesspool full
of barbed wire. Not only did he find himself fatherless but also
very uncomfortable. Once again it was impossible to deny the
fact that he lived in a transition period. What was uncertain
was whether the transition would be made successfully. It was
not even true to say that God was being abolished; it was His
nature that was being changed. Orwell felt that men had made

up their minds about this nature, that the whole quality of our
lives hung upon it:

> 'Brotherhood implies a common father. Therefore it is often
> argued that men can never develop the sense of a community
> unless they believe in God. The answer is that in a half-conscious
> way most of them have developed it already. Man is not an
> individual, he is only a cell in an everlasting body, and he is
> dimly aware of it. There is no other way of explaining why it is
> that men will die in battle. It is nonsense to say that they only do
> it because they are driven. If whole armies had to be coerced, no
> war could ever be fought. Men die in battle—not gladly, of course,
> but at any rate voluntarily—because of abstractions called
> "honour", "duty", "patriotism" and so forth.' (Notes on the
> Way', *Time and Tide*, 6 April, 1940.)

It was a common theme in Orwell's work, that the strongest
force in man's life was not economic or sexual or anything
physical or material at all, but loyalty. In the past men had
regarded themselves as creatures loyal to God, with the
subsidiary loyalty of each man to other men, because they were
all equal lieges in a theological sense. Orwell was prepared to
throw aside the mystical apparatus of religion but it would be
unwise, even impossible, to attempt to strangle the loyalty.
The next step, he felt, requiring only a slight increase of
consciousness, would lead to the extension of this loyalty to
humanity itself. Only in that way could ordinary decent feeling
be safeguarded. At the moment we are moving towards something worse than the Spanish Inquisition, where the total
loyalties of men are dissipated into minor loyalties towards
national and class groups. Unless we reinstate the belief in
human brotherhood, which was always part of the most
enlightened Christian doctrine no matter how frequently it
was denied in practice, the future is black. He even said that
those who believe they have found true Christianity in Soviet
Russia have at least made a step in the right direction by
perceiving that the Kingdom of Heaven must be found on
earth. But their exclusiveness is mistaken.

Orwell insisted, however, despite an occasional relapse into
popular theology, that the great change would be a political
act. It is untrue to say he was obsessed with politics. He realised
very keenly that in the mid-twentieth century the whole of

life has become a political concern. The days when government merely administered justice and collected custom duties are irretrievably past. If we are to work out a better theology for ourselves we will find that it is inextricably mixed with a political policy, that theology and politics, and indeed economics and psychology and anthropology, have merged into one super-science. And the new policy must be Socialist, and Socialism is primarily a fight for justice and liberty. All other considerations are secondary. If a superficially Socialist act, let us say nationalisation of a particular industry, reduces justice and liberty, then it is not truly Socialist. Men will have lost sight of the aim behind a tangle of means. Hence he frequently gave warnings against the false Socialists, the men and women who are not concerned with justice and liberty at all but only with some private little panacea, whether it be the dictatorship of the proletariat or vegetarianism or strength through joy. The main necessity was to hold fast to the true meaning of Socialism and not to be led astray. 'To recoil from Socialism because so many individual Socialists are inferior people is as absurd as refusing to travel by train because you like the ticket-collector's face.' (*The Road To Wigan Pier.*) In the same book he makes a very interesting confession which demonstrates better than anything else he wrote his distrust in the mere mechanics of social development. When he returned from Burma he had no interest in Socialism or in any other economic theory. 'It seemed to me then—it sometimes seems to me now, for that matter—that economic injustice will stop the moment we want it to stop, and no sooner, and if we genuinely want it to stop the method adopted hardly matters.' This is purely and simply an appeal for decency in our political conduct. At times Orwell's thought becomes dangerously nebulous.

It follows from this that the main obstacle to social improvement is not the existence of a small group of rapacious and ruthless power-holders but the indifference of people everywhere. He might have said that by their decency they could move mountains. When the mass of the people decide that they will no longer treat others as enemies but as brothers nothing will stop them. But lack of decency in most cases (not counting the officials of totalitarian parties who have a vested interest in injustice) lies not so much in positive brutality as in a too easy readiness to turn the blind eye to abuses. Recalling the days when pregnant women hauled tubs of coal in the mines, crawling on hands and knees, he remarks that if more efficient methods had not been invented we should still allow this rather than go without coal. Most of these unpleasant things, including the conditions in labour camps and the atrocities of war, are invisible. It requires a simple stop of the imagination to dismiss them entirely from the consciousness. 'Most of the time, of course, we should prefer to forget that they were doing it. It is so with all types of manual work; it keeps us alive, and we are oblivious of its existence. More than anyone else, perhaps, the miner can stand as the type of the manual worker, not only because his work is so exaggeratedly awful, but also because it is so vitally necessary and yet so remote from our experience, so invisible, as it were, that we are capable of forgetting it as we forget the blood in our veins.' (*The Road To Wigan Pier.*)

Such indifference is becoming a marked feature of our lives. It is a loss of decency and only the return or strengthening of decency can turn the tide. There is no mechanical reform that can make people more aware of other people's sufferings or reinforce the emotions of pity and disgust. In a review 'Utmost Edge' (*Observer*, 27 February, 1944) Orwell pursued the subject in political terms:

'In the chaos in which we are living, even the prudential reasons for common decency are being forgotten. Politics, internal or international, are probably no more immoral than they have always been, but what is new is the growing acquiescence of ordinary people in the doctrines of expediency, the callousness of public opinion in the face of the most atrocious crimes and sufferings, and the black-out memory which allows blood-stained murderers to turn into public benefactors overnight if "military necessity" demands it.'

Our political life is riddled with this concept of expediency. No measure is examined according to its moral quality but only as an answer to the question: Will it work? The name given to this type of approach is realism. A realist policy is normally applauded because the public has already accepted realism as the most effective basis for political activity. It implies ruthlessness, the absence of sentimentality, and a high degree of self-seeking. It might perhaps be regarded as a reaction from nineteenth-century hypocrisy, when every imperialist shouldered the White Man's Burden and the poor were kept poor for their own good. But Orwell points out that hypocrisy does at least suggest a moral code, one which the politician would like the public to believe he subscribes to, even if he doesn't. But by the time of the Spanish War Realism had driven such unproductive embarrassments from the field. This was the time when Tory M.P.s cheered the news that British ships had been bombed by Italian areoplanes and when members of the House of Lords lent themselves to organised libel campaigns against the Basque children who had been brought to England as refugees. Realism permits you to change your friends just when it sui+, you. Just as the Tories turned against their old Fascist friends, so the Left easily came to an accommodation with their old Communist enemies.

> 'There has been the same tendency to excuse almost anything "because they're on our side". It is all very well to talk about Lady Chamberlain photographed shaking hands with Mussolini; the photograph of Stalin shaking hands with Ribbentrop is much more recent. On the whole, the intellectuals on the Left defended the Russo-German pact. It was "realistic", like Chamberlain's appeasement policy, and with similar consequences. If there's a way out of the moral pig-sty we are living in, the first step towards it is probably to grasp that "realism" does *not* pay, and that to sell out your friends and sit rubbing your hands while they are destroyed is *not* the last word in political wisdom.' ('Who Are The War Criminals?', *Tribune*, 22 October, 1943.)

To hail decency as a basis for a political policy is unexceptionable but also extremely unhelpful. A programme still has to be constructed and as soon as you dive into the welter of political detail it is frequently very doubtful to know exactly what would be the decent line to follow. But when Orwell puts his finger on the brand of realist behaviour that characterises all modern politics, whether of the Left or of the Right, he is performing a valuable service. It was impossible for him to believe that dishonesty could ever bring satisfactory results. The acceptance of dishonesty by modern politicians as a valid weapon has been passed on to the lower ranks in political life, such as the propagandists. They have justified the popular belief that propaganda means the telling of lies, even if respectable truths are available. But propagandists can be extremely plausible and you have to be alert to detect their dishonesty especially when it lies in the approach or a method of argument rather than in the perversion of facts—which can be checked if you can get access to them. In a fierce attack on Lionel Fielden's *Beggar My Neighbour* Orwell compared the average political propagandist unfavourably with the advertising man:

> 'If you compare commercial advertising with political propaganda, one thing that strikes you is its relative intellectual honesty. The advertiser at least knows what he is aiming at—that is, money—whereas the propagandist, when he is not a lifeless hack, is often a neurotic working off some private grudge and actually desirous of the exact opposite of the thing he advocates.' ('Gandhi in Mayfair', *Horizon*, September, 1943.)

Orwell accuses Fielden of not believing in what he is writing— in other words adopting the role of 'expediency' for reasons known only to himself. He very neatly turned the tables on Feilding by re-writing a shrill anti-European passage by a supposed Indian as a shrill anti-Indian passage by a supposed European. The effect of Fielden's passage was to insult Europeans in general, although he was writing for an English audience. Orwell's point was that Fielden did not believe in what he had written but was incapable of realising that propaganda based on dishonesty was worthless. I have no desire to inculpate Mr Fielden and Orwell himself states that this behaviour is normal in modern propagandist methods. He refers to an Indian nationalist whom he heard addressing a small meeting, at which some American correspondents were present, on the failure of the Cripps Mission:

> 'Within about ten minutes the Indian had converted all of them into ardent supporters of the British Government, because instead of sticking to this subject he launched into an anti-British tirade quite obviously founded on spite and inferiority complex. This is just the mistake that a toothpaste advertiser would not make. But then the toothpaste advertiser is trying to sell toothpaste and not to get his own back on that Blimp who turned him out of a first-class carriage fifteen years ago.'

To summarise briefly, then, Orwell held that the insecurity of the modern world is due as much to the decline in morality or decency, his favourite word, as to any other single cause. The quality of life was affected by this decline in practically every sphere, but it was most noticeable in the attitude to suffering, in the acceptance of realism in politics and of dishonesty in propaganda. These strands acted upon each other and emphasised the trend—governments could switch policy more easily because propagandists were at hand to justify it, they could oppress minorities because the mass of the people were indifferent to others, ordinary people could overlook injustice because they had been taught that it was the inevitable result of realism and therefore necessary—and so on. And Orwell came to the unfashionable conclusion that the first descent down the slippery slope occurred when Christianity virtually lost its grip on ordinary people. Although they were still told that certain things were right or wrong, they were not told it by people whom they really respected. The political leaders, who had built up tremendous prestige for themselves during the last century, quite certainly contradicted in action, if not in word, most of what they had been taught. But another effect of the Christian collapse was that no one any longer had a rational reason for believing that he would persist in a life after death—and rational reasons were the ones that counted for most in this new era. The result of this readjustment of belief about men's expectation was not altogether unexpected. If there was no longer a future life on which to pin one's hopes then men would be all the more anxious to find fulfilment in this. But unless they were carefully guided their search could easily develop into a free-for-all in which every other man's advantage would be your own disadvantage. The new world was preparing for the new religion of power, and the religion of power amounted to a sacred egoism. Men would, it is true, unite for certain purposes but the criterion of action became increasingly personal advantage. There was no scope for decent attitudes here:

'There is little doubt that the modern cult of power-worship is bound up with the modern man's feeling that life here and now is the only life there is. If death ends everything, it becomes much harder to believe that you can be in the right even if you are defeated. Statesmen, nations, theories, causes are judged almost inevitably by the test of material success. Supposing that one can separate the two phenomena, I would say that the decay of the belief in personal immortality has been as important as the rise of machine civilisation. Machine civilisation has terrible possibilities, as you probably reflected the other night when the ack-ack guns started up: but the other thing has terrible possibilities too, and it cannot be said that the Socialist movement has given much thought to them.

'I do not want the belief in life after death to return, and in any case it is not likely to return. What I do point out is that its disappearance has left a big hole, and that we ought to take notice of that fact. Reared for thousands of years on the notion that the individual survives, man has got to make a considerable psychological effort to get used to the notion that the individual perishes. He is not likely to salvage civilisation unless he can evolve a system of good and evil which is independent of heaven and hell. Marxism indeed does supply this, but it has never really been popularised. Most Socialists are content to point out that once Socialism has been established we shall be happier in a material sense, and to assume that all problems lapse when one's belly is full. But the truth is the opposite: when one's belly is empty, one's only problem is an empty belly. It is when we have got away from the drudgery and exploitation that we shall start wondering about man's destiny and the reason for his existence. One cannot have any worthwhile picture of the future unless one realises how much we have lost by the decay of Christianity.' ('As I Please', *Tribune*, 3 March, 1944.)

It is a fruitless task to try and decide whether the mean level of morality is higher or lower now than at some other time in the past. It is possible to have an idea, however, about the probable impact of modern social organisation on the individual's morality. A majority of commentators have agreed that capitalism places a premium on immoral behaviour, particularly in that part of life devoted to earning a living. Capitalist philosophy states openly that the weakest should go to the wall and that native powers should be reinforced by native cunning. It is one thing to believe this theoretically and quite another to know it from experience. Orwell's own contact with the world of labour relations came relatively late in life— during school and his career as a police officer in Burma he had been sheltered from this sector. He first discovered how one's personal morality could be dictated by an impersonal social structure when he worked in Paris as a *plongeur*, i.e., a dishwasher in the hotels. For a time he tried to put his own public school code of ethics into operation, but he found there was no scope for them at all when you were no longer sheltered from the consequences. It was useless behaving decently either to fellow-workers or employers. They would take your job or snatch your money if you gave them half a chance and no one would sympathise with you or think you anything but a fool for giving them the opportunity. His friend Boris was shocked by his naivety and told him it was ridiculous for a *plongeur* to indulge a sense of honour. Orwell was compelled to conclude that Boris was right. It was very pleasant to entertain notions of decent behaviour and fair play, but if you belonged to the submerged section of society it would in all probability lead to starvation. Each man was for himself and you could not even console yourself with the thought of a celestial after-life. Later, he said, he realised how foolish he had been to have any scruples. It was not that his fellow *plongeurs* were essentially depraved, but that they were given no option by their employers. The big hotels were quite merciless towards their employees. They engaged or discharged men as the work demanded, and they always sacked ten per cent or more of their staff when the season was over. Nor did they have any difficulty in replacing a man who left at short notice, for Paris was full of unemployed hotel employees. When he left Paris and lived in England for a while as a tramp he found the same attitude towards right and wrong. They scarcely existed. In their place was the yardstick of expediency. Excluded by respectable society, these men would do anything that might bring them even a petty personal advantage, providing it could be done with impunity. The fact that they did not, that their behaviour was even characterised by an odious humility, was entirely the product of fear. And this fear was bred of hunger. A few sound meals might have transformed them into criminals. Even in Spain, which still retained much of its old feudal quality, the advent of modernism in the form of mechanical warfare, was breaking down the old standards. Despite the generosity and the friendliness, everyone stole. Even at the front the men stole from each other, but the hospital assistants were the worst. They thought nothing of taking wrist-watches from the stretcher-cases. It should be remembered that the prevalence of war in modern times and its spread into every corner of civilian life have helped in the degeneracy of conducted noted by Orwell.

Orwell's peculiar honesty is expressed strongly in his attitude towards religion. He had no faith himself (and was perhaps too prone to believe that no one else had one either) and he was certainly not a churchgoer. But he realised that the great modern complex that has been responsible for the decline in moral standards was religious as much as it was social and political. It was impossible to isolate completely the various strands—commercial predatoriness, political power-lust, Darwinian natural selection, Marxist determinism and the loss of religious faith. They were all part of the same monster, and however much he might hate a particular institution or idea or philosophy he realised that a positive, even a positive evil, is preferable to a vacuum. The culmination of his novel, *A Clergyman's Daughter*, comes when Dorothy realises she has lost her faith. But her innate wisdom told her that it was better to go on living as though her faith still existed, so that there would still be a framework to her life to act as a lifebelt. She would continue to go to church and participate in the ritual in which she no longer believed, because the alternative was to lose her moorings. The church had trained her to behave in a particular way which she felt reasonably good, and the church must continue to help her to conduct herself in the same way:

'She perceived that in all that happens in church, however absurd and cowardly its supposed purpose may be, there is something—it is hard to define, but something of decency, of spiritual comeliness—that is not easily found in the world outside. It seemed to her that even though you no longer believe, it is better to go to church than not; better to follow in the ancient ways than to drift in rootless freedom.'

Part of Orwell's uniqueness as a modern Socialist commentator lies in his insistence on the necessity of a religious attitude, although he himself cannot seriously be thought of as a religious man. He was a highly moral man but not a religious one. Christian socialists are legion, it is true, but religious Socialists whose religion is agnosticism or even atheism are nearly as rare as Orwell. He returned to the charge again and again, tending more and more to equate the quality of decency with a

religious attitude or at least to claim that it was scarcely likely to exist without a religious attitude. Material progress, which had seemed and in fact had been so essential, had been revealed as a ghastly failure *by itself*. It needed something else to soften it and to guide it.

'The essential problem remains. Material progress, which is necessary if the average human being is to be anything better than a drudge, has only been achieved at a fearful price. Somehow the religious attitude of life must be restored, and yet the only body of doctrine available to the Western world is one which the great mass of people are obviously less and less willing to accept.' ('A Muffled Voice', *Observer*, 10 June, 1945.)

But there was a conflict in Orwell's mind, a conflict not so much about what was to be done as the order in which it should be tackled. There does not seem to be any cogent reason why two reforms should not be broached simultaneously, but we have become slaves to the idea of priority, deciding which of two or more measures is the most urgent. Almost from the beginning of his literary career Orwell was convinced that the first task was the abolition of poverty. You could not expect an improvement in the quality of life if the majority of people were compelled to exist in a servile condition. But later the religious query became more and more insistent in his mind, the realisation that man cannot live by bread alone and that some kind of psychological readjustment was essential. In his later years he was increasingly concerned with this problem and with its relation to the first need which he still regarded as absolutely essential:

'As long as supernatural beliefs persist, men can be exploited by cunning priests and oligarchs, and the technical progress which is the prerequisite of a just society cannot be achieved. On the other hand, when men stop worshipping God they promptly start worshipping Man, with disastrous results. The humanist has to decide whether what is needed is re-education and a "change of heart", or whether the indispensable first step is the abolition of poverty.' ('So Runs the World', *Observer*, 22 July, 1945.)

The thing that had probably altered Orwell's emphasis on these matters was the obvious fact that the totalitarian systems had abolished poverty but that their societies were even further from the desired Kingdom of Heaven or Utopia than the inefficient and maladjusted ones of an earlier epoch.

In the above extract it will be noted that Orwell believed that the worship of God had been replaced by the worship of Man. This is true today but there was an intervening stage where the Money God held sway. With the decline of the true religious impulse in the nineteenth century, leaving religious institutions with hardened arteries behind, the search for wealth became the abiding passion. This phase had already passed and today Power rather than Money is the object. Emphasis on Power as the chief social good implies the worship of Man and his attributes. Money, although a constituent of Power, symbolises pleasure. We are passing from the era of hedonism into that of naked power. Wealth is far less important today than privilege. Ambitious men are not concerned with their bank accounts, as were their Victorian forebears, but with the influence they can wield in the right quarters. In fact, a very wealthy man is becoming an anachronism and he is enthusiastically reduced to nonentity by supertaxation. But this is a comparatively recent development and at first Orwell did not notice what was happening. That is why one of his earliest books, *Keep The Aspidistra Flying*, is a long dissertation on money and its supremacy in society, whereas his last book, *1984*, is a dissertation on power. In the first book money is mentioned on nearly every page. In the later one I doubt if it is mentioned more than a couple of times. Orwell was really looking for the single factor that really made a decent life impossible in modern times. His first guess was that money had been elevated into a god and had destroyed the older and truer religion:

> 'What he realised, and more clearly as time went on, was that money-worship had been elevated into a religion. Perhaps it is the only real religion—the only really *felt* religion—that is left to us. Money is what God used to be. Good and evil have no meaning any longer except failure and success.'

And by this route we return to the *plongeur*.

It was at this stage in his thought that Orwell detected a ray of hope for the world. It was simply that he was convinced that the English people had rejected power-worship and that he believed they had a good chance of resisting the pressures making for acceptance.[1] The most promising thing about the

1 In *1984* it is clear that he had given up this hope.

contemporary situation was the failure of totalitarian doctrine to take any root at all in England. He regarded England as an island of resistance against the horrible new European and Asiatic ideologies. The old decency still existed in England and it had been strong enough to reject the ideas that had captured the imagination of young people especially in so many other countries. They were repelled by Mosley's imitative castor-oil technique and although they accepted Hollywood's sock-on-the-jaw ethos they did not assimilate it. The dullness, stolidity and lack of imagination in English life had helped to keep these manifestations of the modern spirit out. Orwell, who was by instinct an extremely patriotic man (another way in which he differed from nearly every other modern Socialist), believed that England still had to play her most important role as a civilising influence:

> 'The power-worship which is the new religion of Europe, and which has affected the English intelligentsia, has never touched the common people. They have never caught up with power politics. The "realism" which is preached in Japanese and Italian newspapers would horrify them. One can learn a good deal about the spirit of England from the comic coloured postcards that you see in the windows of cheap stationers' shops. These things are a sort of diary upon which the English people have unconsciously recorded themselves. Their old-fashioned outlook, their graded snobberies, their mixture of bawdiness and hypocrisy, their extreme gentleness, their deeply moral attitude to life, are all mirrored there.' (*The Lion and the Unicorn.*)

Here we have a catalogue of what Orwell considered the English virtues. I shall refer to them again in detail when I deal with his patriotism, but at this stage it is worth regarding them as an outline of decency, or what Orwell understood by decency. I am not pretending that bawdiness, for instance, is an element of decency but it may be the obverse of something that is quite incompatible with decency—let us say brutality.

The essence of modern power is brutality. Orwell loathed brutality, especially the unnecessary brutality which has become an instrument of government, and he left the Burma Police partly because he could no longer stomach the duties he was expected to undertake. It was the gentleness of English life and English people in their native environment that appealed to him. In Burma he was compelled to do things that nearly every Englishman at home would shrink from. It was in the nature of imperialism that this should be so, not because British imperialism was unnaturally cruel. He stated several times that it was not, that it was certainly much more humane than any totalitarian rule. But it was an impossible situation for a sensitive man to be in, taking part in the administration of imperial government. In the essay 'A Hanging' (*Shooting an Elephant*) he describes how revolted he was by one of his routine duties. He was oppressed by the feeling that the whole thing was a mere ceremony, serving no real purpose: a man's life was being taken in the spirit of cold bureaucracy. Although the warders and police were accustomed to this task they could not hide their discomfort and probably never would, even if they hung a man daily for years on end. The atmosphere was strained, everyone began to behave rather unnaturally, and sighed with relief when it was all over. Then came the reaction and Francis, the head jailer, told of cases where the doctor had to pull the prisoner's legs before he would die.

'We went through the big double gates of the prison into the road. "Pulling at his legs!" exclaimed a Burmese magistrate suddenly, and burst into a loud chuckling. We all began laughing again. At that moment Francis' anecdote seemed extraordinarily funny. We all had a drink together, native and European alike, quite amicably. The dead man was a hundred yards away.'

I mention this little anecdote here to show why Orwell felt he had to get out. By contemporary standards this was not a brutal incident. The assault was on the nerves rather than the flesh. But it was indecent. If you carried on until finally you accepted this sort of thing, or at least pretended to yourself (not to others, you always do that) that you accepted it, your humanity would be gone. And in societies where power is the main goal it becomes quite natural to accept such things. At most they may be regarded as regrettable but always necessary.

Chapter II

An Anatomy

WE KNOW a considerable amount about Orwell's life from his own writings, certainly the minimum necessary to throw light on his social, political and literary ideas. Many of his books are directly autobiographical and most of his novels draw heavily on his personal experiences. When he died he left a request that no biography of him should be written and out of deference to this I shall only include in these pages facts taken from his own work and work about him already published by his friends. Very occasionally I shall augment this with a personal judgment gained from my own acquaintance. It is only decent to honour Orwell's desires in this matter. He used to say that truthful biography was impossible because every life, viewed from the inside, would be a series of defeats too disgraceful and humiliating to contemplate. We can get some idea of what he meant by reading his own account of his schooldays. *Such, Such Were the Joys*, and by considering the fact that so much of his life was spent in seeking out defeat. Even if sought it was nonetheless painful.

He was born at Motihari in 1903. His father was an official in the Opium Department of the Indian Civil Service. Both his parents were Scottish and he had two sisters. When Orwell was only a few years old his father retired on a small pension. He says he never had any doubt that he was going to be a writer:

'From a very early age, perhaps the age of five or six, I knew that when I grew up I should be a writer. Between the ages of about seventeen and twenty-four I tried to abandon this idea, but I did so with the consciousness that I was outraging my true nature and that sooner or later I should have to settle down and write books.

'I was the middle child of three, but there was a gap of five years on either side, and I barely saw my father before I was eight. For this and other reasons I was somewhat lonely and I soon

31

developed disagreeable mannerisms which made me unpopular throughout my schooldays. I had the lonely child's habit of making up stories and holding conversation with imaginary persons, and I think from the very start my literary ambitions were mixed up with the feeling of being isolated and undervalued. I knew that I had a facility with words and a power of facing unpleasant facts, and I felt that this created a sort of private world in which I could get my own back for my failure in everyday life.' ('Why I Write', *Gangrel.*)

The volume of his serious writings in his childhood was not more than half a dozen pages. He wrote his first poem at the age of four or five, his mother taking it down to his dictation. At eleven, when war broke out (he was at boarding school by then), he wrote a patriotic poem which was printed in a local newspaper, followed by another, two years later, on the death of Kitchener. There were also a few nature poems in the Georgian style and two attempts at short stories (which he called 'ghastly failures'). This early work was signed Eric Blair, his real name.

All through his childhood he composed a continuous 'story' about himself:

'As a very small child I used to imagine that I was, say, Robin Hood and picture myself as the hero of thrilling adventures, but quite soon my "story" ceased to be narcissistic in a crude way and became more and more a mere description of what I was doing and the things I saw. For minutes at a time this kind of thing would be running through my head: "He pushed the door open and entered the room. A yellow beam of sunlight, filtering through the muslin curtains, slanted on to the table, where a matchbox, half-open, lay beside the inkpot. With his right hand in his pocket he moved across to the window. Down in the street a tortoiseshell cat was chasing a dead leaf, etc., etc." This habit continued until I was about twenty-five, right through my non-literary years. Although I had to search, and did search, for the right words, I seemed under a kind of compulsion from outside. The "story" must, I suppose, have reflected the styles of the various writers I admired at different ages, but so far as I remember it always had the same meticulous descriptive quality.' ('Why I Write.')

This passage is of especial interest because it shows at what an unusually early age Orwell adopted the habit of a professional writer, the man who consciously tries to make his words as meaningful and significant as possible. He says he discovered the joy of mere words at about the age of sixteen, a reversal, I imagine, of the usual order of experience. As an adult writer Orwell was chiefly remarkable for his lucidity, not for his poetic quality. The latter strain urged him to write enormous naturalistic novels. *Burmese Days* is the nearest he came to this in his published work.

In 1911, when he was eight years old, he was sent to a prep. boarding school on the South Coast and remained there until he was twelve. He has left a fairly full account of this phase in his autobiographical sketch *Such, Such Were the Joys*. His experiences at this school marked him for life and he never escaped their influence. The title is a wry one. There were few joys in his schooldays and he left with what can only be called a deliberately inculcated sense of failure. He went very largely in fear of the headmaster's wife, whom the boys called Bingo. Every boy in the school, he said, hated and feared her, but the top layer of their feelings towards her was a 'sort of guilt-stricken loyalty'. She was frankly capricious. An act which might lead to a caning one day would be laughed off as a boyish prank the next, or even commended because it showed you had guts. The aim of every boy was to be 'in good favour' with Bingo. The discipline of the school was in her hands far more than in those of Sim, her husband and headmaster. The pernicious thing about this school was that it was a snob school, where the sons of wealthy or titled parents received much better treatment than the others. Orwell's pronounced views on the English class system were largely formed from his experiences there. Bingo used her power unashamedly. She established a code of conduct which the boys were too inexperienced to question and ruled them with a kind of Olympian innuendo which affected them far more deeply than any physical system of reward or punishment could have done.

'I am anxious to make it clear that I was not a rebel, except by force of circumstances. I accepted the codes that I found in exist-ence. Once, towards the end of my time, I even sneaked to Brown about a suspected case of homosexuality. I did not know very well what homosexuality was, but I knew that it happened and was bad, and that this was one of the contexts in which it was proper to sneak. Brown told me I was a good fellow, which made me feel horribly ashamed. Before Bingo one seemed as helpless as a snake before a snake-charmer. She had a hardly-varying vocabulary of praise and abuse, a whole series of set phrases, each of which promptly called forth the appropriate response. There was "*Buck* up, old chap!", which inspired one to paroxysms of energy; there was "Don't *be* such a fool!" (or, "It's pathetic, isn't it?"), which made one feel a born idiot; and there was "It isn't very straight of you, is it?", which always brought one to the brink of tears. And yet all the while, at the middle of one's heart, there seemed to stand an incorruptible inner self who knew that whatever one did—whether one laughed or snivelled or went into frenzies of gratitude for small favours—one's only true feeling was hatred.'

A major result of Orwell's education was that he became convinced that it was not possible for him to be good. It was quite natural for him to assume that the rich and titled boys could be good because they were always in Bingo's favour. But being in favour did not depend on volition or intention. Soon after he arrived at Crossgates (as he calls the school) he began wetting his bed. He did not want to wet the bed, but he did and was caned for it. He imprudently told some other boys that it did not hurt and, being overheard by Bingo, was hauled back for another caning. This time Sim broke the riding crop which he used for flagellation. This made everything much worse because undoubtedly it had been broken by Orwell's bottom. The point was that he had sinned and he had no control over his sin. Sin was something that happened to you. After another wetting and another caning the trouble stopped. Perhaps the remedy worked, but only at the price of convincing young Orwell that morality was something you could not control.

Sim had two ambitions. One was to catch titled boys and the other was to win scholarships at public schools, particularly Eton. Orwell was allowed to attend at reduced fees because he was considered 'bright'. He was an investment and he was never allowed to forget it. There were two levels of treatment, depending on the income and background of the boy.

'Sim always gave these boys their titles when mentioning them to a third person, and for their first few days he actually addressed them to their faces as "Lord So-and-So". Needless to say he found ways of drawing attention to them when any visitor was being shown round the school. Once, I remember, the little fair-haired boy had a choking fit at dinner, and a stream of snot ran out of his nose onto his plate in a way horrible to see. Any lesser person would have been called a dirty little beast and ordered out of the room instantly: but Sim and Bingo laughed it off in a "boys will be boys" spirit.

'All the very rich boys were more or less undisguisedly favoured. The school still had a faint suggestion of the Victorian "private academy" with its "parlour boarders", and when I later read about that kind of school in Thackeray I immediately saw the resemblance. The rich boys had milk and biscuits in the middle of the morning, they were given riding lessons once or twice a week, Bingo mothered them and called them by their Christian names, and above all they were never caned. Apart from the South Americans, whose parents were safely distant, I doubt whether Sim ever caned any boy whose father's income was much above £2000 a year.'

The poor boys, of whom Orwell was one, were the sons of clergymen, Indian civil servants and struggling widows. They were discouraged from taking 'extras' and Orwell was never allowed to buy his own cricket bat because 'your parents wouldn't be able to afford it'. This phrase, he said, followed him all through his school days. They brought pocket-money back with them from their holidays and it was handed in for safe keeping. They were never allowed to buy expensive toys, such as model aeroplanes, even when sufficient money stood to their credit. 'Do you think that's the sort of thing a boy like you should buy?' Bingo would ask. She was once heard to say in front of the whole school, 'You know you're not going to grow up with money, don't you? Your people aren't rich. You must learn to be sensible. Don't get above yourself!' Sim's favourite reproach to poor boys was that they would probably end up as 'little office boys at forty pounds a year'. Pocket-money was graded. Millionaires had sixpence a week, the average was threepence, and Orwell and a few others were reduced to two-pence. His parents had given no instruction to this effect, it was merely a way of keeping him 'in his place'. The worst cruelty concerned the birthday cake. It was customary for each boy, on his birthday, to have a large iced cake which was shared out at tea between the whole school. Orwell's parents would willingly have paid for this but it never appeared. Year after year he waited for it to come, never daring to ask.

He says his popularity was not increased by the non-appearance of the cake. To the other boys it seemed to be a case of petty swindling. Orwell suffered not only from the malice of Bingo but from the unthinking censure of the boys, who are traditionally incapable of understanding such situations. When he wrote *Keep the Aspidistra Flying* he gave Gordon Comstock a school background similar to his own.

'They soon found out his poverty, of course, and gave him hell because of it. Probably the greatest cruelty one can inflict on a child is to send it to a school among children richer than itself. A child conscious of poverty will suffer snobbish agonies such as a grown-up person can scarcely even imagine.'

Bingo would never let up. The poor boys were lazy because they were poor (it is well known that poverty is the direct result of laziness) and they had to be stimulated by constant reference to their shameful backgrounds. 'I don't think it's awfully decent of you to behave like this, is it?' she would say. 'Do you think it's quite playing the game by your mother and father to go on idling your time away, week after week, month after month? Do you *want* to throw all your chances away? You know your people aren't rich, don't you? You know they can't afford to send you to a public school if you don't win a scholarship? I know how proud your mother is of you. Do you *want* to let her down?' Sim would make his usual remark about becoming a little office-boy at forty pounds a year. Hot tears would well up. Bingo would carry on remorselessly. 'And do you think it's quite fair to *us*, the way you're behaving? After all we've done for you? You do know what we've done for you, don't you? ... We don't *want* to have to send you away, you know, but we can't keep a boy here just to eat up our food, term after term.' This was a joke, for the boys were half-starved. Sim once came back from a visit to Eton in 'snobbish ecstasies' about the luxury in which the boys lived. (His eldest son was there.) At Eton the boys had fried fish for supper!

The poor boys had to win their scholarships or they were so much waste fodder. Some of them Sim flogged systematically towards the goal. Orwell had no illusions about this method. It worked. Rather than be flogged you will learn Latin verbs. You will never be educated by this method, but you will pass exams. The boys themselves believed in it. One boy Orwell refers to

had no brains to speak of and therefore needed a scholarship
with the utmost urgency, because he had no money as a substitute for intelligence. He went to Uppingham to sit the scholarship, did badly, returned and was flogged. His comment was,
'I wish I'd had that caning before I went up for the exam.' Sim
made no effort to educate, only to cram. The teaching of history
was more like initiation into a mystery cult. Questions were
rapped out, replies flew back. Who plundered the Begums?
Who was beheaded in an open boat? Who caught the Whigs
bathing and ran away with their clothes? Or dates: 1587?
Massacre of St Bartholomew. 1707? Death of Aurangzeb.
Bingo 'took' the higher forms in history and revelled in this
form of instruction.

But bad as this was, it was the snobbery and the use to which
it was put that appalled Orwell most in retrospect. An intelligent person can rise above mal-education but snobbery marks
a person for life, whether he is snob or snubbed. Looking back,
Orwell was amazed to realise how intimately and intelligently
snobbish the boys were, how swift to detect small differences in
accent, manners and cut of clothes. At the beginning and end of
term talks tended to centre around certain magic phrases, 'my
uncle's yacht', 'our place in the country', 'my pony', 'my pater's
touring car'.

'There never was, I suppose, in the history of the world a time
when the sheer vulgar fatness of wealth, without any kind of
aristocratic elegance to redeem it, was so obtrusive as in those
years before 1914. It was the age when crazy millionaires in
curly top hats and lavender waistcoats gave champagne parties
in rococo houseboats on the Thames, the age of diabolo and hobble
skirts, the age of the "knut" in his grey bowler and cutaway coat,
the age of *The Merry Widow*, Saki's novels, *Peter Pan* and *Where the
Rainbow Ends*, the age when people talked about chocs and cigs
and ripping and topping and heavenly, when they went for divvy
weekends at Brighton and had scrumptious teas at the Troc.
From the whole decade before 1914, there seems to breathe forth
a smell of the more vulgar, un-grown-up kinds of luxury, a smell
of brilliantine and creme de menthe and soft-centred chocolates—
an atmosphere, as it were, of eating everlasting strawberry ices
on green lawns to the tune of the Eton Boating Song. The extraordinary thing was the way in which everyone took it for granted
that this oozing, bulging wealth of the English upper and upper-
middle classes would last forever, and was part of the order of

things. After 1918 it was never quite the same again. Snobbishness and expensive habits came back, certainly, but they were self-conscious and on the defensive. Before the war the worship of money was entirely unreflecting and untroubled by any pang of conscience. The goodness of money was as unmistakable as the goodness of health or beauty, and a glittering car, a title or a horde of servants was mixed up in people's minds with the idea of actual moral virtue.'

During term time circumstances enforced a rough kind of democracy, but this began to dissipate as the holidays drew near. Swank became the order of the day. There was a Scottish cult, encouraged by Bingo, who claimed Scottish ancestry and encouraged the Scottish boys to wear kilts. The Scots were admirable because they were grim and dour and irresistible on the field of battle. The real reason for this cult was that only the very rich could enjoy a holiday in Scotland in the approved style. Orwell should, of course, have been among the favoured but he was the wrong kind of Scot, a Poor Scot with a status something like that of a Poor White in South Africa. The privileged made the best use of this situation. Orwell recounts a typical piece of conversation from a boy who is going to Scotland for the 'hols'. 'My pater's giving me a new gun for the twelfth. There's jolly good black game where we go. Get out, Smith! What are you listening for? You've never been in Scotland. I bet you don't know what a blackcock looks like.'

The effect of all this was to turn Orwell against anything to do with Scotland for the rest of his life. Normally a rational man, he encountered a childhood prejudice here which he never overcame. His later work contains many references to his dislike of Scotland and the Scots. For example:

'I confess quite freely to a prejudice against books about Scotland and particularly about the Highland, Celtic, romantic side of Scottish life.' ('History Books', *New Statesman*, 21 September, 1940.)

'The British Empire is simply a device for giving trade monopolies to the English—or rather to gangs of Jews and Scotchmen.' (*Burmese Days*.)

On the 'Scotchification' of England: 'Gordon, Colin, Malcolm, Donald—these are the gifts of Scotland to the world, along with golf, whisky, porridge and the works of Barrie and Stevenson.' (*Keep the Aspidistra Flying*.)

If any boy was suspected of not being sufficiently wealthy he was subjected to a barrage of questions which never failed to draw out the truth in the long run. How much a year has your pater got? What part of London do you live in? How many servants do your people keep? Orwell writes of a little new boy, scarcely more than eight, trying desperately to lie himself into the right group and inevitably failing because he didn't realise that his father's supposed Daimler should have electric lights, not acetylene. And of course, in such an environment the young Orwell's sense of being worthless and no good could only be strengthened. There were qualities besides money, it is true. There were strength, beauty, charm, athleticism and something called 'guts' or 'character', which really meant the ability to impose your will on others. His chief failure was at football, where boisterous, knobbly boys tend to lord it over smaller boys. Virtue, he concluded, lay in winning: 'it consisted in being bigger, stronger, handsomer, richer, more popular, more elegant, more unscrupulous than other people—in dominating them, bullying them, making them suffer pain, making them look foolish, getting the better of them in every way. Life was hierarchical and whatever happened was right. There were the strong, who deserved to win and always did win, and there were the weak, who deserved to lose and always did lose, everlastingly.' Yet however rigid and unbreakable the system appeared to be, it was already beginning to strain at the weak points. A Russian boy asked Orwell how much money his father had a year. Orwell told him, adding a few hundreds in self-defence. The Russian produced a pencil and notebook, did a calculation and said with amused contempt, 'My father has over two hundred times as much money as yours'. That was in 1915. Who had most two years later? And did virtue change in the meantime?

It was obviously not possible to be good. He ought to have felt grateful towards Bingo and Sim but he didn't. He ought to have loved his father but it was impossible to love a gruff-voiced elderly man forever saying 'Don't' whom he had scarcely seen before he was eight. The schoolmasters, the millionaires, the athletes, they were the 'armies of unalterable law' which he read about later. He knew immediately and exactly what they were. Orwell left this school with something worse than an inferiority complex. It was a deep-rooted conviction that he was bad, beyond the pale of decent society, doomed to failure. He was damned according to the law. He was unpopular, he had no money, he was no good at games, he believed he 'smelt' (simply because it was well-known that all unpleasant things 'smelt') and he was horribly ugly because his schoolfellows had told him so. (Not many years later Richard Rees regarded Orwell as a good-looking young man.) 'The conviction that it was *not possible* for me to be a success went deep enough to influence my actions till far into adult life. Until I was about thirty I always planned my life on the assumption not only that any major undertaking was bound to fail, but that I could only expect to live a few years longer.'

At the time, he said, he did not see beyond the moral dilemma presented to the weak in a world governed by the strong: Break the rules, or perish. He did not see that this gave the weak the right to make fresh rules for themselves. If he was more of a rebel than the other boys (as Cyril Connolly, who was Orwell's contemporary at the school, said he was) it was only because by boyish standards he was a poorer specimen. He did not rebel intellectually, only emotionally. 'I had nothing to help me except my dumb selfishness, my inability—not, indeed, to despise myself, but to *dislike* myself—my instinct to survive.' When at last he left Crossgates he felt a genuine sense of emancipation. But it did not take the form of looking forward to fresh conquests in the traditional manner. He was determined, now he had won his scholarship to Eton, to slack off and cram no longer. Between the ages of thirteen and twenty-two he says he hardly ever did a stroke of avoidable work. When he said goodbye to Bingo, who honoured him with his christian name for the occasion, he sensed her patronage. He was not a boy Crossgates was proud to have produced. He could imagine the thoughts that lay behind her smile: 'You haven't made much of a success of your time at Crossgates, have you? And I don't suppose you'll get on awfully well at a public school either. We made a mistake, really, in wasting our time and money on you. This kind of education hasn't much to offer to a boy with your background and outlook.' And so on. He left the school with one deepset conviction: failure lay behind him and failure lay ahead of him, and he saw no point in fighting against it.

I have mentioned above that Cyril Connolly was at school with Orwell and in his *Enemies of Promise* he makes several references to Orwell. We get the impression of a rather lonely dark horse but there is no apparent awareness of Orwell's personal unhappiness. He was convinced that Orwell was a true rebel while he was only a stage one. In this narrative Sim becomes Sambo, Bingo becomes Flip and Crossgates is given the Gothic name of St Wulfric's. He remembers Orwell as 'tall, pale, with his flaccid cheeks, and a matter-of-fact, supercilious voice, he was one of those boys who seem born old. He was incapable of courtship and when his favour went it went for ever. He went through St Wulfric's, despised Sambo and hated Flip, but was valuable to them as scholarship fodder.' Connolly and Orwell each won the Harrow History Prize in consecutive years and also another prize for the 'best list' of books taken out of the library during term. But after this Orwell dropped out of favour for having two volumes of *Sinister Street*. (Probably the kind of book Bingo expected a boy of his background to read.) Both of them wrote poetry, would compare their efforts, be polite to each other and then separate feeling ashamed. Orwell proved to Connolly that there existed an alternative to Character, namely Intelligence, just as another contemporary, Cecil Beaton, added Sensibility.

'The remarkable thing about Orwell was that he alone among the boys was an intellectual, and not a parrot, for he thought for himself, read Shaw and Samuel Butler, and rejected not only St Wulfric's, but the war, the Empire, Kipling, Sussex and Character. I remember a moment under a fig-tree in one of the inland boulevards of the seaside town, Orwell striding beside me, and saying in his flat, ageless voice: "You know, Connolly, there's only one remedy for all diseases". I felt the usual guilty tremor when sex was mentioned and hazarded, 'You mean going to the lavatory?" "No—I mean Death!" He was not a romantic, he had no use for the blandishments of the drill sergeant who made us feel character was identical with boxing, nor for the threats of the chaplain with his grizzled cheektufts, and his gospel of a Jesus of character, who detested immorality and swearing as much as he loved the Allies. "Of course, you realise, Connolly", said Orwell,

"that whoever wins this war, we shall emerge a second-rate
nation." '

This is recognisable Orwell, though he could not have been
more than thirteen years old.

We know far less about his years at Eton because he has only
referred to them in passing. In *The Road to Wigan Pier*, where
he gives a rapid survey of his intellectual and emotional development, he tells us that at the age of fourteen of fifteen he was 'an
odious little snob'. If you have been to an English public
school, he says, you will forget your Greek and Latin within a
few months of leaving, but your snobbishness, unless you
deliberately root it out, will cling like bindweed. There is a
hierarchy in snobbery and Orwell had his place in it in this
period, despite his suffering on account of it. His situation, and
that of all the other boys from families in the same social group,
was neither fish nor fowl:

> 'On the one hand it made me cling tighter than ever to my
> gentility; on the other hand it filled me with resentment against
> the boys whose parents were richer than mine and who took care
> to let me know it. I despised anyone who was not describable as a
> "gentleman", but also I hated the hoggishly rich, especially those
> who had grown rich too recently. The correct and elegant thing,
> I felt, was to be of gentle birth but to have no money. This is part
> of the *credo* of the lower-upper-middle class. It has a romantic,
> Jacobite-in-exile feeling about it which is very comforting.'

The only objective view we have of Orwell at Eton comes from
Connolly, and it is a mere glimpse. We hear that when
Connolly got a bad report (he was 'cynical and irreverent')
his parents were upset and blamed Orwell, who was a 'bad
influence', though they rarely saw each other. Orwell had now
reached the status of evil genius. It might have turned the head
of a more romantic boy. We hear that he was immersed in *The
Way of All Flesh* (Bingo would have foreseen that) and the
atheistic argument in *Androcles and the Lion*. He was beaten at
the age of eighteen for being late for prayers—and by boys of
the same age in their senior election. Orwell himself says he
was 'relatively happy' at Eton. He took classics, was short of
money and made valuable friends such as Richard Rees and
John Strachey. The boys were mildly 'Bolshie' (this was in
1918) and he felt very angry with the old men who had made

such a mess of things. They derided the O.T.C., the Christian religion, even compulsory games and the Royal Family. He remembered two incidents particularly. When the English master set a general knowledge paper which included the question, 'Whom do you consider the ten greatest men now living?' fifteen boys out of sixteen (average age seventeen) included Lenin in their list. In 1919 arrangements were made to celebrate peace in the traditional manner by marching the boys into the schoolyard, carrying torches, and singing jingo songs such as 'Rule Britannia'. The boys guyed the whole proceeding and sang blasphemous and seditious words to the familiar tunes. Orwell was by no means the only one who felt that society needed recasting, but it was unlikely that any of the others felt as keenly as he did that the real fault in the English system was the network of prejudice based on arbitrary money divisions. Eton has always been renowned for its independence of the worst aspect of the public-school system. Stephen Spender said he was 'perhaps the least Etonian character who has ever come out of Eton'. But it is pretty certain that no other public school could have produced him.

In his earliest pamphleteering period, when his main literary task was to attack the class system at every point, Orwell found it impossible to praise Eton, though he never went out of his way to attack it. (In *The Road to Wigan Pier*, for instance, where he criticised his public-school education, he never actually mentioned Eton by name.) In fact, he retained a good deal of affection for his old school and towards the end of his life he made what was for him a handsome gesture of peace. In 'For Ever Eton' (*Observer*, 1 August, 1948) he began with a typical Orwellian attack:

'Whatever may happen to the great public schools when our educational system is reorganised, it is almost impossible that Eton should survive in anything like its present form, because the training it offers was originally intended for a landowning aristocracy and had become an anachronism long before 1939. The top hats and tail coats, the pack of beagles, the many-coloured blazers, the desks still notched with the names of Prime Ministers had charm and function so long as they represented the kind of elegance that everyone looked up to. In a shabby and democratic country they are merely rather a nuisance, like Napoleon's baggage wagons, full of chefs and hairdressers, blocking up the roads in the disaster of Sedan.'

But he ended with a tribute to the spirit of Eton which had allowed him sufficient freedom to develop his native critical sense:

'It has one great virtue . . . and that is a tolerant and civilised atmosphere which gives each boy a fair chance of developing his own individuality. The reason is perhaps that, being a very rich school, it can afford a large staff, which means that the masters are not overworked; and also that Eton partly escaped the reform of public schools set on foot by Dr Arnold and retained certain characteristics belonging to the eighteenth century and even to the Middle Ages. At any rate, whatever its future history, some of its traditions deserve to be remembered.'

When he was not yet twenty he went to Burma in the Indian Imperial Police. As with the Eton years, we know less about his time in Burma than about his early school-days. But in any case, although his Burmese experiences were to be important to him, expecially in his evolving of an attitude towards imperialism, they did not mark him so deeply as his prep. school years. He has given us a brief portrait of his mind about this time in *The Road to Wigan Pier*. He says he was both a snob and a revolutionary—the latter because he had set himself against all authority, He had read all the works of the 'advanced' writers of that time (Shaw, Wells and Galsworthy), called himself a Socialist but had very little idea what Socialism meant. He sympathised with the working classes at a distance but still hated and despised them when he made contact with them. He hated their accents and was revolted by their habitual rudeness. At that time the working people were still expecting some of the wartime promises about reform and better conditions to be made good and they were apt to make their demands rather loudly.

'People had not yet settled down to a lifetime of unemployment mitigated by endless cups of tea. They still vaguely expected the Utopia for which they had fought, and even more than before they were openly hostile to the aitch-pronouncing class. So to the shock-absorbers of the bourgeoisie, such as myself, "common people" still appeared brutal and repulsive. Looking back upon that period, I seem to have spent half the time in denouncing the capitalist system and the other half raging over the insolence of bus-conductors.'

He was in Burma from 1922-7. Although he disliked authority
he had now become the servant of one of the strongest authorities in the world of that time. There is certainly an anomaly
here, but it is easy to explain once you take into consideration
the time and his age. He was a very young man of twenty and he
had to have a job. He was not in a position to reject whatever
came along and wait for the post he really wanted. He had no
phalanx of influence ranged behind him. And then it is not
uncommon for an idealistic young man to believe that he can
soften the rigours of even the worst tyranny by his own conduct.
Until you have served an authority you do not realise how
powerless you are likely to be. He soon realised his unhappiness
and unsuitability for the job. He did not overtly rebel but he
felt unable to act as benevolently towards the native population
in his role of policeman as would have been possible had he been
a doctor or teacher. Undoubtedly Flory in *Burmese Days* represents Orwell at that time—well-intentioned but ineffectual,
leading a double life, externally the good servant, internally
a severe critic of all he represented. But all this latter part he had
to keep to himself. As a result he worked out his own anarchistic
theory that all government is evil, that the punishment always
does more harm than the crime and that people can be trusted
to behave decently if you will only let them alone. Later he
dismissed this as sentimental and even justified the policeman
because of the necessity of protecting peaceful people from
violence.

In 1927 he resigned his post. Even at that youthful age his
appearance revealed both the innate sincerity of the man and
the internal struggle which had started at school and was now
moving to a crisis. Richard Rees said 'his expression could be
remote, intense, dry or comical, but never, literally *never*, self-
important or fugitive or malicious. Most often it was mildly
and rather sadly benign, but whatever it might be, the pleasant
and good-looking face across which it played seemed at some
time to have been frozen with pity and horror, which had left
indelible marks.' The benignity remained to the end, untouched
by the suffering he went through or the bitterness he must have
felt in the remarkable career that was just about to begin. One
thing remained constant, unaffected by his Burmese years, and

that was his personal conviction that failure was the only virtue. He had a horror of success, probably based on his belief that success was always something given you, never a reward for good. This belief was actually growing stronger and by now he felt that even the act of earning a few hundred a year was spiritually ugly, a species of bullying.

It was in this mood that Orwell took the step that made him a writer. He might have written books without it but they would have been genteel and relatively empty. He embraced poverty as other writers have embraced a woman and with the same result: his spirit was fired and he was no longer in any doubt about what his true work was to be. 'What I profoundly wanted at that time', he wrote later in *The Road to Wigan Pier*, 'was to find some way of getting out of the respectable world altogether.' His mind turned to the social outcasts, 'the lowest of the low'. He felt an urge to identify himself with tramps, beggars, criminals and prostitutes that was too strong to be denied. It was to be the act of transfiguration that any true writer must experience, though he did not know it at the time. He probably was not thinking of writing at all, except that he still had the subconscious determination to be a writer. Bingo was still controlling him, more than ten years later. She had said he belonged to the pit and he was overcome by this irresistible compulsion to explore its depths. It was something more than a rejection of 'decent' society (the society he felt so keenly to be indecent), it was something much more passionate, resembling a love affair with the rejected of this world.

In the same book he recounts the trepidation with which he entered the new world. He made long and meticulous preparations. He was about to visit places far more remote than Burma, though they were on his own doorstep. One evening, having equipped himself with the ragged uniform of the tramp, he left Crossgates, Eton and the Burma Police behind him and made his way to a common lodging-house with the sign Good Beds for Single Men in the window:

'Heavens, how I had to screw up my courage before I went in! It seems ridiculous now. But you see I was still half afraid of the working class. I wanted to get in touch with them, I even wanted to become one of them, but I still thought of them as alien and dangerous; going into the dark doorway of that common lodging-house seemed to me like going down into some dreadful sub-terranean place—a sewer full of rats, for instance. I went in fully expecting a fight. The people would spot that I was not one of themselves and immediately infer that I had come to spy on them; and then they would set upon me and throw me out—that was what I expected. I felt that I had got to do it, but I did not enjoy the prospect.'

The 'deputy' of the lodging-house took his ninepence without staring and led him to a firelit kitchen underground. Steve-dores, navvies and sailors were playing draughts and drinking tea. They barely glanced at him. Then a drunken young steve-dore lurched across, thrusting forward his broad red face, looking quarrelsome. Orwell stiffened, waiting for the blow. But the stevedore collapsed on his chest, flung his arms round Orwell's neck and cried, "Ave a cup of tea, chum, 'ave a cup of tea!'

I think that must have been one of the happiest moments in Orwell's life. For the first time he had really been accepted. No one was worrying about how much money he had or where he spent his holidays. No one cared about his 'views', as the others had always been curious about Flory's. The cup of tea was, as he said, a kind of baptism. A criticism has often been made about Orwell that he never selects the most typical group or situation when he is making an enquiry. When he wants to get to know the working class he plunges into the dregs. When he is asked to make a report on working-class conditions he chooses an unemployed mining area. Sociologically the charges have substance, but literature has nothing to do with sociology. Orwell was not hamstrung by considerations of consistency, even the specious consistency of the politician. His slumming was of immense importance to himself, of no importance to the people he mixed with and whose advocates he became. Dicken's work in the blacking factory was of no importance to blacking factories; it meant nearly everything to Dickens and a great deal to the rest of us.

For those who like easily manageable facts, Orwell told T. R. Fyvel that when he returned from Burma he had little money, few social connections and no special trade, and unem-ployment was already becoming a serious problem. But it required more than these humdrum motives to explain Orwell's descent into the underworld and the fascination he felt for it. Anyone who reads *Down and Out in Paris and London*, the book describing his experiences, must note the difference of tenor that distinguishes it from almost any other book of the same kind. The *plongeurs* and the tramps are flies in amber and it is impossible not to share the author's curiosity about the new species he had unearthed. Yet it was not a success. When W. H. Davies, the Supertramp, reviewed it in the *New Statesman* he seemed quite unaware that it was a masterpiece, even if a minor one, and confined a column review to personal information and comment on the life of beggars and Downrighters, with two trivial references to the book itself. Like all his early books, this, his first, did not sell well. He was fond of making financial calculations about authorship and estimated that his literary earnings between 1930 and 1940 averaged a little under £3 a week. On the other hand, he did not have the difficulty in publishing his work that some authors have encountered. When I asked him if he had had trouble starting he said yes, *Down and Out* had been rejected by the first publisher he showed it to. He seemed genuinely astonished! On the other hand, there may have been manuscripts we know nothing about.

During the next few years he eked out a living as a private tutored and underpaid schoolmaster in private schools. He married and for a time kept a village pub and general store. (From the latter source he made about £1 a week.) From 1930–4 he contributed to *The Adelphi*, still using his family name, Eric Blair. (*Down and Out* appeared under the name of Orwell, though a chapter from it had been printed in *The Adelphi* as by Eric Blair.) This seems to have been a period of stasis, writing not very good novels and indifferent poetry. The latter (all we have of Orwell's, except for two in *Tribune*, one which he quoted in his *Gangrel* article and another in 'Looking Back on the Spanish War') is pedestrian and almost lifeless. It trots to a regular metre and is filled with a sense of despair. Eric Blair had come to a temporary stop. He has the air of being lost, of not knowing where to turn next. He had come out of the pit but he has been sucked back into the waste of bourgeoisdom. He has almost become 'a little office-boy at forty pounds a year'.

The poetry is dreary in the extreme:

> And I see the people thronging the street,
> The death-marked people, they and I
> Goalless, rootless, like leaves drifting,
> Blind to the earth and to the sky;
>
> Nothing believing, nothing loving,
> Not in joy nor in pain, not heeding the stream
> Of precious life that flows within us,
> But fighting, toiling as in a dream.

He concludes by urging us 'to learn our world while yet we may.
And shape our souls, however ill'. And later in the same year
(1933) we find him oppressed by the sense of doom:

> And the bird unaware, blessing the summer eternal,
> Joyfully labouring, proud in his strength, gay-plumed,
> Unaware of the hawk and the snow and the frost-bound nights,
> And of his death foredoomed.

In the following year he is oppressed by his 'mortal sickness':

> I feel, and with a sharper pang,
> My mortal sickness; how I give
> My heart to weak and stuffless ghosts,
> And with the living cannot live.

And then, I think, Eric Blair must have had a serious talk
with himself. He was declining into the kind of literary morbid-
ity that is literature's own chief enemy. He was essentially
the kind of writer who requires constant bouts of action to
refresh his sensibility. Now, rotting in the eventless life of an
English village, having his energies sapped by teaching in
schools where the genuine thrill of education is absent, he was in
danger of deteriorating into a soured and hopeless hack. The
change of name may indicate a conscious effort to 'snap out of
it', to leave the miserable Blair behind and to substitute a
pugnacious Orwell. A stylistic development is also discernible.
Most of the Blair contributions are a trifle awkward with
sudden splashes of immaturity which are all the more noticeable when they occur in the midst of his naturally plausible
prose. But in all probability the most powerful reason for the
change was still the shadow of Bingo. He had at last outgrown
his determination to be a failure. He wanted to shut Bingo out
of his life. Although she now meant nothing to him in a

circumstantial sense he was sufficiently sensitive to wince at the thought of her hearing that Blair had become a dish-washer and tramp, and saying with her knowing smile, 'What did I always say? He was never any good.' It was fairly safe to assume that she would never see a copy of *The Adelphi* with his account of life in a spike, but anyone can pick up any book in a shop or a library.

As for the name itself, T. R. Fyvel tells us of Orwell's own explanation:

> ' "Eric", he said—he didn't like the name because of its romantic Norse associations with the sentimental schoolboy histories of his childhood. And Blair was a Scots name . . . he himself felt, and wanted to be, English. "Orwell", that was the name of the English river on whose banks he once lived. And what could be more English, in the patriotic sense, than "George"? This typical explanation was partly true, for England, the country to which he came as a boy, was, and remained, his genuine love. Yet the explanation was only partly evasive: names are highly symbolical things and, as he knew, his own change of *nom de guerre* surely also represented a deliberate act to cut loose from the past, from this childhood, from certain unresolved conflicts which he could never quite shake off.' ('A Writer's Life', *World Review*, June, 1950.)

Towards the end of his life he was planning to change his name by deed poll. He was very impressed by the reverence which primitive feel for their names.

The two novels that followed *Down and Out* (*A Clergyman's Daughter* and *Keep the Aspidistra Flying*) make full use of his experience in these middle years. They do not fuse the material into successful fiction but patches of them are extremely vivid. We are given an insight into what it feels like to work in a third-rate bookshop-cum-library in the second novel (Orwell was an assistant in a Hampstead bookshop for eighteen months during 1932-4) and in the first novel his experience as a schoolmaster are made use of when Dorothy becomes a teacher in a private snob school. It is nothing like Crossgates but the spirit behind it is the same as Crossgates'—the inflated prospectus, the importance of fees, the priority of *morals* over education. (It used to be Character.)

When at last Orwell found an outlet into some kind of action again (as apart from the danger of vegetating and brooding) we can follow his development in his books, as we did in *Down and Out*. In 1936 Victor Gollancz asked him to go to an industrial area and write a personal report for the Left Book Club. The result was *The Road to Wigan Pier*, which aroused an outcry among Socialists. In 1937 he joined the Trotskyist P.O.U.M. and fought in the Spanish Civil War until he was wounded in the neck and escaped from the country with difficulty. The result was *Homage to Catalonia*, which aroused an outcry in the Popular Front circles. The first, as a Book Club edition, naturally found a fairly large public. The second only sold a few hundred copies over the next few years. (But *Coming Up For Air*, which appeared in 1939, was fairly successful and went into several editions.)

Now the interesting point about these two books is that they irritated many people, chiefly Left-wingers, profoundly. And by now Orwell was making no bones about the fact that he was a Socialist. He was in fact starting his career as the devil's advocate for Socialism and it was a valuable role because there had been so few forerunners. Many people began to believe quite genuinely that Orwell's brand of socialism was so aberrant that it was not really socialism at all. Half of *Wigan Pier* was devoted to attacks on middle-class socialists. Half of *Homage to Catalonia* was devoted to attacks on the communists— a much more unpopular act in the days immediately preceding the war than it is now. From 1937 to the end of his life Orwell conducted a running battle with the politicians of his own persuasion, or at least with those who expected to find in him an ally. During this period he discovered for himself that an honest writer cannot be confined within the limits of party discipline. No political party is honest for more than a few months at a time, and those few months represent its heyday. Reviewing *Homage to Catalonia* in the *New Statesman* (30 April, 1938), V. S. Pritchett wrote:

'There are many strong arguments for keeping creative writers out of politics and Mr George Orwell is one of them. If these beings toe the line they are likely to be ruined as writers; if they preserve their independence—and, after all, they have by nature little choice about that—they become an annoyance to the causes they espouse.'

As a general truth this is normally recognised among serious writers, though the general public have great difficulty in understanding it. (But it is the general public that is gulled by political parties.) The matter of interest to us is the particular way in which Orwell fell foul of this principle, as he undoubtedly did. Briefly, Orwell insisted on *seeing for himself*. He did not write about the working class (political fodder in the twentieth century) without first going to live among them and get to know them. His conclusion was that the gulf between the workers and the socialist intellectuals was every bit as great as that between them and the bourgeoisie in general. So he challenged the approach of the intellectuals to the working class and even their sincerity. When he wrote about the Spanish Civil War he did so as one who had taken part in it, and even then he confined himself to that section of Spain he had himself visited. His conclusion was that the Trotskyists were being suppressed by the Communists not because they were insufficiently revolutionary but because they were too revolutionary. Orwell made objectivity and personal experience a severe test of descriptive and polemical writing, and by these standards the greater part of contemporary writing, expecially on the Left wing, was found wanting.

Critics, especially among the Left-wing intelligentsia whom Orwell attacked so vigorously, have frequently claimed that his knowledge of the workers was much less accurate than he claimed. It is true that Orwell's particular brand of plausibility often suggested that he knew more about anything than anyone else. This could be very irritating. It is also true that he knew much less about the tastes and feelings of the workers than the workers did themselves. But he was articulate and they weren't. It was a point that he often made, that as soon as a working man started writing he left the working class in spirit and adopted the mannerisms and attitudes of a bourgeois. Orwell's claim (made, I should add, in no spirit of boastfulness) was that he had discovered from personal experience that the approach of the intellectuals towards the workers was not likely to succeed because it was based on faulty understanding. Despite his mistakes, I believe that of all the prominent literary Left-wingers he was closest to the feelings of the ordinary people (which are normally indifferent and vaguely anarchist). For example, he knew that most people take no formal interest in politics—you don't get that impression from any Marxist writer. He knew that ordinary people refuse to make heroes out of politicians and are not attracted by any stereotyped political policies—at the most they like a 'policy' that can be summed up in homely terms, such as He's a Real Gentleman (Anthony Eden) or Education Counts (Clement Attlee). In fact, Orwell was intellectually a realist in the way that anarchist philosophers and minority socialists often are. But he was also, unlike them, a realist in political action. The anarchists and their allies have made a virtue out of frustration, refusing to modify their impossibly perfectionist demands on imperfect people. (In a passage I quoted above Orwell said that ordinary people had to be protected against violence. The Anarchists tend to argue that there will be no violence in their society so no one will need protection.) Orwell realised that in nearly every political situation action (and he wanted action, at least a partial realisation of ideas) came only from leaders. He was the only prominent Left-winger who could possibly have succeeded in expressing the subterranean feelings of the people in the overt action of leaders. Others were simply trying to persuade the people to follow a prescribed policy of action.

Most converts to Socialism seem to enter the fray ready-armed, i.e., their conversion takes place comparatively early. Orwell's was late, several years after adolescence. Richard Rees tells us that while in Burma he disapproved of an article in a mildly avant-garde magazine, set it up at the end of his verandah and used it for target practice. (He was fascinated by firearms.) A few years later his own work was appearing in the same magazine. We know that he had always intended to write although at about the time he was in Burma he almost lost sight of his determination. When at last he does write we find him contributing to the better-class type of periodical and writing books which are taken seriously by serious critics. There was nothing avant-garde about his technique, but there was a freshness, courage and honesty about the prose that made him acceptable by people who wanted more than 'something to read' to pass the time away. His childhood determination to be a writer had come to the surface again and he had discovered an exciting new world which he wished to inform others about. But these were personal matters. There were certain motives which affected all writers, in his opinion, but which they possessed in varying degrees and with varying emphases. He set these out in his article 'Why I Write' in *Gangrel*:

(i) Sheer egoism, the desire to seem clever, to be talked about, to be remembered after death, to get your own back on grown-ups who snubbed you in childhood, etc. This was shared by the whole of the upper crust in all professions, not merely writers.

(ii) Aesthetic enthusiasm. The perception of beauty in the external world, the feeling of pleasure. Also the joy of arrangement and reduction to order.

(iii) Historical impulse, the desire to transmit truth to posterity.

(iv) Political purpose, using the word 'political' in the widest possible sense. The desire to push the world in a certain direction.

And then he qualified this analysis in a manner most significant for an understanding of his work as a whole. He said that by nature the first three motives originally outweighed the fourth, but events compelled him to become a pamphleteer. 'Every line of serious work that I have written since 1936 has been written, directly or indirectly, *against* totalitarianism and *for* democratic socialism.'

During the period I am discussing, i.e., from the time he gave up tramping until the outbreak of the war, with intervals such as the excursion to Spain, he was leading the rather sordid life of an unsuccessful writer. It is the kind of life that is known to the general public through the medium of books such as Gissing's *Grub Street* (this had a special fascination for him). He has himself left at least two brief descriptions of it, apart from the relevant passages in *Keep the Aspidistra Flying*. Here is one:

'. . . writers resemble one another much more closely in their private lives than in their writings. Behind the most diverse books there is nearly always the same background, the nerve-wracked, dun-haunted figure of the professional writer, paddling about in a dressing-gown in a room full of stale fag-ends and half-empty cups of tea, and struggling with a dreadful book that never gets any further.' ('Two glimpses of the Moon', *New Statesman*, 18 January, 1941.)

He seemed to like the conceit so much that a few years later he elaborated this appalling vision ('Confessions of a Book Reviewer', *Shooting an Elephant*). By now the writer is bald, has varicose veins and wears spectacles, 'or would wear them if his only pair were not chronically lost'. It is half past eleven in the morning and he should have started work two hours ago, but even if he had tried he would have been disturbed by the almost continuous ringing of the telephone, the yells of the baby, the rattle of an electric drill and the heavy boots of creditors clumping up and down the stairs. If things are normal he is suffering from malnutrition. If he has been lucky he will be suffering from a hangover. 'Needless to say this person is a writer.'

This may be an accurate portrait of Orwell settling down to work. It is certainly not a portrait of the average writer known to myself—I can speak for no one else. I know of few writers who could produce a single publishable word in such material and mental chaos. But this is the picture that Orwell cherished. It is part of his obverse romanticism, if I may use the term—I have already said he possessed none of the conventional romanticism. It is also part of his 'world-view' of the writer, a being who is despised and kicked about—in fact, one who is doomed to failure and has accepted failure as part of the order of things. You might be excused for thinking that the seer of such visions or the victim of such circumstances, whichever he was, must be a thoroughly embittered and disgruntled man. But this was not true. There was bitterness within him, of course, but it was felt on behalf of all victims. He was a most selfless man, as I shall show later. All who knew him stress the mildness of his eyes, the hint of suffering in the lines of his face, but a suffering that had drawn out his sympathy. In the only way he could he did his best to help young writers who found circumstances so inauspicious during the war. I have yet to hear of him refusing a contribution to a 'little review', for which he could expect little or no payment, either when he needed money or when he could demand a high price from commercial publications. When T. R. Fyvel took over the literary editorship of *Tribune* from him he found his drawer stuffed full of manuscripts, accepted but useless. Orwell agreed that they were no good but he felt the writers had put all they had got into them. He realised that the early work of some great writers had been atrociously bad.

To return to chronology. I have already said that *Homage to Catalonia* was a commercial failure. It pleased only those who like good writing and the vast majority of people who read books on the Spanish War wanted something else. Only nine hundred copies had been sold by the time he died. On his return to England he lived quietly in Hertfordshire for two years, except for one winter which he spent in Morocco. He had suffered from lung trouble all his life and his war experiences had done the complaint no good. It was his illness which probably caused in him his horror of 'natural' death (shared by Hemingway). He realised that if his own death was to be a 'natural' one it was likely to be unpleasant. He wanted to live, as he often said, but when the time came he would have preferred it to some suddenly. Only Spain would have been too soon, for him and for us. In the essay 'How the Poor Die' (*Shooting an Elephant*) he describes how he was awakened in a French hospital with the news that Numero 57 had just died. The deaths he had seen before had been chiefly Asiatic and violent. This was his first dead European. (I don't know why that impressed him so much. Perhaps it brought home to him that Europeans can and do die.) Numero 57's face was contorted into an expression of agony.

> 'As I gazed at the tiny, screwed-up face it struck me that this dusgusting piece of refuse, waiting to be carted away and dumped on a slab in the dissecting room, wan an example of "natural" death, one of the things you pray for in the Litany. There you are, then, I thought, that's what is waiting for you, twenty, thirty, forty years hence: that is how the lucky ones die, the ones who live to be old. One wants to love, of course, indeed one only stays alive by virtue of the fear of death, but I think now, as I thought then, that it's better to die violently and not too old. People talk about the horrors of war, but what weapon has man invented that even approached in cruelty some of the commoner diseases? "Natural" death, almost by definition, means something slow, smelly and painful.'

When the war came and with it the opportunity of violent death, his main and constant complaint was that the authori-

ties would give him nothing useful to do—by which he meant
some kind of service in the armed forces. He was rejected by the
doctors and was compelled to fall back on work which could
never be of more than second-rate importance to him at such a
time: journalism, film criticism for *Time and Tide* (he objected
strongly to the inferior sherry with which the distributors tried
to buy his honour), editing a series of pamphlets on war aims
with T. R. Fyvel, the Indian Service of the B.B.C. and the
literary editorship of *Tribune*. Just before the end he became
War Correspondent for the *Observer*. He was contemptuous of
the efforts made by some intellectuals to evade war service and
envied them their health.

During 1940-1 he kept a War Diary in which he tried to set
his thoughts about the contemporary situation in order. It is
not an impressive document but it does give us an insight into
his state of mind more effectively than anything else we possess
for any other period. (All other comparable documents are
retrospective and therefore, despite his honesty, not absolutely
reliable.) One of his earliest entries draws attention to the fact
that he had known for some time that war with Germany was
coming and that others, many of them men who should have
known because they had far more facts than he had, had been
taken by surprise.

'S. said to me recently, "Don't you feel that any time during the
past ten years you have been able to foretell events better than,
say, the Cabinet?" I had to agree to this. Partly it is a question of
not being blinded by class interests, etc., e.g., anyone not financially
interested could see at a glance the strategic danger to England of
letting Germany and Italy dominate Spain, whereas many right
wingers, even professional soldiers, simply could not grasp this
most obvious fact. But where I feel that people like us understand
the situation better than so-called experts is not in any power to
foretell specific events, but in the power to grasp what *kind* of
world we are living in. At any rate, I have known since about
1931 (Spender says he has known since 1929) that the future must
be catastrophic. I could not say exactly what wars and revolutions
would happen, but they never surprised me when they came.
Since 1934 I have known war between England and Germany was
coming, and since 1936 I have known it in my belly, and the
chatter of the pacifists on the one hand, and the Popular Front
people who pretended to fear that Britain was preparing for war
against Russia on the other, never deceived me. Similarly, such

horrors as the Russian purges never surprised me, because I had
always felt that—not *exactly* that, but something *like* that—was
implicit in Bolshevik rule. I could feel it in their literature.' (8
June, 1940.)

Two days later he says he is writhing because he can do
nothing more valuable than write book-reviews. He is even
angry that such 'time-wasting' should be allowed. He was still
hoping that he would be taken into the Army, but on 28 June
he knew the worst:

'Horribly depressed by the way things are turning out. Went
this morning for my medical board and was turned down, my
grade being C, in which they aren't at present taking any men in
any corps. . . . What is appalling is the unimaginativeness of a
system which can find *no* use for a man who is below the average
level of fitness but at least is not an invalid. An army needs an
immense amount of clerical work, most of which is done by people
who are perfectly healthy and only half-literate. . . . One could
forgive the government for failing to employ the intelligentsia,
who on the whole are politically unreliable, if they were making
any attempt to mobilise the manpower of the nation and change
people over from the luxury trades to productive work. This
simply isn't happening, as one can see by looking down any
street.'

Orwell's depression was at its greatest during this period.
He was not allowed to serve, he found it quite impossible to
write anything of significance, he despised the journalistic
work he was doing. (He published nothing between *The Lion
and the Unicorn*, 1941, and *Animal Farm*, 1945, except for reviews
and occasional articles.) His very keen sense of nostalgia was
constantly being stimulated—as, for instance, when he discovered
he was lighting the fires with old newspapers whose optimistic
headlines symbolically went up in flames. On 20 January 1941
he noticed that he was making entries far less frequently than
when he started. The feeling of helplessness was growing in
everyone, he thought. The great popular revolution which he
had hoped would make the winning of the war an act of
freedom had not occurred. There would not be the chance of
another without a great disaster preceding it. But his own determination to do what he could against Fascism (remember, he
had by now decided that the major motive in his work was the
defence of democratic socialism against totalitarianism) had not

weakened. Early in the diary he had remarked, 'Horrible though it is, I hope the B.E.F. is cut to pieces rather than capitulate'. And later in the year he made it clear that he did not desire a different fate for himself if events demanded:

'It is impossible even yet to decide what to do in the case of a German conquest of England. The one thing I will not do is to clear out, at any rate not further than Ireland, supposing that to be feasible. If the fleet is intact and it appears that the war is to be continued from America and the Dominions, then one must remain alive if possible, if necessary in a concentration camp. If the U.S.A. is going to submit to conquest as well, there is nothing for it but to die fighting, but one must above all die *fighting* and have the satisfaction of killing somebody else first.' (16 June, 1940.)

But his friends were always urging him to get away while he could if there was any real danger of invasion. In view of his anti-Fascist record he would be a marked man, and anyway, they probably felt he had suffered enough as it was. Eight days later he had grudgingly given way, on specific conditions:

'Both E. and G. insistent that I should go to Canada if the worst comes to the worst, in order to stay alive and keep up propaganda. I will go if I have some function, e.g., if the government were transferred to Canada and I had some kind of job, but not as a refugee, nor as an expatriate journalist, squealing from a safe distance. There are too many of these exiled "anti-fascists" already. Better to die if necessary, and maybe even as propaganda one's death might achieve more than going abroad and living more or less uninvited on other people's charity. Not that I want to die; I have so much to live for, in spite of poor health and having no children.'

As a result of these frustrations we have a vision in January 1941 of a tall, rather emaciated-looking literary gent wearing a shabby mac with its tails ballooning in the wind, ripping posters down from walls. Orwell wasn't being allowed to fight the Germans but nothing would stop him taking action, even if it was minor action against Hitler's friends. The posters belonged to the People's Convention, a communist-led organisation which was demanding a negotiated peace. He was convinced it was a defeatist manoeuvre consciously intended to help Hitler, Stalin's friend. He said that normally it was against his instincts to chalk on walls or to interfere with what other

people had written, but he confessed that he had written
'Visca POUM' on the walls of Barcelona after the P.O.U.M.
had been suppressed, and also 'Sack Chamberlain' on the walls
of London during the summer. Now one's attitude to this type
of activity may be approving or it may be scornful, but the
act itself is entirely Orwellian. It is only necessary to try and
imagine any other leading English writer behaving in the same
way to realise that we are dealing with a distinctive personality.
Chesterton would have torn posters down; Dylan Thomas
might have written an image up; and—————————has probably cut a dirty word into the brick wall of a public place.
But the action conceived as part of a wide, general policy, the
probable feeling that nothing was too insignificant to throw
into the scales against Hitler, were Orwell's alone.

There was one other matter that was causing him great
concern, and at the same time a sense of injustice. How was he
going to live if the government wouldn't employ him and the
war made it impossible for him to follow his calling? The old
spectre of poverty, instead of declining as might have been
expected as his career developed, was actually increased in
size:

> 'The money situation is becoming completely unbearable. . . .
> Wrote a long letter to the Income Tax people pointing out that
> the war had practically put an end to my livelihood, while at the
> same time the government refused to give me any kind of job.
> The fact is really relevant to a writer's position, the impossibility
> of writing books with this nightmare going on, would have no
> weight officially. . . . Towards the government I feel no scruples
> and would dodge paying the tax if I could. Yet I would give my
> life for England readily enough, if I thought it necessary. No one
> is patriotic about taxes.'

The Income Tax people were a great trouble to Orwell at
this period, although it is not easy to understand what income
they were trying to tax. But money and the shortage of money
fascinated him. *Keep the Aspidistra Flying* is, very simply, a book
about money. He had never had enough of it to forget about it.
He was not that conventional character of fiction, the author
who lives on beautiful thoughts or striking conceits. He was
anything but avaricious, yet he could never forget the bare
mechanics of making a living. As a result he would sometimes

consider the financial aspect of a set of circumstances which would not normally occur to others. While everyone else was saying in 1936 what a wonderful venture Penguin books were and how they deserved to succeed, he said this and also something extra. He was not only a reader, he was a writer:

> 'In my capacity as reader I applaud the Penguin Books; in my capacity as writer I pronounce them anathema. Hutchinsons are now bringing out a very similar edition, though only of their own books, and if the other publishers follow suit, the result may be a flood of cheap reprints which will cripple the lending libraries (the novelist's foster-mother) and check the output of new novels. This would be a fine thing for literature, but it would be a very bad thing for trade, and when you have to choose between art and money—well, finish it for yourself.' (*New English Weekly*, 5 March, 1936.)

We fortunately have a full statement by Orwell on what he considered to be a writer's minimum financial needs, thanks to the questionnaire circulated by *Horizon* under the title 'The Cost of Letters' (September 1946). In reply to the first question, How much do you think a writer needs to live on? he replied £10 a week (after tax) for a married man and £6 for a single man. This was a characteristically modest demand. He recognised it was a minimum (and one which he himself only reached towards the end of his career) and went on to say that the *best* income for a writer would be £1000 a year. The implication is that anything above this figure would probably be as damaging as anything below. He then outlined the material needs of a writer, prominent among them being a comfortable, well-warmed room not subject to frequent interruption (the baby and the dun). This in itself, he said, is expensive. Then costs are increased by the need for books and periodicals, plenty of space, the necessity of a considerable correspondence. Part-time secretarial help was almost as essential. 'Most of them probably benefit by travelling.' He added that ideally everyone should have the same income, provided it was fairly high, and thereby removed the whole question from its normal isolation. The writer is a member of the community and instead of legislating particularly for the writer we should legislate for everyone, including the writer.

The second question was, Do you think a serious writer can

earn this sum by writing, and if so, how? No, said Orwell. A few hundred people in Britain live by writing books and most of them probably write detective stories and the like. 'In a way it is easier for people like Ethel M. Dell to avoid prostitution than it is for a serious writer.'

If not, what do you think is the most suitable second occupation for him? Something non-literary, also congenial. 'I can just imagine, for instance, a bank clerk or an insurance agent going home and doing serious work in the evenings; whereas the effort is too much to make if one has already squandered one's energies on semi-creative work such as teaching, broadcasting or composing propaganda for bodies such as the British Council.'

Do you think literature suffers from the diversion of a writer's energy into other employments or is it enriched by it? It is enriched, so long as the other employment doesn't use up all his time and energy. A writer needs contact with the ordinary world.

Do you think the State or any other institution should do more for writers? The only thing the State could usefully do is divert more public money into buying books for public libraries. Under Socialism the writer should be State-supported, but in the present economy he should not be under obligation to any organised body. Private patronage is undesirable. The public is the most satisfactory patron but it doesn't spend money on books. Its expenditure should be increased, unknown to it, via rates and taxes.

Finally, are you satisfied with your own solution of the problem and have you any specific advice to give to young people who wish to earn their living by writing? Satisfied in a financial sense during the last few years. 'I had to struggle desperately at the beginning, and if I had listened to what people said to me I would never have been a writer. Even until quite recently, whenever I have written anything which I took quite seriously, there have been strenuous efforts, sometimes by quite influential people, to keep it out of print. To a young writer who is conscious of having something in him, the only advice I can give is not to take advice . . . if one wants to be primarily a *writer*, then, in our society, one is an animal that is tole ated but not encouraged—something rather like a house sparrow—and one gets on better if one realises one's position from the start.'

In these answers there was a reference to the public as a non-book-buying entity—a poor outlook for writers if the 'free market' is to become their new condition of patronage. In an article 'Books v. Cigarettes' (*Shooting an Elephant*) Orwell makes one of those little financial calculations that never failed to amuse him. He was stimulated to do this by hearing of a workman who had said he couldn't afford to buy books. He then counted and priced the books in his own flat and arrived at the following figures: 442 books, total cost price (*not* market value) £82 17s. 6d. He had an equal number stored in another place, making grand totals of nearly 900 books at £165 15s. This was the accumulation of about fifteen years, i.e., £11 1s. a year spent on books. Then there are newspapers and periodicals and paper-bound books which one loses or which disintegrate, and he prices them at £8 and £6 a year respectively. Total yearly expenditure, £25. But he was spending more than that on tobacco, nearly £40 a year. Even before the war his tobacco consumption would have cost £10 a year, and a pint of beer a day would have brought the two items to £20 a year. In 1938 the expenditure on tobacco and alcohol in the country as a whole worked out at nearly £10 a head. In 1944 the figure had risen to £23. Allowing for the children, non-smokers and non-drinkers, £40 seemed a reasonable individual figure. In other words, the cost of his own book-buying, which was so much greater than the average, was about equivalent to the combined cost of smoking and drinking. As far as he could discover, the average person was only buying three books a year before the war, amounting to an expenditure of £1 or less.

During the war Orwell consistently overworked. He was an enthusiastic member of the Home Guard (though very critical of its organisation) and the additional strain must have been a heavy one. The constant artificial light in stuffy rooms which was characteristic of wartime London must have further weakened him. Like many others, he was working long into the night and when his work was finished he could often only get a few hours' disturbed sleep on a camp-bed. In the last year of the war his wife died—probably from sheer lack of strength, he told a friend. His generosity and his serious attitude towards the struggle led him to forego part of his rations, 'so that there should be more for other people'. He wanted the war to be a great communal enterprise and he did not wait for the government to decree it. By the time the war was over he was in great demand, he was earning large sums of money, but it came too late to save his health. He was writing regularly for *Tribune*, the *Observer*, *Partisan Review*, the *New Leader* and reviewing for the *Manchester Evening News*. *Animal Farm* was an immediate success (although he found difficulty at first in finding a publisher for it) and was made a Book of the Month choice in America. At the age of forty-two he could at least regard himself as well-off. His literary and political interests were wider, if anything, than they had ever been before: the Communist totalitarian threat, the political dangers deriving from the growing ascendancy of scientists, post-war exhaustion in England, the adulteration of the English language by journalists, propagandists and advertisers. In 1947 he realised that this sudden popularity was not necessarily an advantage to a writer. He wanted to write the book for which all his earlier work had been a preparation, so he retired to Jura, one of the most inaccessible islands of the Hebrides, saying he wished to escape, with his adopted son, from possible atomic war (a most unlikely story). The scenery was delightful. Primitive conditions, a damp house and long, arduous journeys to the mainland scarcely helped his physical recovery. In 1949 he was ordered South and entered a sanatorium in Gloucestershire. A little later he was removed to University College Hospital, London. Somehow he managed to finish *1984*. 'It wouldn't have been so gloomy', he said, 'if I hadn't been so ill.'

The disease from which he was suffering was consumption of the lung. After his tenth year he was seldom in good health during the winter. One of the reasons for his unpopularity at school had been his ill-health, which did not allow him to participate on a level with other boys, and which, in any case, no one really believed in.

'I had defective bronchial tubes and a lesion in one lung which was not discovered till many years later. Hence I not only had a chronic cough, but running was a torment to me. In those days,

however, "wheeziness" or "chestiness", as it was called, was
either diagnosed as imagination or was looked on as essentially a
moral disorder, caused by overeating. "You wheeze like a con-
certina", Sim would say disapprovingly as he stood behind my
chair. "You're perpetually stuffing yourself with food, that's
why." My cough was referred to as a "stomach cough", which
made it sound both disgusting and reprehensible. The cure for it
was hard running, which, if you kept it up long enough, ultimately
"cleared your chest".' (*Such, Such Were the Joys.*)

And of course, he had never given way to it or even tried to
coax it. He seemed to regard it as a challenge which it would be
unmanly not to take up. His ruined lung was dragged through
hotel kitchens and spikes and common lodging-houses and war
trenches and Home Guard exercises, and then finally to the
harsh landscapes of the Hebrides.

During his last days he was still reading the newspapers
carefully, on the look-out for journalistic misuse of words. He was
contemplating a study of Joseph Conrad, meditating on the
interaction of the English and continental mind, anarchism, the
sensitivity of Jewish intellectuals. He had decided to forsake
his old polemical method of writing and to concentrate on
human relations, and had even sketched out a story in the new
manner. He was considering sending his son to a good public
school, though he hoped they would have been abolished by the
time he was ready. (By this I imagine he meant he hoped the
State schools would have incorporated the better aspects of the
public schools.) Little practical details could always hold his
attention. Towards the end he amused himself with the different
ways of making tea. All his life he seems to have tinkered with
manual jobs, which he enjoyed doing but did badly. Once
when I visited him he had just bought a Handyman's book. On
the other hand, he was helpless with machinery and disliked it.
Flory in *Burmese Days* had been 'a fool about machinery'.

During these last months he married again. His second wife
was Sonia Brownell who had been editorial assistant on *Horizon*,
which had published so much of his best work and had given
him so much encouragement under the guidance of his old
school friend, Cyril Connolly. Meanwhile, the one lung that
remained to him was not much worse but it was not responding
well to streptomycin treatment. His body was wasting and

plans were being made to remove him to a Swiss sanatorium when he died suddenly after a haemorrhage on 23 January, 1950.

Chapter III

Views on the Raj

YOU COULD make a rough plan of Orwell's literary career by listing in chronological order the 'subjects' which he tackled in his effort to understand the world about him. The first of these was Imperialism and it was unlike the others because it was not deliberately chosen. He became part of the imperialist machine by enlisting in the Burma Police. I doubt if he did this out of any curiosity about how a modern empire is administered. He was fresh from school, could not be too choosey about jobs, and probably had the young man's ideas of adventure in a distant Oriental land. So he went to Burma and discovered that it was part of his job to be hated:

> 'In Moulmein, in Lower Burma, I was hated by large numbers of people—the only time in my life that I have been important enough for this to happen to me. I was sub-divisional police officer of the town, and in an aimless, petty kind of way anti-European feeling was very bitter. No one had the guts to raise a riot, but if a European woman went through the bazaars alone somebody would probably spit betel juice over her dress. As a police officer I was an obvious target and was baited whenever it seemed safe to do so. When a nimble Burman tripped me up on the football field and the referee (another Burman) looked the other way, the crowd yelled with hideous laughter. This happened more than once. In the end the sneering yellow faces of the young men that met me everywhere, the insults hooted after me when I was at a safe distance, got badly on my nerves. The young Buddhist priests were the worst of all. There were several thousands of them in the town and none of them seemed to have anything to do except stand on street corners and jeer at Europeans.' (*Shooting an Elephant.*)

He could not understand this at the time. He thought he had gone to Burma to help a backward people. He had had no education in imperialism (a lot of insidious propaganda, of

67

course) and had to think things out in the utter silence imposed
on every thoughtful Englishman in imperial service. He did not
even know that the British Empire was dying, nor that it was
'a great deal better than the younger empires that are going
to supplant it'. All he knew was that he was stuck between the
hatred for the empire he served that was growing in him and his
rage against the people who made his job so difficult. With one
part of his mind he thought of the British Raj as an unbreakable
tyranny imposed on helpless people, with another he thought
the greatest joy in the world would be to drive a bayonet into
a Buddhist priest's guts. He said any Anglo-Indian official will
admit to this twin attitude towards his job—but only if you
catch him off duty. On duty he is correct and admits
neither.

The majority of Anglo-Indians, he said, are not nearly so
complacent about their position as people at home believe.
From the most unexpected quarters you will suddenly hear an
outburst such as: 'Of course, we've no right in this blasted
country at all. Only now we're here for God's sake let's stay
here.' No modern man really believes it is right to invade a
foreign country and hold it down by force. Foriegn oppression
is a much more understandable evil than economic oppression.
Millions of Englishmen tamely admit to being robbed to keep
a few worthless idlers in luxury, but they rise like one man
against the very idea of being governed by, say, Chinese. Many
of the people at home who complain bitterly about British rule
in the colonies live on unearned dividends without a single
qualm of conscience. But all this secret realisation of guilt is
broken on one economic rock: Am I expected to throw up a
good job? The power of inertia is not the least one upholding
imperial rule.

'The result is that every Anglo-Indian is haunted by a sense of
guilt which he usually conceals as best he can, because there is no
freedom of speech, and merely to be overheard making a seditious
remark may damage his career. All over India there are Englishmen who secretly loathe the system of which they are part; and
just occasionally, when they are quite certain of being in the right
company, their hidden bitterness overflows. I remember a night
I spent on the train with a man in the Educational Service, a
stranger to myself whose name I never discovered. It was too hot

to sleep and we spent the night in talking. Half an hour's cautious questioning decided each of us that the other was "safe"; and then for hours, while the train jolted slowly through the pitch-black night, sitting up in our bunks with bottles of beer handy, we damned the British Empire—damned it from the inside, intelligently and intimately. It did us both good. But we had been speaking forbidden things, and in the haggard morning light when the train crawled into Mandalay, we parted as guiltily as any adulterous couple.' (*The Road to Wigan Pier*.)

Orwell discovered through personal experience the faulty bases of imperial rule. Officially the unpleasant truth was concealed behind a big lie. The British were bringing Progress to backward peoples. This Progress was haphazard and dependent on the other and real interest of the imperialists, exploitation. Whether a particular part of the country actually benefited from British Rule had very little to do with its needs and almost everything with its strategic situation. Whether the forms of Progress really made life easier for its recipients was a moot point. Kyauktada, for instance, where the action takes place in *Burmese Days*, had been selected for 'improvement' because it proved a convenient spot for a railway terminus. In 1910 it became the headquarters of a district and a seat of Progress—'interpretable as a block of law courts, with their army of fat but ravenous pleaders, a hospital, a school and one of those huge, durable jails which the English have built everywhere between Gibraltar and Hong Kong'. These institutions are necessary in a modern society but their value is corrupted by the hypocrisy which lies behind them. It was the hypocrisy that Flory loathed. He admitted that he was there to make money and resented the 'white man's burden' humbug. This was the subject of many friendly arguments between him and his Indian friend, Dr Veraswami, who would have supported British power (and, of course, his own job and prestige) to the last British Tommy. He was genuinely puzzled by Flory's talk of 'living a lie'. Flory tried to explain:

'. . . the lie that we're here to uplift our poor black brothers instead of to rob them. I suppose it's a natural enough lie. But it corrupts us, it corrupts us in ways you can't imagine. There's an everlasting sense of being a sneak and a liar that torments us and drives us to justify ourselves night and day. It's at the bottom of half our beastliness to the natives. We Anglo-Indians could be

almost bearable if we'd only admit that we're thieves and go on
thieving without any humbug.'

Although Kipling is rarely spoken of these days, he was
responsible more than anyone else for popularising the notion
of the noble white man providing salvation for the noble but
unfortunate savage. Yet Orwell points out that Kipling never
really understood the real basis of imperialism. Kipling was
a romantic who was never inside imperialism; one might say he
made occasional forays from the periphery. He could not understand what was happening because he never had any grasp of
the economic forces underlying imperial expansion. He never
realised that an empire is primarily a money-making concern—
in fact, many people inside the system never fully understood
this. Naive boys when they leave school, they go out to the
colonies and live in an enclosed society with its club and its
round of parties and they never reach the intellectual maturity
that is forced upon those who stay at home. Kipling saw
Imperialism as a kind of forcible evangelising. You turn a
Gatling gun on a mob of unarmed 'natives', then you establish
the 'law', which includes roads, railways and a courthouse. The
commercial houses and plantations seem unimportant and
unimpressive alongside these achievements. And in the long
run the motives which brought the Empire into existence
would end by destroying it. Malayan jungles were cleared for
rubber estates. During the last war they were handed over
intact to the Japanese. In the event the sanctity of property was
more important than the prolongation of the Empire.

If you examined this Empire of 1910 without prejudice and
sentimentality you soon realised that most of the officials were
superfluous. It was true, they were no worse than any other
body of random men. To complete their careers they spent
thirty years, not very well paid, in an alien country and came
home with wrecked livers and a pineapple backside from sitting
in cane chairs, to settle down as the bores of some second-rate
Club. But there was no point in idealising them. The idea was
prevalent that the men in 'outposts of Empire' were at least
able and hard-working. Apart from the scientific services such
as the Forest Department and the Public Works Department,
Orwell said, this was untrue. Most of the other jobs could be

done by any native official. In fact, most of the real work of administration was done by native subordinates. Few of the British officials worked as hard or as efficiently as the postmaster of a provincial town in England. But the real backbone of the despotism was the Army. In British colonies the Army is not very noticeable, but everyone knows it is there. 'Given the Army, the officials and the business men can rub along safely enough even if they are fools. And most of them *are* fools. A dull, decent people, cherishing and fortifying their dullness behind a quarter of a million bayonets.' (*Burmese Days.*)

The officials realised this, though they only admitted it by implication. There is an interesting conversation between Westfield, District Superintendent of Police, and Ellis, manager of a local company. Each realises and feels acutely his position. They realise they are not necessary to the development of Burma and their refusal to admit it irritates them and leads to fairly frequent outbursts. They feel the country is not governed firmly enough. Westfield believed that the good old days of the Indian Empire were numbered. Its ruin, according to him, was due to too much legality imposed by a timid government at home. Only the reintroduction of martial law could save the Empire from decay—by which he meant a situation in which he was no longer needed. 'All this paper-chewing and chit-passing. Office babus are the real rulers of this country now. Our number's up. Best thing we can do is to shut up shop and let 'em stew in their own juice.' He had the Anglo-Indian's familiar and really compulsive view that the withdrawal of the British was bound to lead to internecine warfare to such a degree that a chastened community would invite the sahibs back. Ellis adopted the opposite viewpoint. 'We could put things right in a month if we chose. It only needs a pennyworth of pluck. Look at Amritsar. Look how they caved in after that. Dyer knew the stuff to give them. Poor old Dyer! That was a dirty job. Those cowards in England have got something to answer for.'

Ellis had been driven nearly insane by his sense of frustration and his hatred of the people he had gone out to 'help'. The smallest incident would rouse in him a fury which he was finally unable to restrain. When the servant at the Club told him he

'found it very difficult' to keep the ice cool Ellis shouted at
him in sudden rage. It was not because the ice was melting,
although that helped to make life difficult, but because the
servant, a 'native', used a standard English phrase instead of the
pidgin he was expected to use. He was talking like an 'uppity
nigger' in the States. How much longer would they be able to
control these people and keep their jobs if the servants began to
talk as though they had swallowed a dictionary? The great
days of the Empire had been when they were leading the natives
towards the light of civilisation. It became distinctly unbearable
when the light actually came within the range of vision.

What was this civilisation? Orwell knew that there were some
extremely valuable things in Western culture, but how many
reached the shores of Burma, let alone up-country stations?
One of the chief criticisms of British colonial rule, especially in
India, has been its failure to export the better aspects of English
life. Burma received irritable officials, Scotch whisky and Club-
lounging and never saw any worthwhile samples of English art
and culture. How could it? What could these men bring that
wouldn't be better left behind? Time and again Flory had to
run from the Club before he started throwing bottles around.
'Dull boozing witless porkers! Was it possible that they could
go on week after week, year after year, repeating word for
word the same evil-minded drivel, like a parody of a fifth-rate
story in *Blackwood's*? Would none of them ever think of anything new to say? Oh, what a place, what people! What a
civilisation is this of ours—this godless civilisation founded on
whisky, *Blackwood's* and the Bonzo pictures! God have mercy on
us, for all of us are part of it.'

Each man felt he was driven against his will. Technically
he was a leader, but his energy and initiative had been drained
away and in practice he was almost as powerless as the people
whom he helped to keep in order. Not only was he stunted in
his development, remaining permanently stuck in intellectual
adolescence, but the whole of his life followed a plan which he
could no longer alter. This did not apply merely to the round of
duties and the round of Club-lounging, it even applied to those
details in which he prided himself that he was his own master.
Orwell said the real futility of the white man's dominion became

apparent when, by turning tyrant, he destroyed his own freedom. He gave an example of this from his own experience in
Shooting an Elephant. An elephant had run amok and the incident
had been reported to him. Going out with his rifle he was
followed by a huge crowd, anxious to see the white man shoot
the elephant. When at last he found the beast he realised that it
was not necessary to shoot it. Its frenzy had passed and also
an elephant was a creature of considerable value to its owner.
He did not want to shoot it, but all around him was the
impalpable yet forcible pressure of the crowd urging him on.

'Here was I, the white man with his gun, standing in front of
the unarmed native crowd—seemingly the leading actor of the
piece; but in reality I was only an absurd puppet pushed to and
fro by the will of those yellow faces behind. I perceived in this
moment that when the white man turns tyrant it is his own
freedom that he destroys. He becomes a sort of hollow, posing
dummy, the conventionalised figure of a sahib. For it is the
condition of his rule that he shall spend his life in trying to
impress the "natives", and so in every crisis he has got to do what
the "natives" expect of him. He wears a mask, and the face grows
to fit it. I had got to shoot the elephant. I had committed myself
to doing it when I sent for the rifle. A sahib has got to act like a
sahib; he has got to appear resolute, to know his own mind and
do definite things. To come all that way, rifle in hand, with two
thousand people marching at my heels, and then to trail feebly
away, having done nothing—no, that was impossible. The
crowd would laugh at me. And my whole life, every white man's
life in the East, was one long struggle not to be laughed at.'

Even when the sahib was shooting at 'natives' instead of ele-
phants it was the expected sahib action. Now that the behaviour
of sahibs to natives has changed there has been a corresponding
change in the native's assessment of the sahibs. In the past, if a
schoolboy jeered at a European he was beaten (as by Ellis in
Burmese Days). This was indefensible conduct and arose out of
the sahib's sense of moral deficiency. Today nothing happens,
the boy may pass in peace. As a result the boy thinks the sahib
is losing his grip and jeers more than ever. And he is right, the
sahib *is* losing his grip. If only he had been morally strong enough
in the first place to rule without undue violence and decent
enough to admit that he was in the country with the ultimate
purpose of losing his grip, he would not suffer so much from

outraged prestige as he does today. When he makes the change of attitude today (largely because he is compelled to by world opinion) he is surprised that his action is not extolled by the native population. All these men were so muddled, so haphazardly selected for their jobs, so ignorant of what an Empire really is, they were bound to feel at odds when old ways gave place to new.

In *Burmese Days* Orwell listed the beatitudes of the pukka sahib. They were:

> Keeping up our prestige.
> The firm hand (without the velvet glove).
> We white men must hang together.
> Give them an inch and they'll take an ell.
> *Esprit de corps.*

In practice these principles were supported by a large number of minor fallacies, most interesting of which is the sunstroke fallacy, to which Orwell alludes several times. The European with his thinner skull (the implication being that he is a more delicately and sensitively constructed creature), is much more susceptible to sunstroke than the thick-skulled native. It is a measure of his superiority. This belief was especially cherished by the Eurasians, those unhappy people whose main object in life was to be accepted by the European community but who were consistently snubbed by everyone. One of them, ever anxious for a chat, could not resist warning Flory and Elizabeth of the danger they ran. 'Also, sir-madam, may I advise to you, wearing only Terai hat is not judicious in April, sir. For the natives all well, their skulls are adamant. But for us sunstroke ever menaces. Very deadly is the sun upon European skull.' Another favourite gambit of his was a discussion of his prickly heat; natives were supposed not to suffer from it.

Now Orwell was convinced that this was a typically British superstition. No doubt there are cranial differences between the races but few people who take this attitude towards sunstroke have troubled to acquaint themselves with them nor do they understand the factors that produce sunstroke. I myself have twice had mild attacks of it, once in Gibraltar and once in the Sudan, but so have many thousands of Moslem pilgrims at Jedda. Orwell felt that he was confirmed in his doubts when

Wingate's men, the Chindits, forsook the pith helmet for the
slouch hat in Burma, He himself first saw through this superstition when he lost his topi in a river and marched bareheaded
all day without ill-effects. A little research proved that the topi
was a recent invention. The early European in India did not
wear it.

'But why should the British in India have built up this superstition about sunstroke? Because an endless emphasis on the
differences between the "natives" and yourself is one of the
necessary props of imperialism. You can only rule over a subject
race, especially when you are in a small minority, if you honestly
believe yourself to be racially superior, and it helps towards this if
you can believe that the subject race is *biologically* different. There
were quite a number of ways in which Europeans in India used
to believe, without any evidence, that Asiatic bodies differed
from their own. Even quite considerable anatomical differences
were supposed to exist. But this nonsense about Europeans being
subject to sunstroke, and Orientals not, was the most cherished
superstition of all. The thin skull was the mark of racial superiority,
and the pith topi was a sort of emblem of imperialism.' ('As I
Please', *Tribune*, 20 October, 1944.)

There are two interesting footnotes to this. First of all, it is
rare these days to see an Englishman wearing a topi in the
tropics, but increasingly common to see it worn by the native
population. Secondly, only a few months before he wrote the
above Orwell had referred in the *Observer* to 'the incredible
insensitiveness to pain of the Mongolian peoples'. This does
not invalidate his sunstroke argument, but I am not sure how
much this also may not be a superstition. Orientals appear to
suffer pain more stoically than we do but they may possess
greater self-control.

Orwell never stated in any detail why he left Burma. At
different times he gave different reasons, including 'other
reasons', but the main one was his dislike of imperialism which
had become unbearable. In *Partisan Review* (September-
October 1942) he stated, 'it is quite true that I served five years
in the Indian Police. It is also true that I gave up that job,
partly because it didn't suit me but mainly because I would not
any longer be a servant of imperialism. I am against imperialism
because I know something about it from the inside. The whole
history of this is to be found in my writings, including a novel

which I think I can claim was a kind of prophecy of what happened this year in Burma.' But beyond this Orwell does not tell us much about his feelings in Burma. Most of his criticisms and reactions to imperialism are of the rather conventional type that I have quoted. And towards the end of his life he made a blunder which leads one to imagine that his feelings about Burma were mixed, even muddled. In reviewing Graham Greene's *The Heart of the Matter* in the *New Yorker* he says that Greene's hero, Major Scobie, 'would not be an officer in a colonial police force if he were the kind of man we are told he is—that is, a man whose chief characteristic is a horror of causing pain'. This is a remarkable statement coming from a man who was himself an officer in a colonial police force and whose chief characteristic was a sense of decency!

However, Orwell's own story is that he considered imperialism wicked and doomed and that he had been dirtied by serving it. This explains the next phase in his development, which I have referred to in the previous chapter, his desire to mingle with the oppressed in expiation of his sin. He had been identified with the oppressors, now he must identify himself with the oppressed. It is my belief that Orwell was very late in reaching maturity. Even by the time he left Burma at the age of twenty-four he had not really discovered his true self. His novel, *Burmese Days*, though not published until 1934 (it was probably written some years earlier), was not particularly Orwellian. A score of other young writers of the time might have written it, given the same same experiences and background. It has none of Orwell's customary sympathy for the victims of circumstances. Later he would have realised that the British officials in Burma were as much victims of circumstances in their way as the Burmese themselves. But there is little realisation of this in the book. They are referred to as 'witless porkers' and only on one occasion, I believe, was there a grudging admission that they were fundamentally decent human beings who had been pitched into a job that was too big for them. And there is probably a good reason for this. Orwell's critical apparatus was by no means trained or settled when he was in Burma. He went out with a probably genuine belief that he would be able to do what Kipling had told him everyone else was doing—carrying a portion of the White Man's Burden. He discovered that no real attempt was being made to carry the Burden at all and after five years he was bitterly disillusioned. *Burmese Days* was written in the full flush of disillusionment, without the softening influences of his earlier naivety or his later maturity. Here and there remnants of the earlier attitude broke through and produced rather uncomfortable strains in the novel's texture. Malcolm Muggeridge, revaluing *Burmese Days* in the *World Review* Orwell memorial issue (June 1950), says it is an over-simplification to say that Orwell's later views were the product of revulsion from his Burmese experiences. He genuinely did hate cruelty and overt authority, but he also romanticised the Raj and its mystique. This, I take it, was the hangover of his youthful attitude and we must be careful how to apply it. I have said (quoting Connolly) that Orwell had nothing of the schoolboy's normal romanticism. I don't think it is true to say that he romanticised the Raj, but I do think he probably romanticised the part he could play in humanising the Raj. Muggeridge points out that the most vivid episodes in the novel are those which lend themselves most naturally to romantic treatment, Flory's hunting expedition with Elizabeth and the attack on the English club. The description of the Europeans in their club is always a little unreal, a little too intense. He projected thoughts and feelings too easily into action. 'A tremendous struggle went on inside Orwell', writes Muggeridge, 'between one side of his character, a sort of Brushwood Boy side, which made him admire the insolence and good looks of Verrall, and a deep intellectual disapprobation of everything Verrall stood for.' Crossgates was being enacted all over again. Verrall was the 'good type of boy', the boy who was always 'in favour'. the boy whose pater had a Daimler with electric lights and who regularly holidayed in Scotland. Orwell envied him and would have admired him if he hadn't suffered so much from a sense of inferiority.

The admiration for Kipling had left its mark on Orwell. 'When I used sometimes to say to Orwell', writes Muggeridge, 'that he and Kipling had a great deal in common, he would laugh that curious rusty laugh of his and change the subject.' There was, perhaps inevitably, a strain of romaniticism in

Orwell's make-up. The traditional brand of imperial romanticism has persisted so long, bolstered as it was by the genius of
Kipling, it sometimes becomes difficult to realise that another
brand can exist. Flory was in some ways the villain-type of the
old melodrama (semi-socialist, would-be highbrow, unpleasant
to look at) but it is he who saves the English community from
the Burmese mob. Not, be it noticed, the stiff-lipped District
Commissioner nor the self-assured Chief of Police. Flory was
not a satisfactory alternative, from the popular romantic point
of view, because he is never entirely sure of himself and he
tends to do things by halves. He had too many complications
to be a Henty hero. Yet the fact remains that this despised,
unpukka type took action when action was needed. It is equivalent to an art collector winning the girl in a Hollywood film.
And this new type of hero was, in a way, prophetic. The old
heroes are on the way out, the Political Service are being
pensioned off, and *Blackwood's* will have to look somewhere else
for its darlings. The Englishman in the tropics is becoming
increasingly a technician, a man who can do something which
the native people cannot do, but had nevertheless been to a
shockingly unfashionable school. There will be a crisis in the
Blackwood's boardroom.

I have strayed rather a long way from imperialism in pursuit
of romanticism. Orwell's views on the British Empire mellowed
as he got into perspective and was able to step back and look at
it from a distance with the advantage of actual knowledge
still in him. In his essay on 'Rudyard Kipling' (*Critical Essays*)
he made the claim on behalf of the nineteenth-century Anglo-
Indians that at least they had got things done, even if in other
respects they were not a very attractive crowd. This is, or was,
an activist or Western virtue—I say 'was' because one of the
things that is happening today is that the passivist East no
longer appears to be passive. There are two aspects of imperialism which it is as well to keep separate. First of all, that it is
morally wrong, and secondly, that it is technically necessary.
That is, providing we accept technical progress as necessary as
most people do today. (Those who oppose the concepts are
very small minority groups and isolated individuals.) Today we
believe that the correct method of developing backward

countries which have not the power to develop themselves is by
some form of international trusteeship and capital investment.
But it would have been useless proposing this in the nineteenth
century, the very idea was beyond the reach of the great
majority of imaginations. It is only necessary to compare the
Sudan with its neighbour, Ethiopia, to see the great difference
that imperialism makes to the material progress of backward
countries. Admittedly, material progress is not of prime importance but we happen to live in a world in which all parties,
capitalists and communists, whites and blacks, townsmen and
countrymen, rich and poor, have pinned their hopes, or many
of them, on material progress. Writing of Kipling's vision of
Empire, Orwell says:

> 'The nineteenth-century Anglo-Indians, to name the least
> sympathetic of his idols, were at any rate people who did things.
> It may be that all they did was evil, but they changed the face
> of the earth (it is instructive to look at a map of Asia and compare
> the railway system of India with that of the surrounding countries),
> whereas they could have achieved nothing, could not have
> maintained themselves in power for a single week, if the normal
> Anglo-Indian outlook had been that of, say, E. M. Forster.'

Another fact that is rarely taken into consideration by
critics of imperialism is that there is an ebb and flow in imperialist morality. That imperialism itself is immoral there is no doubt,
but once it exists there are variations in its practice and its
conscience. This ebb and flow had been particularly noticeable
in Indian administration, ranging from the uninhibited corruption of Clive's day to the comparative enlightenment of
Macaulay's. Orwell contrasted the imperialists of Kipling's day
favourably with their modern successors. The first were rough,
uncompromising men who did a few good jobs among the bad,
most of them unpleasant, whereas the later ones (this was
before the concept of Empire changed to that of Common-
wealth) were as often as not rather loquacious men whose view
of Empire came from a city boardroom. In an earlier essay on
Kipling (*New English Weekly*, 23 January, 1936) he wrote:

> 'What is much more distasteful in Kipling than sentimental
> plots or vulgar tricks of style, is the imperialism to which he chose
> to lend his genius. The most one can say is that when he made it
> the choice was more forgivable than it would be now. The

imperialism of the 'eighties and 'nineties was sentimental, ignorant and dangerous, but it was not entirely despicable. The picture then called up by the word "empire" was a picture of overworked officials and frontier skirmishes, not of Lord Beaverbrook and Australian butter. It was still possible to be an imperialist and a gentleman, and of Kipling's *personal* decency there can be no doubt.'

It is only a choice of evils, of course, but in the early days the imperialist was the pioneer, who no longer exists. It is a human characteristic to feel a sentimental attraction towards the pioneer, just as the Americans have a distinct tenderness for the gun-toting waggoners and hunters who ran the Indians off the prairies and herded them into Reservations, a tenderness that is to be found at every level of their literature.

The 'bad' period of Imperialism in India was the latter half of the nineteenth century, and there were very practical reasons for this as there usually are for most changes of psychological attitude. Kipling's active career followed this period and ended before the boardroom phase became dominant. Even during this phase there were enlightened men in the Indian service but they were unable to make much headway. One of these was Lord Beveridge who believed that the aim of British rule should be 'to prepare for its own extinction'.

'A generation earlier these views would have seemed reasonable to Macaulay; a generation later, much of what Henry Beveridge advocated was within sight of happening. But the period covered by his career, 1858-93, was a bad period in Indian-British relations. Among the British, imperialist sentiment was stiffening and an arrogant attitude towards "natives" was becoming obligatory. The greatest single cause was probably the cutting of the Suez Canal. As soon as the journey from England became quick and easy the number of Englishwomen in India greatly increased, and for the first time the Europeans were able to form themselves into an exclusive "all white" society.' ('A Lost World', *Observer*, 1 February, 1948.)

But there was a worse change coming, and again it was the result of an advance in physical control of Nature. The telegraph made it possible for the Empire to be governed by Whitehall. On the whole, this has been to the advantage of the native population in areas of white settlement (in Kenya, for instance, the settlers regard Whitehall as the major barrier to a society where white dominance shall be absolute), but in countries like India where there was no settlement, only government by officials under contract, the remoteness of Whitehall hindered the projects of the better type of official more than it hindered those of the rapacious type. As a result it became increasingly difficult to recruit the best type of man for the colonial service. Orwell describes this trend at some length in *The Lion and the Unicorn* and it is worth quoting because it throws some light on the frustrations he experienced personally while in Burma.

'Thirty years ago the Blimp class was already losing its vitality. The middle-class families celebrated by Kipling, the prolific lowbrow families whose sons officered the army and navy and swarmed all over the waste places of the earth from the Yukon to the Irrawaddy, were dwindling before 1914. The thing that had killed them was the telegraph. In a narrowing world, more and more governed from Whitehall, there was every year less room for individual initiative. Men like Clive, Nelson, Nicholson, Gordon would find no place for themselves in the modern British Empire. By 1920 nearly every inch of the colonial empire was in the grip of Whitehall. Well-meaning, over-civilised men, in dark suits and black felt hats, with neatly-rolled umbrellas crooked over the left forearm, were imposing their constipated view of life in Malaya and Nigeria, Mombasa and Mandalay. The one-time Empire-builders were reduced to the status of clerks, buried deeper and deeper under mounds of paper and red tape. In the early 'twenties one could see, all over the Empire, the older officials, who had known more spacious days, writhing impotently under the changes that were happening. From that time onwards it has been next door to impossible to induce young men of spirit to take any part in imperial administration. And what was true of the official world was true also of the commercial. The great monopoly companies swallowed up hosts of petty traders. Instead of going out to trade adventurously in the Indies one went to an office stool in Bombay or Singapore. And life in Bombay or Singapore was actually duller and safer than life in London. Imperialist sentiment remained strong in the middle class, chiefly owing to family tradition, but the job of administering the Empire had ceased to appeal. Few able men went East of Suez if there was any way of avoiding it.'

There is no doubt that the awareness of this was strong in Burma. All the club members who had not yet learnt to bury their frustration were liable to burst into vituperation against what they called paper-chewing. The mind of the Indian official, unless he was a clod, was a pretty mess. He had dreamed of being an empire-builder and he found himself an office boy, compelled to go on trek occasionally for the sake of his soul, if not for the Travel Allowance. He was expected to keep up the pretence of sharing the famous Burden but in his heart he didn't believe in it. He hated the natives in proportion to the amount of legality he had to observe in dealing with them. He would have liked to have cleared out but wasn't sure where he would find another job. And then, the crowning blow, he was expected to fraternise with men he had always despised. It was becoming the practice to open the British clubs to certain selected members of the native population, and circulars were being sent round recommending such action. Apart from Flory, everyone in Kyauktada club was opposed to this. The true significance of *Burmese Days* is pinpointed in one moment of irony. While Maxwell, acting Divisional Forest Officer, was being killed and his body cut to pieces, the other club members were concerning themselves with the blackballing of Dr Veraswami, whom Flory had proposed for membership. In a rage Ellis scatters the black and white balls over the floor. At that moment the bearers come in, carrying Maxwell's body, and one of them stumbles and nearly falls as he treads on a white ball. The irony is two-fold. To the pukka sahib Maxwell is dead because the natives have been given too much freedom. To Orwell it has happened because they have been shut out too long.

In Orwell's view the failure of the British imperial method lay in its stupidity rather than in any sinister intention to oppress people for its own sake. He knew that British Imperial rule was relatively mild, that compared with some other rules, self-rule as well as alien rule, it was benevolent. Amritsar became a bye-word merely because it was the single incident of its kind in nearly two centuries. He always bore in mind that the British Empire was policed by an army that would have been considered ridiculously small by some European despots with few foreign possessions of their own. He was scornful of those who called British rule in India 'Fascist' because it was an obvious misuse of a word which had a fairly exact meaning if you took the trouble to look for it. The imperial relationship is not a simple one and probably no people could ever make a success of it in human terms. The Indian peasant regarded all Englishmen as oppressors and most Englishmen despised the Indian as primitive. These attitudes were rooted in the two cultures and could not be eliminated by a fiat of will. In his 'Letter to an Indian' (*Tribune*, 19 March, 1943) Orwell wrote:

> 'We are all nearer to the blimp than we are to the Indian peasant, but don't expect people to like being told so. Opinions sentimentally held are liable to be suddenly reversed. I know more than one intellectual who has started out with a burning zeal to "free India" and ended up by feeling that there is a lot to be said for General Dyer.'

The British ruled India and ninety-nine per cent of them were abysmally ignorant of it. India had in fact become a bore and a joke, thanks to the revulsion against Kipling and the presence of pickled Anglo-Indian officials living in retirement up and down the land. So there was really no public consciousness of India, only of the Empire, and 'Empire' was one of those sacred words like 'mother' and 'king' and 'navy'. In the last resort no one wanted the Empire to disintegrate, although some, particularly Left-wing intellectuals, were rather shamefaced about it. It was realised in a vague way that the high standard of living enjoyed by the population as a whole had something to do with possessing an Empire. 'Under the capitalist system, in order that England may live in comparative comfort, a hundred million Indians must live on the verge of starvation—an evil state of affairs, but you acquiesce in it every time you step into a taxi or eat a plate of strawberries and cream.' (*The Road to Wigan Pier.*) The Indians also realised this and knew that whatever his personal opinion, every Englishman was an active though unthinking oppressor.

Chapter IV

The Meaning of Poverty

IF IMPERIALISM was the first of the 'subjects' Orwell applied himself to, the second was poverty. There was a considerable difference of approach, inasmuch as his approach to poverty was deliberate and intentionally undertaken. In no fewer than four books (*Down and Out in Paris and London, A Clergyman's Daughter, Keep the Aspidistra Flying* and *The Road To Wigan Pier*) he examined poverty under modern conditions and wrote his report. In each of these books there is a different slant. *Down and Out*, the best, is an account of his personal search for poverty. ('Poverty is what I am writing about', he said in the concluding paragraph of the first chapter.) In the two novels he puts the information he has gathered to fictional use. *A Clergyman's Daughter* is a hotchpotch and the poverty theme is interlinked with another, loss of faith and the necessity to maintain one's early world-view. *Keep the Aspidistra Flying* is entirely about lack of money, the basis of poverty, and at times reaches a level of fanatical bitterness. *The Road to Wigan Pier* was commissioned. Orwell was asked to write a book about the condition of the working class and characteristically chose its most depressed section, the unemployed miners, as his subject.

Orwell saw poverty in plenty in Burma but it does not appear to have roused his conscience specifically because Oriental poverty is taken for granted and its causes are different from those that account for European poverty. (You would expect Orientals to be poor because they are exploited. But why should there be abject poverty in the exploiting nations?) I have only traced one reference to poverty in *Burmese Days*, and it is a reflection in the mind of Verrall, the only really pukka sahib in the novel. 'Like all sons of rich families, he thought poverty disgusting and that poor people are poor because they prefer disgusting habits.' This is undoubtedly Orwell's starting point. He makes no bones about the fact that until he reached manhood he shared the views of his class about working people because his home and educational backgrounds made it inevitable.

When he left his own society and became poor by an act of will he discovered a completely new world which had no relation at all to the comfortable middle-class assumptions about it. No one reading *Down and Out* can miss the degradation that runs through the life he describes like a thick vein. Whether this degradation had been sought by vicious characters or not, there it is, something completely alien from the decency of normal well-fed life. He describes a horrifying argument between an old-age pensioner of seventy and a young stevedore in a common lodging-house. The old man was almost crying with grief and rage and furiously abused the stevedore, who taunted him back. This was the kind of exchange between them:

'*The old-age pensioner:* You ————!

The stevedore: Shut yer mouth, you ole ————, afore I set about yer!

The old-age pensioner: Jest you try it on, you ————! I'm thirty years older'n you, but it wouldn't take much to make me give you one as'd knock you into a bucketful of piss!

The stevedore: Ah, an' then p'raps I wouldn't smash you up after, you ole ————!'

This went on for five minutes, and ended with the old man breaking down and crying with his face in his hands. This is horrible enough, but it becomes quite ghastly when we discover that the quarrel was about a shilling's worth of food. The old man had lost his store of bread and margarine and would have nothing to eat for the next three days. The stevedore had mocked him. The question that immediately arises, and was certainly never far from Orwell's mind, is this: Were these people naturally depraved or had they been driven into depravity by poverty? Why they should be poor is another matter altogether.

Hunger is always an element of true poverty. The old-age pensioner was hungry all the time and it was the expectation of increased hunger, amounting to starvation, that first roused his spirit and then broke it. Normally hunger produces inertia, the kind of feckless behaviour that used to be attributed by common consent to the very poor. After two days without food Orwell discovered that he had a mind to do nothing but lie in bed and read the *Memoirs of Sherlock Holmes.*

> 'It was all that I felt equal to, without food. Hunger reduces one to an utterly spineless, brainless condition, more like the after-effects of influenza than anything else. It is as though one had been turned into a jellyfish, or as though all one's blood had been pumped out and luke-warm water substituted. Complete inertia is my chief memory of hunger.'

This is well known by revolutionary parties, such as the Communists. There used to be a Hunger Theory which welcomed the worst excesses of capitalist disorganisation, on the grounds that the more miserable the people became the more likely they would be to revolt. Later this theory was rejected as really hungry people are much too spiritless to do anything about it. Orwell describes one of the tramps, an Irishman named Paddy, as abject and envious, with the character of a jackal. But it was malnutrition and not vice that had destroyed his manhood. He had lived for two years on bread and margarine until both his mind and body were composed of inferior stuff. He was only half a man.

The natural result of this is that the well-fed tend to cease to regard the underfed as properly human. The mental and physical differences between the two classes are in fact so great that this is scarcely surprising. The treatment the poor receive from institutions and officials is different in kind from that received by the well-fed. The assumption is that they are a lower form of life, even if human life, can bear more discomfort and pain with less suffering, have no delicacy of feeling and possess a much coarser neural system than other men. In his essay 'How the Poor Die' (*Shooting an Elephant*) Orwell describes how he entered a Paris hospital in 1929 and was put in a ward with a lot of paupers. Every day a doctor made his rounds, followed by a troop of students, who examined all the interesting cases. 'I myself, with an exceptionally fine specimen of a bronchial rattle, sometimes had as many as a dozen students queueing up to listen to my chest.' He said they seemed to have a lack of any perception that he or the other patients were human beings.

As a non-paying patient, in the uniform nightshirt, you were primarily *a specimen*. I believe things are better now, but certainly in the past no one seemed to take it amiss that the medical profession should behave in this way to the poor. If you had pointed out that one person was treated like a human being because he had money and another like a specimen because he had none, the doctor might have felt ashamed or tried to deny it or admitted that he had never thought of it in that light before. But undoubtedly the mere fact of poverty decreased the human value of a man in the minds of the well-to-do.

Down and Out is easily obtainable and anyone who is interested in poverty must read it at some time or another. What he is certain to feel as he reads is that it describes a life which few of us had ever imagined existed, and that this life is coexistent with our own. This is an extraordinary state of affairs. We sometimes see these people, we are occasionally disgusted by them, we even write letters to the papers making well-meaning suggestions as to what should be done with them (we automatically assume that they are passive material), but until we read Orwell we have practically no conception of the lives they lead or the kind of people they are. It is true, the worst abuses of poverty in England have disappeared, but poverty itself cannot be banished *sine die*. It can come back, like the Plague. A future historian, particularly if he is an Arthur Bryant, may typify English society in the twentieth century by an account of Coronation Day or the Eton-Harrow cricket match, but a Trevelyan could equally go to Orwell and produce a picture that might serve as a study of Hell. There is one remarkable chapter in *A Clergyman's Daughter* about the outcasts in Trafalgar Square on a winter's night which is even more vivid than anything in *Down and Out*. The greater part is written in dialogue form (Orwell was probably influenced by Joyce), but here is a brief descriptive passage:

'They run, or shamble, as fast as they can to the corner of the Square where three youths are distributing surplus posters given away in charity by the morning newspapers. Charlie and Ginger come back with a thick wad of posters. The five largest men now jam themselves together on the bench, Deafie and the four women sitting across their knees; then, with infinite difficulty (as it has to be done from the inside), they wrap themselves in a monstrous cocoon of paper, several sheets thick, tucking the loose ends into their necks or breasts or between their shoulders and the back of the bench. Finally nothing is uncovered save their heads and the lower part of their legs. For their heads they fashion hoods of paper. The paper constantly comes loose and lets in cold shafts of wind, but it is now possible to sleep as much as five minutes consecutively.'

The imperial city of London, *circa* 1930, while you and I were warmly tucked between the sheets. Now and again a policeman comes and this motley cocoon has to disentangle itself and pretend it is out for a moonlight stroll. The policeman is shame-faced but he has to enforce the law. And the millionaire press barons send out posters as blankets from the heart of their charity.

These people drag out their terrible and hopeless existence (for what hope has any of landing a good job and finding himself a wife and home when he has literally nothing to start from?) because they have no money. Because they have no money they have no food and because they have no food they have no fighting spirit left. Of course, there were exceptions. Odd individuals may not be too far gone in degradation. But the majority would stay where they were, a blot on society but too feeble to be a danger. They were also a very small minority. But what Orwell discovered when he was collecting material for *The Road to Wigan Pier* was that this kind of life and the mental attitude it engendered only differed in degree from the lives lived by millions of unemployed men, with their families and children. They had not sunk so low, that was the main difference, but they were low enough. They had roofs over their heads (frequently leaky), they had a small amount of money and therefore a small amount of food (but never enough) and they had a little coal, varying in amount according to whether they lived on a coalfield or not. But the effect of poverty was the same. It produced a deadening, debilitating effect, worse for the men than for the women, because the women still had their housework and child-rearing to do. The best intellects will not stand up against such conditions, said Orwell. He had met unemployed men with genuine literary ability and he had read work by others that was far superior to the stuff that was praised so fervently by the reviewers, but they could never keep it up. Why not? Natural laziness, was the comfortable middle-class answer. The true answer is that to write well, to do anything well, you need peace of mind. You can't settle to anything, you can't command the spirit of hope that is necessary for creation, with the dull evil cloud of unemployment hanging over you. Then what about the man who cannot read without discomfort?

'Take a miner, for instance, who has worked in the pits since childhood and has been trained to be a miner and nothing else. How the devil is he to fill up the empty days? It is absurd to say that he ought to be looking for work. There is no work to look for, and everybody knows it. You can't go on looking for work every day for seven years.'

He mentions some of the alternatives—allotments and occupational centres. But these are palliatives and never very satisfactory ones. The inescapable conclusion is that under these conditions the mind is bound to corrode very rapidly. Even a trained middle-class mind would do so if subjected to the same influences.

These are old issues, but they embody experience which should not be forgotten. Also we are reminded from time to time, by documents such as the annual reports of the National Assistance Board, that such conditions and their psychological consequences are still in our midst. Extreme poverty and prolonged unemployment bring on a feeling of impotence and despair which make normal life impossible. We know that in a capitalist society there must be unemployment; what would we do without the 'labour reserve', a charming term to conceal mass misery? These people are distant from us and their reality is that of a statistical unit. But the victim doesn't feel like a statistical unit. He believes he is a human being, as human as any other, and he is sometimes driven half frantic by the knowledge that other men are still going to work. It is not the work he craves as such—most work in an industrial society has no implicit value. It is merely a means of livelihood. But constant unemployment and chronic poverty induce a feeling of impotence and despair which is far worse than any physical hardship. The horror of poverty, once it has become a habitual environment, is that it unfits a man for a better life once it is available to him. There is a great deal of grumbling these days about the failure of the poor to live gracefully once they are in better circumstances. Those who share this feeling should read *The Road to Wigan Pier* and if they are honest they will gain understanding. One of the lessons Dorothy learnt in *A Clergyman's Daughter* was that there exists an eleventh commandment: Thou Shalt Not Lose Thy Job. More than the loss of livelihood was at stake. There were also the loss of self-respect and faith in the future.

One is compelled to treat Orwell on poverty seriously because he is not sentimental about it. There are, broadly speaking, two attitudes to poverty: the indifference of the comfortable who don't like being troubled with anything unpleasant, sometimes amounting to the charge that poverty is always the reward of laziness, and the sentimentality of philanthropists and those with a political interest in the working class. Orwell had not become a politician when he took his plunge into poverty. Early in *Down and Out* he described his financial position, which amounted to about a shilling a day for a limited period, and added that if not actual poverty it was on the fringe of it. A shilling was worth more than it is today, but even so I think most people would have regarded such resources as well within the poverty line. Orwell was not concerned with people who 'haven't much money' or 'not enough money'. These phrases belie any standards, for some of the richest people in the world have complained about lack of money. He was concerned with those who tried to eke out existence on a shilling a day or less (1930) or a family of five with 37s. 6d. a week from the Unemployment Assistance Board (1936). And once you have reached this level (unless you happen to live in a community where everyone is in the same position, as on some of the coalfields) you find yourself faced with a bewildering set of complications which arise entirely out of the fact that, although you are now poor, you pretend not to be poor simply because in the past you had known better times. With a shilling in your pocket you try to give the impression that you have five. Later this will be knocked out of you but at first it represents the main problem. You stop sending clothes to the laundry; you meet the laundress in the street, you think up some lie, she thinks you're sending it

elsewhere and becomes your enemy for life. You can't answer
letters you would like to answer because of the cost of postage.
At meal-times you pretend to set off for a restaurant and later
smuggle home scraps of food that you have managed to accumu-
late. Orwell learnt his first lessons in poverty in Paris and the
examples he gives of subterfuge are different from those that
would be necessary in England, but there would still be subterfuge. In this respect, once again, he refused to romanticise
poverty. He showed it up for the dirty, wretched state it is. He
would have nothing to do with the familiar convention of the
poor man keeping his head in the air, looking the world in the
eyes, and even revelling in a mystique of the great virtue
residing in poverty. His own experience was that poverty led to
a net of lies, gross self-pity and acute boredom. These characteristics varied according to whether one was alone in poverty
or with others. The only consolation, he said, was a sense that
the future had been annihilated, a feeling of relief at reaching
bottom.

The impact of poverty inevitably varies according to environment. In a community where poverty is the norm and is never
unexpected it is least difficult to bear. A gentleman plunging
into poverty will have moments of exhilaration. Poverty is
worst for those who have feared it all their lives but have
managed to stave it off for years. He gives an example in
Coming Up For Air:

'A small shopkeeper going down the hill is a dreadful thing to
watch, but it isn't sudden and obvious like the fate of a working
man who gets the sack and promptly finds himself on the dole. It's
just a gradual chipping away of trade, with little ups and downs,
a few shillings to the bad here, a few sixpences to the good there.
Somebody who's dealt with you for years suddenly deserts and
goes to Sarazin's. Somebody else buys a dozen hens and gives
you a weekly order for corn. You can still keep going. You're still
"your own master", always a little more worried and a little
shabbier, with your capital shrinking all the time.'

And your neighbours, the other shopkeepers, notice everything.
It is better in a way when everyone is going downhill together,
you have the solidarity of a sinking ship. Because of this Orwell
found that extreme poverty was less in evidence in the industrial
North than in London. Everything is shabbier, there are fewer

motor-cars and well-dressed people, but also fewer who are obviously destitute.[1] London is a whirlpool which draws the destitute towards it. You can go to pieces and no one will notice it. But in communities where there is a strong neighbourhood feeling this is rarely allowed to happen.

Dealing with such a complex subject, with its various levels, causes and environments, it is not surprising that at times Orwell was inconsistent in his judgments. In one place, for instance, you will find him claiming that poverty frees people from ordinary standards, in another that the poor cling to the pretence of civilised behaviour even in the most abject circumstances. You have to bear the context in mind. The eccentricity is to be found in the common lodging houses and cheap pensions, where the poor live as individuals and need only mingle with their own kind. The clinging to convention will be found in the homogeneous communities where the family feeling is still strong. But as a general rule he appeared to believe that poverty, leading as it did to the lowest kinds of job, resulted in a general degeneration of manners. He noticed this in himself, and Orwell always had a high regard for good manners. In one hotel he said the kitchen staff became neurasthenic with fatigue and quarrelling became continuous. The cook, who was short, would ask Orwell to reach him down a saucepan, and he would snap back, 'Get it down yourself, you old whore!'

> 'We quarrelled over things of inconceivable pettiness. The dustbin, for instance, was an unending source of quarrels—whether it should be put where I wanted it, which was in the cook's way, or where she wanted it, which was between me and the sink. Once she nagged and nagged until at last, in pure spite, I lifted the dustbin up and put it out in the middle of the floor, where she was bound to trip over it.
> ' "Now, you cow", I said, "move it yourself."
> 'Poor old woman, it was too heavy for her to lift, and she sat down, put her head on the table and burst out crying. And I jeered at her. This is the kind of effect that fatigue has upon one's manners.'

It is worth remembering that Orwell was a public schoolboy and came from what is automatically referred to as a 'good'

---

1 These observations were made during the era of depression. Such variations continue to exist, but may alter geographically.

home. He was also noted for his natural gentleness of manner.

So here we have another progression: poverty, unpleasant work, deterioration of manners. Some people are driven by poverty to do work of which the rest of the world is quite ignorant. When he was in the North he met a tribe of newspaper-canvassers whose job 'seemed to me so hopeless, so appalling that I wondered how anyone could put up with such a thing when prison was a possible alternative'. They were employed by weekly or Sunday papers and were sent from town to town with maps and a list of streets which they had to 'work' each day. If they failed to secure a minimum of twenty orders a day they got the sack. If they got the twenty they received £2 a week and a tiny commission on anything over. Orwell got to know two of them:

> 'Both of them were middle-aged men with families to support, and one of them was a grandfather. They were on their feet ten hours a day, "working" their appointed streets, and then busy late into the night filling in blank forms for some swindle their paper was running—one of those schemes by which you are "given" a set of crockery if you take out a six weeks' subscription and send a two-shilling postal order as well. The fat one, the grandfather, used to fall asleep with his head on a pile of forms. Neither of them could afford the pound a week which the Brookers charged for full board. They used to pay a small sum for their beds and make shamefaced meals in a corner of the kitchen off bacon and bread-and-margarine which they stored in their suitcases.'

The question was bound to arise sooner or later: is such poverty necessary? The political economist would immediately reply that it wasn't and outline some scheme by which it could be eliminated. But Orwell didn't mean that. He knew it wasn't economically necessary. Was it socially necessary? Or, to put it in another way, why did those people who controlled society and had sufficient wealth to give everyone a decent minimum, consider it necessary for a small part of the population to live in such hopeless squalor ? His reply was that the *plongeur* (to take one example) was simply supplying a luxury which very often was not a luxury. He compared him with the rickshaw puller of the East. The latter was an emaciated wretch, weighing about eight stone, often diseased, sometimes fifty years old, who trotted for miles on end in the hot sun or rain, coughing his lungs out and getting thirty or forty rupees a month. Or the gharry pony. This was a gaunt and vicious beast that worked itself to the knacker's yard on 60 per cent whip and 40 per cent food. They are thrashed so hard that the pain behind outweighs the pain in front. These two are instances of unnecessary work, only existing because so many Orientals consider it vulgar to walk. And although they are luxuries, they are very poor luxuries. It was the same with the *plongeur*. He was the slave of his hotel or restaurant. They helped provide a luxury which was usually no luxury, because the food you get in a hotel is usually inferior to the food you get at home. In a 'smart' hotel the staff work more and the customers pay more and only the proprietor benefits. Hotels and restaurants are necessary, but if the work were done with simple efficiency the *plongeurs* would only need to work six or eight hours a day instead of the customary ten or fifteen.

But why does the *plongeur* exist if his work is largely useless? Orwell's reply was that at bottom the rich are afraid of the mob and think it can only be kept out of mischief if kept constantly busy. Fear of the mob was a perennial theme in nineteenth-century literature and if it is no longer so apparent in our own it is not necessary to assume that it no longer exists. Orwell said that if an honest rich man were asked for his observations on the existence of conditions such as have been described above, he would reply something like this:

'We know that poverty is unpleasant; in fact, since it is so remote we rather enjoy harrowing ourselves with the thought of its unpleasantness. But don't expect us to do anything about it. We are sorry for you lower classes, just as we are sorry for a cat with the mange, but we will fight like devils against any improvement of your condition. We feel that you are much safer as you are. The present state of affairs suits us, and we are not going to take the risk of setting you free, even by an extra hour a day. So, dear brothers, since evidently you must sweat to pay for our trips to Italy, sweat and be damned to you.'

Extending this to society as a whole, you have the spectacle of large masses of the population toiling at jobs which are not only unproductive but actually destructive: armaments. It is said that no one wants war but everyone continues to prepare for it.

From this observation Orwell drew one of the bases of the society described in *1984*, a state of perpetual warfare which kept the proletariat physically and emotionally engaged.

But the poor have an immense fund of resilience. One of the discoveries he made on his tour of the distressed areas was that millions of people were accepting life on P.A.C. yet were managing to avoid going to pieces spiritually. After several years, living on the dole ceased to be shameful. Because of this there was a decline in the *consciousness* of misery. A working man does not disintegrate under the strain of poverty as a middle-class person does. Unemployment did not prevent the workers from marrying—a proof of their essential good sense, according to Orwell, though a constant source of irritation to the old ladies of Brighton. It was an affirmation of their belief, despite all pressures, that they were still human beings. Instead of raging against the fates the unemployed lowered their standards and so continued to live a reduced version of their former lives.

Parallel with this is the friendliness and even generosity which Orwell found among the poor. They retained their sense of community and did not allow hardship to destroy their decency. The standards they lowered were physical, not moral. (Here again there is an apparent inconsistency, for I have already showed that Orwell believed poverty led to a decline in manners. But that was the result of the job, not of poverty itself, the effect of working under beastly conditions and subject to exceptional fatigue. The point was that you only took that kind of job if you were poor. No rich man was subject to anything like it.) Orwell tells us of the deputy of a lodging house and his wife who were prepared to make you a cup of tea at any time of the day or night. The tramps were always offering each other fag-ends. There was one touching story of a tramp whose box of fag-ends was confiscated by the Tramp Major at a spike. Orwell had managed to keep his tobacco, gave some to the other and thought no more about it. But when he was leaving next day the tramp came running after him and said he had had his tobacco returned and one good turn deserved another. 'And he put four sodden, debauched, loathly cigarette-ends into my hand.'

It was questionable how much thinking or reflection about

their lot the poor did. In the past the hope of Heaven had been strong and conscious but it is doubtful if it had been replaced by anything comparable. There was increased intellectual awareness among the unemployed, Orwell claimed, of the social factors that had caused their condition, but even so it could not have been widespread. The day-dreaming which might lighten the burden of the poor was an unconscious process. On the whole, the poor had learnt to accept their lot without the consolations that had formerly been considered necessary. Also, the preoccupation of the poor with matters which seem ridiculously petty to the rest of us was only intensified by the increasing complexity of modern life. The poor probably had to spend more rather than less time and energy adapting their straitened resources to the needs of modern society. There was correspondingly less time left over for the consideration of their spiritual condition, which must appear to them as a luxury.

'To the well-fed it seems cowardly to complain of tight boots, because the well-fed live in a different world—a world where, if your boots are tight, you can change them; their minds are not warped by petty discomfort. But below a certain income the petty crowds the large out of existence; one's preoccupation is not with art or religion, but with bad food, hard beds, drudgery and the sack.' ('Poverty—Plain and Coloured', *The Adelphi*, April, 1931.)

The kind of problem that tended to fill the horizon of the poor was, for example, that of keeping warm. Orwell met men who spent threepence or fourpence (twopence at matinees) to go to the pictures to escape the winter cold, even men who were on the verge of starvation. In Sheffield he went to a public hall to hear the silliest lecture he had ever heard, given by a clergyman, and found it impossible to sit it out. But the hall was crowded with unemployed men who would sit through the most appalling drivel for the sake of warmth. So great is the ignorance of the real nature of poverty among the well-fed that the men at the pictures would be blamed for wasting their money and the men at the lecture would be praised for concerning themselves with higher things, when all they were really concerned with in each instance was their frozen feet. Then there was the never-ending housing problem. People would put up with almost anything to have a roof over their heads ('I have been into appalling houses, houses in which I would not live a week if you paid me, and found that the tenants had been there twenty and thirty years and only hoped they might have the luck to die there': *The Road to Wigan Pier*). By the time you have fought for the simple comforts which the well-fed regard as their birthright you will be an exceptional person if you still have enough energy or even curiosity to spend on the search for truth and beauty. The very poor work in a kind of treadmill. They continually cover the same ground and in time they forget that any other kind of activity exists. The well-fed are equally blind. The business man who has just been laughing with Gracie Fields, the art-collector who has just bought a Vlaminck, will argue blithely that the poor deserve no help because they will not help themselves. But their blindness is more culpable.

There is another aspect of poverty which is entirely modern. Although at the time when Orwell was writing the poorer sections of the working class had no money which could be regarded as surplus, the fact remained that they had a considerable spending power if you considered them in bulk. If everyone spent his money 'correctly', i.e., necessities first and luxuries after, there would have been little luxury spending in working-class areas. But people do not behave in this way. There is something naturally attractive about luxury, however tawdry, and nearly everyone at some time or another will forego something he really needs to buy something he merely wants. The advertisers were quick to grasp this point, and various psychological pressures were laid on the poor to buy commodities which were useless or even harmful at the expense of others which, on a sane valuation, they should not be without. From Boyd Orr's point of view priorities were often hopelessly wrong. Again the poor would be blamed ('wasting money on rubbish'). But there was not much honesty in blaming the poor when the advertisers (who unquestionably belong to the well-fed section of society) used all their arts to assist this process. Although many people will tell you that they take no notice of advertising, every commercial artist and copywriter and advertising agent knows that very few people indeed are able to resist their appeals. Advertisers are the last people to spend money without getting a satisfactory return. Orwell said that the two things

that have made the greatest difference in the circumstances of
the poor have been the movies and the mass-production of cheap
smart clothes. A man may be chronically hungry, but for a few
pounds, with the help of the hire-purchase system, he can buy a
suit which for a short time and at a distance looks tolerably
smart. You may be unemployed and have three-halfpence in
your pocket but you will feel a kind of exhilaration in your
private day-dream of yourself as Clark Gable or Greta Garbo
(they were the stars of the period—today I imagine it would be
Robert Mitchum and Rita Hayworth). The curious but not
unexpected result of this is that luxuries are often cheaper than
necessities.

> 'One pair of plain solid shoes costs as much as two ultra-smart
> pairs. For the price of one square meal you can get two pounds of
> cheap sweets. You can't get much meat for threepence but you
> can get a lot of fish and chips. Milk costs threepence a pint and
> even "mild" beer costs fourpence, but aspirins are seven a penny
> and you can wring forty cups of tea out of a quarter-pound packet.
> And above all there is gambling, the cheapest of all luxuries.
> Even people on the verge of starvation can buy a few days' hope
> ("Something to live for, as they call it") by having a penny on
> the sweepstake.'

The prices have changed and, at the moment of writing, there
are far fewer people really poor in England than there were
before the war. But poverty can come again, though servility is
more likely to precede it, and I am chiefly concerned here with
the social reactions to poverty, the way in which a society
adapts itself to not enough money and too many wants. I should
also add that many of the things listed in the above are not
technically luxuries. But Orwell's chief point was that it was
always becoming easier to buy the inferior and unnecessary
article than the valuable and the needed. Many working-class
families never bought fresh milk but there was always a steady
sale of aspirins.

Then there is the queer spectacle of modern electrical science
showering miracles upon people with empty bellies. You may
shiver all night for lack of bedclothes, but in the morning you
can go to the public library and read the news that has been
telegraphed at great expense for your benefit from San Fran-
cisco and Singapore. Twenty million people were underfed, he

said, but practically everyone had access to a radio. What we have lost in food we have gained in electricity.

'Do you consider all this desirable? No, I don't. But it may be that the psychological adjustment which the working class are visibly making is the best they could make in the circumstances. They have neither turned revolutionary nor lost their self-respect; merely they have kept their tempers and settled down to make the best of things on a fish-and-chip standard. The alternative would be God knows what continued agonies of despair; or it might be attempted insurrection which, in a strongly governed country like England, could only lead to futile massacres and a regime of savage repression.

'Of course the post-war development of cheap luxuries has been a very fortunate thing for our rulers. It is quite likely that fish and chips, art-silk stockings, tinned salmon, cut-price chocolate (five two-ounce bars for sixpence), the movies, the radio, strong tea and the Football Pools have between them averted revolution. Therefore we are sometimes told that the whole thing is an astute manoeuvre by the governing class—a sort of "bread and circuses" business—to hold the unemployed down. What I have seen of our governing class does not convince me that they have that much intelligence. The thing has happened, but by an unconscious process—the quite natural interaction between the manufacturer's need for a market and the need of half-starved people for cheap palliatives.' (*The Road to Wigan Pier.*)

One aspect of this silent revolution that interested Orwell particularly was the consequent decline in taste. He was more concerned with food than aesthetics, and it was taste in food that he meant. The less a person can spend on food the more tempted he is to buy something 'tasty'—and 'tasty' food is not always rich in calories. The press at the time was full of advice to the working class on how to buy their food—wholesome things like oranges and wholemeal bread and raw carrots were urged upon them. Orwell says the ordinary human being would rather starve than live on brown bread and raw carrots. A millionaire may enjoy breakfasting off fruit juice and Ryvita biscuits but the unemployed man doesn't. If you are underfed, bored and miserable, you don't *want* to eat dull wholesome food. Chips, ice-cream and the eternal tea helped to fill the stomach and rot its lining and reduce the body's energy and resistance. White bread and marge and sugared tea don't nouish you to any extent but they are *nicer*, more comforting, than brown bread and dripping and cold water. With a couple of aspirins to soothe. All wrong, of course. But not evidence of depravity, merely the results of almost unbearable poverty and, to some extent, ignorance—but the poverty is more powerful than the ignorance.

Practically all through this chapter I have used the word 'poverty', which is abstract. I have tried (quoting Orwell) to give it form, to express it in terms of not much flesh and thin blood. But poverty in a modern society can be expressed in another way: simply lack of money. In the past it was lack of goods, but now money has interposed itself between the person and the goods. This has had an evil effect, for when the poor were short of goods there was never any question of the goods they needed. Luxuries were not available. But in a comprehensive money economy you have the factor of choice, which does not improve the condition of the poor, as I have shown, although it acts as psychological balm. One of Orwell's books on poverty, *Keep the Aspidistra Flying*, is specifically about lack of money. It is an unpleasant book to read because it wallows in self-pity, one of the inevitable consequences of poverty, as has been stated before. It is the only one of his books in which self-pity is obtrusive. He seems to have surrendered to it for the space of one volume (it had been accumulating from earlier books from which it had been excluded) and thereafter he rejected it. Flory in *Burmese Days* exhibited a considerable amount of self-pity but it did not derive from poverty.

Lack of money is the keynote of this novel and the message is that without money you cannot possibly live a decent life or find any fulfilment whatsoever. Everything to which you put your hand (culture, sociability, love, respect) will be doomed to failure if you have not sufficient money to support your pretensions. In the frontispiece he adapted the famous passage from I Corinthians XIII ('Though I speak with the tongues of men and of angels, etc.'), consistently changing the word 'charity' to 'money'. 'And now abideth faith, hope, money, these three; but the greatest of these is money.' We get a hint of this growing obsession in a poem published in *The Adelphi* in the preceding year (November 1935), only to find later that it is incorporated in the novel. It is about the clerks, not their

treason but their poverty. It explains why they abase themselves
to the money-god:

> Thinking, each one, Here comes the winter!
> Please God I keep my job this year!
> And bleakly, as the cold strikes through
> Their entrails, like an icy spear,
>
> They think of rent, rates, season tickets,
> Insurance, coal, the skivvy's wages,
> Boots, school bills, and the next instalment
> Upon the two twin beds from Drage's.
>
> For if in careless summer days
> In groves of Ashtaroth we whored,
> Repentant now, when winds blow cold,
> We kneel before our rightful lord;
>
> The lord of all, the money-god,
> Who owns us, blood and hand and brain,
> Who gives the roof that stops the wind,
> And, giving, takes away again.
>
> ('St Andrew's Day, 1935.')

In the novel itself we get a catalogue of what money can do—
which is everything—or conversely, what can't be done without
money—which again is everything. You cannot be cultured
without money: 'In a country like England you can no more be
cultured without money than you can join the Cavalry Club'.
Charm is impossible without money. Watching a 'nancy'
browsing among the books in the shop, Gordon is swamped with
bitterness. 'The skin at the back of his neck was as silky-smooth
as the inside of a shell. You can't have a skin like that under five
hundred a year. A sort of charm he had, a glamour, like all
moneyed people. Money and charm; who shall separate them?'
Another equation. What is personality? It is income. Gordon
develops this theme at some length in his ceaseless attempt to
persuade his girl, Rosemary, that all his shortcomings are simply
due to his lack of 'ready'.

'Don't you see that a man's whole personality is bound up with
his income? His personality *is* his income. How can you be attractive to a girl when you've got no money? You can't wear decent
clothes, you can't take her out to dinner or to the theatre or away
for weekends, you can't carry a cheery, interesting atmosphere

about with you. . . . If you haven't got money there isn't even anywhere where you can meet. Rosemary and I never meet except in the streets or in picture galleries. She lives in some foul women's hostel, amd my bitch of a landlady won't allow women in the house. Wandering up and down beastly wet streets—that's what Rosemary associated with me. Don't you see how it takes the gilt off everything?'

Whenever Rosemary treats him badly he feels it is because he has no money. It even applies to men—you can't be friendly with a man if he has more money than you have. At Gordon's lodgings there was a cheerful traveller named Flaxman who invited him out for a drink. But it is impossible for Gordon to accept because he only has $2\frac{1}{2}$d. in his pocket, and so he is compelled to snub him. 'He was for ever snubbing friendly advances. Of course it was money that was at the bottom of it, always money. You can't be friendly, you can't even be civil, when you have no money in your pocket.'

The climax comes when Gordon arranges to take Rosemary into the country. It is the only opportunity they will ever have to be alone. But except for a few brief moments of exhilaration it is a dreadful failure. To begin with, he has to borrow 5/- from his sister, who cannot afford it. He really needs more but hasn't the heart to ask. He can just manage the trip if he goes without tobacco and cuts down on food for the rest of the week. It is Sunday and they find that they are compelled to lunch in a pretentious riverside hotel. Gordon feels the waiter senses his poverty and despises him. This leads him to 'show off' and order wine. When the meal is over he has 8d. left. They return on Rosemary's money, which she willingly spends but which he regards as charity. The whole expedition has been a ghastly flop. In the end this unremitting emphasis on money, one-sided as it may seem, becomes impressive because its sheer weight overwhelms you. And it does reflect faithfully the experience of many young men, for after the book had been published they wrote to him saying that they had been through exactly the same ordeal, with all pleasure in the companionship of the girl spoiled by the constant worry about being able to manage without being caught out. Orwell also contrasts the attitude of the woman with that of the man. Rosemary does not agree with Gordon's diagnosis. A woman never does. She always says that

in some way—but in a way that she cannot make real to a man
—money is not important. But the sex war which is depicted
so brutally in this novel was already hinted at in *Down and Out*.
As soon as he put his tramp's clothes on he noticed that women
shrank away from him, as though he were a dead cat.

After *The Aspidistra* Orwell never returned to the money
theme with the same venom but nor did he forget it entirely.
A commonplace incident could easily revive his emotion on the
subject. One day towards the end of the war he saw a woman
with a baby and a child of six leave one of the large London
termini with her husband, who was carrying a broken suitcase,
tied with rope, and a cot. They tried to board a bus but the
conductor would not allow the cot to be brought on. Finally the
woman and children stayed on the bus and the man set off for
home on foot, still carrying the case and cot. There is no need to
guess at Orwell's reaction:

> 'Our society is not only so arranged that if you have money
> you can buy luxuries with it. After all, that is what money is for.
> It is also so arranged that if you don't have money you pay for it at
> every hour of the day with petty humiliations and totally unneces-
> sary discomforts—such as, for instance, walking home with a
> suitcase cutting your fingers off when a mere half-crown would
> get you there in five minutes.' ('As I Please', *Tribune*, 6 October,
> 1944.)

I must have given the impression that for Orwell poverty
represented a life of unrelieved misery. I think this is a truthful
impression if we go by the four books alone, and I have no
intention of recanting. Three of these books are extremely
gloomy affairs and I doubt if there is a single lightening of the
gloom throughout. Orwell took poverty seriously and refused
to romanticise it. I think he was entirely justified in this because
before the second world war the extent of poverty and the
intensity of poverty in a wealthy country like England was a
disgrace to our civilisation. In *Down and Out* the gloom is mitigated by a considerable amount of humour. It was Orwell's
first essay in the subject and his freshness was not completely
worn away. All the same, he never fell into the trap of claiming
that poverty 'wasn't so bad' or that nothing matters 'if you have
a sense of humour'. A sense of humour is important but it should
not be used as a weapon for the defence of an evil system. Yet

Orwell did not believe that poverty crushed every other value out of existence. It was almost unbearable in northern Europe, more so in England than in France, for climatic reasons. But the climate was really less important than the texture of the society. Capitalist society tends to be a friendless affair, particularly when it is industrial. Friendship and the feeling that you are not alone is the most powerful antidote to poverty. That is why poverty was less horrible in the north of England than in the south. But later he came across a society where poverty was worse than anything in England in a physical sense yet not nearly so damaging in a spiritual sense. This was in Morocco. It is true, the climate was in their favour, but much more important was the closely-woven nature of Arab society.

His best account of poverty in Morocco is to be found in the essay 'Marrakech' (*New Writing*, New Series, No. 3, 1939). He tells how he was feeding a gazelle in a public garden with bread. An Arab navvy, an employee of the municipality, stopped his work and watched him in amazement, and then said in French, '*I* could eat some of that bread'. Once when he stopped to light a cigarette in the Jewish quarter there was immediately a frenzied rush of Jews, even old grandfathers, clamouring for cigarettes. In a moment his whole packet had gone. His comment was, 'None of these people, I suppose, works less than twelve hours a day, and everyone of them looks on a cigarette as a more or less impossible luxury'. In fact, poverty is so widespread you no longer notice it.

> 'It is only because of this that the starved countries of Asia and Africa are accepted as tourist resorts. No one would think of running cheap trips to the Distressed Areas. But where the human beings have brown skins their poverty is simply not noticed. What does Morocco mean to a Frenchman? An orange-grove or a job in Government service. Or to an Englishman? Camels, castles, palm-trees, Foreign Legionaires, brass trays and bandits. One could probably live here for years without noticing that for nine-tenths of the people the reality of life is an endless back-breaking struggle to wring a little food out of an eroded soil.'

And elsewhere he says: 'Except for the climate, every feature that attracted the tourist depended on the fact that the average human being's earnings were round about a penny an hour'. ('In the Darlan Country', *Observer*, 29 November, 1942.)

And yet despite this he believed that these people were happier than the average Englishman—or Londoner, at least:

> 'I may have seemed to paint a picture of general misery but I must record that in 1938 or 1939 the people in Morocco struck me as being happier than, for instance, the people in London. One saw everywhere the most shocking destitution and drudgery, but also, on the whole, one saw happy faces and magnificent bodies. The Chleuh, even poorer than the Arabs of the plains, were one of the most debonair peoples I have seen. One must remember that Morocco is still almost entirely in the fuedal stage, barely touched by industrialism with its conveniences and its discontents. ('Background of French Morocco', *Tribune*, 20 November, 1942.)

I can only confirm this from my own personal experience in a similar comparison. I have little doubt that the people of the Sudan, though not so poor as those of Morocco yet so much poorer than those of England, are happier than the English. They have not yet been overwhelmed by the complexity of Western civilisation, though they give every signs of wishing to be. I remember a letter from my wife, who had just returned to England, saying that as soon as she saw the tense English faces at the terminus she wanted to turn round and catch the first plane back. So I think I know what Orwell meant. It is something that the average book-trained Left-winger cannot understand or admit. When the article from which I have just quoted first appeared I heard a Socialist M.P. get really upset about it. He seemed to think Orwell was equating poverty with happiness in the manner of a sentimental or crafty Tory. But Orwell was merely proving that he did not regard poverty as a bar to happiness. On the other hand, he did believe that poverty could be a most powerful ingredient in unhappiness.

Orwell never fell into the unfortunate modern habit of tying his judgment to his political opinions. The Left-winger begins by deploring social conditions, and adopts a new social theory. From there he moves to a new but false position, from which he believes that where his new social theory is not in practice everything must be wrong. (Communist art must be better than capitalist art, capitalist illness is more painful than socialist illness, and so on.) Instead of using his personal judgment he uses an artificial measure. By refusing to do this Orwell made himself

many enemies. He even claimed that the peasants of Tras-Os-
Montes in Portugal were happy, which was more than could be
said for the people of Sheffield and Manchester. This was heresy,
for the peasants lived under the Salazar regime. Happiness has
become secondary to doctrine.

Chapter V

Saints and Sinners

I HAVE given the reasons why I believe Orwell left comfortable society and joined the outcasts, yet we cannot leave this aspect of his life until we have probed a little deeper. As we follow him from the Paris kitchens to the Jura farmhouse the question inevitably arises: Was there a neurotic or even pathological vein in his personality? I am no psychologist and cannot pretend to examine this question clinically. But I think it is possible to go a little deeper into his motives and to discover if there might not be a compulsive element which helped to dictate his career.

If we partially identify Orwell with Flory in *Burmese Days* (I think this is justifiable because Orwell was not a novelist by nature and always wrote either of himself or his anti-self) we will find his fascination with the morbid and subterranean already existing in Burma. The thing that Elizabeth could not forgive in Flory and which made their break certain was his 'deliberate seeking after the squalid and the "beastly" '. He represented this to her as the inevitable result of his natural curiosity about other people; if their conditions are squalid then you cannot avoid contact with their squalor. But Elizabeth shrunk from squalor just as naturally as he was attracted by it. In her view he was deliberately wallowing in the unpleasant and abusing what she considered the normal human instinct for happiness. In his view she was turning away from Christ on the cross, though he never used those terms. But whether we call ourselves Christians or not our tradition is permeated with Christian imagery.

Everyone who has written on Orwell has noticed the constant mortification to which he subjected himself and has tried to explain it. Tom Hopkinson attributes it to Orwell's lack of historic sense, by which only the present seems significant to him. The future (about which Orwell never stopped worrying) was simply the projection of the present; the past, with the sense of perspective that it gives, hardly existed for him.

'This concentration on the present, this belief that the historic moment is *now*, led Orwell—backed by his own uncommon courage—to do at any point in life the thing that seemed to him most important. If fear of poverty is the enemy, the thing to do is to face it, reducing one's self to the lowest state, learning what happens when the last coat is pawned, the last franc spent, the bugs on the wall are massing in battalions and one's temperature indicates pneumonia. If on the Spanish war hangs the hope of human freedom, then the inevitable step is to take part: the fact that one may be an incompetent soldier, and that one will certainly come under suspicion of authority for the rest of one's life for having done so, can be neither here nor there.' (*George Orwell*, The British Council and the National Book League.)

Whether this is true or not, it is certainly not the kind of truth a man knows about himself. Every man believes he has a valid sense of history. Orwell criticised both H. G. Wells and James Burnham for the very fault that Hopkinson charges him with—being bogged so deep in the present that their prophecies of the future are warped at birth. But neither Wells nor Burnham found it necessary to bury their noses in the dungheaps which they saw around them. In *The Road to Wigan Pier* Orwell wrote: 'I find that anything outrageously strange generally ends by fascinating me even when I abominate it', and gives as an instance the Burmese landscapes, which used to give him nightmares and finally obliged him to write about them in a novel! At least two qualities were necessary to produce his practice of self-mortification: an extreme sensitivity to anything 'outrageously strange' (to which I would add in most cases 'and outrageously unjust') and a passion for first-hand understanding. This covers most of the cases but not all. It does not explain why, with his health ruined, he longed to join the Army during the war and did join the Home Guard, and worked hard at it, nor why he chose to end his days in Jura. Hopkinson's 'historic present' may account for his desire to immerse himself in the Army but it doesn't touch Jura. Nor was there anything there that he urgently needed to examine and know at first-hand.

There is still something else, some primary factor, which must be taken into account. And because this other factor is primary we will have to leave it there. We get nowhere by using names such as 'masochism'.

Orwell himself was convinced of the ambivalence existing in the average man's mind. There were two attitudes, for instance, to women. One, perhaps the strongest in our culture, is expressed by Blake's 'the naked female human form divine'. But the view which stands in opposition to this is obsessed with the more disgusting attributes of this female form, attributes which it shares with the male, and which disqualify it from any justified deification. This is certainly the minority view, although it is probably more widespread than at first appears, because it is conventionally reprehensible. When a man concentrates on this view to the exclusion of the other, as did Swift, he is likely to be a remarkable person. At least, his views will be unfamiliar. Swift sees nothing but dirt, folly and wickedness. We know there is more to existence than this, but we acknowledge that they have their place.

'Part of our minds—in the normal person it is the dominant part—believes that man is a noble animal and life is worth living: but there is also a sort of inner self which at least intermittently stands aghast at the horror of existence. In the queerest way, pleasure and disgust are linked together. The human body is beautiful: it is also repulsive and ridiculous, a fact which can be verified at any swimming pool. The sexual organs are objects of desire and also of loathing, so much so that in many languages, if not all languages, their names are used as words of abuse.' ('Politics v. Literature', *Shooting an Elephant*.)

And he gives many more examples.

I think there is a clue to Orwell himself in this passage. As a twentieth-century writer he tends to be more interested in society than in individuals. He is applying the sensitive nose of a Swift to the body social, not liking much what he smells, but still, like Swift, unable to leave it alone. Every now and again he has to return for another sniff. (I use the sense of smell for illustrative purposes, but he did, in fact, have one of the sharpest noses in our literary history. If a place has a smell peculiar to it, such as a kitchen or a battlefield, Orwell always lets us know.) But Orwell must never be regarded as a social Swift.

The fact that he could diagnose Swift's view of human beings makes it quite impossible that he also should be dead to all but the unpleasant. Like other people he experienced pleasure linked with disgust, but his disgust was immeasurably stronger than theirs. His saving grace was that he could always distinguish between the two and never surrendered so completely to the disgust that he could believe the pleasure was an illusion.

Orwell believed he was exercising his social duty when he examined the slums. I am not sure whether there is actually such a thing as social duty or whether it is one of those fantasies in which modern man delights or, conversely, with which he tortures himself. It is much more likely to be a socialisation of the old Christian injunction to love one another, only the embarrassing associations of love are removed. But whatever it is, Orwell believed there was a social duty and he was nothing if not dutiful. In some ways he tried to live the ideal life for a modern man, which is why some of his friends have actually used the term 'saint' to describe him. In *The Road to Wigan Pier* he wrote:

> 'You cannot disregard them (the victims of poverty) if you accept the civilisation that produced them. For this is part at least of what industrialism has done for us. Columbus sailed the Atlantic, the first steam engines tottered into motion, the British squares stood firm under the French guns at Waterloo, the one-eyed scoundrels of the nineteenth century praised God and filled their pockets; and this is where it all led—to labyrinthine slums and dark back kitchens with sickly, ageing people creeping round and round them like black beetles. It is a kind of duty to see and smell such places now and again, especially smell them, lest you should forget that they exist; though perhaps it is better not to stay there too long.'

I have only one quarrel with that. It implies that if you do not accept modern civilisation you have the right to turn your back on its products. In the first place you can't do that, and in the second place it encourages people to become selective in what they accept and reject, absolute rejection being impossible. And in the third place it allows people to reject the civilisation when what they are really rejecting is the poverty, or their exquisite feelings about poverty, and the cart is then before the horse.

Orwell used his experiences of poverty to write *A Clergyman's*

Daughter and was immediately faced with a problem which is
strongly indicative of his own psychological needs. The difference between Orwell and Dorothy is that he sought poverty and
she was forced into it by circumstances. This did not satisfy him.
He wanted a closer parallel with his own experience. The factor
that was missing was mortification. He therefore makes of
Dorothy a character who has chosen the way of mortification
irrespective of any circumstantial reactions. She is the victim of
her own puritanical ethos—only we feel she was not innately
masochistic but was at the mercy of her upbringing. But it does
not matter whether her mortification is innate or acquired, the
important thing is that when we first meet her she is in the habit
of applying to herself a rota of little pains. 'She detested cold
baths; it was for that very reason that she made it a rule to take
all her baths cold from April to November.' 'She made it a rule,
whenever she caught herself not attending to her prayers, to
prick her arm hard enough to make blood come.' '. . . She was
not having bacon this morning—a penance she had set herself
yesterday for saying "Damn" and idling for half an hour after
lunch.'

With Gordon Comstock in *Keep the Aspidistra Flying* Orwell
comes much closer to his own case. Gordon actively chose the
gutter. It was either that or the stars, and the stars were an
awful long way away. When he lost one job and found another
he was offered ten shillings a week less. 'Ten bob less—ten bob
nearer the mud. It was what he wanted.' The parallel seems to
have been fairly exact: both Orwell and Gordon were deliberately choosing failure. The variation only occurred after this
phase was complete, when Gordon chose the aspidistra and
Orwell began to struggle toward the stars. He did not do it
consciously but in fact he did reach up much higher than most
of his contemporaries. Here we have a description of Gordon's
state of mind when his descent began to accelerate:

'Before, he had fought against the money-code, and yet he had
clung to his wretched remnant of decency. But now it was pre-
cisely from decency that he wanted to escape. He wanted to go
down, deep down, into some world where decency no longer
mattered; to cut the strings of his self-respect, to submerge himself—to *sink*, as Rosemary had said. It was all bound up in his
mind with the thought of being *under ground*. He liked to think

about the lost people, the underground people, tramps, beggars, criminals, prostitutes. It is a good world that they inhabit, down there in their frowsy kips and spikes. He liked to think that beneath the world of money there is that great sluttish under-world where failure and success have no meaning; a sort of kingdom of ghosts where all are equal.'

The recurrence of the word 'decency' here is interesting and may provide a further clue to the state of Orwell's mind. I have described how he revered decency, but perhaps there was a period when he associated it with the well-to-do middle-class world which had caused him so much pain. He may have con-sidered it a sham and only later decided that it was real, although vague, blind and often ineffective. Also notice how, once Gordon had achieved complete failure, he hoped that the very idea of failure would be wiped out. There could be no failure at the bottom simply because there was no success.

Sir Richard Rees was one of his friends who used the term 'saint' with reference to Orwell. He likened him to the saint who kissed lepers. He had only to think of something apparently beyond endurance and he could not rest until he had endured it. When a weak chest and the Spanish war wound confined his activities to the Local Defence Volunteers, and the name was changed to Home Guard, he remarked plaintively, 'They'd better call us the Fireside Fusiliers'. His Hebridean home was on the most depopulated island of the group, at the end of eight miles of moorland track and more than twenty-five miles from the nearest doctor. If he had any squeamishness left in him he conquered it by cleaning and skinning rabbits, gutting fish, handling the tripes of deer, and discussing the technique of caponising cockerels and slaughtering or castrating pigs. But this had nothing to do with a sense of failure. If that had operated before it had certainly ceased by now. Even if there was still a sense of failure lurking within him, caponising cockerels would not dismiss it. This was the other aspect, the mortification. And it derived from what V. S. Pritchett called a 'guilty conscience', the conscience which we all feel at times but which was developed in Orwell to a remarkable degree.

'His was the guilty conscience of the educated and privileged man, one of that regular supply of brilliant recalcitrants which Eton has given us since the days of Fielding; and this conscience could be allayed only by taking upon itself the pain, the misery, the dinginess and the pathetic but hard vulgarities of a stale and hopeless period.' ('George Orwell', *New Statesman*, 28 January, 1950.)

Yet Orwell never pretended that he hated life. He felt he was doing something towards the purification of life, so that it might be the more fully enjoyed. When he had a bullet through his neck in Spain he thought he was dying. He describes his feelings minutely. He did not adopt postures of relief at throwing off the 'mortal coil' but said that his first thought was for his wife. 'My second was a violent resentment at having to leave this world which, when all is said and done, suits me so well.' He also makes the funniest remark in the whole of his work hereabouts. Although he had a dry sense of humour it rarely entered into his writing. He only made one joke which made me laugh, and I shall refer to it lovingly in a later chapter. But there is rich humour, presumably unknown to him, when he complains rather petulantly that unpleasant things are always happening to him and wonders why it is!

The literary editor of the *Observer* must be congratulated for sending *My Caves*, by Norbert Castoret, to Orwell for review. Caving was one of the activities he had not taken part in, to the best of my knowledge, but most people probably think of it as an unpleasant business, only fit for spelaeological fanatics. Orwell or a sub-editor headed the review 'Down Under'. Orwell gravely listed some of the dangers and the disagreeableness of caving and then added (as though we needed telling): 'However, human beings vary in their notion of what constitutes pleasure'. But while this is amusing in the context Orwell was fascinated by the things that gave pleasure. His own view was that the aim of the common man was self-preservation and a good time, nothing 'higher'. But it was the constitution of the 'good time' that varied so immensely. There were certain propositions he felt applied to all normal men, and he made a catechism of it:

> 'Is the common man heroic? Not consciously.
> 'Is he anxious to die for a Cause? No.
> 'Does he want to be faithful to his wife? No.
> 'Does he ever want to work? Not very much.'
> ('The End of Henry Miller', *Tribune*, 4 December, 1942.)

This gives us a negative description of the ordinary man's desires. But you can only generalise about negatives. As soon as you try to declare positives you find the variety. When he reviewed some of the depressing novels which our society produces in such large numbers (his own among them, of course) he felt they reflected the self-mortification of our age. The old Christian cult had merely been displaced:

> 'The *ideal rongeur* has merely changed its shape. Instead of being the ideal Christian sanctity, it is now the ideal—equally unattained by most people—of a life fully lived. In Baudelaire's day you woke in the brothel and lamented your lost innocence. Now, on the other hand, you are wheeled in your bath-chair down the Bournemouth parade, thinking with mingled desolation and relief of the adultery you failed to commit in '97. It is perhaps a spiritual come-down.' ('Some Recent Novels', *New English Weekly*, 1 August, 1935.)

This was a negative mortification, based on regrets, just as so many modern pleasures are based on rejections. Orwell felt it was typical of the modern spirit, rarely sufficiently serious about anything to do it wholeheartedly.

In his 'Reflections on Gandhi' (*Shooting an Elephant*) he considers the relationship between saint and sinner in some detail. The saint is a person who has set his mind on some good and will not serve from its pursuit. The essence of being human, on the other hand, is that one does not seek perfection, that one is perfectly willing to commit a sin for the sake of a human loyalty, and will not push asceticism to the point where friendly intercourse becomes impossible. 'No doubt alcohol, tobacco and so forth are things that a saint must avoid, but sainthood is also a thing that human beings must avoid.' It is well to remember that Orwell was aware of this gap between ordinary humanity and the saints, and that although by taking the guilt of his class upon himself he became a type of modern saint he did not try to impose a similar mode of behaviour upon his fellowmen. He was not agitated by the sins of the flesh and could therefore smoke and drink with a clear conscience. He was a social saint, wishing to share the pains of society, or rather the victims of society. He rejected the yogi view that every man is a failed saint, a man who would be a saint if it were not so difficult. The mortification of our time is imposed and not sought. 'Many people genuinely do not wish to be saints, and it is probable that some who achieve or aspire to sainthood have never felt much temptation to be human beings.' And then he says that the probable motive for 'non-attachment' is a desire to escape from the pain of living, and above all from love, which, sexual or non-sexual, is hard work.

This is at least a reasonable hypothesis. In 'Lear, Tolstoy and the Fool' he broaches the question again. Saint and human being, he says, differ in kind and not simply in degree. Each is an imperfect form of the other. The human being wants the best life possible on earth; the saint, or Tolstoy's kind of saint, wishes to provide an alternative and better life. It is usually part of his doctrine to claim that celibacy is a 'higher' form of life than marriage. The object should be to cut ourselves off from the surface of life, and no tie is stronger than that of sexual love. The aim is the Kingdom of Heaven, but the ordinary person is not interested in the Kingdom of Heaven. He likes his life on earth, even if the balance is usually in favour of pain and suffering. Therefore, says Orwell, the true hedonist is the Christian who is always struggling to escape life and find refuge in the Kingdom of Heaven. There is no middle way; one must either choose this world or the next.

'The enormous majority of human beings, if they understood the issue, would choose this world. They do make that choice when they continue working, breeding and dying instead of crippling their faculties in the hope of obtaining a new lease of existence elsewhere.'

If we are to regard Orwell as a saint it must be as a new kind of saint, what I have previously called a social saint, without religious promptings. He shared the taste of the ordinary man for life in this world, yet he seemed to go out of his way to endure its pains. He did not wish to cut himself off from life but appeared to have the conviction that he could help recreate a better life. There is something magical in this view, in the belief that one can abolish or transmute or rise above a complex of circumstances by total immersion. It is a kind of social baptism. It may contain something akin to Henry Miller's belief that one can ultimately destroy sex by a complete abandonment to it. It is not new, for many of the saints of the Christian past were men who had been notoriously loose livers in their youth. The agent of sanctity is utter and irrevocable disgust. It is possible that Orwell believed he could purify himself in the world's pain and filth, and so prepare himself for his championship of those who could not take the same path. But he differed from the conventional saint in that he never expected others to change their natures.

His view that the Christian saints were the biggest hedonists of all must, I think, be challenged. It was not an idea that came to him late in life. We find it expressed by Mr Warburton in *A Clergyman's Daughter* when he says the saints are 'out for an eternity of bliss'. But hedonism does not concern itself with long-term aims. The hedonist is aware only of his immediate environment and sensations. He is the petty, average man, wishing to avoid pain now at all costs but never considering whether pain avoided now will have to be endured later with interest. The Lives of the Saints contain a catalogue of human suffering and mortification that no hedonist could possibly accept. He wishes to be sure of his pleasures and is not willing to postpone them to a future that must be hypothetical, however strong his faith. The hedonist has no faith, unless we accept a desire for carnal pleasure as a faith. He postpones unpleasant duties in the hope that later they will no longer be duties and he will be able to sidestep them. He may know that a cold bath will invigorate him, but he will choose a hot one for its immediate return. Orwell expanded the meaning of the term when he called Christian saints hedonists, and without justification.

It is the common man who is hedonistic and Orwell showed time and again that he realised this and did not base his social arguments on false premises. At the same time, he was aware of a contrary streak, a kind of mass masochism which appeared in different societies at different times and with varying intensities, and which alone made it possible for modern dictators to debase standards of living for no appreciable advantages and to reduce the sense of security which is normally a human need. I will refer to this characteristic of modern man in a later chapter. I wish to end this chapter with a vision of the future paradise which Orwell believed most men entertain today. It is a concentrated picture of social emptiness that is quite as horrifying in its way as the picture of social discipline in *1984*. In either case we have the uncomfortable feeling that a people is committing suicide unknowingly.

'On a pleasure cruise or in a Lyons Corner House one already gets something more than a glimpse of this future paradise. Analysed, its main characteristics are these:
  (a) One is never alone.
  (b) One never does anything for oneself.
  (c) One is never within sight of wild vegetation or natural objects of any kind.
  (d) Light and temperature are always artificially regulated.
  (e) One is never out of the sound of music.'

He adds that music (the same for everybody) is the most important ingredient. Its function is to prevent thought and conversation and to shut out natural sounds, just as the radio already does in many homes today.

'It is difficult not to feel that the unconscious aim in the most typical modern pleasure resorts is a return to the womb. For there, too, one was never alone, one never saw daylight, the temperature was always regulated, one did not have to worry about work or food, and one's thoughts, if any, were drowned by a continuous rhythmic throbbing. . . .
  '. . . in exploring the physical universe man has made an attempt to explore himself. Much of what goes by the name of pleasure is simply an effort to destroy consciousness. If one started by asking, What is man? What are his needs? How can he best express himself? one would discover that merely having the power to avoid work and live one's life from birth to death in electric light and to the tune of tinned music is not a reason for doing so. Man needs warmth, society, leisure, comfort and security: he also needs solitude, creative work and the sense of wonder. If he recognised this he could use the products of science and industrialism eclectically, applying always the same test: does this make me more human or less human? He would then learn that the highest happiness does *not* lie in relaxing, resting, playing poker, drinking and making love simultaneously. And the instinctive horror which all sensitive people feel at the progressive mechanisation of life would be seen not to be a mere sentimental archaism, but to be fully justified. For man only stays human by preserving large patches of simplicity in his life, while the tendency of many modern inventions—in particular the film, the radio and the aeroplane—is to weaken his consciousness, dull his curiosity and, in general, drive him nearer to the animals.' ('Pleasure Spots', *Tribune*, 11 January, 1946.)

In another place Orwell claimed that there was a tendency for modern writers to creep inside the whale, i.e., the womb, a warm, soft place. This view of the future paradise is at the other extreme from the present hell of abject poverty and war—and yet the two are part of the same extension, one leads to the other, one understands the other. He discovered that experience of hell produces visions of a false paradise which is just as deplorable. The next Orwell may have to mortify himself in tepid bathing pools and jig out his guilt to the bim-bam-bim of the juke-box.

Chapter VI

Victims

IF ORWELL saw a victim he would drop whatever he was doing to go to his assistance. It must have been an instinct.

Sir Richard Rees points out that all the characters in his novels are victims like himself. The leading characters are guinea-pigs on which life is experimenting. Dorothy, the clergyman's daughter, is a victim of her narrow upbringing. Gordon Comstock is a victim of poverty. Tubby Bowling is a victim of a society running mad. Winston Smith is a victim of the complete totalitarian state. There is no happy or fulfilled character in these novels. There is nothing unusual in this, of course, for there are few happy or fulfilled characters in any modern novel. When we come across them we tend to distrust them. But there is an intensity in Orwell's work which differentiates it from most contemporary fiction. His novels are studies of victimisation pure and simple. In most others the victimisation is incidental, often implied but frequently ignored on the surface. Even the successful characters in Orwell's novels are to be pitied. The most successful is U Po Kyin in *Burmese Days*, but none of us envy him. The powerful O'Brien in *1984* is powerful in the way that a prison warder is powerful.

In *Homage to Catalonia* Orwell says he began his service in Spain with a prejudice aaginst the P.O.U.M.—I.L.P. viewpoint because 'I naturally reacted against the viewpoint of which I heard most'. At that stage the Communists were the victims, not because they were weak, but from where he stood they did not get full representation. This suggests a simple mechanism in Orwell's mind which had nothing to do with morality. I don't think it should be stressed, but it did reinforce his natural desire to support the weak. Normally the weak are the victims not only of circumstances but also of propaganda and therefore he supported the weak not only because they were weak but also because the scales were loaded against them. As time passed, however, the strong became weaker and the forces of propaganda sometimes turned against those whom they had supported in the past. This is most clearly seen in Orwell's attitude towards the British Empire. He himself was a vigorous critic of it, as we have seen, but towards the end of his life he became more generous in his criticisms because it had become fashionable to criticise the Empire.

He attacked the view that the victims of life, as a result of their victimisation, cease to feel it as keenly as we should do in similar circumstances. This argument usually comes from a bad conscience. Once, travelling by train through the northern coalfields, he saw a young woman kneeling on the stones, poking a stick up the leaden waste-pipe which ran from the sink inside and which must have been blocked. It was a very cold March day with blackened snow on the ground. This woman had a round pale face, 'the usual exhausted face of the slum girl who is twenty-five and looks forty, thanks to mis-carriages and drudgery; and it wore, for the second in which I saw it, the most desolate, hopeless expression I have ever seen'. It was not the ignorant suffering of an animal, he said. She knew what was happening to her, the hopelessness of her destiny. It is easy to say that this is Orwell's imagination at work. It is. But imagination is one of the most valuable faculties we have, and the important thing to realise is that he believed in it passionately. No one can prove he was wrong.

As he grew older his outlook widened and he realised that while slum-dwellers are the especial victims of poverty we are all of us the general victims of the society we have half inherited, half created. He believed that the immense popularity of books like *No Orchids for Miss Blandish* and American magazines like *Action Stories* was due to the subconscious sense of victimisation that so many people possess. It is conventional to call this atti-tude 'escape', but escape from what? Escape from the feeling of powerlessness that is prevalent in a power-hungry society. Men engaged in the most terrible war in history would lie in their trenches avidly reading of some puny gun-battle in Chicago. Their actual participation in war only reinforced their

sense of weakness. In the imagination they could enlarge themselves and take a leading, positive role. In real life one is
usually a passive victim, whereas in the adventure story one
can think of oneself as being at the centre of events.

When Orwell was a boy and a young man there were obviously people who felt they were in command of their lives.
Their numbers were rapidly declining as he grew older. In
Coming Up For Air he attempts to show how even a normally
unthinking, good-time-loving insurance agent begins to feel
society closing in on him in a way that he is powerless to prevent. He takes a few days off to go back to the scenes of his
childhood and the only impression he gets is of change for the
worse. The old carefree life of fishing and dreaming would no
longer be possible. Something had started in the modern world
that would have to play itself out, and this something with its
harshness and vulgarity and ugliness would lead to war and the
police state.

> 'I'll tell you what my stay in Lower Binfield had taught me and
> it was this. *It's all going to happen.* All the things that you've got at
> the back of your mind, the things you're terrified of, the things
> that you tell yourself are just a nightmare or only happen in
> foreign countries. The bombs, the food-queues, the rubber
> truncheons, the barbed wire, the coloured shirts, the slogans, the
> enormous faces, the machine-guns squirting out of bedroom
> windows. It's all going to happen, I know it—at any rate, I knew
> it then. There's no escape. Fight against it if you like, or look the
> other way and pretend not to notice, or grab your spanner and
> rush out to do a bit of face-smashing along with the others. But
> there's no way out. It's just something that's got to happen.'

Bowling worked this out for himself. It seeped through his pores
in a way he could never have analysed. Dorothy, the clergyman's daughter, did not have this sensation of approaching
apocalypse, but it is we, the readers, who sense it or something
like it when we read the opening paragraph of that novel.

> 'As the alarm clock on the chest of drawers exploded like a
> horrid little bomb of bell metal. Dorothy, wrenched from the
> depths of some complex, troubling dream, awoke with a start
> and lay on her back looking into the darkness in extreme exhaus-
> tion.'

There is a great deal of Orwell in that. We are obviously being
introduced to a victim of circumstances, the bomb is already

prominent in Orwell's consciousness, Dorothy's dream is complex and troubling, and she awakes from sleep in exhaustion.

When Bowling got away from his home and work for a few days he never felt he had really escaped them. 'They', a great amalgam of forces which wished to do him down, would be after him. He felt there was a huge army following him, all of them furious at the thought that he should even think of enjoying himself. They had built up a complicated system of loyalties, most of them unnecessary and without value, and they were determined that he should honour them. His wife was in front, with the kids, and his wife's forbidding friends. Then came his employers and then his colleagues at the office and thousands of others just like them, down-trodden pen-pushers who were horrified by any repudiation of the pram or the lawn-mower. In the rear were the Nosey Parkers, the people who never see you but insist on legislating for you, the Home Secretary, Scotland Yard, the Temperance League, the Bank of England, Lord Beaverbrook, Hitler and Stalin on a tandem, the bench of bishops, Mussolini, the Pope—all after him and all shouting: 'There's a chap who thinks he's going to escape! There's a chap who says he won't be streamlined! He's going back to Lower Binfield! After him! Stop him!'

This was the kind of man Orwell felt especially drawn to protect. To a very large extent he was that man himself. He is always ready in defence of the man who is being chased or bullied. His genuine love of Dickens can be explained less on literary grounds than on moral grounds. Dickens himself always supported the underdog. He even (like Orwell) changed sides when the underdog became an upperdog. He loathed the Catholic Church but began to sympathise with it when it was being persecuted, as in *Barnaby Rudge*. He loathed the aristocracy but his sympathies changed when they were overthrown, as in *A Tale of Two Cities*. Orwell's attitude to the British Empire and even to Blimps was beginning to modify just before his death. If he had lived ten years longer he would have been alert to protect them from unfair criticism.

There is no doubt that Orwell realised this characteristic in himself—in fact, he drew attention to it on at least one occasion, as I have already shown. And there is nothing surprising in it

because it is in the Western tradition to support the underdog.
In the essay on Dickens he draws attention to popular Western
folklore, from Jack the Giant-killer to Mickey Mouse, with its
constant reiteration of the same theme, the victory of the weak
over the strong. Justice is in this case a secondary consideration.
After the defeat of plutocracy it would be logical to wish the
defeat to be maintained, but instinct will not always allow it.
When 'bad rich man' becomes 'defeated rich man' his badness
tends to be forgotten. In practice, however, one is not often
called upon to make the choice. The weak are usually the poor;
they are weak because they are poor. But Orwell believed a
psychological change was taking place in the modern world,
and that while the common man still lived in the mental world
of Dickens and instinctively supported the weak against the
strong, the intellectuals, who are the vanguard in the progress
of new mental attitudes, had abandoned this world-view. Nearly
all modern intellectuals, he felt, had gone over to some form of
totalitarianism, with its basis in power irrespective of morality.
The modern Marxist or Fascist considers the Dickens viewpoint
as the supreme instance of 'bourgeois morality' or 'sentimentality', yet never stopped to consider that the people whom they
pretended to idealise were utterly 'bourgeois' in their outlook.
There is a great deal of truth in this, and Orwell was only able
to discover it by his first-hand researches. Although the living
conditions and the social behaviour of the working class differs
so greatly from that of the middle class, in their morality they
form a unity and this unity is expressed in the 'bourgeois
morality' of the Marxists. In their attitude to truth, honour and
decency the two classes were indistinguishable. Morally, the
Marxists legislated for a class that did not exist, or only existed
in the theses of middle-class intellectuals. As this gap widened
the intellectuals withdrew from the cultural unity that existed
in England and among other things they lost the traditional
sympathy for the weak. They wrote and spoke a great deal
about the condition of the weak but there was little human pity
('bourgeois sentimentality') behind this attitude. The weak
were to be the instruments of the intellectuals in their bid for
power. I shall go into Orwell's attitude towards the intellectuals
more fully in a later chapter.

I will complete this chapter with a tabulation of those groups and individuals whom Orwell felt the urge to protect at some time or another in his literary career. I shall do it as nearly as possible in chronological order.

(1) *Those marked out by some physical disability.* The best example of this is Flory in *Burmese Days.* Flory had 'a hideous birthmark stretching in a ragged crescent down his left cheek, from the eye to the corner of the mouth. Seen from the left side his face had a battered, woebegone look, as though the birthmark had been a bruise—for it was a dark blue in colour.' This mark not only stained his face, it stained his mind. He was always anxious to keep it out of sight and kept his left cheek turned from whomever he was with. He felt it was a mark that singled him out from his fellowmen, and any personal failure could ultimately be attributed to it. He was probably convinced that it was the cause of his loss of Elizabeth. A normally attractive man can afford to hold certain unconventional ideas, but a man who is marked in this way must atone by complete conventionality. Such victims are doomed from birth. As if in recognition of this, the birthmark practically disappeared when Flory died, leaving no more than a faint grey stain.

(2) *The Partido Obrero de Unificacion Marxista (P.O.U.M.)* Orwell fought in the P.O.U.M. militia but never joined the party. *After* it was suppressed he said he wished he had joined it. But he had another motive for identifying himself with P.O.U.M.—quite apart from the political rights and wrongs of the situation. The P.O.U.M. were in a weak position because they had no footing in any press outside their own country, and inside Spain press censorship was under Communist control. (Incidentally, the P.O.U.M. had a high standard of morality and did not indulge in personal attacks on leaders of other factions, which was unusual.)

(3) *Owners whose property had been destroyed.* In Spain again. 'Sometimes it gave you a sneaking sympathy with the Fascist ex-owners to see the way the militia treated the buildings they had seized.' (*Homage to Catalonia.*)

(4) *Clients of Building Societies.* They try to persuade themselves that they're buying their houses painlessly, without noticing the draught, but the fact is 'we aren't householders, that we're all

in the middle of paying for our houses and eaten up with the ghastly fear that something might happen before we've made the last payment. . . . We're all bought, and what's more we're bought with our own money.' (*Coming Up For Air*.)

(5) *The lower middle class wife*. The milk bill! The coal bill! The rent! The school fees! 'Next week we'll be in the workhouse.'

'She's got this feeling that you *ought* to be perpetually working yourself up into a stew about lack of money. Just working up an atmosphere of misery from a sense of duty. . . . She loves getting into a panic because something or other is "serious". . . . If you made a list of Hilda's remarks throughout the day, you'd find three bracketed together at the top—"We can't afford it", "It's a great saving" and "I don't know where the money's coming from".' (*Coming Up For Air*.)

(6) *Small Nations in general*. The small Baltic countries, for instance, sound like paradises. 'They seem to possess everything except the power to defend themselves.' ('Good Travellers', *Time and Tide*, 2 December, 1939.) The dilemma of the small nations was this: when they are independent they are unable to protect themselves; when they are not independent they are invariably misgoverned.

(7) *Poland in particular*. The dominant atmosphere of power worship in the modern world had no time for a small power like Poland. The prevalent idea was that 'Fascist Poland did not deserve to survive'. The implication was always that Poland was worse than Nazi Germany. Both were Fascist, but the Poles committed the unforgivable sin of being weak. Nevertheless they put up a better resistance than the French and they did not change sides in the middle. '. . . this nation of thirty million souls . . . deserves its independence in any world where national sovereignty is possible.' ('On the Brink', *New Statesman*, 13 July, 1940.)

(8) *Ernest Raymond*. He wrote a silly book called *Tell England* and was thereafter damned. Orwell often tried to convince his friends that Raymond's *We, the Accused* was a remarkable novel but was always met by 'the cold, shocked stare of the mentally superior person'.

(9) *Adolf Hitler*.

'I should like to put it on record that I have never been able to dislike Hitler. Ever since he came to power—till then, like nearly everyone, I had been deceived into thinking that he did not matter—I have reflected that I would certainly kill him if I could get within reach of him, but that I could feel no personal animosity. The fact is that there is something deeply appealing about him. One feels it again when one sees his photographs—and I recommend especially the photograph at the beginning of Hurst and Blackett's edition [of *Mein Kampf*], which shows Hitler in his early Brownshirt days. It is a pathetic, doglike face, the face of a man suffering under intolerable wrongs. In a rather more manly way it reproduces the expression of innumerable pictures of Christ crucified, and there is little doubt that that is how Hitler sees himself. The initial, personal cause of his grievance against the universe can only be guessed at; but at any rate the grievance is there. He is the martyr, the victim, Prometheus chained to the rock, the self-sacrificing hero who fights single-handed against impossible odds. If he were killing a mouse he would know how to make it seem like a dragon. One feels, as with Napoleon, that he is fighting against destiny, that he *can't* win, and yet that he somehow deserves to. The attraction of such a pose is of course enormous; half the films that one sees turn upon such a theme.' ('Hitler', *New English Weekly*, 21 March, 1940.)

(10) *The Blacks.* In 'Notes on the Way' (*Time and Tide*, 30 March, 1940) he relates how he saw a coolie carrying a long tin uniform-case and endangering people's heads with it at Colombo. A police sergeant kicked him. The passengers murmured approval. Suppose such a scene were transferred to Paddington or Liverpool Docks. But it couldn't happen. An English luggage porter would probably hit back if he were kicked. Nor would the policeman attempt such a thing. And if he did the onlookers would be disgusted. Even the most selfish millionaire would feel momentary resentment if he saw such a thing. The people who approved of this incident were ordinary, decent, middling people, with incomes of about £500 a year. 'They were white and the coolie was black. In other words, he was sub-human, a different kind of animal.'

(11) *The Intellectuals!* A surprise, after all the unpleasant things Orwell said about this class. But it is an instance of how his feelings could swing once he thought there was injustice or hardship. But the intransigence of the modern intellectual is due to his victimisation.

'Since about 1930 everyone describable as an 'intellectual'' has lived in a state of chronic discontent with the existing order.

Necessarily so, because society as it was constituted had no room
for him. In an Empire that was merely stagnant, neither being
developed nor falling to pieces, and in an England ruled by
people whose chief asset was their stupidity, to be "clever" was
to be suspect. If you had the kind of brain that could understand
the poems of T. S. Eliot or the theories of Karl Marx, the higher-
ups would see to it that you were kept out of any important job.
The intellectuals could find a function for themselves only in the
literary reviews and the Left-wing political parties.' (*The Lion and
the Unicorn.*)

(12) *'Great men' in the future.* This is only true if you believe
that the future is predetermined, but apparently more and
more people do hold that belief today, when faith in individual
judgment is declining. The 'great man' believes rather more
than others that he can control his destiny, but this is of course
an illusion—given the above premiss. ('Thomas Hardy Looks
at War', *Tribune*, 18 September, 1942.)

(13) *The British in Burma!* When the British were driven out
of Burma by the Japanese Orwell came to their defence in the
particular context of evacuation. It was not true, he said, that
they had abandoned the Indians to their fate, as was being
alleged by some commentators. Many Europeans left Burma
on foot, as most Indians did; it would not have been possible to
fly out all the Indians; fifty thousand of them were repatriated
by the British and Indian navies. ('War in Burma', *New Statesman*, 14 August, 1943.)

(14) *The Jews.* Orwell was naturally anti-anti-semitic, but
the problem troubled him and he had no ready-made solution.
(I doubt if it was of major interest to him, he very rarely
referred to it in his writings.) He said that the explanations of
anti-semitism usually fell into two schools, which might be
called the 'traditional' and the 'economic'. Left-wing thinkers
usually regard the Jew as a convenient scapegoat, but it is never
made clear why the Jews, rather than some other minority
group, should always be chosen. Nor is it clear why anti-
semitism should flourish among people who have no economic
grievance, or why it should be mixed up with irrelevant magical
beliefs. The other theory, which regards anti-semitism as a relic
of the Middle Ages, explains these difficulties no more successfully. The Jews have clung to their religious and cultural

identity in an alien environment—'but so have many other
small groups all over the world, and it is very doubtful whether
modern Europe cares enough for doctrinal questions to want to
persecute people merely because they are not Christians'.
('Chosen People', *Observer*, 30 January, 1944.) Why did it ever
start? Why, if it is the survival of medieval superstition, should
it have survived when so many other supersititions perished?
All he can do is suggest a thorough enquiry be made.

Orwell's attention seemed to be drawn by particular problems or circumstances for a brief period, and then they would
pass from his view. The abiding problems were poverty and
oppression on a large scale. (The Small Nations period was, not
unexpectedly, 1939-40. The Jewish period was early 1944.) A
month later he returned to this problem in *Tribune* ('As I
Please', 11 February, 1944). This time he was concerned with
the ineffectiveness of the normal approach to anti-semitism:

> 'The weakness of the Left-wing attitude towards anti-semitism
> is to approach it from a rationalistic angle. Obviously the charges
> made against the Jews are not true. They cannot be true, partly
> because they cancel out, partly because no people could have such
> a monopoly of wickedness. But simply by pointing this out one
> gets no further. The official Left-wing view of anti-semitism is that
> it is something "got up" by the ruling classes in order to divert
> attention away from the real evils of society. The Jews, in fact, are
> scapegoats. This is no doubt correct, but it is quite useless as an
> argument. One does not dispose of a belief by showing that it is
> irrational. Nor is it any use, in my experience, to talk about the
> persecution of the Jews in Germany. If a man has the slightest
> disposition towards anti-semitism, such things bounce off his
> consciousness like peas off a steel helmet. The best argument of all,
> if rational arguments were ever of any use, would be to point out
> that the alleged crimes of the Jews are only possible because we
> live in a society which rewards crime. If all Jews are crooks, let us
> deal with them by so arranging our economic system that crooks
> cannot prosper. But what good is it to say that kind of thing to the
> man who believes as an article of faith that Jews dominate the
> Black Market, push their way to the front of queues and dodge
> military service?'

Orwell never gave much attention to the Jewish problem,
not because he did not consider it important, but because to
approach it in his natural way, as he approached poverty and
the Spanish war, would have involved at least two years of

complete absorption in it, involving living in a ghetto. There is
a limit to what one man can do.[1]

(15) *Small Quislings.* Orwell shared with many other people
disgust for the way in which minor quislings were hounded
down after the war.

'Few things in this war have been more morally disgusting than
the present hunt after traitors and quislings. At best it is largely
the punishment of the guilty by the guilty. In France, all kinds of
petty rats—police officials, penny-a-lining journalists, women
who have slept with German soldiers—are hunted down while
almost without exception the big rats escape. In England the
fiercest tirades against quislings are uttered by Conservatives who
were practising appeasement in 1938 and Communists who were
advocating it in 1940.' ('In Defence of P. G. Wodehouse',
Critical Essays—1945.)

---

1 Orwell explored this subject further in an article entitled 'Anti-Semitism in
Britain' (*Such, Such Were the Joys*). He summarised his opinion as follows: there is
more anti-Semitism in Britain than we care to admit; it has the effect of making
people callous to Jewish sufferings in other countries; it is quite irrational and
will not yield to argument; the persecutions in Germany have obscured the
whole picture; the subject needs serious investigation.

Chapter VII

The Assault on Liberty

AS YOU read his books you can watch Orwell's political development from scratch. He did not emerge fully-fledged. In Burma he does not seem to have been very interested in political matters and his later views were partly formed by his experience of poverty rather than the descent into poverty deriving from political curiosity. He approached politics through poverty, but later, when the new totalitarian regimes replaced poverty by security in return for social servility and political discipline, he realised that the crux of modern politics is liberty. The old English doctrine that liberty was more important than equality was challenged by the Marxists. Orwell noticed, however, that the equality established by a totalitarian regime did not last very long, and the people realised too late that they had traded their liberty and received nothing in return. Therefore liberty must be retained at all costs and the fight for equality should take place on entirely different ground. There should be no bargains, no pretence that security was equivalent to equality.

George Woodcock, in 'Orwell and Conscience' (*World Review*, April 1950), called Orwell a 'Liberal survivor'. Although he called himself a Socialist and in general supported the programme of the Labour Party (at least, during the war) he was intellectually the disciple of men such as Emerson and Ruskin. After the first World War these men were regarded as hopelessly old-fashioned, 'bourgeois idealists' who never came to terms with the *real* world. They were swept aside by the amoralist doctrines of political expediency. Orwell's contribution to modern political thought was the reintroduction of the despised value which used to be called Truth. The moderns said truth was variable and relative, and even spoke of 'proletarian truth'. Orwell said this was rubbish. A thing was either true or not true and any attempt to evade this self-evident proposition was dishonest. (He could never really come to terms with his enemies because they did not use the same vocabulary: they could turn aside the charge of dishonesty by claiming that it, too, was entirely dependent on circumstances.) Woodcock pointed out that specialisation has reached such a pitch today that the expert can only express himself to the uninitiated by means of gross simplifications. Politicians use simplifications to conceal their true purpose. No one man can bring to order the whole of knowledge. The most he can do is create by an imaginative effort a vision of the whole. The vision will be generalised but it will contain innumerable implications. Orwell attempted to create this new vision, and he knew that it could only be done through imagination and feeling. This explains his constant lack of precision. Without being a poet he sought a poetic picture of society. In this picture broad truths could be recognised although analysis would break them down and demonstrate their logical inconsistency. His instinct told him that if the scientific method were wholly adopted in the social and political field the old generalised guides and sanctions would be destroyed and in their place would come a piecemeal approach which would be compelled to make expediency the measure, as there would be nothing else. Expediency is the temporary judgment of fallible men. If the habit of applying broad principles accepted by all men were destroyed, its place would be taken by the application of narrow principles designed merely to benefit the particular men who happened to hold power.

Orwell did say many times that there is less freedom in the world today than in the world of thirty or forty years ago. He did not, however, claim that there was sufficient freedom in that past epoch. It was a convention of Western society to revere the concept of freedom, but the reverence was frequently hypocritical. However, it was better for a man to pretend to admire freedom then to state quite openly that he thought it should be abolished. It is when men begin to talk about 'freedom' as a 'bourgeois value' that they win adherents and then start tearing down the bourgeois freedom and replacing it with proletarian dictatorship or fulfilment through a Leader, which in some mystical way is actually supposed to be more free than freedom itself. Hypocrisy is the product of fear, and hypocritical advocates of liberty are a sure sign that there is still health in the community.

Orwell discovered in Burma how free the English were. In Burma every thought and every word were censored. In England it was difficult even to imagine such an atmosphere. 'Everyone is free in England; we sell our souls in public and buy them back in private, among our friends.' But there was no freedom in Burma, for white and brown alike. The white man was part of a despotism and therefore had no more freedom than its overt victims. (Freedom must not be confused with standard of living.) The official was a cog and when the machine moved the cog moved with it. There were individual freedoms, of course. You were free to be a drunkard, an idler, a coward, a backbiter, a fornicator. But there was one freedom you were not allowed and it was the most important of all. You were not allowed to speak freely. If you cannot speak freely you soon lose the faculty of thinking freely. You fall back on the code of the pukka sahib.

If you are a cog in a machine you are certainly not a full human being. There was freedom in England, but Orwell first experienced the real excitement of freedom in Catalonia. There the people had suddenly attained freedom for the first time, they had jubilantly ceased to be cogs, and had discovered each other anew as human beings. It was a bit crude at times (in the barbers' shops there were Anarchist notices solemnly proclaiming that barbers were no longer slaves) but there was no doubting the exhilaration. It might seem rather pathetic to what Orwell called 'the hard-boiled, sneering civilisation of the English-speaking races', but that would be because they had inherited freedom from their fathers and had half-forgotten its value. This Spanish freedom was anchored in the equality they had taken for themselves. Liberty and equality are different concepts but neither flourishes perfectly without the other. And just as the party hacks and the advanced professors had decided that social discipline was really more valuable than freedom, so they were now busy 'proving' that equality is not a part of

Socialism, which is a kind of planned state-capitalism with the grab-motive left intact. But it is not easy to deceive ordinary people about the nature of a thing once it has been driven deep into their consciousness, and the popular view of Socialism had sunk in some fifty years ago. To most people Socialism meant equality. Equality took precedence of liberty because they already had liberty. And there in Spain they had them both for a brief period.

> 'In that community where no one was on the make, where there was a shortage of everything but no privilege and no boot-licking, one got, perhaps, a crude forecast of what the opening stages of Socialism might be like. And, after all, instead of dis-illusioning me it deeply attracted me.' (*Homage to Catalonia.*)

Orwell was unusual in his time for keeping alive the idea of liberty, not at the expense of equality, but to the extent of over-shadowing it. He knew that tags like socialism and capitalism will not rouse men to action but that tags like liberty and loyalty do. Men go into battle with various phrases on their lips but these rarely reflect the ideas in their hearts. Ideas are trans-muted into slogans by propaganda. Loyalty and liberty are personal things and men are not so foolish, as they are some-times represented, as to be unable to sense the reality behind an abstraction.

The actual savouring of liberty is a rare thing. It is far more common for people to possess liberty without appreciating its value. It is felt to be a man's right and when he has it he is no more conscious of it than of the air he breathes, unless he has recently come out of a dungeon. That was the condition of the Spanish people during the early months of their Civil War. But the majority of men are either in the dungeon or well out of it. Those who are still imprisoned can even acquire a taste for servility. Some stimulus is required to set men on the search for liberty, especially if they have never had it. They only regard it as their right when they have it. The first slaves Orwell became intimate with were the *plongeurs* of the Paris hotels. He discovered they had a pride of their own but it was a perverted pride in their drudgery. It lay in being equal to whatever demands were laid upon them, however unreasonable. The only attainable virtue is the power of working like an ox. It is

the ambition of every *plongeur* to be a *debrouillard*, a man who
does whatever he is told, even the seemingly impossible. This
is surely what we mean by the phrase 'slave mentality'. The
idea of freedom, of having the right to choose between reasonable alternatives, does not exist for them. Their work is servile
and without art; they are paid just enough to keep them alive;
their only holiday is the sack. They can rarely marry, but if they
do their wives are also compelled to work. The only possible
escape is into prison. It was probably while working in Paris
that Orwell first perceived the idea that was to become increasingly important to him in later years: that there was a
rough equality among the *plongeurs* but that it was of no use to
them at all without liberty. There was nothing in nature or
politics to prevent a community of slaves from enjoying perfect
equality.

His main interest where freedom was concerned was its
power in England. In one country after another he saw freedom
being destroyed. In some of these countries, it is true, it had
scarcely taken root. But there was a long tradition of freedom
in England and he was constantly speculating on the extent to
which it would be able to resist the new forces. He tended to be
pessimistic but was agreeably surprised when the war came to
find that most of the old liberties were retained. His conclusion
was that freedom had become a habit and it was misleading to
assume that it could therefore be filched without being noticed.
In *Coming Up For Air* he had stated his belief that freedom
scarcely existed in the £5-£10-a-week class. They were ridden
by economic fears and worries, accentuated by the need to
maintain respectability, which often left them poorer in 'real'
surplus money power than the workers. Their only freedom lay
in their dreams. But at this stage he was still concerned with the
economic basis of freedom, which is admittedly important, but
the situation that was developing was one in which the political
liberties were assuming a growing importance, and for two
reasons. In the first place, modern states of every political complexion were learning how to provide security for their citizens,
and in the second place it was the political liberties that were
being actively attacked.

Political liberty is a complex thing, and some of the strands that make it up may be stronger than others. Orwell believed, for instance, that there was great respect for freedom of speech in England but very little for freedom of the press. In one of his 'London Letters' to *Partisan Review* (July-August, 1941) he said that there had been much tampering, direct and indirect, with the freedom of the press during the last twenty years, but it had never roused a flicker of popular protest. No one could seriously maintain that there was a free press in England. The press that exists is fairly free, but there is a large potential press that simply doesn't exist at all. England, he said, was a lowbrow country and the common man did not think the printed word mattered greatly. On the other hand, the kind of situation where a man is afraid to open his mouth for fear of the Gestapo is simply unimaginable in England. Any attempt to introduce it would be broken not so much by conscious resistance as by the inability of ordinary people to grasp what was wanted of them. When there is unemployment working men will sometimes be careful not to express 'red' opinions in the hearing of his boss, but no one would both about being overheard by a policeman.

English freedom, in fact, does depend on public opinion to a much greater extent than we normally imagine. Orwell makes a very good but seldom noticed point in this context, namely, that no country can enforce laws, or enforce them for very long, if the public really disapprove of them. This is perhaps another way of saying a people gets the government it deserves but it is not meant as justification. The aims of political science should be political justice. If Orwell had not believed this passionately there would have been no cogent factor to prevent him accepting any government that managed to impose itself on a non-vigilant people. In the last resort he believed that the British people had vast psychological power, although it was largely unconscious and obeyed a rule of thumb rather than any enunciated principles. (They had been enunciated, of course, *ad nauseam* by theorists and journalists, but few people troubled to read them.) It was this resource that enabled the British people to resist Fascism during the war, although it was, not surprisingly, weakened.

'The relative freedom which we enjoy depends on public

opinion. The law is no protection. Governments make laws, but whether they are carried out, and how the police behave, depends on the general temper of the country. If large numbers of people are interested in freedom of speech, there will be freedom of speech, even if the law forbids it; if public opinion is sluggish, inconvenient minorities will be persecuted, even if laws exist to protect them. The decline in the desire for intellectual liberty has not been so sharp as I would have predicted six years ago, when the war was starting, but still there has been a decline. The notion that certain opinions cannot safely be allowed a hearing is growing. It is given currency by intellectuals who confuse the issue by not distinguishing between democratic opposition and open rebellion, and it is reflected in our growing indifference to tyranny and injustice abroad. And even those who declare themselves to be in favour of freedom of opinion generally drop their claim when it is their own adversaries who are being persecuted.' ('Freedom of the Park', *Tribune*, 7 December, 1945.)

He thought the passion for intellectual liberty was declinnig, though he had expected the declinc to be sharper. But the really sinister aspect of this trend lay in the fact that the decline was to be found almost completely in the very class which one would imagine to be the chief defenders of intellectual liberties. It was the intellectuals who were forsaking the liberty of their own field and trying to establish a new and alien mental tyranny. The ordinary people, who had little respect for intellect, clung to intellectual liberty not because they had learnt at school to value it but because they regarded it as an essential part of life. If you told them they were guardians of intellectual liberty they would think you were making fun of them, but they would assert vigorously their right to say what they thought. Orwell was particularly horrified when he attended a P.E.N. Club discussion on Freedom of Expression. There were between thirty and forty eminent speakers, all celebrating Milton's work for intellectual freedom, and the speeches were later collected and published in book form. What struck Orwell, in the midst of the platitudes, were the large number of contemporary attacks on freedom of expression which the speakers did not deign to refer to. They did not refer to the centralised ownership of the British press, with its consequent power to suppress any bit of news that it chose; the question of who really controlled the B.B.C.; the buying-up of young writers by film units and the M.O.I.; the methods by which British correspondents in foreign countries were squeezed into telling lies or concealing truths; the corruption of literary criticism by the publishing trade; the vague semi-official pressure that prevents books on unpopular themes from being published; and the spread of totalitarian ideas, mostly emanating from the U.S.S.R., among English intellectuals. You could not expect the ordinary man to know about these things, or even to care overmuch if he did know, because it was not his territory. But those people whose duty it was to safeguard these freedoms were not doing it. Equivalent abuses in other fields would have been checked immediately. Orwell concluded that this meeting had in effect been a demonstration in favour of censorship.

'There was nothing particularly surprising in this. In our age, the idea of intellectual liberty is under attack from two directions. On the other side are its theoretical enemies, the apologists of totalitarianism, and on the other its immediate, practical enemies monopoly and bureaucracy. Any writer or journalist who wants to retain his integrity finds himself thwarted by the general drift of society rather than by active persecution. The sort of things that are working against him are the concentration of the Press in the hands of a few rich men, the grip of monopoly on radio and the films, the unwillingness of the public to spend money on books, making it necessary for nearly every writer to earn part of his living by hackwork, the encroachment of official bodies like the M.O.I. and the British Council, which help the writer to keep alive but also waste his time and dictate his opinions, and the continuous war atmosphere of the past ten years, whose distorting effects no one has been able to escape. Everything in our age conspires to turn the writer, and every other kind of artist as well, into a minor offiical, working on themes handed to him from above and never telling what seems to him the whole of the truth. But in struggling against this fate he gets no help from his own side: that is, there is no large body of opinion which will assure him that he is in the right. In the past, at any rate throughout the Protestant centuries, the idea of rebellion and the idea of intellectual integrity were mixed up. A heretic—political, moral, religious or aesthetic—was one who refused to outrage his own conscience. His outlook was summed up in the words of the Revivalist hymn:

> Dare to be a Daniel,
> Dare to stand alone;
> Dare to have a purpose firm,
> Dare to make it known.

To bring this hymn up to date one would have to add a "Don't"
at the beginning of each line. For it is the peculiarity of our age
that the rebels against the existing order, at any rate the most
numerous and characteristic of them, are also rebelling against the
idea of individual integrity. "Daring to stand alone" is ideologic-
ally criminal as well as practically dangerous. The independence
of the writer and the artist is eaten away by vague economic
forces, and at the same time it is undermined by those who should
be its defenders.' ('The Prevention of Literature', *Shooting an
Elephant.*)

It was during the thirties when the Western intellectuals
began to abdicate their role as defenders of intellectual freedom
in large numbers. The big test came with the Moscow Trials.
Orwell was less horrified by the trials themselves (he even considered them necessary in a totalitarian society) than by the
eagerness of Western intellectuals to justify them. Correspondents of Liberal newspapers, whose predecessors would have been
the first to denounce the methods and procedure used at
Moscow, pronounced themselves 'completely satisfied' by the
confessions of men who had been dragged into the light after,
in some cases, years of solitary confinement. One eminent
lawyer even produced the theory that the loss of the right to
appeal was a great advantage to the accused! This kind of
cynicism had been encountered before, but never by men who
prided themselves on being 'progressive'. The majority of
intellectuals, Orwell felt, had decided that democracy had
failed and intellectual freedom was a hindrance to good government.

Although totalitarianism was a new system produced by a
new situation, its attitude to intellectual liberty was as old as
liberty itself. The Stalinists and Fascists were only doing what
religious orthodoxies had done for years. Because religion has
made a compact with the State in most modern countries, there
exists the fiction that religion supports that degree of intellectual
liberty that is allowed by the State. In England, for instance,
the Church of England is so tolerant many people feel its
tolerance has actually become theological laxness. Support is
given to this view because most members of the Church are
merely Sunday Christians and would be quite incapable of
repeating its tenets if challenged. But if we consider a man who

takes his religion seriously he would know the tenets and he would believe them—and he would be intellectually crippled in the process. Orwell said that in practice books by orthodox believers usually show the same cramped, blinkered outlook as books by orthodox Stalinists, or others who are mentally unfree. In fact, while reading these books the most powerful impression one gets is of what is unsaid or distorted rather than of what is sincerely said. Such people do not believe in the power of the individual to acquaint himself with the truth, and are prepared to abuse their own sense of truth in accordance with 'inspired' doctrine. The Christian Churches still demand assent to doctrines which no one seriously believes in, and the totalitarian parties are doing the same. Belief in life after death is as alien to the modern mind as mystical Leader-worship, but both are considered necessary for purposes of loyalty and administration. Men feel a need for a 'purpose', find refuge in a Church or Party and nibble round their intellectual absurdities.

Parallel with this, and enforcing it, has been the growth of the implication that theology and politics are exact sciences and should therefore be left to experts. It is certainly possible to use a scientific approach to these fields, for a particular intellectual method can be used at any time. But the use of scientific method does not convert the subject under examination to an *exact* science. Catholic apologists profess to be astonished when a layman or a scientist offers an opinion on such questions as the existence of God or the immortality of the soul. They say that the scientist is only an expert in one particular field and is necessarily ignorant in all others. This is an old dodge for confining the study of important questions to cabals who know what their conclusions will be before they have even initiated their 'enquiry'. In politics the common man is urged to let the expert think for him, with the plausible rider that a full-time student of politics must inevitably approach nearer the truth than a part-time, semi-informed amateur. 'Leave it to the experts' is one of the subtlest slogans of tyranny.

Orwell believed that intellectual liberty was an essential condition not only of political truth but also of the best work in art. When he recognised that 'a fairly large proportion of the distinguished novels of the last few decades have been written by Catholics and have even been describable as Catholic novels', there seemed to be a contradiction. But although many of the best novels have been by Catholics, none of them could be described as great. In fact, compared with other epochs, the best of today are but a poor best. In a thin period the Catholic may be at an advantage in having a fixed moral and theological background to work against. On the other hand, this background will inhibit him from writing anything in the first class because of its artificiality and unacceptability by the majority of men. Secondly, Orwell doubts whether the writers in question would be considered 'good' Catholics from the point of view of the hierarchy. The usual criticism of them is that they concentrate monotonously on the evils of human nature, which gives a very biased impression of what their religion claims to offer mankind. Nearly all the better modern novels by Catholics are concerned with the sense of sin, which implies in the authors a constant and theologically unhealthy concern with whatever is forbidden. An equivalent would be for Marxist novelists to write continually about the salvation of heretics. They don't, probably because the political parties are so much younger than the Catholic Church and have by no means passed through the first flush of enthusiasm in which it is 'not done' to harp on failure.

Orwell's most important treatment of the decline of intellectual liberty in modern times is to be found in his essay 'The Prevention of Literature' (*Shooting an Elephant*). This liberty has always had its enemies, and in the recent past they were to be found among Conservatives, Catholics and Fascists, each of them centred round an orthodoxy. But today intellectual liberty has to be defended against the Communists and 'fellow-travellers', who a short time ago had been regarded as champions of liberty. It was not the English Communist Party that was important but the poisonous effect of the Russian *mythos* on English life. The favourite method used in the attack on liberty lay in the suppression and distortion of facts to such an extent that it was doubtful whether a true history of our times would ever be written. He gave as an instance the suppression of the fact that large numbers of Soviet Russians had welcomed and supported the invading German armies during the last war, and that some Russian prisoners and Displaced Persons refused to return to Russia after the war or were returned against their will. This was well known by British journalists on the spot but was hardly ever mentioned in the British press, where it was fashionable to maintain that Russia had had no quislings. This is not due to a conscious policy of falsification but because most journalists at the time were sympathetic to the Soviet Union and acquiesced in dishonesty on the grounds of expediency. He also referred to a pamphlet written by Maxim Litvinoff in 1918 (which he actually possessed) in which high praise was given to the parts played by Trotsky, Zinoviev and Kamenev in the revolution, with no mention of Stalin. A modern Communist would say that such a publication would be better suppressed and in addition would accept a garbled version denigrating Trotsky and giving full praise to Stalin. Such forgeries are common. Once again, it is not the existence of such forgeries that is alarming (they have always existed) but the failure of the Left-wing intelligentsia to protest. It is felt that it is better to distort the truth than 'play into the hands' of some opposition group.

This type of orthodoxy makes good writing impossible, Orwell said. The mere prevalence of certain ideas can spread a kind of poison that makes one subject after another impossible for literary purposes. The enemies of intellectual liberty always present their case as a plea for discipline versus individualism. Having 'proved', by careful selection and with reference to specific contexts, that individualism is a social evil, they then proceed to treat any aspect of individualism (e.g., individual truth) as false or dangerous. The issue of truth-versus-untruth is therefore kept in the background. Anyone who tries to present the truth as he sees it is branded as an egoist. As the first concern of an honest writer is truth, he finds it quite impossible to write about many political issues because he knows he will not find a market.

'The Catholic and the Communist are alike in assuming that an opponent cannot be both honest and intelligent. Each of them tacitly claims that "the truth" has already been revealed, and that the heretic, if he is not simply a fool, is secretly aware of "the

truth" and merely resists it out of selfish motives. In Communist
literature the attack on intellectual liberty is usually masked by
oratory about "petty-bourgeois individualism", "the illusions of
nineteenth-century liberalism", etc., and backed up by words of
abuse such as "romantic" and "sentimental", which since they
do not have any agreed meaning are difficult to answer. In this
way the controversy is manoeuvred away from its real issue. One
can accept, and most enlightened people would accept, the Communist thesis that pure freedom will only exist in a classless
society and that one is most nearly free when one is working to
bring such a society about. But slipped in with this is the quite
unfounded claim that the Communist party is itself aiming at the
establishment of the classless society, and that in the U.S.S.R. this
aim is actually on the way to being realised. If the first claim is
allowed to entail the second, there is almost no assault on common
sense and common decency that cannot be justified. But meanwhile, the real point has been dodged. Freedom of the intellect
means the freedom to report what one has seen, heard and felt,
and not to be obliged to fabricate imaginary fact and feelings.
The familiar tirades against "escapism" and "individualism",
"romanticism" and so forth are merely a forensic device, the aim
of which is to make the perversion of history seem respectable.'

In the essay on Dickens Orwell said he was the type of
writer who was 'hated with equal hatred by all the smelly little
orthodoxies which are now contending for our souls'. Dickens
was a man who was *generously angry*, a nineteenth-century
liberal, a free intelligence, who fought hard against abuses but
always fought in the open and was never frightened. He contrasts such a man with the modern critic who requires guidance
from a higher authority before he knows what ought to be
attacked, and who can never be quite sure where the boundaries
of orthodox opinion lie. A Dickens will fight what he knows to
be evil; the other will fight against what he is told is evil,
knowing that it may cease to be evil tomorrow and that it was
accepted yesterday. One result of this tendency has been the
declining importance of what a man *does* compared with what
he *is*. A man may do the same thing twice and the first time it
will be good and the second time bad. It therefore becomes
much safer to mark down the man himself as bad, and not the
action. But as it is often impossible to know exactly what a man
is, in practice the important thing becomes what he is suspected
of being. Millions of people have been and are being imprisoned

today simply because they are believed to hold certain beliefs. If they don't hold the beliefs attributed to them they are soon persuaded to admit that they did. Truth is not important. Victims are necessary. Commenting on one of these victims, Mr Arthur Koestler, Orwell remarked that he should consider himself lucky that when he was interned in England he had fallen into the hands of amtaeurs, who not only let him out again, but did not force him beforehand to confess to poisoning sheep, committing sabotage on the railways or plotting to assassinate the King. In England a man's actions were still significant.

Orwell was perfectly well aware that intellectual liberty did not harmonise very well on a narrow view with social, technical and political efficiency. You paid for liberty with a measure of chaos.

> 'How are freedom and organisation to be reconciled? If one considers the probabilities one is driven to the conclusion that Anarchism implies a low standard of living. It need not imply a hungry or uncomfortable world, but it rules out the kind of air-conditioned, chromium-plated, gadget-ridden existence which is now considered desirable and enlightened. The processes involved in making say, an aeroplane are so complex as to be only possible in a planned, centralised society, with all the repressive apparatus that that implies. Unless there is some unpredictable change in human nature, liberty and efficiency must pull in opposite directions.' (Review of *A Coat of Many Colours*, by Herbert Read, *Poetry Quarterly*, Winter, 1945.)

It is the idea of social and technical efficiency that has caught the imagination of so many of the younger generations in recent years. On the whole you will find reverence for liberty, with the corresponding preparedness to accept lower technical standards, among older men and women. The young are prepared to swallow authority to get the efficiency. Orwell recalls how Thomas Mann was booed by a youthful audience in 1923 while defending the Weimar Republic against militarism, authoritarianism and nationalism. A man of fifty was saying in effect, Stay alive! and the young men replied, in effect, We want to be killed! 'The middle-aged man is for liberty, the young are for authority . . . the general tendency in every country of the world has been the same.' ('The Faith of Thomas Mann', *Tribune*, 10 September, 1943.)

There is in fact a blind force, only half-recognised, driving modern society towards the abdication of liberty. This is most clearly seen in the progress of the totalitarian states, but its universality is masked in their case because we have excellent reason to believe that the loss of liberty is actually sought as part of a political programme. But even in a relatively free society, where freedom is cherished and is watched vigilantly, the mere conditions of modern life tend to reduce the liberty of the individual. Orwell noticed this process at work when he made his study of conditions among the northern unemployed. Some of the slums had been pulled down and the tenants rehoused on new estates. There was no doubt that the new houses were much better than the old, but nearly everyone agreed that they were comparatively cold and uncomfortable and 'unhomelike'. In some almost intangible way the original atmosphere of home, its freedom and friendliness, had been whittled away. One of the more obvious causes of this deterioration was the absence of pubs. Presumably this was intended to improve the moral and financial condition of the tenants, but it struck a serious blow at communal life. The right to enjoy communal life implies certain amenities. These were lacking, a freedom was curtailed, and it was all done to improve the quality of life on the estate. Orwell said he sometimes thought that the price of liberty was not so much eternal vigilance as eternal dirt. Hygiene is one of the modern efficiencies which can make life horribly dreary. On some estates new tenants were systematically deloused before entering their new homes. All their possessions were taken away, fumigated and sent on to the new house. 'Bugs are bad, but a state of affairs in which men will allow themselves to be dipped like sheep is worse.' (*The Road to Wigan Pier.*) If the authorities were accused of nibbling at popular rights and liberties they would be genuinely upset. Such acts belong to the temper of our time and we are scarcely aware of their true nature.

The temper of the time is authoritarian and the Communist and Fascist, although possessing different aims, accept this temper. The liberal intellect fights against it but is handicapped because it is easier to surrender to something as intangible as atmosphere than it is to oppose it. The Communists in particular have made a joyous surrender and have shown their enthusiasm by deliberately setting out to destroy even the traces or memory of freedom. It is not sufficient to attack the free man, the free institution, the free act. They also consider it necessary to attack and destroy history. Organised lying is not a temporary expedient as some Communists naively imagine. No one who believes that a correct knowledge of the past is important could possibly lend himself to even temporary distortion. A totalitarian state is really a theocracy and the ruling caste must be regarded by its subjects as infallible. Mistakes must not be admitted, and where they have been made they must be erased from the records. Every change in policy demands a corresponding change of doctrine and a revaluation of prominent historical figures. This applies not only to recent history (e.g., the sudden change in the nature of the last war in 1941) but also to remote events (e.g., the transformation of Ivan the Terrible from a bloody tyrant to a noble founder of the Russian state). Totalitarianism demands a continuous alteration of the past. Friends of totalitarianism claim that as all history is inevitably biased and inaccurate, we might as well accept one bias as another. If absolute truth is impossible we might as well adopt expedience as a guide. This view of totalitarian methods played an important part in *1984*. Orwell mentioned the possibility of a schizophrenic system of thought, in which the laws accepted in normal life and in the exact sciences could be disregarded by the politician, historian and sociologist. There are already many people who would think it scandalous to falsify a scientific textbook but knowingly accept historic falsification.

Once this type of society prevails literature will be doomed. Literature, particularly prose, cannot flourish where the author is subject to mental inhibitions. The results will be either unredeemed dullness or neurosis. And once the freedom of literature is destroyed there will be little hope for freedom of speech. As I have pointed out, Orwell did not believe the English people felt much conscious concern for either literature or the press but the effect of their freedom on mental habits is incalculable. Nearly everyone reads newspapers and many read books, and whatever the quality preferred these publications are set against a background of free discussion and reporting. If this were taken away it would be immensely difficult to maintain the freedom of spoken discussion and speculation. It is easy for a politician to follow the 'party line' (thousands held three quite distinct attitudes towards Nazi Germany in succession, from 1939 to 1941), but a writer depends on his feelings. If he is compelled to adapt his political thinking to a fluctuating line (and every writer today is compelled to think politically, directly or indirectly) he must either tell lies about his subjective feelings, or suppress them altogether.

> 'In either case he has destroyed his dynamo. Not only will ideas refuse to come to him, but the very words he uses will seem to stiffen under his touch. Political writing in our time consists almost entirely of prefabricated phrases bolted together like the pieces of a child's Meccano set. It is the unavoidable result of self-censorship. To write in plain, vigorous language one has to think fearlessly, and if one thinks fearlessly one cannot be politically orthodox. It might be otherwise in an "age of faith", when the prevailing orthodoxy has been long established and is not taken too seriously. In that case it would be possible, or might be possible, for large areas of one's mind to remain unaffected by what one officially believed. Even so, it is worth noticing that prose literature almost disappeared during the only age of faith that Europe has ever enjoyed. Throughout the whole of the Middle Ages there was almost no imaginative prose literature and very little in the way of historical writing: and the intellectual leaders of society expressed their most serious thoughts in a dead language which barely altered during a thousand years.' ('The Prevention of Literature.')

This is not mere speculation. We have been warned. Orwell gives examples. German literature almost disappeared under Hitler and the situation was not much better in Italy. (There is almost certainly a close correlation between the decay of literature and the degree of social discipline.) Judging by translations Russian literature has deteriorated at an increasing tempo since the Revolution. (Some readers may remember the crude Russian novels which were translated into English during the war. Also, although Orwell doesn't mention it, it is worth recalling the fact that the high-water mark of Russian literature took place under a tyranny, it is true, but a hopelessly inefficient tyranny. The Tsars wanted to inhibit intellectual freedom but they never had

the skill to do it.) The Left-wing, 'proletarian' literary movement in Western Europe and America produced few memorable
books. The literary great of modern times have been almost
exclusively free intellects: Proust, Joyce, Lawrence, Hemingway. How many people during the last three hundred years,
asks Orwell, have been at once good novelists and good
Catholics? The fact is that certain themes cannot be celebrated
in words, and tyranny is one of them. Prose literature is the
product of rationalism, of the Protestant centuries, of the
autonomous individual. It is significant to note in this context
that many modern writers have made fierce attacks on rationalism and Protestantism. Superficially they are the enemies of
poetry and sensibility, but it is more important to remember
that they are the champions of free examination and free judgment. A new form of literature, not involving individual feeling
or truthful observation, may conceivably arise, but it is not
imaginable at present. If liberal culture perishes the literary art
will perish with it. An honest man, thinking honestly, can
scarcely deny all this. But there is always the thought in men's
minds that the next tyranny will be somehow different, that it
will not destroy as its predecessors attempted to destroy. It is
from this vague and lazy hope that modern totalitarianism
derives so much of its power.

The intellectual world is weakened by its own divisions.
Scientists in particular are uncritical admirers of the U.S.S.R.
because their aim is efficiency and they have not the cultural
breadth to realise that efficiency of the modern technological
type can only be obtained at the expense of something else. In
any case, this 'something else' is not a quality for which most
scientists have much admiration. They understand the importance of liberty in their own sphere and they appear to believe it
possible that a selective attack on liberty would leave their own
position untouched. In a country like the U.S.S.R., with its
great need of scientists, they are privileged persons providing
they steer clear of the dangerous subjects. Even in Nazi Germany scientists, providing they were not Jews, were well
treated and as a community offered no resistance to Hitler. To
a modern autocratic ruler blueprints are necessary in a way
that novels are not—or rather, good novels. Entertainment is

as essential as machinery, but the machinery must be good. It doesn't matter how bad the entertainment is from the tyrant's point of view. In fact, the worse the better.

> 'No tirades against "individualism" and "the ivory tower", no pious platitudes to the effect that "true individuality is only attained through identification with the community", can get over the fact that a bought mind is a spoiled mind. Unless spontaneity enters at some point or another, literary creation is impossible, and language itself becomes ossified. At some time in the future, if the human mind becomes something totally different from what it now is, we may learn to separate literary creation from intellectual honesty. At present we know only that the imagination, like certain wild animals, will not breed in captivity. Any writer or journalist who denied that fact—and nearly all the current praise of the Soviet Union contains or implies such a denial—is, in effect demanding his own destruction.'

And so ends this most important essay, which should appear in all future anthologies on the nature of literary art, along with the earlier ones by Sidney and Shelley.

I sometimes meet people, and Orwell undoubtedly met them too, who console themselves with the thought that the modern tyrannies are evanescent and will pass away by a natural law. In fact, there is a retired schoolmaster in *Coming Up For Air* who refuses to take Hitler seriously and at the mere mention of his name refers to the shattered empires of Cambises and Sardanapulus. What Orwell recognised keenly was that with his new weapons of science and technology the modern tyrant is in an infinitely better position than his predecessors to perpetuate his tyranny. Although all tyrants to date have come and gone there is simply no evidence to prove that this is an unbreakable law. Another advantage possessed by the modern tyrant is the realisation that his position will be much stronger if he gives the people economic security, and that this is at least possible by centralised planning. It is not necessary to control the populace by terror (although in a transition stage such as the present this is still done) when it is much easier to lull them through the satisfaction of their elementary desires. The Romans attempted it, but now it can be done far more efficiently. But even if tyranny is to be perpetual there are still some who will find consolation in the belief that no one can touch the mind, that the mind's freedom is secret, and that independence is entirely spiritual, *1984* was an attempt to show that not even the mind was impregnable. This point of view also ignored the fact that all education in the totalitarian state is controlled by the state, and by the time it is over there is very little *desire* for liberty that has not been destroyed. Only an exceptionally vigorous and fertile mind could overcome this disability. But the individual is not autonomous. No one thinks in isolation. All 'individual' thought is fed upon the thought of others. What will happen to thought if the works of the great philosophers and writers are unobtainable? How will thought develop without constant stimulation from other free minds? It is almost impossible to think without talking. 'If Defoe had really lived on a desert island he could not have written *Robinson Crusoe*, nor would he have wanted to. Take away freedom of speech and the creative faculties dry up.' ('As I Please', *Tribune*, 28 April, 1944.)

Once the tyranny is firmly in the saddle the free intellect will be doomed and 'secret' freedom will be a mockery. But such a society has not yet been established, and Orwell believed there were certain loopholes in existing society which the intellectuals could turn to their advantage. For instance, the British Government started the last war with the more or less openly declared intention of keeping the literary intelligentsia out of it, yet after three years nearly every writer in the country, however undesirable his political history of opinions, had been sucked into one of the Ministries or the B.B.C. This was by no means a pleasant experience for the writers, but it did demonstrate that the Government found it difficult or even impossible to get on without them. The ideal, from the government point of view, would have been to entrust propaganda to 'safe' people of the A. P. Herbert or Ian Hay type, but there weren't enough. One result of this was that British propaganda was modified and much of it must have been highly distasteful to the people who sponsored it, but it was impossible for them to control in detail everything that went out under their name. Orwell felt that the bigger the machine of government became the more loose ends and forgotten corners there were in it.

'This is perhaps a small consolation, but it is not a despicable one. It means that in countries where there is already a strong liberal tradition, bureaucratic tyranny can perhaps never be complete. The striped-trousered ones will rule, but so long as they are forced to maintain an intelligentsia, the intelligentsia will have a certain amount of autonomy. If the government needs, for example, documentary films, it must employ people specially interested in the technique of the film, and it must allow them the necessary minimum of freedom; consequently, films that are all wrong from the bureaucratic point of view will always have a tendency to appear. So also with painting, photography, script-writing, reportage, lecturing and all the other arts and half-arts of which a complex modern state has need.' ('Poetry and the Microphone', *Such, Such Were the Days.*)

It would be wrong, however, to overstress the value of such loopholes. It was only because the British Government was psychologically unprepared for war that they existed. The genuine intellectual can be superseded by the spurious one, given sufficient time to train the latter. You cannot train a great writer or film director for nothing, but you can train a perfectly adequate one for the mundane purposes of government propaganda. In general Orwell believed that during war there was a progressive degradation because such things as individual liberty and a truthful press are not compatible with military efficiency. In his view this was a superficial judgment, but it was the accepted official one, the one that modern governments always act upon. He believed the opposite, that the tremendous controversies which always rage in a democratic country at war, the endless discussion of strategy by more or less ignorant people, the free expression of near-seditious opinions, are sources of strength in the long run. It means that the conduct of war shall not be entirely in the hands of the experts, who are generally right on minor points and wrong on the major ones. Such an outlook is always rejected by totalitarian leaders, who much prefer the easily governable expert, the general and the scientist, to the many-headed public, just as the Catholic Church set expert theological opinion against individual judgment. As literary editor of *Tribune* Orwell maintained his faith in the free play of individual judgment to the extent of publishing a long anti-war poem called *The Little Apocalypse of Obadiah Hornbrook*. The readers of *Tribune* could be assumed to support the war but their resolution would not be weakened

by reading criticisms of it. Orwell's faith was that they would
bo enabled to adopt a more intelligent attitude towards it.
He did not distrust the intelligence as did so many of his
contemporaries.

In the last analysis he believed that our only claim to victory
would come through winning it by telling fewer lies about it
than our enemies. Victory was a moral condition as well as
military. It would be a sterile victory if it were based on lies and
ignorance. He thought that by far the worst feature of totalitarianism was not the atrocities it committed but its attack on
the concept of objective truth. He was surprised and pleased to
find that despite the lying and self-righteousness that war encouraged the respect for truth had maintained itself in British
public life. He even believed that the press was slightly freer
that it had been before the war, that it was possible to print
things in 1944 that would have been impossible ten years
earlier. War-resisters had not been badly treated and it was
safer to express unpopular opinions than it had been in the last
war. 'There is some hope, therefore, that the liberal habit of
mind, which thinks of truth as something outside yourself,
something to be discovered, and not as something you can make
up as you go along, will survive.' ('As I Please', *Tribune*, 4
February, 1944.) During war people either stopped thinking
or they were stimulated to think more carefully than was their
custom. Even the Brains Trust, which he disliked, played its
part. He refused to attack it because that was already being
done by Right-wing intellectuals, and for a very good reason
from their point of view. 'These people see the Brains Trust as
a symbol of freedom of thought, and they realise that, however
silly its programmes may be in themselves, their tendency is to
start people thinking.' ('As I Please', *Tribune*, 16 June, 1944.)
Orwell would support any move to enlarge freedom of thought
and expression. He knew that it was the basis of the Western
liberal culture that was being attacked on all sides. To support
it was not sentimentalism, as more and more cynics can be
heard proclaiming. It was simply good sense—unless, of course,
you really believe that it would be better for nine-tenths of the
population to sink into a servile condition. But in that case,
don't make the mistake that so many hopeful Communists have

made, when they helped the glorious revolution on its way and then found, to their horror, that they were not being taken into the privileged class. The essence of a privileged class is that it is small. The candidates are many.

Chapter VIII

The Class System

WHEN HE was a boy Orwell was once watching a village cricket match. One of the batsmen was given out, hit wicket, at the moment the ball entered the wicket-keeper's hands. The batsman started for the pavilion but his captain, the local squire, ordered him to return. The umpire reversed his decision. This seemed to Orwell at the time the most shocking thing he had ever seen. Later, he said, so much do we coarsen with the passage of time, he would have felt no anger but would merely have enquired whether the umpire was also the squire's tenant. He was reminded of this incident when Churchill refused to accept the Parliamentary decision on equal pay for women and ordered it to be left lying on the Statute Book (April 1944). Some years after this he was in digs in Portobello Road. His landlady had been lady's maid to a titled woman. One day they found themselves locked out. Orwell suggested borrowing a ladder from the jobbing builder who lived next door and entering the house at an upper window. His landlady looked uncomfortable and replied, 'I wouldn't like to do that. You see, we don't know him. We've been here fourteen years and we've always taken care not to know the people on either side of us. It *wouldn't do*, not in a neighbourhood like this. If you once begin talking to them they get familiar, you see.' They therefore borrowed a ladder from a relative of her husband, and carried it nearly a mile with great labour and discomfort.

These two incidents represent the disadvantages of the class system at their worst. In return for certain intangible, psychological benefits many people are prepared to accept injustice and inconvenience. It is the lower class that suffers from the injustice in most cases, but the inconvenience is shared out fairly equally.

The division of society into classes was one of those subjects, like poverty and intellectual liberty, that Orwell studied closely and carefully. His views on it are well worth considering partly because they were based on knowledge, partly because of his honesty. Everyone has knowledge of a small sector of the class structure but few people bother to examine the other sectors. Most of them have absolutely rigid views about other classes, usually based on ignorance and prejudice. Similarly, few people are honest about class because they are not equipped for it. The class system in England is one of the most vicious sources of social evil because it nearly always generates fear and hatred between one class and the next. There is no doubt about Orwell's ideal society. He would have abolished class feeling, or at least reduced it to a rational and non-explosive minimum. He was much too intelligent to think that classes could be abolished. They could not be abolished by statute, and they could not be abolished by evolution in a society where the modes of life must necessarily differ from one work-group to the next. But it should be possible and certainly desirable to abolish the hatred and distrust that existed between class and class. These were not based on essential social factors but were the product of a certain type of social evolution. The English class system and its attendant snobbery is really the result of centuries of social stability, which in turn are the gift of the English Channel and the British Navy. Every other ancient state has had a more troubled history than England, and in no other state, ancient or modern, is there a class system so designed to make a real community impossible as in England.

The first book in which Orwell deliberately studied class relations was *The Road to Wigan Pier*. Before that they had only been referred to in passing. Although he was a radical in politics he was a conservative in taste, including the kind of life he preferred to live. He came from the middle class and he knew that he belonged to it irrevocably. He was always saying that it was impossible to cast aside the world-view acquired during childhood and early manhood. Opinions can change, of course, but you cannot pick yourself up by your bootlaces and shift the vantage point of ten or twenty years ago. For this reason he never claimed that he had become a member of the working class, despite his poverty, as was so fashionable during the thirties. He could not stomach the humbug of calling himself a proletarian. Perhaps there was a certain inconsistency when he said, as he often did, that every writer was *ipso facto* a bourgeois. Writing was simply not a proletarian occupation. Yet according to his own lights a writer from a working-class family must possess a proletarian world-view. However, his own attitude is shown clearly by an incident related by Sir Richard Rees. When he was collecting material for *The Road to Wigan Pier* he made friends with a working-class intellectual and Marxist theoretician. When he started on the routine abuse of the bourgeoisie Orwell said, 'Look here, I'm a bourgeois and my family are bourgeois. If you talk about them like that I'll punch your head!' He probably would, too.

John Beavan, in his revaluation of *The Road to Wigan Pier* (*World Review*, June 1950), said that Orwell never crossed the barrier of class. He always remained the lodger and saw the working class as through the glass wall of an aquarium.

'Orwell's quest for the worker was a failure. He never attained a deep understanding of the ordinary English wage-earner and his aspirations; and he never appreciated, therefore, the virtue of the Labour Party and the Trade Union Movement which fulfil so successfully the English wage-earner's needs.... He was concerned with the mental and moral health of the entire Left. He was a Lollard of social democracy, a preacher of the pure faith at war with the corruption and hypocrisy of the Church.'

There is much truth in this, particularly in the last sentence, but it was really what Orwell had been saying implicitly throughout his career. He knew that he could not merge with the working class (he never even gave any signs of wanting to) and that he would always be a spectator. But that is true of any observer in any subject. Our views on the Middle Ages are limited and at the same time various because we are all viewing them from a distance. It is possible to mingle with the proletariat but quite impossible to merge with it by an act of will. It is like the Englishman who leaves home and spends the greater part of his life in Germany, speaking German, eating German, sleeping German and playing German—but never thinking German or becoming a German, always remaining obviously an Englishman. The answer is not, however, to retreat because perfection is out of the question. There is no logical reason why, because classes must exist, each class should retire into contemptuous isolation. Classes help to provide social variety. If we do not take advantage of this variety through sympathy, understanding and imagination we destroy one of the most valuable qualities in living. Orwell has been criticised for not taking a proletarian job in his scrutiny of the working class. It would have aided him in his understanding but it would not have broken down the barrier, and he knew it. The barrier is far too impalpable for that.

He made mistakes about working-class mentality but fewer than most people of middle-class origin. He hardly ever romanticised the working class but he had certain blind spots which allowed romanticism to creep upon him. For instance, in his 'London Letter' to *Partisan Review* (November-December 1941) he mentioned a favourite theme of his when he referred to the million British working men who had rifles in their bedrooms and didn't in the least wish to give them up. 'The possibilities contained in that fact hardly need pointing out.' This was wishful thinking and it was largely a product of his wartime frustration. Normally he was perfectly well aware that the British working man takes no formal interest in politics, hates social disorder, and would much rather have a fishing-rod or a lathe by his bedside than a rifle. The political situation at the time was not at all explosive. But it was rare for Orwell to go astray in this manner.

One of the features of working-class life which struck him as forming a major contrast with bourgeois life was the extent to which the worker was subject to petty and, one would think, unnecessary inconveniences and indignities. He mentions in *The Road to Wigan Pier* a miner who was half-blind with nystagmus, contracted at his work. He had been drawing compensation of twenty-nine shillings a week, but the colliery company were talking of putting him on a 'partial compensation' of fourteen shillings a week, depending on whether the doctor passed him as fit for light work. The fact that there was no light work available did not deter the company. The man could draw the dole and the company would save money. Payment of compensation is an honourable arrangement, but it is always

humiliating for a man who has had work for the greater part of
his life to start drawing the dole. Even when he was receiving
his pension he could not demand it as a right, which he was
surely entitled to. He could not draw it when and how he
wanted it. He had to go to the colliery once a week at a time
named by the company, and when he got there he was kept
hanging about in the cold. He wasted an afternoon and spent
sixpence in bus fares. Even a 'down-at-heel' member of the
bourgeoisie (Orwell's own description) such as himself received
better treatment than that. He did not earn much more than a
miner, but it was at least paid into a bank in a gentlemanly way
and he could draw it out whenever he chose. Even when his
account was empty the bank people were still passably polite.
A thousand such influences constantly press the working man
into a passive role. He does not act but is acted upon. He feels
he is the slave of some mysterious authority and has a firm conviction that 'they' will never allow him to do this, that or the
other.

It would be easy to catalogue what Orwell considered the
main differences between the two classes. A second one which
he referred to more than once was the long middle age of the
working man compared with the bourgeois. He records in his
Notebook how he registered with the 38 group (13 April, 1941)
and was appalled to see how faded most of the men were. When
you see a group like this, picked out by age, you notice how
rapidly the working class grow old. It isn't that they live less
long than the middle class but that they have an enormous
middle age, stretching from 30 to 60.

Another difference lies in the position of the man in his
family. In a working-class home the man is always the master
and not, as in so many middle-class homes, the woman or the
baby. You will rarely see the working-class man doing any
housework. Not even unemployment changes this. This seems
unfair, as the man is idle and the woman has as much work as
ever, or even more, as she has to manage on less money. Yet she
rarely protests. Both feel that a man who does housework loses
some of his manhood. This is not true in a middle-class home
and is less true today in working-class homes, owing to increasing bourgeoisification.

Orwell believed that the manual labourer in work had a
better chance of a happy life than an educated man. In a
comparatively prosperous working-class home there is a warmer
and more human atmosphere than is to be found in most
bourgeois homes. (I think Orwell found this the most attractive
aspect of working-class life. In a bourgeois home there is too
often a mental looking-over-the-shoulder for comfort.)

> 'I have often been struck by the peculiar easy completeness, the
> perfect symmetry as it were, of a working-class interior at its best.
> Especially on winter evenings after tea, when the fire glows in the
> open range and dances mirrored in the steel fender, when Father,
> in shirt-sleeves, sits in the rocking chair at one side of the fire
> reading the racing finals, and Mother sits on the other with her
> sewing, and the children are happy with a pennorth of mint
> humbugs, and the dog lolls roasting himself on the rag mat—it is
> a good place to be in, provided that you can be not only in it but
> sufficiently *of* it to be taken for granted.' (*The Road to Wigan Pier*.)

It is the contrast between an interior by Le Nain and one by
Campbell Taylor. There is a sense of yearning in it, yearning
for something that Orwell himself never knew and which he
knew he could never get for himself. He is still outside the
aquarium.

I have referred to the bourgeoisification of the working class,
a trend that has accelerated since the war. It already existed
before the war but it was much stronger in the South than in
the North. The kind of warmth expressed in the above extract
was much more typical of a Northern home than of a Southern
one, Orwell thought—though he would probably have agreed
that the comparison should be made with a Southern urban
home. For climatic reasons the parasitic dividend-drawing
class tend to settle in the South. In a Lancashire cotton town
you could go for months on end without hearing an 'educated'
accent, whereas 'there can hardly be a town in the South of
England where you could throw a brick without hitting the
niece of a bishop'. In the North there is no petty gentry to set
the pace of bourgeoisification. The Northern accents persist
while the Southern ones are collapsing before the onslaught of
the B.B.C. (In fact, I understand that some educational authorities in the North are encouraging a twin-dialect standard, one
for the home and the other for 'public relations'.) An 'educated'

accent in the North stamps you as a foreigner rather than a member of the petty gentry as it does in the South.

The adoption of an 'educated' accent is part of a social climbing process that is commoner in the South than in the North. In *Coming Up For Air* Tubby Bowling, a Southerner, describes how his Army commission in the first war carried him out of the shop-keeping orbit in which he had been brought up. He realised later that he might have started a little business when he was demobbed, but it never occurred to him at the time. The Army had turned him into an imitation gentleman and gave him a fixed idea that there would always be a bit of money coming from somewhere without doing anything positive to earn it. He had worn pips on his shoulder and such gentlemen didn't slave in shops. This process (the Army is by no means completely responsible, of course) had produced a kind of spurious middle class whose interests were really identical with those of the working class but which was quite unaware of the fact and certainly didn't wish to be aware of the fact. This group always sided with the capitalist class in moments of crisis and in Germany, for instance, had provided the background of the new National Socialist Party. The process was also aided by the tactlessness of Socialist propaganda with its continual attacks on the bourgeoisie. This only helped the sense of bourgeois solidarity among those who realised that their footing in the middle class was recent and not very firm.

Family loyalty and ultimately group loyalty, said Orwell, are much stronger among the working class than in the middle class. A working man has not that deadly weight of family prestige hanging round his neck like a millstone. Orwell believed that a middle-class person goes to pieces far more easily under the stress of poverty than a working man and he attributed this to the behaviour of his family—to the fact that he has scores of relations nagging and badgering him night and day for failing to 'get on'. The success ethos is more important among the bourgeoisie than in the proletariat. The fact that the working class know how to combine and the middle class don't is probably due to their different conceptions of family loyalty.

'You cannot have an effective union of middle-class workers, because in times of strikes almost every middle-class wife would be egging her husband on to blackleg and get the other fellow's job. Another working-class characteristic, disconcerting at first, is their plain-spokenness towards anyone they regard as an equal. If you offer a working man anything he doesn't want, he tells you that he doesn't want it; a middle-class person would accept it to avoid giving offence. And again, take the working-class attitude towards "education". How different it is from ours and how immensely sounder! Working people often have a vague reverence for learning in others, but where "education" touches their own lives they see through it and reject it by a healthy instinct. The time was when I used to lament over a quite imaginary picture of lads of fourteen dragged protestingly from their lessons and set to work at dismal jobs. It seemed to me dreadful that the doom of a "job" should descend upon anyone at fourteen. Of course I know now that there is not one working-class boy in a thousand who does not pine for the day when he will leave school. He wants to be doing real work, not wasting his time on ridiculous rubbish like history and geography. To the working class, the notion of staying at school till you are nearly grown-up seems merely contemptible and unmanly. The idea of a great big boy of eighteen, who ought to be bringing a pound a week home to his parents, going to school in a ridiculous uniform and even being caned for not doing his lessons! Just fancy a working-class boy of eighteen allowing himself to be caned! He is a man when the other is still a baby.' (*The Road to Wigan Pier*.)

As with all the examples of Orwell's diagnosis of class differences, these two may no longer be true or as true as they were. He was giving a picture of the classes as he saw them in the thirties, when there was considerable social strife and consequently more friction and greater variation of behaviour and attitude. What he called bourgeoisification has already modified the truth of what he wrote in 1937. But it was attitude rather than material condition that interested him. He was appalled by the shams in middle-class life, and he believed that in both their valuation of appearances and their attitude towards education the working class were more realistic and therefore more sincere than the middle class.

There were really three educational groups, and each marked its subjects for life. The working-class boy wanted to get out as soon as he could. The son of really rich parents considered it natural to stay on until early manhood. The intermediate class, the solid bourgeoisie and the aspirants from below, used education as a kind of social gesture. Tubby Bowling admitted that the sons of shopkeepers and farmers stayed at school two years longer just to show they weren't proletarians. They didn't enjoy those last years, they didn't consider them valuable, especially if they were following their parents in the family business, but they were useful as a kind of social distinction. As for the upper-class attitude towards education, they were largely contemptuous of it. Bowling believed they never recovered from their public-school drilling: 'either it flattens them out into half-wits or they spend the rest of their lives kicking against it'. In his article on 'Boys' Weeklies' Orwell returned to the charge that education in England is mainly a matter of status. The great gulf between bourgeoisie and working class is (or was—it has of course been lessened) that the former pay for their education. Within the bourgeoisie there is another gulf between 'public' school and 'private' school. Because of the status, not because of the education, the public schools have been glamorised in boys' papers. From his own experience he found that boys who were likely to go to public schools themselves read the *Gem* and the *Magnet* until they were about twelve years of age; they might continue for another year from habit but they would not take them seriously. Boys at 'private' schools read them much longer. When Orwell taught at a private school he found that boys of fifteen and sixteen were still reading these papers and taking them seriously. There was also little doubt that they were popular among working-class schoolboys and even continued to be read after they had left school. While continued education had no attraction for the working class, the schools of the rich possessed glamour because of their class status.

Orwell was convinced that the English upper class habit of sending children away to boarding school at the age of nine, eight or even seven is a thoroughly bad one. If the working class had a more realistic attitude towards life than the upper class, as he believed it had, it was partly due to the fact that its children maintained contact with the sanity of the home. At Crossgates he developed all kinds of ridiculous ideas, fears and prejudices that would never have been allowed to develop if there had been someone in whom he could have confided. At such an early age this can only be a parent, and of the two parents probably only the mother. Boarding schools, he said, were worse than day schools. Our national admiration for boarding schools is an admiration for qualities that are not really admirable in themselves but which act as a kind of social heraldry. He came to this conclusion at the end of *Such, Such Were the Joys*, after concentrated consideration of his own schooldays, and the judgment is correspondingly biased. Orwell's style was more rational than his thought. He was liable to be carried away by one particular factor which occupied his mind to the exclusion of all else, and at such times his judgment was least reliable.

English education was the result of the class system and in turn the education fortified the system. There is a striking example of this in *Down and Out*. We sometimes use the word 'declassed' but it is doubtful if it has any reality. A man may appear to sink in the social scale but inwardly he will still consider himself a member of the class where he originated. He will cling to this and the opinions of others will not sway him. I have already mentioned how difficult it is to change in the other direction: the Bowlings who felt they had had a push upwards during the war were always uneasy at heart, always conscious that other people were seeing through them. The incident I refer to took place in a common lodging house. A man who had heard Orwell speaking to one of the tramps suddenly leant over his bed and began babbling in an educated, half-drunken voice:

> ' "An old public school boy, what? Don't meet many of the old school here. I am an old Etonian. You know—twenty years hence this weather and all that." He began to quaver out the Eton Boating Song, not untunefully:
> "Jolly boating weather,
> And a hay harvest——."
> ' "Stop that —— noise!" shouted several lodgers.
> ' "Low types", said the old Etonian, "very low types. Funny sort of place for you and me, eh? Do you know what my friends say to me? They say, M——, you are past redemption. Quite true, I *am* past redemption. I've come down in the world; not like these ——s here, who couldn't come down if they tried. We chaps who have come down ought to hang together a bit." '

What was more, there were others who were ready to assist the fallen maintain their high opinion of themselves. On the whole the tramps were not interested in the social backgrounds of their members. When they discovered that someone had once been a 'toff' they saw nothing surprising in it and they tended to show respect rather than take the opportunity to wipe out old class scores. At one spike each tramp had to register his trade and Orwell gave 'journalist' because he had sometimes earned money from newspaper articles. The Tramp Major called for him, commented on his trade and said, 'Then you are a gentleman?' Orwell supposed he was. The Tramp Major replied, 'Well, that's bloody bad luck, guv'nor, bloody bad luck that is.' After that he treated Orwell with great deference, did not search him and even gave him a clean towel for himself. 'So powerful is the word "gentleman" in an old soldier's ear.'

It is impossible to discuss the English class system without eventually coming up against the magic word 'gentleman'. I am not going to waste time in trying to define it. The word is a totem in itself and is probably charged with more emotional values than any other word in the language. It represents a vague yet powerful idea, generated by one class and to a very large extent accepted by the others. A few generalisations are possible. It is used in its simplest form by the working class to denote a person of the middle class who almost invariably possesses money and has a certain degree of 'good breeding'—but that is another phrase of almost insurmountable vagueness. A young gentleman must be rich. An old gentleman can be poor—but he is not called poor, his 'circumstances' are always 'straitened'. Among all the guff that is written about his concept the only one that is worth noticing is the statement that a gentleman (broadly speaking, the kind who is recognised as a gentleman by other people) never uses the word. The people who use it constantly and even neurotically about themselves are those who are usually terrified that their footing in the privileged class is insecure. This sub-group of the middle class is always fighting shadows and would prefer the compliment of being called gentlemen to the solid benefit of adequate meals such as are had in a fairly prosperous working-class family.

It was this struggling group which interested Orwell most of all. He belonged to it, he knew its gods and its fears, he had an intimate understanding of it which he could not possibly have of any other group. He called it the lower-upper-middle class. (No one has ever divided the English social system into such fine gradations as Orwell.) What we usually refer to as the lower-middle class is the shopkeeping, farming community, raised above the proletariat sometimes by income, nearly always by pretence, rarely by social manners. Without another Orwell it is difficult to know what has happened to the lower-upper-middle class these days—sociological studies do not help because the principle of class in this group was far more a state of mind than anything else. But before the war this was the class which saw itself as a community of gentlemen, and they were characterised by a determination to live like gentlemen, irrespective of money power.

'Before the war you were either a gentleman or not a gentleman, and if you were a gentleman you struggled to behave as such, whatever your income might be. Between those with £400 a year and those with £2,000 or even £1,000 a year there was a great gulf fixed, but it was a gulf which those with £400 a year did their best to ignore. Probably the distinguishing mark of the upper-middle class was that its traditions were not to any extent commercial, but mainly military, official and professional. People in this class owned no land, but they felt that they were landowners in the sight of God and kept up a semi-aristocratic outlook by going into the professions and the fighting services rather than into trade. Small boys used to count the plum-stones on their plates and foretell their destiny by chanting "Army, Navy, Church, Medicine, Law"; and even of these Medicine was faintly inferior to the others and only put in for the sake of symmetry. To belong to this class when you were at the £400-a-year level was a queer business, for it meant that your gentility was almost purely theoretical. You lived, so to speak, at two levels simultaneously. Theoretically you knew all about servants, and how to tip them, although in practice you had one or, at most, two resident servants. Theoretically you knew how to wear clothes and how to order a dinner, although in practice you could never afford to go to a decent tailor or a decent restaurant. Theoretically you knew how to shoot and ride, although in practice you had no horses to ride and not an inch of ground to shoot over. It was this that explained the attraction of India (more recently Kenya, Nigeria, etc.) for the lower-upper-middle class. The people who went there as soldiers and officials did not go there to make money, for a soldier or an official does not make money; they went there because in India, with cheap horses, free shooting, and hordes of black servants, it was so easy to play at being a gentleman.' (*The Road to Wigan Pier.*)

At heart these people were not and could not be happy. Gordon Comstock in *Keep the Aspidistra Flying* belonged to them and he had been trained to indulge tastes which he could not afford. The Comstocks belonged to 'the most dismal of all classes . . . the landless gentry'. It was always a great psychological comfort to think of your family as an 'old' one, but in fact the majority of them were not 'old'. Just as some of the most respected families in England today rose from the Northern working classes less than two hundred years ago, so the Comstocks and many others like them had risen on the wave of Victorian prosperity but had not been able to maintain their prosperity. They 'sank again faster than the wave itself'. There were three alternatives for the wretched offspring. India, pretence-in-poverty, or a frank acceptance of poverty. The latter was of course rare. And it was also possible, where the talent existed, to sink family and class pride and become a merchant or an artist. This was the only possibility of happiness.

One result of this situation was a curiously ambivalent attitude towards titled people. This class felt that they really belonged to the group which flowered into Marquises and Viscounts but it was often galling to be ignored by the great. A modern Viscount, with his roots in coal or cotton, with none of the lower-middle class nonsense about class origins beating in his head, is more likely to be polite and gracious to a rich farmer or business man than to the ragtag of the bourgeoisie. The community at Kyauktada in *Burmese Days* were sent into a flutter when they discovered that the new policeman, Verrall, was an Honourable! But Verrall didn't care a damn for any of them and very soon was detested by all the men and hopefully admired only by the two women, with matrimony in view. Orwell commented that titled people are always adored or hated. If they accept you they show charming simplicity; if they ignore you they show loathsome snobbishness.

It is clear from the above that the English class system cannot be defined in terms of money, although it provides a rough guide. Orwell's view of class was a money-stratification, but it is interpenetrated by a shadowy caste system, 'rather like a jerry-built modern bungalow haunted by medieval ghosts'. It is only because of this that the upper-middle class could extend downwards to the verge of poverty, to incomes much lower than were to be found in what is normally called the middle class proper. There are countries where you can predict a man's opinions from his income, but in England you always have to take tradition into consideration as well. This produces great social variation and surprises but at the cost of snobbishness and a tremendous waste of effort appeasing ghosts and feeding pretences. Orwell said that a naval officer and his grocer may easily have the same income but their opinions will differ on practically everything this side of something really serious, such as a general strike. But if the possession of money is not the characteristic of this section of the upper-middle class it certainly is the ideal towards which they strive. The life they wish to live demands easy money; the lives they actually live are reflections dimmed by lack of it. The best evidence of this lies in a consideration of the books they read. It lay at the back of the enormous popularity of a writer like Wodehouse. He was funny, yes, but so was W. W. Jacobs. Wodehouse's amusing young men lived the fantasy lives that the lower-upper-middle class regarded as their right.

> 'Behind the farcical incidents there is manifest a vision of life in which the dividends flow in for ever and ever, and the M.C.C. will out last the Pyramids . . . what is finally noticeable, as in all Mr Wodehouse's books, is the complete parasitism of outlook. After reading him steadily for a quarter of a century I cannot remember a single one of books in which the *jeune premier* really works for his living. His heroes either have private incomes, like Bertie Wooster, or they end up with some kind of sinecure job in the retinue of a millionaire. And that, however lightly he may choose to treat it, is obviously the way in which he considers it desirable for a young man to live.' ('Wishful Thinking and the Light Novel', *New Statesman*, 19 October, 1940.)

There is so much contempt between class and class generated in England that it is surprising that political hatred is not much greater than it is. Orwell believed there was a certain feeling of family loyalty which cut across the class system and held the hatred in check—and also, incidentally, helped to perpetuate the system. The tradition of security from foreign invasion was probably responsible for this, and the family loyalty is really an aspect of insularity which in the last resort puts a foreigner below members of other classes. But in normal times, when foreigners are not available to be pitied or despised, the whole astonishing battery of English uncharitableness is switched against another class. And one of the big guns of the English middle class in their war against the working class is the triumphant assertion that the latter smell! When Orwell referred to this normally unpublicised belief in *The Road to Wigan Pier* he roused a wail of shocked horror from people who considered he had let the side down by selling secrets to the enemy. But he was bringing into the open a conviction that was a middle-class heirloom, one which many members of the middle class recognised as true though it may have made them feel so uncomfortable that they refrained from mentioning it. (Orwell quoted from Somerset Maugham to show that he was no stranger to this belief.) There is no barrier so unpassable as a physical one, he said. In this way the middle class could really put their claim that the poor were a different species on a factual basis. You can get over race-hatred, religious hatred, differences of education, temperament, intellect, even morals, but physical repulsion will baffle you.

'You can have an affection for a murderer or a sodomite, but you cannot have an affection for a man whose breath stinks— habitually stinks, I mean. However well you may wish him, however much you may admire his mind and character, if his breath stinks he is horrible and in your heart of hearts you will hate him. It may not greatly matter if the average middle-class person is brought up to believe that the working classes are ignorant, drunken, boorish and dishonest; it is when he is brought up to believe that they are dirty that the harm is done. And in my childhood we *were* brought up to believe that they were dirty. Very early in life you acquired the idea that there was something subtly repulsive about a working-class body; you would not get nearer to it than you could help. You watched a great sweaty navvy walking down the road with his pick over his shoulder; you looked at his discoloured shirt and his corduroy trousers stiff with the dirt of a decade; you thought of these nests and layers of greasy rags below, and, under all, the unwashed body, brown all over (that was how I used to imagine it), with its strong, bacon-like reek. You watched a tramp taking off his boots in a ditch— ugh! It did not seriously occur to you that the tramp might not enjoy having black feet. And even "lower class" people whom you knew to be quite clean—servants, for instance—were faintly unappetising. The smell of their sweat, the very texture of their skins, were mysteriously different from yours.'

Every middle-class person has a dormant class prejudice, he said, which requires only a small thing to arouse it. By the time a member of this class reaches the age of forty he usually believes that he is sacrificing himself to keep those below him in idleness and comfort. He does not see the working man as a submerged slave but as a sinister creature who, with all his fellows, is slowly engulfing the superior class in a flood, sweeping all culture and decency out of existence. This fear becomes more and more real and eventually takes on a pathological quality. There is continual anxiety that the working class is becoming too prosperous. Orwell refers to a joke in *Punch* which showed four or five miners sitting in a cheap motor-car. A friend asks them where they borrowed it and they reply, 'We've bought the thing!' That is the 'joke'—but to some people it is also a hideous threat. And so the middle classes cultivated the legend that the typical working man rode to the Labour Exchange on a motor-bike, kept coals in his bath, and 'If you'll believe it, my dear, they actually *get married* on the dole!' The net result of all this is that when a middle-class person tries to get to know a working man and his family the wall of the aquarium against which he bangs his nose is partly constructed by himself.

The meeting of proletarian and bourgeois is apt to resemble the clash of alien cultures. This usually results in war and the term class-war is not an exaggeration. The fact that it is not conducted with tanks and high explosives should not mislead us. Tubby Bowling recalls the days when he was courting Hilda, who came from the Anglo-Indian colony in Ealing. At first he was prepared to be impressed by a family which boasted majors, colonels and even an admiral. But in the end he had to admit that they never started getting to know each other. Among business people, his own type, he was a good judge of character, but he had never had any experience of the officer-rentier-clergyman class and was even inclined to kow-tow to them as his social and intellectual superiors. In the end he had to dismiss them as decayed throw-outs. They, in their turn, probably thought he was a rising young business man who would soon be pulling in what they all wanted and hadn't got. But it couldn't last. The only things that should matter between people, character and personality, were never considered.

The bitterest feeling of all exists between the shabby-genteel and the working class. After all, it is the former who believe that every improvement in the latter's living conditions is obtained at their expense and the gap between them is so small they are terrified it may be closed for good. The shabby-genteel are like a family of 'poor whites' in a street of Negroes. You cling to your gentility the more fiercely because it is the only thing that differentiates you. You are hated for your accent and stuck-up-ness which place you in the boss class, though you know quite well that you are not in the boss class at all. Orwell's first heroes were working men (men who let him ride on a drill, who caught ewes to give him a drink, who taught him to say 'b——') but later he was told he must not play with their children because they were 'common'. (He adds that although this was snobbish it was also sensible because no middle-class parent can afford to let his child develop a vulgar accent.) So the working classes became enemies who hated the middle classes, and as the reasons were beyond a child's comprehension he put it down to the natural malice of the working man. These inferior people had coarse faces, hideous accents and gross manners, they hated everyone who was not like themselves, and they never lost a chance to insult you. Orwell recalls that there was far more overt class-hatred before the first War than there was after it. A well-dressed person walking down a slum street was bound to be insulted. Today, he said, he was more likely to be fawned upon. Whole quarters of big towns were considered unsafe because of 'hooligans'. One of the terrors of Orwell's childhood was the gang of 'cads' who were liable to set upon you in over-whelming numbers. In term time, on the other hand, it was the 'cads' who were usually outnumbered. He recalled two savage mass-battles in the winter of 1916-17. Once again he produces a *Punch* joke as evidence (this time from the sixties): it shows a nervous-looking gentleman riding through a slum street and a crowd of street boys closing in on him and shouting, ' 'Ere comes a swell! Let's frighten 'is 'oss!' And Orwell comments that today (or in 1937 at least) they would hang around for a tip. The brutality has now disappeared from the relationship but this does not mean that it is any easier. It is merely a reflection of the progressive softening of English manners and customs.

Defining and describing the class system is rather like mapping a delta which is liable to change its shape from year to year. It is also a complex of minor relationships and unspoken conventions. Item, although a man from Mars might be tempted to think that a paid companion and a parlourmaid should be of equal status he would be mistaken. Item, members of the upper class have the right to slum, i.e., to preach at and pray over anyone whose income falls below a certain level. Item, when class collides with sex the poor girl (like the coloured girl) is 'fair game': her feelings do not matter or perhaps she doesn't have them. Item, the working classes consider it perfectly honourable to victimise the bourgeois who is not protected by wealth. Item—but that's enough to be going on with. I have taken these examples from Orwell's work and there are many more, enough to provide a much fuller examination of the system than I have room for here. Not all can be treated as safe generalisations, but all have local application at particular times. For instance, the last example applies especially to the clergyman who is contemptuous of his parishioners but who cannot afford to compel them to lick his boots. You will find him a *A Clergyman's Daughter*.

Although Orwell developed a voracious curiosity about the working class and followed it up with a genuine pity for the condition of the less fortunate members of the class which it took him several years and at least four books to lay to rest, he always came back to the incontrovertible *fact* that he himself was a bourgeois and would always remain one. His sympathy and understanding of his own class was ultimately stronger than that of the working class whom, as a Socialist, he sincerely believed to be oppressed, although in widely varying degrees. Although there is a clearly discernible development in his political ideas it is less abrupt than in the case of many other writers, purely because he retained certain basic ideas from his early days. In 1937, for instance, he was still in his 'proletarian' period[1] but he could still understand without the kind of whipped-up bitterness peculiar to some of his contemporaries, the difficulties of the situation in which the bourgeoisie found itself. By its nature the class is always between the devil and the deep blue sea and it is too much to expect the ordinary man of any class to be divinely forgiving and supernaturally intelligent. During the thirties there was a strong temptation in the middle class to adopt some kind of Fascist attitude towards the rest of society. Orwell's peculiar gift was to be capable of understanding this position and realising that it could not be evaporated by verbal polemic.

'The peasant and the worker hate feudalism and clericalism; but so does the "liberal" bourgeois, who is not in the least opposed to a more modern version of Fascism, at least so long as it isn't called Fascism. The "liberal" bourgeois is genuinely liberal up to the point where his own interests stop. He stands for the degree of progress implied in the phrase *la carriere ouverte aux talents*. For clearly he has no chance to develop in a feudal society where the worker and the peasant are too poor to buy goods, where industry is burdened with huge taxes to pay for bishops' vestments, and where every lucrative job is given as a matter of course to the friend of the catamite of the duke's illegitimate son.' ('Spilling the Spanish Beans', *New English Weekly*, 29 July, 1937.)

It is perfectly easy to see how dangerous such an attitude is, but it is nothing like so easy to get rid of it. The same is true of any class opinion or attitude. It is part of you, grafted on to your skin shortly after birth, and a surgical operation is needed to get rid of it. Even then there will be a scar. In *The Road to Wigan Pier* he says you cannot wish class distinctions away. Or, more accurately, if you do manage to wish them away (it will be more like hard labour than wishing) you must realise that you will be abolishing a part of yourself. You may not like what is left. In fact, the wishing away of class distinctions is a process that has actually begun, not merely among Left-wing critics but over a much wider field. Nearly everyone today is proud to announce that he is not a snob. Unlike his neighbours, he can see through the absurdity of wealth, rank, titles, etc. It is particularly noticeable in novels—the sneering at huntin',

1 By this I mean 'interest in the proletariat', not 'merging with the proletariat', which he never attempted. I use it in the sense we give to 'blue' when we speak of Picasso's 'blue' period.

shootin' and fishin', at the old ladies in Cheltenham boarding houses, at the military caste, at 'county' society. But the evanescence of this trend is made clear by one of Orwell's examples: during the thirties it became fashionable to despise royalty. Now it requires courage to criticise the Royal Family in public.

When reviewing *The Unquiet Grave* by Palinurus in the *Observer* (14 January, 1945), Orwell brands the author as an example of the upper-class man who is no longer sure of himself. Palinurus contemplates the modern world without enthusiasm and even with aristocratic disdain—but also with self-accusation and the consciousness of being an end-product, a mere ghost, 'like the cultivated pagans of 400 A.D.'. This book, he said, exhibits that queer product of capitalist democracy, the inferiority complex resulting from a private income. The constant hammering of the dividend-drawers has had its effect, if not the effect intended: they have not disappeared but they have grown unsure of themselves. They have been told for so long how unnecessary they are. They cannot help wanting their comforts and privileges but they are ashamed of wanting them. They feel they have a right to them, yet they also feel they are doomed to disappear. This in fact is the dilemma of the Western intellectual as a whole. The class of intellectuals tended to be drawn from the comfortable and well-to-do, but in addition they were irritated by either a desire for responsibility or an over-active sensibility to abuse of their original class. They were suspended in a commercial society, not indispensable, dependent on others for their living standards, and constantly reproached for their uselessness or hypocrisy. One of the social developments of the recent past, said Orwell, has been the emergence of an intelligentsia enjoying security but possessing no responsibility. The intellectual is in the position of a young man living on an allowance from a father whom he hates. The result is a deep feeling of guilt and resentment, not combined with any genuine desire to escape. But there must be some form of psychological escape or self-justification and it was this inner compulsion, in Orwell's view, that produced the modern phenomenon of transferred nationalism. During the thirties it became fashionable among intellectuals to transfer their loyalties to Soviet Russia, but after the outbreak of war the trend was towards pacifism, anarchism and Eastern mysticism. It accounted for the craze of 'spirituality' by which you could condemn the activist, materialist West and keep your money. This was one outlet for a sub-section of the class which Orwell knew best and to which he belonged. He himself, as I have said, was a class freak, having the mind of an intellectual (which was conventional enough, as his class produced the intellectuals anyway) but the emotions and realistic attitude of a completely different class. All around him he saw unhappy people, nagged by their consciences but enjoying their social position, taking refuge in the doctrine that only a 'change of heart' could benefit mankind, because they knew inside themselves that a 'change of heart' alone was insufficient and they did not really want the kind of change that was certain to strike a death blow at their own status.

He knew that there was nothing constant about the class system. The changes were not easy to describe but he had seen them happening and he knew they would continue to happen. He did not believe that a 'withering away' of the classes was inevitable. In fact, he felt that modern conditions were bringing a new class into existence, one which gained its recruits from the technicians of both middle and working classes. I have already referred to what he called the bourgeoisification of the working class, and this was happening most quickly in the new towns, largely in the South, based on modern light industry and engineering. Nothing could stop the spread of middle-class ideas and habits among the working class. Comparing the new type of magazine with the old, he was struck by its higher intellectual level. In the past the upper classes had been the magazine-reading public and the upper classes are not interested in new ideas—why should they be? But now the lower classes could read there was an enormous new market, yet it could not be satisfied with the kind of brainless drivel that had been sufficient for the old type of reader. Orwell certainly did not claim that the working man was a natural intellectual and he knew that a lot of rubbish was still being published specifically for their benefit. But the working man who reads at all usually likes to read something crammed with information. He has no understanding of art, but he does feel that when he pays money for reading matter he should get something almost tangible for it—and the nearest thing to that was information. Hence the enormous increase of trade and technical journals and the improved standard of the popular weeklies. But the new information and the new ideas from which they could not be separated were not of interest to one class alone. The widespread interest taken in aircraft, for instance, helps to create a common ground between the classes that had not existed before. And then the nature of social organisation inevitably brings people together, the fact that the whole community share more and more amenities: street-lighting, roads, pure water, police protection, libraries. Rich and poor tend to read the same books, their clothes and houses tend to differ less than they did in the past. Another important point is that modern industrial methods demand less muscular effort than formerly, and the characteristic physical differences between the classes are beginning to be less noticeable.

'After 1918 there began to appear something that had never existed in England before: people of indeterminate social class. In 1910 every human being in these islands could be "placed" in an instant by his clothes, manners and accent. That is no longer the case. Above all, it is not the case in the new townships that have developed as a result of cheap motor-cars and the southward shift of industry. The place to look for the germs of the future England is in the light industry areas and along the arterial roads. In Slough, Dagenham, Barnet, Letchworth, Hayes—everywhere, indeed, on the outskirts of great towns—the old pattern is gradually changing into something new. In those vast new wildernesses of glass and brick the sharp distinctions of the older kind of town, with its slums and mansions, or of the country, with its manor houses and squalid cottages, no longer exist. There are wide gradations of income, but it is the same kind of life that is being lived at different levels, in labour-saving flats or Council houses, along the concrete roads and in the naked democracy of the swimming pools. It is a rather restless, cultureless life, centring round tinned food, *Picture Post*, the radio and the internal combustion engine. It is a civilisation in which children grow up with an intimate knowledge of magnetoes and in complete ignorance of the Bible. To that civilisation belong the people who are most at home in and most definitely *of* the modern world, the technicians and the higher-paid skilled workers, the airmen and their mechanics, the radio experts, film producers, popular journalists and industrial chemists. They are the indeterminate stratum at which the older class distinctions are beginning to break down.' (*The Lion and the Unicorn.*)

Whether these people would eventually form a new self-contained class or would gradually assimilate the whole population, Orwell did not say. Judging by *1984* it is fairly safe to assume that they would provide the core of the Outer Party. Orwell always argued that the classless society was one of the first necessities of the free community. He knew that it could not come by wishing, but sometimes, particularly before the onset of depression in his last years, he seemed to think that it might come as a natural product of modern conditions. What he never seemed to consider, and this is a serious fault in his writing on this subject, was the quality of the final society. The classless society is only worth encouraging if it enjoys a culture at least as high as middle-class culture today. The new class he watched taking shape had nothing that we would refer to as culture; he himself called it 'cultureless'. If he had lived I am certain that he would have tackled this aspect of class, for there are a few hints that his mind was being drawn in that direction. The most pointed is to be found in his essay 'Raffles and Miss Blandish' (*Critical Essays*) which is dated 1944. When he examines *No Orchids For Miss Blandish* he is examining the kind of literature which the new class tends to demand for recreative reading. (They will also read and understand *Autocar*.) And the cultural atmosphere of such books is completely arid. *Raffles*, on the other hand, though naive and 'soft', comes from a world of powerful and decent values. The thought must have suddenly occurred to Orwell that there may be some organic relationship between snobbery and culture—in the previous book there is neither—because he ends the essay with these words: 'one is driven to feel that snobbishness, like hypocrisy, is a check upon behaviour whose value from a social point of view has been underrated'.

Orwell did have a temporary experience of a society where the class system had momentarily broken down and where snobbery had vanished, and he found it immensely stimulating. This was in Catalonia in the early days of the Civil War. Ordinary people looked you in the face and treated you as an equal. Servile and even ceremonial forms of speech temporarily disappeared. No one said 'Senor' or 'Don' or even 'Usted'. Everyone was 'Comrade' and 'Thou', and they said 'Salud' instead of 'Buenos dias'. Except for a small number of foreigners there were no 'well-dressed' people at all. Practically everyone wore rough working-class clothes or blue overalls or some variant of the militia uniform. This aspect of social levelling is of course repugnant to many people, but Orwell revelled in it. If you divide people into those who like sartorial display and those who don't he was passionately on the side of the latter. He said he found this atmosphere queer and moving. There was a great deal he did not understand, in some ways he did not even like it, but he recognised immediately that it was a state of affairs worth fighting for. He thought the proletarian revolution was complete and did not realise that large numbers of well-to-do bourgeois were simply lying low and disguising themselves as workers for the time being.

In Aragon he found the same thing. The entire population, though originally of different social origins, were living at the same level and mingling on terms of equality. The prevailing atmosphere was that of Socialism, i.e., the popular idea of Socialism, not the twisted variants that have been produced by intellectuals who have overthrown the idea of equality for the sake of efficiency. The most noticeable thing was the disappearance of the normal motives of normal bourgeois life—snobbishness, money-grubbing and fear of the boss. No one was anyone else's master. He knew it could not last—all but a small percentage of the influential people on earth wish to retain a class system of one kind or another—but it lasted long enough to have a powerful effect on anyone who experienced it. Many aspects of this new life were unpleasant, but you could not avoid the knowledge that you were in contact with something strange and valuable. Perhaps the greatest change of all was that hope had become more normal than the familiar apathy and cynicism of bourgeois life. He added that the word 'comrade' really stood for comradeship and not, as in most other countries, for humbug.

But when the communist Popular Army took control all this came to an end. I will describe later how, in Orwell's opinion, the communists destroyed the social revolution that P.O.U.M. had really attempted to bring about. With the victory of the communists in Catalonia there was a return to normal. The smart restaurants and hotels once again catered for rich people with unlimited supplies of food, while for the working-class population prices jumped without a corresponding rise in wages. The beggars, who had disappeared, now returned. Outside the delicatessen shops gangs of barefoot children swarmed round anyone who came out and clamoured for food. The revolutionary forms of speech were dropping out of use. Even tipping returned. The cabaret and high-class brothels, which had been closed by the workers' patrols, reopened. The cigarette racket was the worst. Franco controlled Spanish supplies but there was a steady importation of smuggled foreign cigarettes at extremely high prices, beyond the reach of the working man. He had to be satisfied with a foul mixture containing sliced liquorice root. In general, you could get anything you wanted if you had the money. This open contrast of wealth and poverty had been impossible a few months earlier.

I mention these things here for this reason. Orwell loathed the class system but he knew that it would be a tremendously difficult job getting rid of it. Spain demonstrated this in practice. But he had known for some time that the mere assertion of class abolition was meaningless. It had been vigorously proclaimed in Russia but the claim merely masked the reality of a new hierarchy. In various of his writings, mainly book reviews, he had criticised the new regime in Russia, but it was in *Animal Farm* that he gave the strongest expression to his disappointment. The revolution at Manor Farm had not long been stabilised before the 'bourgeois' conception of titles and awards, so heartily condemned a short time before, was introduced. Snowball and Boxer became Animal Heroes of the First Class. The dead sheep became Animal Heroes of the Second Class. The animals had such an attitude of piety towards their new leaders that the reintroduction of 'class' quite escaped their notice. A little later Napoleon, Squealer, and Minimus, the court poet, were being protected by trained dogs with the faithful pigs in the background. Napoleon made fewer and fewer public appearances, and when he did he was escorted by the dogs.

But more often he simply issued orders through the other pigs. Next came the appointment of a black cockerel who marched in front of him and acted as a kind of trumpeter, letting out a loud 'cock-a-doodle-doo' before Napoleon spoke. He adopted separate apartments in the farmhouse, took his meals alone with two dogs to wait upon him, and always ate from the Crown Derby dinner service which had been in the glass cupboard in the drawing-room. It was also announced that a gun would be fired every year on his birthday. Finally special privileges were instituted for the pigs. They took their exercise in the garden and were discouraged from playing with the other animals. The rule was laid down that if a pig and any other animal met on the path, the other animal must stand aside, and all pigs were granted the special privilege of wearing green ribbons on their tails on Sundays.

There is therefore a conflict in all Orwell's writing on class. There is no doubt about his desire for the abolition of the system. But on the one hand there was his belief that modern conditions favoured the gradual decrease of class differences, and on the other his awareness that the desires of the leaders of practically all the political factions were opposed to this automatic trend. In *The English People* he enumerated the chief factors that were tending to make the various classes of Englishmen less different from one another. They were the improvement in industrial technique, so that heavy work no longer gives a distinctive carriage to the working man; improvements in housing, as a result of which most people now live in similar types of house; the mass production of furniture, which reinforces the second factor; and the mass production of cheap and reasonably smart-looking clothes so that the cloth cap, for instance, is no longer a badge of status. These are natural trends but their effect is resisted by the majority of political leaders who discover the opportunities afforded by power are too great a temptation to forego.

In his wartime Notebook he referred now and again to the breaking-down of privilege which he believed was occurring. For instance, in June 1940 he attended a group conference of the L.D.V. in the Committee room at Lord's. The last time he had been there had been at the Eton-Harrow match in 1921.

At that time he would have felt that to go into the Pavilion without being a member of the M.C.C. would have been 'on a par with pissing on the altar', and even later he would have had some vague idea that it was a legal offence for which he could have been prosecuted. People were also talking more readily to each other on the streets, without first enquiring into each other's pedigrees. He himself spoke to a young working man who was quite bitter about the homelessness of people in South London while empty houses in the West End remained un-requisitioned. He felt this was a good sign because a mental awakening of this kind might push the class revolution to its conclusion.

Orwell wanted complete equality and believed that if there were certain things that everyone could not have, then no one should have them. This is a most unpopular view and I doubt if such a society would ever be accepted by the majority. It certainly requires a majority to establish it, unlike most social changes. Orwell left out of account one very strong human impulse, although he referred to it elsewhere in his writings on poverty. This is the willingness to gamble rather than to accept a dead level. Nearly everyone would rather go without something but retain the chance of a lucky break rather than share out goods on a basis of mathematical equality. The important thing, however, is not to exaggerate this impulse to the point where you claim that any social condition is permissible and acceptable providing the lucky break exists. The poor are not that foolish. Orwell was once rebuked by a young woman who worked in an exclusive shop off Bond Street. Why not level up, she said, instead of down? This is a familiar question and though we may not agree with Orwell's views on social levelling he did explode this rather facile notion.

> 'In some cases you can't level "up". You can't give everyone a Rolls-Royce car. You can't even give everyone a fur coat, especially in wartime. As to the statement that everyone ought to go to Eton or Harrow, it is meaningless. The whole value of those places, from the point of view of the people who go there, is their exclusiveness. And since certain luxuries—high-powered cars, for instance, fur coats, yachts, country houses and whatnot—obviously can't be distributed to everybody, then it is better that nobody should have them.' ('As I Please', *Tribune*, 18 February, 1944.)

But he knew that the abolition of the class system was still far distant. One year after he broke the Lord's tabu he was writing to *Partisan Review* telling them that centralised control was a certainty in Britain and that it was more likely to be under the control of wealthy men and aristocrats than the representatives of the common people. They would use their power to keep the structure of government on a class basis, manipulate taxation and rationing in their own favour, and avoid a revolutionary war strategy, but they would not return to capitalism of the old chaotic kind. He felt that the developing situation did not mean more economic freedom or profits for the individual business man, but it did mean something much more essential to the perpetuation of the class system—you were less likely to get an important job unless you had been to one of the right schools. And he was probably right in his diagnosis. Despite the intervention of the Labour Government and a considerable degree of socialisation, the old English class system remains untouched. Some of the class differences which I have quoted in this chapter from Orwell's work have disappeared or declined in importance, but in general the system has shown remarkable powers of endurance. Orwell's examination of the subject leaves us with two interesting questions which it is impossible to answer yet with any certainty: will the new class of light-industry technicians and their allies continue to gather strength, and will the political leaders accept the levelling that this implies?

Chapter IX

Evolution of a Socialist

ORWELL WAS primarily a political writer and all his best
work deals directly or indirectly with political or social problems. (In the twentieth century social problems are, of course,
political problems.) In his early work politics are rarely discussed directly. There is often a political implication but it is
never laboured and it is not until *The Road to Wigan Pier* and,
more emphatically, *Homage to Catalonia* that political aspects
begin to be stressed. In *Burmese Days*, for instance, he makes
passing comments about the political scene but he never follows
them up or incorporates them in a body of political opinion.
In this book we find him expressing a viewpoint that became a
central part of his political thought later, but at this early stage
it is a mere by-product that occasionally floats to the surface. It
is that in India you were not judged for what you did but for
what you *were*. Macgregor, the Deputy Commissioner, had his
doubts about Dr Veraswami. There was no question of the
doctor having committed an overt act of disloyalty—the question was rather was he the *kind* of man who might hold seditious
opinions? Later Orwell seized on this point as one that helped
to contribute to the peculiar horror of life in a totalitarian
society. Depending on the society the question was always, Is
this man a bourgeois or a proletarian, a liberal or a fascist?
Actions did not matter; states of mind did.

In *Down and Out* he says he knew nothing of politics, but he
was under suspicion in Paris. He had been seen coming out of
the office of a Communist weekly paper and he had had a lot of
trouble with the police. This kind of atmosphere encouraged a
conspiratorial attitude towards politics. During Orwell's youth
there had been a popular brand of fiction which treated political
activities in a conspiratorial way, and it had always seemed

rather ridiculous. But like some other forms of popular literature, it was becoming true. One experience of his reproduced
the atmosphere perfectly. His Russian friend Boris encouraged
him to write articles for a Communist secret society. When
Orwell visited headquarters he was asked for the password
(which he didn't know). This difficulty was overcome, but then
he was reprimanded for not carrying a parcel. The office was
over a laundry and everyone visiting it was supposed to carry a
parcel which was intended to lull the suspicions of the police.
When they discussed the nature of the articles he was supposed
to write he was invited to write about *Le Sport*. Football and
Communism had some mysterious connection on the continent,
he discovered. All the time it was necessary to pretend you
were something quite different from your real self. The conspiratorial atmosphere was maintained in the hotels, for some
of the waiters were spies. It was apparently a favourite resort
of the spy to get a job as a waiter. Later he commented in a
book review on the fact that conspiracy is now normal in
politics.

By the time he is writing *The Road to Wigan Pier* he calls
himself a socialist. There is no doubt that the conversion was
the result of his experiences of poverty. Even in *Down and Out*
he had made some suggestions about the employment of tramps
which were at least semi-political. But in *Wigan Pier* he is not a
formal politician. He has joined a political group, the Socialists,
but he is less concerned with their political progress than with
their internal fitness for attempting political progress. As
Pritchett said, he had become the conscience of the Left.
Everyone else was talking about aims and methods; he was far
more concerned with the personnel that was to undertake the
aims and methods. There is no hint of conspiracy in all this. In
fact, Orwell never showed any sign of interest in conspiracy.
He was a partisan of the good old-fashioned political practice
of ordinary decent people trying to carry out an ordinary
decent policy. He thought it odd that a theory such as Socialism,
which promised so much to ordinary people and promised it
rationally, should find so many enemies among the very people
it was intended to help. In his opinion the answer was that they
didn't object to Socialism but they did object to Socialists. And

he agreed with them. He usually agreed with the simple opinions held by simple people but he had the intellectual equipment to make them sound much more impressive than they usually did.

He discovered five reasons why ordinary people often resisted Socialism. First was the point I have already mentioned. As with Christianity, the worst advertisement for Socialism is its adherents.

'The first thing that must strike any observer is that Socialism in its developed form is a theory confined entirely to the middle class. The typical Socialist is not, as tremulous old ladies imagine, a ferocious-looking working man with greasy overalls and a racuous voice. He is either a youthful snob-Bolshevik who in five years' time will quite probably have made a wealthy marriage and been converted to Roman Catholicism; or, still more typically, a prim little man with a white-collar job, usually a secret tee-totaller and often with vegetarian leanings, with a history of Noncomformity behind him, and, above all, with a social position which he has no intention of forfeiting. This last type is sur-prisingly common in Socialist parties of every shade; it has perhaps been taken over *en bloc* from the old Liberal Party. In addition to this there is the horrible—the really disquieting—prevalence of cranks wherever Socialists are gathered together. One sometimes gets the impression that the mere words "Socialism" and "Com-munism" draw towards them with magnetic force every fruit-juice drinker, nudist, sandal-wearer, sex-maniac, Quaker, "Nature Cure" quack, pacifist and feminist in England.'

These people are keen logicians, though their logic is often weak. Another reason why the working man is often not a Socialist is that he is rarely logically consistent. He is not fas-cinated by the perfection of a plan as is the book-trained middle-class intellectual. To the working man Socialism means very little more than getting a decent wage and enough spare time to enjoy himself. He really does not mind what the system is so long as he gets these things. That is why the intellectual will often consider nationalisation the crux of Socialism while the working man only wants it if it brings immediate and palpable results. Orwell said the ordinary working man is often a truer Socialist than the Marxist because he never forgets that Socialism should mean justice and common decency, but on the other hand he does not realise that you cannot improve sections of society without affecting the rest of society at the same time. Then the working man is rarely a bigot. Orwell draws an analogy between Roman Catholicism and Socialism. It is the Catholic convert, the Chesterton type, who can never forget that he is a Catholic, who is compelled to prove that beer-drinking is Christian and tea-drinking is pagan. The working man has not time for this kind of preciousness. It is only the 'educated' man, particularly the literary man, who attempts to enclose the whole of life within the confines of a theory. It is the same with the Communist.

Orwell doubted very strongly whether the Marxist intellectual was actuated by a love of the working class. He doubted if the type loved anybody. Then what was his motive? He believed it was simply a hypertrophied sense of order. The intellectual dislikes the present order not because of the misery it causes but because it is untidy. 'What they desire, basically, is to reduce the world to something resembling a chessboard.' He instances the barren Socialism of Shaw. No genuine working man cares tuppence about social tidiness, and all Shaw's working men were figures of fun. The world was to be reorganised in the interests of non-existent men and women. Ordinary people recoil from the Socialist vision of a completely ordered world. They have been taught to identify Socialism with mechanical progress, something quite soulless and empty. 'Please notice', he writes, 'that this essentially fat-bellied version of "progress" is not an integral part of Socialist doctrine; but it has come to be thought of as one, with the result that the temperamental conservatism which is latent in all kinds of people is easily mobilised against Socialism.'

Towards the end of this book he states what he thinks is the best strategy for Socialist propaganda. In the past it has tended to make the worst of all possible worlds. It antagonises the working class by its theoretical inhumanity and it antagonises the middle class by abusing them as 'bourgeois', which is of course used as a term of reproof. If you are born a bourgeois, he says, there is nothing you can do about it. You have to remain one. Why not try to recruit the middle classes? They have ultimately as much to gain from a decent Socialism as the workers. Economically a bourgeois was in the same boat as a miner, a navvy and a farm-hand. Remind him of that and he will fight at their side. But if you constantly remind him that culturally he is different from them he will become their enemy. And he was not a solitary phenomenon. He shared his position with every bank clerk worrying about the sack, every shopkeeper on the brink of bankruptcy. But Socialist propaganda always concentrated on the differences between people, never on what they had in common.

One very dangerous result of this situation was that many people were driven into Fascist attitudes when a little tact would have brought them into the Socialist fold. Many Fascists were not fundamentally evil people. They really believed they were defending Christian civilisation against the materialistic Utopia of Socialist propaganda. The Socialists never made it sufficiently clear that their essential aims were justice and liberty. Unable to tear themselves away from economic facts, they had forgotten that man has a soul.

'As a result Fascism has been able to play upon every instinct that revolts against hedonism and a cheap conception of "progress". It has been able to pose as the upholder of the European tradition, and to appeal to Christian belief, to patriotism and to the military virtues. It is far worse than useless to write Fascism off as "mass sadism", or some easy phrase of that kind. If you pretend that it is merely an aberration which will presently pass off of its own accord, you are dreaming a dream from which you will awake when somebody coshes you with a rubber truncheon. The only possible course is to examine the Fascist case, grasp that there is something to be said for it, and then make it clear to the world that whatever good Fascism contains is also implicit in Socialism.'

The popular idea of Socialism, which is especially strong in England, is that it is basically a fight against tyranny. But the majority of orthodox Marxists will not accept that definition, or will only accept it as a phase in some long-term strategy. Their Mecca, Soviet Russia, is the most rigid tyranny on earth, and even before the war was not surpassed by Nazi Germany. Her only superiority lay in the socialisation of production, which led the innocent to believe that the Socialist virtues were to be found there. Orwell said that when he heard Marxists talking, and still more when he read their books, he got the impression that the whole Socialist movement was no more than a kind of exciting heresy-hunt—'a leaping to and fro of frenzied witch-doctors to the beat of tom-toms and the tune of "Fee, fo, fi, fum, I smell the blood of a right-wing deviationist!" ' How many people who rage against deviationists know *why* they are supposed to be evil as distinct from knowing the marks of the species?

The next step was Spain, and again the central fact of Orwell's Socialism was a perfectly simple faith in the power of common decency and the need to defend it. He said that when he went there, and for some time afterwards, he was not only not interested in the political situation but unaware of it. He knew nothing about the nature of the war, except that it was against Fascism, and he had decided that Fascism was an enemy of common decency. He had accepted the *News Chronicle-New Statesman* version of the war as the defence of civilisation against a maniacal outbreak by an army of Colonel Blimps in the pay of Hitler. In other words, he held the view of a typically uninformed Englishman, the kind of view that working men hold in their millions. But later he discovered that the Communists in Spain were putting their political spite against the Trotskyists before anti-Fascist unity. It was this that made the situation seem so bewildering. After all, despite their differences, all the various groups were supposed to be Socialist in one form or another, and one would have expected them to resist the common enemy first before they got down to settling their own differences. Trotskyism was branded by a Valencia Communist paper as 'an official capitalist organisation, a Fascist terrorist band occupied in crime and sabotage against the people'. The P.O.U.M. was supposedly in league with the Fascists and was part of Franco's Fifth Column. No evidence was ever produced; it was simply asserted with an air of authority. In their anger with the P.O.U.M. Communist writers even divulged military secrets in the press. (Orwell gives evidence of this.) Ralph Bates even wrote that P.O.U.M. troops were playing football with the Fascists in no-man's-land at a time when Orwell knew their troops were suffering heavy casualties and a number of his personal friends were killed or wounded.

The real, though unspoken, charge against the P.O.U.M. was that they were revolutionary extremists. One would not

expect this to be regarded as a vice by Communists but in fact
they were not anxious for the revolution in Spain to become too
emphatic. The Communists alleged that anyone who professed
revolutionary extremism was a Trotskyist, and all Trotskyists
were in Fascist pay. Only the law of libel held back their
denunciations and accusations. When Maxton, the I.L.P.
leader, went to Spain he was denounced by the Spanish Communist press as a 'Trotsky-Fascist' and spy of the Gestapo. But
the English Communists were careful not to echo this charge
because they have a wholesome dread of the law of libel. In
England Maxton was merely a 'reactionary enemy of the
working class', which is too vague to be actionable. The other
charge would have had to be proved in the law courts in England and the Communists did not feel prepared to repeat it.
In Spain Orwell learnt the real difference between the Anarchists and Communists, a distinction that is quite unknown to the
average Englishman. Although the Anarchists were rather
vague in their principles, there was no doubt about the genuine-
ness of their hatred of privilege and injustice. The Communists
were much more interested in centralism and efficiency than in
liberty and equality. This in itself explains why Orwell veered to
the Anarchist camp once he had discovered what they stood for.

Yet at first he was inclined to prefer the Communist viewpoint to that of P.O.U.M. simply because the Communists had
a definite practical policy, 'an obviously better policy from the
point of view of the common-sense which looks only a few
months ahead'. (Hemingway also supported the Communists
because they alone seemed to be getting on with the war.) The
day-to-day policy and propaganda of the P.O.U.M., said
Orwell, were unspeakably bad. But it did not take him long to
come round to the view that any policy which ignored liberty
and equality must fail in the long run—or rather, it might
succeed, but the resultant situation would be no improvement
on the previous one. He would not say anything against the
rank-and-file Communist, especially those who died so heroic-
ally around Madrid. They were often dupes of those who
directed policy, believing propaganda and never noticing how
ill it agreed with the practical issue of events. It was even possible to come across men in this war who did not know what

their affiliations were. Most of these were Andalusians, the most ignorant people in Spain. They knew they were fighting against people called Fascists and that they were fighting for a better life, but whether they were Anarchists or Communists it was beyond their powers to say.

The chief lesson that Orwell learnt in Spain was that there was the beginning of a dangerous split in the world working-class movement. In fact, the split was already a definite fact and it has widened since. The attacks and libels against convinced Socialists that he came across in Spain would soon make the split irreconcilable. He believed that the only way of avoiding a complete split was through exhaustive discussion. The real difference between the Communists and their enemies was that the Communists believed in the Popular Front, i.e., Fascism could be defeated through an alliance with sections of the capitalist class, while their opponents believed that this manoeuvre simply gave new opportunities for the revival of Fascism. 'The question has got to be settled', he wrote in *Homage to Catalonia*; 'to make the wrong decision may be to land ourselves in for centuries of semi-slavery.' The Popular Front could not succeed because it was an alliance of enemies. One partner was bound to swallow the other. The Spanish situation was difficult for foreigners to understand because the Communists were on the extreme Right of the Government side, not on the extreme Left as they are usually believed to be. This should not have caused surprise, he said, because the Soviet alliance with France had made it clear that official Communism had become a counter-revolutionary force. Moreover, the whole of Comintern policy was subordinated to the defence of the U.S.S.R. This was excusable, in view of the world situation, but it should not have blinded people to the fact that Russia had relinquished her earlier title to revolutionary leadership. Russian policy in Spain was dictated, he said, by the fact that Russia's ally, France, would never allow a revolutionary regime to be set up in Spain nor would she allow the liberation of Spanish Morocco. 'In reality it was the Communists above all others who prevented revolution in Spain. Later, when the Right-wing forces were in full control, the Communists showed themselves willing to go a great deal further than the Liberals in hunting down the revolutionary leaders.'

For this reason he said later that Attlee was right to resist the Popular Front in England. (Review of *Mr Attlee: an Interim Biography*, by Roy Jenkins, *Observer*, 4 July, 1948.) The Popular Front would simply have weakened the Labour Party without bringing any electoral advantage. In an article entitled 'Spilling the Spanish Beans' (*New English Weekly*, 29 July, 1937) he said that the Popular Front was

> 'a combination with about as much vitality, and about as much right to exist, as a pig with two heads or some other Barnum and Bailey monstrosity. . . .
>
> 'In any serious emergency the contradiction implied in the Popular Front is bound to make itself felt. For even when the worker and the bourgeois are both fighting against Fascism, they are not fighting for the same things; the bourgeois is fighting for bourgeois democracy, i.e., capitalism, the worker, in so far as he understands the issue, for Socialism.'

It was one thing to understand what had been happening after the event, but quite another and more difficult thing to understand while the events were happening. Even Orwell himself admitted that at the time he made none of the correct political reflections. He was only conscious of weariness and a strong desire for the whole thing to be over and done with. It must have been far more bewildering for the uneducated, apolitical common man, caught in the net and buffeted this way and that by competing propagandas. It was particularly bad in Spain because of the political intolerance that everyone took for granted—an intolerance, he pointed out, that does not yet exist in England. It is true that it is wise for a Communist coal-miner to keep his opinions to himself when his boss is about, but it is not yet considered natural to 'liquidate' or 'eliminate' anyone who disagrees with you. In Spain this was becoming a commonplace, as many an unfortunate P.O.U.M. member discovered to his cost. One of the most dangerous possessions Orwell had was a photo of a group of militiamen with a P.O.U.M. flag in the background, and which his wife made him tear up. 'That was the kind of thing that got you arrested nowadays.'

Spain strengthened his uncomplicated faith in decency, equality and justice, as I have said before. It was not enough to accept the Communist doctrine that economic equality would bring the political virtues in its train (apart from the fact the Russian Communists had already abandoned economic equality). It was necessary to eliminate great variations in wealth, but that in itself was not enough.

'I do not believe that a man with £50,000 a year and a man with fifteen shillings a week either can, or will, co-operate. The nature of their relationship is, quite simply, that the one is robbing the other, and there is no reason to think that the robber will suddenly turn over a new leaf. It would seem, therefore, that if the problems of western capitalism are to be solved, it will have to be through . . . a movement which is genuinely revolutionary, i.e., willing to make drastic changes and to use violence if necessary, but which does not lose touch, as Communism and Fascism have done, with the essential values of democracy.'

Tubby Bowling in *Coming Up For Air* believed that Fascism in England would not make the slightest difference to ordinary fellows like himself. They were just the fodder of politics and their treatment did not vary from one system to another. There would be a lot of face-bashing, certainly, but the bashers and the bashed would all come from the politically engaged sections of the population. This was one instance in which the character was less wise than his creator.

Orwell was always at his best when he interpreted foreign events in English terms. The struggle of Communist and Trotskyist and Fascist is remote to the Englishman and the only way to bring home its reality and its enormity is to suppose them translated to English soil. In an article entitled 'Impenetrable Mystery' (*New English Weekly*, 9 June, 1938) he gives a remarkable description of Trotsky-type trials in English terms. This is worth quoting at some length because it is in these passages that Orwell's imaginative faculty receives its fullest expression. There is no doubt that after the early years it was the political scene which roused his literary skill to its peak.

'Mr Winston Churchill, now an exile in Portugal, is plotting to overthrow the British Empire and establish Communism in England. By the use of unlimited Russian money he has succeeded in building up a huge Churchillite organisation which includes members of Parliament, Roman Catholic Bishops ad practically the whole of the Primrose League. Almost every day some dastardly act of sabotage is laid bare—sometimes a plot to blow up the House of Lords, sometimes an outbreak of foot-and-mouth disease in the Royal racing stables. Eighty per cent of the Beef-eaters at the Tower are discovered to be agents of the Comintern. A high official of the Post Office admits brazenly to having embezzled postal orders to the tune of £5,000,000, and also to having committed *lese majesté* by drawing moustaches on postage stamps. Lord Nuffield, after a seven-hour interrogation by Mr Norman Birkett, confesses that ever since 1920 he has been fomenting strikes in his own factories. Casual half-inch paras in every issue of the newspapers announce that fifty more Churchill-ite sheep-stealers have been shot in Westmorland or that the proprietress of a village shop in the Cotswolds has been transported to Australia for sucking the bullseyes and putting them back in the bottle. And meanwhile the Churchillites (or Churchillite-Harmsworthites as they are called after Lord Rothermere's execution) never cease from proclaiming that it is *they* who are the real defenders of Capitalism and that Chamberlain and the rest of his gang are no more than a set of Bolsheviks in disguise.'

Orwell adds, perhaps unnecessarily, that it couldn't happen here. But he is astonished that the Communists should regard an equivalent situation in Russia as a good advertisement for Communism.

By the time the war came Orwell's political viewpoint was clarified but he had been unable to solve the basic dilemma of social and political progress. He had adopted Socialism but he had rejected the Communist method of achieving it because it threw out the baby with the bath-water: the chance of decency, justice and equality went gurgling down the drain in the wake of capitalism. But capitalism had to be eliminated before Socialism could take its place. How could the values of a decent life be retained while the imperfect framework was swept away? He dismissed the 'change of heart' theory because this was the alibi of people who did not wish to change the *status quo*. In the essay on Dickens he said that two viewpoints are always tenable: how can you improve human nature without changing the system, and what is the use of changing the system before you have improved human nature? They appeal to different indi-viduals and they tend to alternate in point of time. The moralist and the revolutionary are constantly undermining one another.

Of one thing he was certain and that was the general truth

contained in Marxism. He could not accept the theory in its entirety, but equally it was impossible to dismiss it in its entirety. He was always suspicious of people who explained everything in terms of blood, religion, the solar plexus and national souls because it was obvious that they were avoiding something. This something was the 'dreary' Marxist economic interpretation of history. They did not avoid it because it was untrue but because it had too much truth in it for their own comfort. Although Marx himself is a difficult author to read and understand, a crude version of his theory is believed in by millions of people—particularly middle-class people. The underlying thesis is so simple it provides a permanent opportunity to avoid any real thought. If you hold such-and-such opinions it is because you have such-and-such an amount of money in your pocket. Many writers gave their true feelings away when they expend immense energy in attacking a theory which they claim to be obviously untrue. The reason is because 'it is *not* altogether untrue, in fact, is quite true enough to make every thinking person uncomfortable'. ('The Lure of Profundity', *New English Weekly*, 30 December, 1937.)

One difficulty in the way of every sincere Socialist was the common assumption that Soviet Russia was a Socialist state, with the consequent association of the two in the public mind. Hostile criticism of Russia should not affect true Socialist theory at all, but in fact it was always accepted as propaganda against Socialism. This in itself made honest discussion of Socialism a very difficult matter, leading all argument away on the trail of red herrings. There was a further complication arising out of the difficulty of discovering the truth about Soviet Russia. This meant that much criticism of Socialism was not only false but was even false criticism of Russia—criticism based on a double fallacy. There were two opposed attitudes towards the Soviet Union, favourable and unfavourable, and both were based on the view of Russia as a revolutionary force. In fact, she was a counter-revolutionary force. By 1937 Communists everywhere were in alliance with bourgeois reformism and were using the whole of their powerful machinery to crush or discredit any party that showed signs of revolutionary tendencies (as in Spain). In this hotchpotch of lies, distortions

and deliberate falsification, backed by much genuine ignorance
and unconscious dishonesty, Orwell was trying to discover the
correct method of achieving Socialism. He knew what Socialism
should be; he was puzzled to know how to bring it about.

Chapter X

Political Commentary

DURING THE war years and after Orwell produced a large mass of political journalism, in addition to his two books, *Animal Farm* and *1948*. I propose to deal with the two latter separately and in this chapter will set out the political ideas expressed in his journalism. They provide the background to the more important books. For the sake of convenience I will deal with these ideas under separate heads.

POWER

Power has replaced wealth as the main object of desire in the modern world. Any approach to politics must be conducted through an examination and understanding of this power urge.

Orwell did not believe that the distinction between violence and non-violence was of first importance. The determining factor in any political situation was the strength of the appetite for power. His quarrel with the pacifists was partly attributable to this particular emphasis. It is wrong to equate power-lust with blustering and bullying, even with the use of violence. If it is possible to attain power without the use of violence there are many people who would prefer it that way. Some people dislike armies and police forces but are more intolerant and inquisitorial in outlook than the normal person who believes it is necessary to use violence in certain circumstances. He believed that creeds like pacifism and anarchism encouraged mental intolerance, while at the same time renouncing violence. Orwell's illustration of this type of mind was taken, rather unexpectedly, from the life of Tolstoy. Tolstoy was a would-be saint who became convinced of his own rightness, especially towards the end of his life when he lost all sense of proportion. He thought it part of his mission to prevent people enjoying

Shakespeare, drinking alcohol or smoking tobacco. He did not attempt to enforce these tabus physically but did all he could to discredit relatively harmless pleasures by dubious appeals to morality.

It is obvious that Orwell has widened the normal concept of power by including within its limits the attitude of a pacifist such as Tolstoy. He did not concern himself much with the consideration of brute power—he preferred a subtler challenge and in any case many other writers were doing that. He disliked pacifism because he thought it was a mistaken policy but also because he thought it concealed a lust for power as strong as that of any Fascist. In other words, the contemporary struggle between violence and non-violence becomes much more significant if we regard it as the conflict of rivals who use different methods to attain the same end. And, like Lord Melbourne, he could see no future for moral force when opposed by physical force. He thought the pacifist faith in moral force a pathetic illusion and once said that Hitler would willingly have paid his opponents to adopt methods of moral resistance. He also used this argument against H. G. Wells, who was anything but a pacifist. Wells was so dazzled by the prospect of a World State that he thought it was only necessary to march seven times round the national boundaries blowing trumpets, and the walls would fall down. But no new political system, including the World State, can be established without first winning power, and to win power it is necessary to oppose a greater force to a weaker. To defeat a chauvinism you must employ a stronger chauvinism. To reach Utopia, or the nearest resemblance to Utopia, it is necessary to appeal to the crudest and even basest emotions: racial pride, leader worship, religious belief, love of war. Without such stimuli the people will not produce the effort required to win power. 'No one in our time believes in any sanction greater than military power; no one believes that it is possible to overcome force except by greater force. There is no "law", there is only power. I am not saying that that is a true belief, merely that it is the belief which all modern men do actually hold. Those who pretend otherwise are either intellectual cowards, or power-worshippers under a thin disguise, or have simply not caught up with the age they are living in.' ('Rudyard Kipling', *Critical Essays*.)

I should add that this belief of Orwell's was purely intuitive and had no factual basis—or rather, he did not produce one. It is an offensive view to many people. It belonged to Orwell's own least tolerant period, the frustrated early years of the war when some of his views were tinged with hysteria.

CAPITALISM

Capitalism is where we start from. In his Introduction to *British Pamphleteers* Orwell lists some of the 'achievements' of capitalism: 'the horrors of the Industrial Revolution, the destruction of one culture after another, the piling-up of millions of human beings in hideous ant-heaps of cities, and, above all, the enslavement of the coloured races'.

Orwell did not waste time attacking capitalism for its own sake—once again, this field was crowded and he always looked for the subtler contrasts and relationships. For instance, when he writes in *The Lion and the Unicorn* that British capitalism does not work, it is not simply that he can make the trite follow-up that Socialism would work, but that he could add that Fascism also would and did! He deplored the tendency among Socialists to regard the success of Socialism as inevitable and to see Fascism as merely a variant of capitalism, which was therefore doomed. Fascism worked because it was a planned system geared to a definite purpose, world-conquest, and it did not allow any private interest to stand in the way. British capitalism did not work because it was a competitive system in which private profit was and must be the main objective. It was a system in which all the forces were pulling in opposite directions and the interests of the individual were as often as not totally opposed to the State.

British capitalism was on the defensive and consequently showed a high degree of cunning, accepting allies wherever it could find them. This was particularly true during the war. Orwell noticed how, unlike some other Right-wing publications, the Beaverbrook press appeared to be enthusiastically pro-Russian, even to the extent of playing down the suggestion that Trotsky was a victim of the G.P.U. In his Notebook for 22 August, 1940, occurs the following passage:

'The men responsible for the *Standard's* present pro-Russian policy are no doubt shrewd enough to know that a Popular Front "line" is not really the way to secure a Russian alliance. But they also know that the mass of Leftish opinion in England still takes it for granted that a full anti-Fascist policy is the way to line up Russia on our side. To crack up Russia is therefore a way of pushing public opinion leftward. It is curious that I always attribute these devious motives to other people, being anything but cunning myself and finding it hard to use indirect methods even when I see the need for them.'

This passage is more than 'devious', it is unusually obscure. It is only fair to recognise that it is a note, but all the same the reasoning is difficult to follow. We know that Orwell considered Russia a counter-revolutionary force and the Beaverbrook journalists, particularly the alert staff of 1940, would also recognise this. But why should the *Standard* wish to push public opinion leftward? It doesn't really matter at this date. What is more interesting is the conception of a political and economic system with its back to the wall, trying to perpetuate itself by any shift that comes to hand. The last sentence draws our attention to a dilemma that must have worried anyone who has taken an interest in politics. We always attribute the most diabolical cunning to the other fellow and persuade ourselves that although we can appreciate his tricks we would be incapable of performing them ourselves. Is this true? It would be worth a psychologist's while to examine the peculiar mental state of the politician, both professional and amateur.

The same doubts had to be entertained when Churchill accepted the Russian alliance without qualifications. At the same time he stressed his abhorrence of Russian Communism. Orwell felt sure that the normal sentimental Socialist would be appalled, being naive enough to believe that an alliance must be based on love. Orwell applauded Churchill's honesty. Orwell's thinking at this stage had become ingrown (as I have said before, it was his worst period). As suspicion piled on suspicion there was a kind of intellectual incest which produced weird monsters of thought. He did not appear to believe that anyone was capable of thinking straight politically. Every Socialist insisted that every capitalist must acquiesce in Socialism to make an alliance effective. Every capitalist must pretend to every Socialist that he had sloughed off his skin of anti-Socialism. On the whole I think people in 1941 were far more realistic. No one was expecting a perfect marriage—apart, that is, from the lunatic fringe, to whom Orwell was paying far more attention than it merited. He ended a note on this subject by referring to the squeal that he was certain correspondents would raise in the *New Statesman*. In fact there were no letters in the next issue of the *New Statesman*. The editorial referred to the speech as a 'great and historic event'. There were no letters in the next two issues either. Orwell's prophecy seemed plausible but it was really stimulated by too much concern with political oddities.

The main point that emerges from a consideration of these minor events is that in a capitalist society like Britain's political straightforwardness is rare. Everyone pretends he is something other than what he is. The Conservative has not enough confidence in his views to be conservative but poses as a progressive. In fact, Orwell claimed that a true Conservative no longer existed. He was either a Liberal, a Fascist or the accomplice of the Fascists, but he did not dare to come out into the open. Whatever the faults of the Communists and Fascists, they at least believed in themselves and left no doubts as to their true beliefs. There was a time when British Conservatives had hoped desperately that the new continental movements were temporary aberrations, and that disillusioned people would return gratefully to the blessings of capitalist society. But it had become clear that this was not happening. The U.S.S.R. could not be called Socialist without changing the accepted meaning of the word, but on the other hand it had not reverted to capitalism. It was something new. Nazi Germany had left the old-style capitalism behind and had become a planned economy with an adoptive oligarchy in control. In Russia the capitalists were destroyed first and the workers crushed later. In Germany the workers were crushed first but the private capitalists were being rapidly eliminated. Even in the United States capitalism had changed; there was no longer the old blind faith in *laissez-faire*. The question for the future was not whether capitalism could be salvaged. It certainly could not. The question was whether it would be replaced by oligarchy or a true democracy.

Orwell believed that British capitalism was moribund and yet he had one good word to say for it—and strangely enough, it was for an aspect that most Left-wingers sneered at. He was grateful to British capitalism for allowing democratic procedure and sentiment to persist. Most Socialists regarded British democracy as a sham by which the ordinary people were duped, but Orwell claimed that it was real and could be put to good use. He made this point in 'Fascism and Democracy', his contribution to *The Betrayal of the Left* (edited by Victor Gollancz).

'When the real English Socialist movement appears . . . it will cut across the existing party divisions. It will be both revolutionary and democratic. It will aim at the most fundamental changes and be perfectly willing to use violence if necessary. But also it will recognise that not all cultures are the same, that national sentiments and traditions have to be respected if revolutions are not to fail, that England is not Russia—or China, or India. It will realise that British democracy is *not* altogether a sham, *not* simply "superstructure", that on the contrary it is something extremely valuable which must be preserved and extended, and, above all, must not be insulted.'

SOCIALISM

Orwell believed that Socialism was the only political system based on hope. All others were movements of despair and derived from disillusion. He called their advocates neo-pessimists and traced them back to Georges Sorel and T. E. Hulme. They were an ill-assorted crowd and among them were Pétain, Berdyaev, 'Beachcomber' and Aldous Huxley and they had links with Catholicism, Conservatism, Fascism, Pacifism and Anarchism. It was necessary to dissociate Socialism from Utopianism. Most of the attacks on Socialism were made by people who confused the two—probably deliberately. Nearly all neo-pessimist apologetics consisted in setting up a man of straw and knocking him down again. The man of straw was called Human Perfectibility, which was alleged to be the aim of Socialism. The answer to this, he said, was that Socialism is not perfectionist, perhaps not even hedonistic. Socialists only claim that they can make the world better, not perfect. Any thinking Socialist will admit that when economic justice has been achieved there will still be a major problem to be solved, that of man's place in the universe. In some ways Socialism was as much a religious theory as an economic. But the average man is not going to think about religious or metaphysical problems while he is hungry or oppressed. It is all summed up in Marx's saying that after Socialism has arrived human history can begin.

There are Socialists of many different kinds and all of them tend to equate Socialism with their own pet theories of progress or reconstruction or, in some cases, of perfectibility. Orwell was no exception. He rejected the idea of perfectibility and his own personal view of Socialism was not simply of a technique for greater economic efficiency or justice. Many Socialists would have regarded him as a Liberal who had annexed a title to which he had no right; he himself believed that the Marxian type of Socialist had even less right to the title. He admitted that in the narrow sense Socialism had nothing to do with liberty, equality or common decency of any description. If you adopted this viewpoint (he did not, but thousands did) then you could not grumble if a State was internally Socialist and externally imperialist. Technically it would be possible to 'socialise' England and still continue to exploit the Crown Colonies for the benefit of the home population. Soviet Russia had adopted a Socialist economic system but her foreign policy exploited the discontents of other people for the benefit of her own security. In 1940 he felt certain that Germany was moving rapidly towards Socialism and yet side by side with it was a perfectly clear and open determination to turn the subject peoples into a reserve of slave labour. The Socialist society that was the aim of the pioneers could not possibly be attained without an equal emphasis on the political virtues of democracy.

While England was expecting invasion and before Russia had entered the war he believed that there was a good chance of a genuine Left-wing government being set up. But he thought the many people who would have welcomed this were in error in believing that they would get any support from Russia. Quite simply, the Russians did not want Socialism anywhere, the more so as they had failed to introduce it in their own country. He believed that Stalin was hostile to any country that was genuinely undergoing revoltuion. For him this was the chief lesson of his Spanish experiences.

Looking at the situation as a whole, Orwell believed that the

Socialist revolution had failed. He did not think the situation was beyond redemption but a great effort on the part of Socialists would be necessary before it would be possible. The failure of Socialism was due less to the power of the opposition than to the seduction of Socialists themselves from the straight and narrow path. He gave his reasons in a review of Oscar Wilde's *The Soul of Man Under Socialism* (*Observer*, 9 May, 1948). Wilde had said he did not consider it necessary in a Socialist state for an inspector to call each morning to see that each person got up to do his eight hours' labour. Orwell agreed, but added that unfortunately that was exactly what far too many Socialists did consider necessary. Socialism, in the sense of economic collectivism, was conquering the world at great speed, yet a free and just society such as the early Socialists envisaged was as far away as ever.

'If one looks more closely one sees that Wilde makes two common but unjustified assumptions. One is that the world is immensely rich and is suffering chiefly from maldistribution. Even things out between the millionaires and the crossing-sweeper, he seems to say, and there will be plenty of everything for everybody. Until the Russian Revolution this belief was very widely held— "starving in the midst of plenty" was a favourite phrase—but it was quite false, and it survived only because Socialists thought always of the highly developed Western countries and ignored the fearful poverty of Asia and Africa. Actually, the problem for the world as a whole is not how to distribute such wealth as exists but how to increase production, without which economic equality merely means common misery.

'Secondly, Wilde assumes that it is a simple matter to arrange that all the unpleasant kinds of work shall be done by machinery. The machines, he says, are our new race of slaves: a tempting metaphor but a misleading one, since there is a vast range of jobs—roughly speaking, any job needing great flexibility—that no machine is able to do. In practice, even in the most highly-mechanised countries, an enormous amount of dull and exhausting work has to be done by unwilling human muscles. But this at once implies direction of labour, fixed working hours, differential wage rates and all the regimentation that Wilde abhors. Wilde's version of Socialism could only be realised in a world not only far richer but also technically far more advanced than the present one. The abolition of private property does not of itself put food into anyone's mouth. It is merely the first step in a transitional period that is bound to be laborious, uncomfortable and long.'

If this were the whole truth the Socialist future could no longer
attract us. Wilde's chief mistake was not to take into account
the transitional period, or at least to think it will be much
shorter than seems likely. But fundamentally Wilde was right
because once Socialism is established there is no logical reason
why a harsh social discipline should be retained. But all the
dangers and disappointments we face today spring from the
transitional period. The inhumanity generated by the necessities of the period tend to become permanent. This appears to
have happened in Soviet Russia. A dictatorship supposedly
established for a limited purpose has dug itself in, and Socialism
comes to be thought of as meaning concentration camps and
secret police forces. This was one of the dangers of accepting
Russia as a Socialist state. Orwell did not appear to believe
that the transition period would necessarily last much longer,
however, for by 1984 there is to be potential plenty for everyone and plenty has in fact to be reduced by constant warfare in
order to keep a hold on the people.

But even if it was going to be difficult to institute Socialism
he still did not doubt that it was the only possible solution. In
fact, in 'Toward European Unity' (*Partisan Review*, July-
August, 1947) he said that a socialist United States of Europe
was the only worthwhile political objective today. Such a
federation would contain about 250 million people, including
perhaps half the skilled industrial workers of the world. The
difficulties, he knew, were tremendous; one of them was the
apathy and conservatism of people everywhere, but there were
also certain actively hostile forces which he listed as follows:

(1) Russian hostility. The Russians would not welcome any
    European union that was not under their control. There is
    also the danger that the European masses will continue to
    believe in the Russian myth—though this danger must have
    lessened since Orwell wrote.

(2) American hostility. American capitalism would certainly not
    welcome a socialist Europe. In addition, the Americans have
    the power to break up a European coalition by drawing
    Britain out of it.

(3) Imperialism. True Socialism cannot be built on colonial
    exploitation. If all the European colonies gain their autonomy
    and manage their own affairs the standard of life in Europe
    is bound to fall. Also, to hold its own a United States of

Europe must include Africa and the Middle East, but on equal terms. (The nature of colonial exploitation has changed, but it still remains true that when African and Asiatic workers are paid decent wages prices will rise steeply in Europe. Orwell throws Africa and the Middle East rather blithely into the European Union. The Africans and Arabs would want to examine this proposal very carefully.)

(4) The Catholic Church. It is not reactionary in the ordinary sense and is capable of coming to terms with Socialism, but its influence is always against freedom of thought and speech, against human inequality and against any form of society that tends to promote earthly happiness.

But despite these difficulties Orwell believed there were grounds for optimism. For one thing, a major war during the next twenty years was inconceivable (for psychological reasons) and during such a period all kinds of things might happen to change the existing situation. A powerful Socialist movement might arise in the United States, for instance. Russia itself might change. The tendency of one generation to reject the ideas of the last may be an abiding human characteristic. By 1960 there may be millions of young Russians who are no longer willing to put up with dictatorship and loyalty parades. And finally, if the world did fall apart into three superstates, there was always the hope that the liberal tradition in the Anglo-American section would be strong enough to make life tolerable and even offer some hope of progress.

LEFT-WING PARTIES

In his essay on Rudyard Kipling (*Critical Essays*) Orwell wrote:

'All left-wing parties in the highly industrialised countries are at bottom a sham, because they make it their business to fight against something which they do not really wish to destroy. They have internationalist aims, and at the same time they struggle to keep up a standard of life with which those aims are incompatible. We all live by robbing Asiatic coolies, and those of us who are "enlightened" all maintain that those coolies ought to be set free; but our standard of living, and hence our "enlightenment", demands that the robbery shall continue.'

This was a recurring theme in Orwell's work. In *The Lion and the Unicorn*, for instance, he says that the Labour Party is not genuinely Socialist because it will not face up to this divergence between aim and practice. It has only been Socialist in internal policy and as Socialism is an international movement its intentions have always been suspect. It is primarily a party of the Trade Unions, devoted to raising wages and improving working conditions. (This is not entirely true; there is often a wide difference of opinion between Trade Unions and constituency parties, but the latter would be powerless without the support of the former.) Wages can only be maintained if British capitalism remains prosperous, and British capitalism can only remain prosperous if the Empire is maintained. In the past the wealth of England was largely drawn from Asia and Africa. Thus the standard of living of the British worker has depended indirectly on the sweating of Indian coolies. At the same time the Labour Party was committed to Socialist phraseology and the freeing of India. Orwell believed that an agricultural country like India would not be able to retain its independence, even if granted, in the age of the tank and the bombing plane, but would be absorbed by Japan or divided by Japan and Russia. These ideas of Orwell are being tested now, and like most of his political prophecies they have gone awry. This view was published in 1941, before India was freed. When India did gain its independence Japan was powerless and so far Russia has made no overt attempt to fill the vacuum caused by the retreat of British power.

The only party Orwell ever showed any enthusiasm for was Common Wealth—and it is significant that Common Wealth lived for a very short time and is now no more. His enthusiasm is typically guarded, but he was attracted by the synthesis of patriotism and the international outlook, the following of the British tradition, the ethical tone of the propaganda and the attempt to win over the middle classes. 'I think this movement should be watched with attention', he wrote to *Partisan Review*. 'It might develop into the new socialist party we have all been hoping for, or into something very sinister: it has some rather doubtful followers already.'

COMMUNISM AND SOVIET RUSSIA

Orwell was as vehemently anti-Communist as he was pro-Socialist. Like many other Socialists he was at first guarded in

his comments because it was so difficult to discover the truth
about Soviet Russia. There existed overwhelming evidence, he
said, to prove that the inhabitants of Soviet Russia were the
hungriest, the best fed, the happiest, the most miserable, the
freest, the least free, the most advanced and the most backward
population in the world. But by 1941 he was convinced that the
immense loyalty that the Soviet Union had inspired among the
working-class populations of other lands had been dissipated
by the selfishness of its international policy. He believed the
time would come when we would regard Stalin's foreign policy
as merely opportunistic and stupid instead of diabolically
clever, as it was claimed to be at the time. Here again, it was the
sacrifice of Spain that affected Orwell's judgment most strongly.
When he reviewed John Plamenatz's *What is Communism?* in the
Observer (15 February, 1948) he made it clear that he regarded
the Communist experiment as a lost revolution. This was partly
due to the fact that the kind of revolution that Marx had
envisaged could not take place because Russia was not industrialised. It was brought about by a group of professional
revolutionaries.

> 'Placed as they were, the Russian Communists necessarily
> developed into a permanent ruling caste, or oligarchy, recruited
> not by birth but by adoption. Since they could not risk the growth
> of opposition they could not risk genuine criticism, and since they
> silenced criticism they often made avoidable mistakes; then,
> because they could not admit that the mistakes were their own,
> they had to find scapegoats, sometimes on an enormous scale.'

But Orwell's strongest criticism of the Communists was of
their failure to interpret human motives. They always wrote
off religion, morality, patriotism and similar values as 'superstructure', a sort of hypocritical cover-up for the pursuit of
economic interests. They never stopped to ask why it was
necessary for the superstructure to exist. If no man is ever
motivated by anything except class interests, why does every
man constantly pretend that he is motivated by something else?
A possible answer is that human beings can only put forth their
full powers when they believe they are *not* acting for economic
ends. But this in itself is enough to suggest that superstructural
motives should be taken seriously. They may be causes as well

as effects. A Marxist 'analysis' of any historical event tends to be a hurried snap-judgment based on the principle of *cui bono?*, something rather like the 'realists' of the saloon bar who *always* assume that the bishop is keeping a mistress and the trade union leader is in the pay of the boss. Along these lines it is impossible to have an intuitive understanding of men's motives and therefore impossible to predict their actions. As a result the predictions of the Marxists in recent years have not only been wrong but more sensationally wrong than those of much simpler people who have relied on intuitive judgment. The outstanding failure of the Marxists was their failure to see in advance the danger of Fascism. Long *after* Hitler came to power official Marxism was declaring that Hitler was of no importance and could achieve nothing. On the other hand, people who had hardly heard of Marx but knew the power of faith had seen Hitler coming years earlier.

Orwell gave an example of the ineptness of Marxist propaganda in his Notebooks. He saw the slogan 'Cheese—not Churchill' chalked on a wall in South London. (He admitted that it might have been the work of a Blackshirt, but the point is that it could well have been written by a Communist.) He was struck by the silliness of it, the psychological ignorance of people who had not grasped the fact that while some people would die for Churchill no one would die for cheese. But such ignorance was actually created by the study of Marxism. Loyalty to Churchill was superstructure. Only a passionate desire for cheese could drive men on to social justice.

FASCISM

The whole theory of authoritarian government, said Orwell, was summed up in Lear's couplet

'It's a fact the whole world knows,
That Pobbles are happier without their toes.'

And this is exactly why Hitler achieved such success, why he had the greater part of the German nation at his feet: he deprived them of things they really wanted.[1] One of the most interesting discoveries Orwell made was that those modern

---

1 Olaf Stapledon's Third Men did without toes quite happily, but I assume that at this stage in our evolution we are still quite attached to them.

political movements that make hedonism one of their aims tend to fail (e.g., Socialism) while those movements that demand sacrifice tend to succeed (e.g., Fascism and Communism), He recognised Hitler's astuteness in rejecting hedonism. Nearly all Western thought since the last war had tacitly assumed that human beings desired nothing beyond ease, security and the avoidance of pain. Such a view of life left no room for patriotism and the military virtues. The Socialist who found his children playing with soldiers was usually upset, but he could never thing of a substitute. Tin pacifists were not a satisfactory one. Hitler knew intuitively that human beings don't only want comfort, safety, short working hours, hygiene, birth-control and, in general, common sense; they also, at least intermittently, want struggle and self-sacrifice, not to mention drums, flags and loyalty parades.[1] However they may be as economic theories, Fascism and Nazism are psychologically far sounder than any hedonistic conception of life.

> 'All three of the great dictators have enhanced their power by imposing intolerable burdens on their peoples. Whereas Socialism and even capitalism in a more grudging way, have said to people, "I offer you a good time", Hitler has said to them, "I offer you struggle, danger and death", and as a result a whole nation flings itself at his feet.' ('Hitler', *New English Weekly*, 21 March, 1940.)

A little later Churchill was to base his war administration on this same capacity of people to endure hardship, providing there is some foreseeable goal.

During the 'thirties Socialists in particular were always careful to distinguish between Communism and Fascism. However much they might have in common as totalitarian states, the theory was that they were fundamentally quite different because they were built on opposed economic premises. Orwell was one of the first Left-wingers to stress the psychological sameness of the two systems, a point of view that is now much more widely held. However different they may have been in the beginning the tendency was for them to become more alike. Under Communism the State begins by taking complete

---

1 'It dawned upon me up there in the moon as a thing I ought always to have known, that man is not made simply to go about being safe and comfortable, and well fed and amused. Against his interest, against his happiness he is constantly being driven to do unreasonable things.' (H. G. Wells, *The First Man in the Moon*.)

control of industry, reduces the capitalist to the status of a manager, and rations consumption goods so strictly that it is impossible to spend a large income even if you have one. The result is the structure of Socialism plus the comfortless equality of war-communism. Simply in the interests of efficiency the Nazis found themselves doing the same thing, whatever ideas they had when they started out—expropriating, nationalising, destroying the very people they had ostensibly set out to save. And despite their avowed political views this process did not really worry them because their aim was power and not any particular form of society. They were not much concerned with whether they were Reds or Whites, providing they remained on top.

Orwell really believed that the extensive theorising of both Fascists and Communists had become a sham, whatever it was in the beginning. This became particularly evident when you considered the type of people who became Fascist or sympathetic to Fascism, not because they believed in one political form rather than another but because they were being driven to support a positive movement by the pressure of events. In 'Looking Back on the Spanish War' (*Such, Such Were the Joys*) he drew up a list of people who were apparently extremely diverse in their political attitudes but had one thing in common: each regarded Fascism as the ultimate champion of their own kind. The list included Hitler, Pétain, Montague Norman, Pavelitch, William Randolph Hearst, Streicher, Buchman, Ezra Pound, Juan March, Cocteau, Thyssen, Father Coughlin, The Mufti of Jerusalem, Arnold Lunn, Antonescu, Spengler, Beverley Nichols, Lady Houston and Marinetti! All these were people with something to lose or people who longed for a hierarchical society and dreaded the prospect of a world of free and equal human beings. They would have supported any system which left power in their hands, regardless of the economic form of the system. Today it is not uncommon to meet Conservatives with a sincere admiration for Soviet Russia, simply because they regard the Russian method as the only way of ensuring power in the modern world.

The path to Fascism was often unconscious and was even followed unknowingly by people of the highest integrity. In his essay on W. B. Yeats (*Critical Essays*) Orwell claimed that Yeats was well on the way to Fascism by an aristocratic route long before Fascism was heard of. Yeats, said Orwell, was a hater of democracy, of the modern world, science, machinery, the concept of progress—above all, of the idea of human equality. Such people had existed in the past, but in our world they were all necessarily gathered under the wing of Fascism, the one movement that consciously attempted to formalise these phobias. Yeats was not able to foresee the actual form that Fascism would take; he appreciated its reality, 'great wealth in a few men's hands', but he did not realise that the political Fascists would find it necessary to claim that they were fighting for justice. This was a concession to the modern spirit, for even oligarchy must win mass support. Yeats himself believed passionately in social injustice, the unspoken ideal at the heart of Fascism. He justified this view by claiming that the mass of people could not distinguish between good and evil. What he did not foresee was that an unjust society in the modern world would not be aristocratic but would be ruled by 'anonymous millionaires, shiny-bottomed bureaucrats and murdering gangsters'.

The habitual mistake of the Socialists, said Orwell, was their insistence that Fascism was merely an economic policy, a last-ditch defence of capitalism. By insisting on this they constantly underrated its political strength. Laski himself was guilty of this mistake, simplifying the issue until it became quite unreal. The thesis was that since Fascism was obviously not Socialism, it followed that it must be a form of capitalism. Capitalism, by definition, could not 'work', therefore Fascism could not 'work'. Socialist strategy was therefore to wait for Fascism to be undermined by its 'internal contradictions', to use a favourite Marxist phrase. This view simply ignored all the psychological strengths of Fascism, particularly its recruitment of all those discontents and resistances of quite ordinary people who felt bewildered by the complexity of a machine civilisation.

Holding this view, Orwell believed that Fascism had an insidious attraction for many people who were superficially appalled by its brutality. During the war he felt convinced that many of the younger intellectuals were becoming subjectively pro-Fascist, following their social instincts without fully realising their nature. In 1942 he wrote to *Partisan Review* that the quisling intellectual had become a phenomenon of the last two years. The fate of the intellectuals in France had reassured many of the younger generation, who saw that the Germans had a place in their scheme of things for the compliant writer or artist. With the careers of Drieu de la Rochelle, Pound and Celine in mind, he even felt he could make out a preliminary list of English intellectuals who would 'go over' if they had to make a choice. But by 1945 he had regretted some of the charges he had made against these people, sometimes by name, and apologised in his 'London Letter'. There is no doubt, however, that he believed the overt attitude of many people to Fascism was quite unreal and that the hidden appeal of the movement was far stronger than the average Socialist had any knowledge of.

PACIFISM

Orwell devoted a lot of time and space during the war to a consideration of Pacifism and Anarchism, and his conviction was that a totalitarian tendency was implicit in both of them. He illustrated this in his essay 'Politics *v.* Literature' (*Shooting an Elephant*). He recalled how the General Assembly of the Houyhnhnms 'exhorted' Gulliver's master to get rid of him. The significance of an 'exhortation' among the Houyhnhnms was that it could not be disregarded. In a society in which there is no law and in theory no compulsion, the only arbiter of behaviour is public opinion. But public opinion, because of the tremendous urge to conformity among gregarious animals, is less tolerant than any system of law. 'When human beings are governed by "thou shalt not", the individual can practise a certain amount of eccentricity; when they are supposedly governed by "love" or "reason", he is under continuous pressure to make him behave and think in exactly the same way as everyone else.' Orwell could have illustrated this restrictive tendency from the annals of the Godwin group, where there was more real fear of 'public opinion' than the normal individual ever has of the law in a democratic state. This is an important social discovery, that the greatest freedom can be discovered in a formally prohibitive framework.

If we accept the truth of this we might argue that most pacifists are unaware of the implications of their faith and would be alarmed if they ever realised them. But Orwell went further than this; he believed that most pacifists were in fact emotionally totalitarian in outlook and that they were more conscious of the implications than they liked others to know. In June 1943 *Tribune* published a verse 'Letter to an American Visitor' by a young pacifist using the pseudonym Obadiah Hornbooke.[1] Orwell answered this in the same form and pointed out how the pacifists continually attacked the British war effort, which was at least partially democratic (remarkably so, considering the circumstances) but he never seemed to show any concern over the tyrannies of Hitler and Stalin.

> But you don't hoot at Stalin—that's not done—
> Only at Churchill; I've no wish to praise him,
> I'd gladly shoot him when the war is won,
> Or now, if there were someone to replace him.
> But unlike some, I'll pay him what I owe him;
> There was a time when empires crashed like houses,
> And many a pink who'd titter at your poem
> Was glad enough to cling to Churchill's trousers.
> Christ! how they huddled up to one another
> Like day-old chicks about their foster-mother!

Apart from the emotional motivation of pacifism, Orwell was convinced that it was also objectively pro-Fascist. He called this elementary common sense. If you hamper the war effort of one side you automatically help that of the other. 'The idea that you can somehow remain aloof from and superior to the struggle, while living on food which British sailors have to risk their lives to bring you, is a bourgeois illusion bred of money and security.' ('Pacifism and the War', *Partisan Review*, September-October 1942). He did not feel that this objective support of Fascism was as innocent as it was professed to be. He noted how many French pacifists went over to Hitler after the fall of France and claimed that in England there was a small overlap of membership between the Peace Pledge Union and the Blackshirts. He found it difficult not to feel that pacifism was secretly inspired by an admiration for power and successful

1 This is the original spelling. A second poem by the same author was attributed to 'Obadiah Hornbrook'.

cruelty. He objected to the intellectual cowardice of people who were objectively and to some extent emotionally pro-Fascist but took refuge behind the formula, 'I am just as anti-Fascist as anyone, but——.' As a result pacifist propaganda was just as dishonest and intellectually contemptible as war propaganda. Both concentrated on putting forward a 'case', obscuring the opponent's point of view and avoiding awkward questions. The line normally followed was that 'those who fight against Fascism go Fascist themselves'. To avoid the obvious objections to this argument the pacifists used the following tricks:

'1. The fascising processes occurring in Britain as a result of war are systematically exaggerated.

'2. The actual record of Fascism, especially its pre-war history, is ignored or pooh-poohed as "propaganda". Discussion of what the world would actually be like if the Axis dominated it is evaded.

'2. Those who want to struggle against Fascism are accused of being wholehearted defenders of capitalist "democracy". The fact that the rich everywhere tend to be pro-Fascist and the working class are nearly always anti-Fascist is hushed up.

'4. It is tacitly pretended that the war is only between Britain and Germany. Mention of Russia and China, and their fate if Fascism is permitted to win, is avoided.' (' Pacifism and the War', *Partisan Review*, September-October, 1942.)

The article from which I have been quoting was actually part of a controversy between Orwell and three British pacifists. One of them, D. S. Savage, called Orwell a 'politician', with a politician's outlook on the world. He consequently saw pacifism as a political phenomenon. Savage denied this. He said it was primarily a moral phenomenon. Programme and organisation, the bases of political movements, are quite subsidiary matters to the pacifist, who is concerned with the individual conscience. Orwell replied that he simply wasn't interested in pacifism as a moral phenomenon. The brutal fact was that you could not overcome the Germany Army by lying on your back, however much you may have deplored its methods. He said he was always compelled to laugh when he heard Gandhi named as an example of the success of non-violence. Twenty years previously it had been cynically admitted in Anglo-Indian circles that Gandhi was very useful to the British Government. 'Despotic governments can stand "moral force" till the cows come home;

what they fear is physical force.' He added that though he was
not much interested in the theory of pacifism he was interested
in the psychological processes by which pacifists who started
out with a horror of violence ended with a marked tendency to
be fascinated by the success and power of Nazism.

Orwell was appalled by what he felt was the indecency of the
pacifist position. They were in the peculiar situation of being
able to conduct their propaganda only because they were protected by the people they attacked. Without 'a screen of guns'
pacifism could not have existed. Obadiah Hornbrooke had
written:

> Our work is plastered and ourselves resented—
> Our heads are bloody but we have not bent them.
> We hold no licenses, like spaniels;
> We live like lions in this den of Daniels.

Under any circumstances this would have been arrogant.
Orwell attacked with all he'd got.

> Your hands were clean and so were Pontius Pilate's,
> But as for 'bloody heads', that's just a metaphor;
> The bloody heads are on Pacific islets
> Or Russian steppes or Libyan sands—it's better for
> The health to be a C.O. than a fighter,
> To chalk a pavement doesn't need much guts,
> It pays to stay at home and be a writer
> While other talents wilt in Nissen huts;
> 'We live like lions'—yes, just like a lion,
> Pensioned on scraps in a safe cage of iron.
>
> For while you write the warships ring you round
> And flights of bombers drown the nightingales,
> And every bomb that drops is worth a pound
> To you or someone like you, for your sales
> Are swollen with those of rivals dead or silent,
> Whether in Tunis or the B.B.C.,
> And in the drowsy freedom of this island
> You're free to shout that England isn't free;
> They even chuck you cash, as bears get buns,
> For crying Peace! behind a screen of guns.

In 'Reflections on Gandhi' (*Shooting an Elephant*) he compared
Gandhi favourably with Western pacifists because he did at
least realise that it was sterile and dishonest to pretend that
both sides are as bad as each other in war and that it doesn't

matter who wins. The Western pacifists believed in their hearts (according to Orwell) that a tyranny was preferable to capitalist democracy but they would not say it openly. The Western pacifist always refused to answer awkward questions. For instance, during the late war everyone had to make up his mind about one question: 'What about the Jews? Are you prepared to see them exterminated? If not, how do you propose to save them without resorting to war?' Orwell had never heard a Western pacifist answer this question honestly, though he had heard plenty of evasions, usually of the 'you're another' type. Gandhi, in fact, did have a positive answer to this question, though it was a completely staggering one.[1] Even so, Orwell could not believe that Gandhi's methods could possibly have succeeded against a ruthless enemy. When Louis Fischer urged the Western powers to adopt Gandhiism against Russia in 1948 Orwell pointed out that Gandhi's methods were irrelevant to the existing situation because they depended on publicity. Gandhi had never had to deal with a totalitarian power. He had dealt with an old-fashioned and rather shaky despotism which treated him in a fairly chivalrous way and allowed him to appeal to world opinion at every step. He could not have applied his strategy of fasting and civil disobedience in a country where political opponents simply disappeared and the public never heard anything that the Government did not want it to hear.

Even if the attempt is made to apply pacifism to foreign politics, it either stops being pacifist or becomes appeasement. Pacifist policy must be based on the belief that all people will respond to a generous gesture—but how true is this? How will lunatics respond? Was Hitler sane? Might not one whole culture be judged insane by the standards of another?

Orwell was convinced that a pacifist policy was an incitement to slavery and twice he pointed out what he called a moral to pacifists: that the names of very few slaves had been recorded for posterity and that the best-known, Spartacus, had been a slave who refused to be a slave any longer and adopted a policy of violent resistance. During the war no group of people irritated Orwell more than the pacifists. While many of his

1 He advocated mass suicide.

points were shrewd he did tend at times to lose his usual sense of proportion. Later his natural fairness asserted itself again and twice he apologised for the exaggerations for which he felt guilty—once in a latter to *Partisan Review* and once in his *Tribune* column, 'As I Please'. Here he attacked the slack use of the word 'objectively' as in the statement, 'Pacifists are objectively aiding the Nazis', and the conclusion that personal hostility to Fascism was therefore irrelevant. He admitted that he had been guilty of saying this more than once. After the excitements and frustrations of war had passed, Orwell probably continued to believe that a pacifist outlook did inevitably help the enemy but his genuine belief in the right of the individual to his own opinion and not one imposed by others came uppermost once again and drove away his personal desire to destroy pacifist doctrine. He could not be totalitarian for long.

PATRIOTISM AND NATIONALISM

The thing that distinguished Orwell from his fellow Socialists more than anything else was his patriotism. Most Socialists, knowing that Socialism was international in its impact, assumed that it must be an enemy of patriotism. Orwell shrewdly saw that patriotism could be one of the most powerful weapons at the disposal of both Socialism and an international outlook. Love of country need not be incompatible with loyalty to mankind. In fact, he believed that a man who loved his own country and fellow-countrymen would have a better understanding of what the wider loyalty implied and demanded. But more than this, Orwell believed that in the modern world, where so many areas were subject to a hopeless tyranny, a patriotic feeling towards a relatively mild administration such as existed in England was a positive condition of revolutionary strategy. In 'Patriots and Revolutionaries' (*The Betrayal of the Left*) he drew attention to the intense patriotism of the English working class. They wished to defeat Hitler but they could not do it without a socialist revolution (so he believed at the time). The deduction from this was obvious.

'We have got to make far clearer than it has been made hitherto the fact that at this moment of time (1941) a revolutionary has to be a patriot, and a patriot has to be a revolutionary. "Do you want to defeat Hitler? Then you must be ready to sacrifice your social prestige. Do you want to establish Socialism? Then you must be ready to defend your country." That is a crude way of putting it but it is along those lines that our propaganda must move.'

It was necessary, however, to distinguish between patriotism and nationalism. By patriotism he meant devotion to a particular way of life, which one believes to be the best in the world but has no wish to force upon other people. Patriotism is of its nature defensive, both militarily and culturally. Nationalism, on the other hand, is inseparable from the desire for power. The purpose of every nationalist is to secure more power and more prestige, not for himself but for the unit in which he has chosen to sink his own individuality. He defined nationalism as power-hunger tempered by self-deception. Every nationalist is capable of the most flagrant dishonesty but he is also unshakably certain of being in the right.

In his 'Notes on Nationalism' (*Such, Such Were the Joys*) he gives examples of the kind of self-deception practised by nationalists. He divided nationalists into three groups: Positive (Neo-Tory, Celtic, Zionist), Transferred (Communist, Political Catholic, Colour Group and Class Group) and Negative (Anglophobe, Anti-Semite, Trotskyist). For each of these types there are facts which it is impossible for them to accept, even in their secret thoughts. He gives the following examples:

'*British Tory*. Britain has come out of the war with reduced power and prestige.

'*Communist*. If she had not been aided by Britain and America, Russia would have been defeated by Germany.

'*Irish Nationalist*. Eire can only remain independent because of British protection.

'*Trotskyist*. The Stalin regime is accepted by the Russian masses.

'*Pacifist*. Those who "abjure" violence can only do so because others are committing violence on their behalf.'

The group in which Orwell took the most interest was the Communist. During the nineteen-thirties most of the transferred nationalist sentiment in Britain accrued to the Communists and Soviet Russia. By about 1930 there was no activity, with the possible exception of scientific research, the arts and Left-wing politics, that a thinking person could believe in. The civilisation of the West had been so successfully debunked that few intelligent people could gain any satisfaction from a normal bourgeois career as soldier, clergyman, stockbroker or Indian Civil Servant. All the old values—patriotism, religion, the Empire, the family, the sanctity of marriage, the old school tie, birth, breeding, honour, discipline—had come to look pretty tawdry. But by getting rid of these things you did not get rid of the need to believe in something. Some frustrated young men had entered the Catholic Church, although its appeal did not persist for long. But it was significant that this Church had a worldwide organisation and a rigid discipline, and had more power and prestige than any other. But the organisation that did win allegiance on a really large scale from among these dispossessed young men was the Communist Party. It gave them something to believe in and it was something that had not yet been discredited as the Catholic Church had on so many occasions. It was to them a Church, an army, an orthodoxy and a discipline. It even gave them a new Fatherland (they had rejected their own) and after 1935 a Führer. All the loyalties and superstitions that the intellect had seemingly banished could come rushing back under the thinnest of disguises. Russia and Stalin filled the vacuum created by the corrosion of bourgeois values—a situation corresponding fairly closely to the modern 'failure of nerve'. God was Stalin, the devil was Hitler, Heaven was Moscow and Hell was Berlin. A new cosmogony and pantheon ready-made. Orwell concluded that the Communism of the British intellectual was easily explicable. It was merely the patriotism of the deracinated.

POLITICAL PROPHECY

Orwell was much addicted to political prophecy and his prophecies were usually wrong. This is rather troubling to someone, such as myself, who believes he had a sane and balanced outlook on the political arena. On the other hand there is no logical reason why an analytical understanding of politics should contain within it the capacity to foresee the future. In fact, there is a certain amount of comfort to be gained from his failure as a prophet: it encourages us to believe that the society he describes in *1984* is the less likely to occur.

In 'Toward European Unity' (*Partisan Review*, July-August, 1947) he said that if he were a bookmaker he would give odds against the survival of civilisation during the next few hundred years. He foresaw three possibilities:

1. The U.S.A. might use the atomic bomb while the Russians hadn't got it, and thus eliminate them. This possibility no longer exists.
2. The cold war will continue until several countries have atomic bombs, which they will then let loose. This will be the end of machine civilisation and the world will be once again inhabited by a few million people practising subsistence agriculture.
3. Fear of the atomic bomb will result in the division of the world into two or three superstates, with a semi-divine caste at the top and abject slavery at the bottom. (This is the alternative he selected for *1984*.)

He sometimes wondered if it was childish or morbid to terrify himself with visions of such a future. He decided that it wasn't because in 1925 the world of today would have seemed a nightmare that could not possibly come true. This is merely a statement that the world of 1984 is not impossible, not a piece of evidence that it is likely.

And yet it is strange that he believed most political prediction was the product of wishful-thinking. Many people have noticed how bitter the Orwell of *1984* seemed compared with the author of, say, *Animal Farm*, which is aglow with good humour, and they have attributed it to his bad health. It is possible that pain had caused him to hate the world and helped project his nightmare. During the war he noticed that military prediction was a direct reflection of a person's political beliefs. Communists, for instance, were certain that Rommel would take Cairo because they wanted him to (to discredit the British), while *he* felt sure that Rommel would not take Cairo because he didn't want him to. He realised that all his predictions were coloured by his love of England while the predictions of Communists were coloured by their hatred of England. He admitted that there were other occasions when his love of England caused him to form a false picture of political developments. He hated to see England humiliated or humiliating anyone else. He wanted to see England win the war but he hoped post-war England would not be stained by the class distinctions and imperialist exploitation that had existed before the war. For this reason he over-emphasised the anti-Fascist character of the war, exaggerated the social changes that were occurring and underrated the strength of the forces of reaction.

One would have expected Orwell to have been quite confident of a Labour victory in the 1945 election. He certainly wanted it and no one who mixed with the electorate at large was surprised by it, but only by the size of it. Yet he predicted in a letter to *Partisan Review* (Summer 1945) a narrow Conservative win, although he realised the tide was turning against them. In his later years, however, he suffered the disability of all prominent journalists and politicians—he lost touch with a sufficiently large number of average people to be able to form an accurate judgment of their opinions. Also, realising his tendency to foresee what he wanted to happen, he probably allowed too much compensation when making forecasts. It was partly his honesty which led him to retreat to Jura. He was isolated there, it is true, but at least he was not subject to the hothouse atmosphere of Fleet Street.

By the winter of 1945 he was admitting in another London Letter that he had been quite wrong in believing that it would be impossible to win the war without first making it a revolutionary war. It was this belief, he said, that led him to over-value Common Wealth. He consoled himself with the belief that everyone was wrong. No one, neither Socialist nor capitalist nor imperialist, had been right in his predictions. He had been equally wrong in his assessments of other probabilities. After the dissolution of the Comintern he had believed that the British Communist Party, left without guidance, would either wither away or become less rigid and less Russophile under more enlightened leadership. Neither of these things happened. At first sight it is surprising that political prophecy is just as inaccurate in these days of scientific political study as it always was in the past. In fact, although it is impossible to measure, it is probably more inaccurate. But on reflection it seems very likely that this is a direct result of scientific, analytical study of human behaviour. Orwell himself attributed it to the intellectual habit of making *a priori* judgments and then casting around for facts to support them. Although it would be possible to make the necessary calculations to decide whether the U.S.S.R., Britain or the U.S.A. had contributed most to the defeat of Germany, in practice no one would do this because he would regard the whole question as a matter of prestige. This is the reason why none of the 'experts' were able to forecast the Russo-German pact of 1939; friends of Russia were unable to envisage an agreement with the Fascist beasts and the enemies of Russia were usually people who inwardly regarded Germany as a defence against Bolshevism.

This is perhaps not a very agreeable section to the fervent admirer of Orwell—although it was easy to admire his writing without sharing his political views. But Orwell's natural honesty makes it very easy to forgive and forget. Writing in 'As I Please' on 17 December, 1943, he said:

> 'One way of feeling infallible is not to keep a diary. Looking back through the diary I kept in 1940 and 1941 I find that I was usually wrong when it was possible to be wrong. Yet I was not so wrong as the Military Experts. Experts of various schools were telling us in 1939 that the Maginot Line was impregnable, and that the Russo-German pact had put an end to Hitler's eastward expansion; in early 1940 they were telling us that the days of tank warfare were over; in mid-1940 they were telling us that the Germans would invade Britain forthwith; in mid-1941. that the Red Army would fold up in six weeks; in December 1941 that Japan would collapse after ninety days; in July 1942 that Egypt was lost—and so on, more or less indefinitely.
>
> 'Where now are the men who told us those things? Still on the job, drawing fat salaries. Instead of the unsinkable battleship we have the unsinkable Military Expert.'

You may also remember that in 1939 it was alleged that oil shortage would not allow Germany to continue the war for more than two years at the most; and in 1943 it was alleged that the Japanese were capable of holding out for thirty years at the least. Orwell may have been wrong, but he did a service in drawing attention to the misdeeds of the military tipster, who was protected by the same kind of amnesia that protects Old Moore and the newspaper stargazers.

Chapter XI

'Animal Farm'

IN HIS revaluation of *Animal Farm* in *World Review* (June 1950) Tom Hopkinson says that this novel is one of the two modern works of fiction before which the critic must abdicate. The other is Koestler's *Darkness at Noon*. There is so much truth in this that I find it very difficult to say anything useful about the book and yet a study of Orwell cannot ignore it altogether. It has been constantly compared with *Gulliver's Travels*, not because there is any real similarity of treatment but because each is a political satire and *Animal Farm* will probably appeal to posterity in the same way that Swift's book appeals to us today, as a charming fairy tale especially suitable for children. Politics is a grim study and it has its revenge by winning the admiration of children for some of its major literary productions. It should be remembered that many of our nursery rhymes, when they are not the product of sexuality, are the product of political controversy.

All the useful things that can be said about *Animal Farm* at this early stage have already been said. Perhaps, three hundred years later, critics will find hidden significances which we cannot grasp as contemporaries, just as *Gulliver's Travels* continues to yield its meanings, some of them having been elucidated by Orwell himself. It is the work of a man whose literary personality has evolved into maturity and good-temper, even when dealing with matters about which he feels keenly. It is the task of the artist to uphold the right of individual judgment, but this is normally done shrilly and with exaggeration. Orwell had reached the point where his emotions were held in check by his reason at a fine point of balance. It is not a position that can be maintained for long. By the time he wrote *1984* his emotions had spilled over and weighed down what he would have called his common sense. He did not retreat into shrillness but into its opposite, a monotony of the spirit.

Animal Farm is written on many levels. It is already a children's story in its own right. It is an attack on Stalinism—and it should be pointed out that it is an attack from the Left. Right-wing journalists tried to extract more comfort from it than was warranted. I have shown how Orwell believed that one of the difficulties Socialists had to content with is the familiar belief that Soviet Russia is Socialist, and that therefore any criticism of Russia is a criticism of Socialism. *Animal Farm* is a Socialist's mockery at the expense of Soviet Russia. It contains very little real comfort for an English Conservative because it will make very few converts. Most Englishmen believed in *Animal Farm* before it was written, but they were delighted by the form in which their beliefs appeared. The book is also a lament for the fate of revolutions and the hopes contained in them. It is a moving comment on man's constant compromise with the truth. In a very short compass it contains most of Orwell's main ideas about men and politics.

In *Horizon* Cyril Connolly welcomed the book for three reasons. It broke down some of the artificial reserve with which Russia was always written about. Orwell would have put it more strongly, as he did in his reply to Obadiah Hornbooke and in many of his reviews. It restored the allegorical pamphlet to its rightful place as a literary force and it proved that Orwell had not been entirely seduced away by the opinion-airing attractions of weekly journalism from his true vocation, which was to write books. There is considerable substance in this last point. *Animal Farm* appeared in 1945 and was the first book of his since *The Lion and the Unicorn* (1941). Between these two publications appeared many of his London Letters to *Partisan Review* and his reviews and 'As I Please' column in *Tribune*, writing which was nearly always spoilt by a too-clever-by-half attitude and an irritating brand of plausibility which often did anything but convince. *Animal Farm* proved that his literary powers remained undamaged.

There is only one thing to do with *Animal Farm* at this stage, apart from reading it. (That is both easy and pleasant and anyone who reads this book as an open-sesame to Orwell will be disappointed. My main aim is to collate his scattered journalism and relate it with his more easily obtainable books. I'm damned if I'm going to encourage laziness.) The only thing I can usefully attempt to do is to help those readers who have not got the political background necessary to a full appreciation of the book. It is too often assumed that the post-Revolution history of Russia is known to everybody. My own generation was stuffed with Five Year Plans and Moscow Trials and Right-Wing Deviationists and Left-Wing Infantilists, but there is at least one younger generation which knows nothing of these things, except by hearsay, as everyone knows of the retreat from Moscow and Marie Antoinette's dairy, i.e., doesn't know them at all but shares a kind of cultural memory. The average Boots subscriber or Public Library borrower does not know whom Snowball, Squealer and Boxer represent. They don't have to know, but all good books improve on a wider acquaintance.

This will not be exegesis. Here and there I intend to quote from two books critical of the Soviet Union to illustrate the significance of Orwell's satire. Orwell had read both these books and he received one. They are *The Life and Death of Stalin* by Louis Fischer (which I shall refer to as Fischer) and *The Real Soviet Russia* by David J. Dallin (Dallin). I am only quoting from two books because I simply wish to illustrate the political attitude expressed in *Animal Farm*. In other words, an exhaustive treatment or a critical survey is not part of my purpose. It is merely to transfer the allegory of *Animal Farm* into the political realities (or possibly illusions) which it represents.

When the animals of Manor Farm rose against the farmer and threw him out they reorganised the farm on the basis of the equality of all animals. So great was the enthusiasm, the symbols of revolution and equality acquired a stronger hold on the animal mind than the realities of the situation. Boxer the carthorse, for instance, threw his straw hat (which had been used to keep the flies out of his ears) on the fire. This made life rather more unpleasant for Boxer but he was determined to destroy anything which had become associated with slavery. He was a Stakhanovite who would suffer any hardship to prove he was not a slave. Not all had this spirit of mingled pride and servility. Mollie, the white mare, had to be reproached for her continued love of finery and coloured ribbons. It was stressed that all free and equal animals should not only do without decoration but were better naked.

The leaders of the revolution were Snowball and Napoleon, sometimes referred to in history books and newspapers as Trotsky and Stalin. Snowball was an intellectual pig who was capable of enshrining the principles of the revolution in Seven Commandments. The majority of animals could not grasp these principles, however (partly because of the high illiteracy rate), and Snowball therefore farrowed them all down into one admirably simple slogan: 'Four legs good, two legs bad', which was equivalent to saying that all animals were not equal because bourgeois human animals were intrinsically inferior to proletarian inhuman animals. But this idea delighted the sheep, who learnt to refer to themselves as 'masses', a term borrowed from physics and having a modern feel to it.

The revolution had not eliminated stupidity, of course, and some of the more stupid animals believed that all animals had the same physical needs. Squealer, who edited *Pravda*, explained that Science (a substitute for Mr Jones's effete God) had proved that brain-workers (pigs, on the whole) needed special foods. As a result, milk and apples were reserved for the pigs. If they didn't have the vitamins contained in these succulent foods Mr Jones would come back. That was so obvious it didn't need proof, only assertion.

Then came the dispute between Snowball-Trotsky and Napoleon-Stalin. Snowball was a brilliant speaker, but Napoleon cut the cackle and quietly won support behind the scenes. Snowball was full of schemes for the scientific improvement of the farm. Napoleon had no schemes but always said Snowball's would come to nothing. Snowball was finally chased from the farm by specially trained dogs and was seen no more; but like Julius Caesar, his spirit lived on. Napoleon was now immersed in plans for improving administration. He saw how ridiculous it was to expect the average ignorant animal to know what was best for him, and substituted a special committee of pigs for the weekly meeting. The dog-Ogpu and the pig-Commissars were really much more efficient than the incompetent rank-and-file. Besides, they were leading lives of self-sacrifice because all their activity was devoted to the welfare of the farm. It wasn't really necessary for the others to participate. Squealer explained all this very patiently and honest old Boxer adopted a new motto, 'Napoleon is always right'.

One of Snowball's chief crimes had been to suggest the building of a new windmill. This was typical of Snowball's method of sabotage: no one wanted a windmill, it was in fact an attempt to reintroduce slavery. Soon after Snowball's banishment, however, Napoleon decided to build the windmill after all. It then became known that he had in fact made the original suggestion but Snowball had stolen his plans—further proof of his Fascist humanity, if such were needed. Some of the animals were puzzled to know why Napoleon had opposed his own plans. Squealer explained that this was known as Tactics. It had been absolutely necessary to rid the farm of Snowball and this had provided the opportunity. The animals were delighted by Napoleon's cunning and frequently called it wisdom.

('Stalin's programme of rapid industrialisation and collectivisation was taken from the "platform" of the Trotskyist opposition, but only after the suppression of the opposition at the end of the 'twenties. The authors of the policy were Trotsky, Zinoviev and Preobrazhensky . . .'—Dallin.)

In a continued campaign to destroy even the memory of slavery Napoleon now instituted a sixty-hour week. (Just a little later the oppressed creatures on French Farm were compelled to adopt a forty-hour week, despite all resistance—a typical example of bourgeois farm practice.) Sunday work was also introduced, although this was entirely voluntary, Animal Farm being now the home of the free. Animals who refused Sunday work had their rations reduced by one-half.

The next step was to start trade with some of the other farms in the neighbourhood. This again worried some of the animals, who believed in their pathetic ignorance that they had agreed at some time in the past never to resume dealings with human beings. Napoleon announced that no ordinary animal need ever meet a human being (an agent was to be employed) and Squealer explained how the supposed ban on intercourse with human beings was another of the lies circulated by Snowball.

The animals made a similar mistake when the pigs moved into the farmhouse and started sleeping in beds. Nobody but Snowball could have been malicious enough to suggest that sleeping in beds was wrong. So long as there were no sheets it was a perfectly normal practice for brain-workers who needed peace and quiet. Snowball's infamy became apparent when the windmill was blown down. A price was actually set on the head of this modern Aeolus who was prepared to ruin the work of simple farm animals out of a spirit of petty personal spite.

Despite the efforts of the animals and Boxer's new determination, 'I will work harder', the food situation got worse and worse. The corn ration was drastically reduced and the potato crop was frosted in the clamps, which had not been covered thickly enough. Stories about starvation on Animal Farm began to circulate among the bourgeois human neighbours. Mr Whymper, the agent, was taken on conducted tours through the farmyard and was shown bins overflowing with corn (there was sand underneath, but he didn't know that) and introduced to selected animals, mostly sheep, who could be relied upon to mention the recent increase in rations. (It is believed that Mr Whymper was a member of the Society for Cultural Relations with Soviet Russia.) Shortly after this came the first real signs of discontent. Peasant-hens were ordered to surrender all eggs to the community. There followed a wave of egg-smashing until Napoleon ordered the hens' rations to be stopped. They held out for five days, then went back to their nesting boxes, while the dead ones were buried (victims of coccidiosis) and the truth was kept from Mr Whymper.

It was hardly possible to keep up with Snowball's activities by now. He was everywhere—stealing into the farm by night, stealing corn, upsetting milk-pails, breaking eggs, actually milking the cows during their sleep. In all these forays he was assisted by Fascist rats which still managed to persist on the farm despite the stern discipline and the obvious advantages to all animals of porcine benevolence. It was then discovered that Snowball had actually sold himself to Frederick of Pinchfield Farm, who was plotting to attack them and take away their land. He had even been in league with Jones from the start! Frederick had a toothbrush moustache and a flop of hair over one eye—Orwell does not tell us this, but Frederick was well known. It was absolutely necessary that all animals should show increased vigilance against the machinations of Snowball and his cosmopolitan allies.

('. . . the *Propagandist* openly demanded action against two dangers existing on the ideological front. The first was "baseless cosmopolitanism", a synonym for Trotskyism.'—Dallin.)

Once again the animals discovered how easily memory can play tricks. They seemed to remember Snowball fighting bravely at the Battle of the Cowshed and now Squealer was telling them that in fact Snowball had tried to lure them to their doom. Boxer was puzzled. He thought he could remember Snowball shedding his own blood and receiving the award of Animal Hero, First Class. Squealer explained with admirable patience. Jones's shot had only grazed Snowball (it was all prearranged) and had it not been for Napoleon Snowball would have led the animals into ignoble retreat. Boxer still felt troubled until he heard that Comrade Napoleon himself had stated (categorically) that Snowball was a traitor. Since nothing like Napoleon had been known since God retired from human affairs, this was proof enough. The situation had now become so serious Napoleon ordered Snowball's agents, still at large on the farm, to be arrested. These were four pigs who had objected to the cancellation of the Sunday meetings and three hens who had been ringleaders in the egg rebellion. These seven suddenly confessed that they had been in touch with Snowball ever since his expulsion and had their throats torn out by the Ogpu-dogs. Then others came forward with similar confessions and the air was heavy with the smell of blood.

The animals were extremely perturbed. It seemed obvious to Boxer that the fault lay in themselves and that the only way of purging the sense of sin they all felt was through harder work. But Clover, the other cart-horse, felt that something serious had gone wrong. They had not carried through a revolution so that they might set about killing each other. She realised now that no one dared speak his mind, that fierce dogs roamed everywhere and the strong no longer protected the weak as they had done immediately after Jones's expulsion. Of course, life was still better than it had been in Jones's day but somehow it wasn't good enough. Clover dejectedly began to sing *Beasts of England*, the Interanimale song, and the others took it up. Then came Squealer, attended by two dogs, announcing that by special decree of Comrade Napoleon the song *Beasts of England* had been forbidden. There were perfectly sound reasons for this. The song had been a song of rebellion, expressing their longing for a better society. Now the rebellion was completed and the better society had come, so that the song was an anachronism. A new song was substituted but it never took their imagination like the first one had done.

All through this time the original Seven Commandments had been altered to suit new demands. Now, for instance, the Sixth Commandment had had two words added, or perhaps they had been there originally but had slipped from the animals' memory: 'No animals shall kill any other animal *without cause*'. Sometimes the animals felt that they were working even longer hours than they had done in Jones's day but they were reassured by Squealer's announcement that the production of every class of foodstuff had risen by 200 per cent or 300 per cent or even 500 per cent—very gratifying figures, though the animals felt they would like more food as well as figures.

There was no doubt about it, the wonderful advances that had been made on Animal Farm were entirely due to the wisdom and leadership of Comrade Napoleon. Hens would proclaim their debt to Napoleon when they laid five eggs in six days and cows would praise Napoleon for the excellence of the drinking water in the pool. Minimus, a poet and cousin to Mayakovsky, composed a remarkable ode which began:

> Friend of the fatherless!
> Fountain of happiness!
> Lord of the swill-bucket! Oh, how my soul is on
> Fire when I gaze at thy
> Calm and commanding eye,
> Like the sun in the sky,
> Comrade Napoleon!

> ['The world has no person
> Dearer, closer.
> With him, happiness is happier,
> And the sun brighter.'
> (*Hymn to J. V. Stalin*—Fischer.)]

There followed some extremely complicated dealings with Frederick. Of all the humans Frederick was the most utterly human and no decent animal would ever have anything to do with him. But once again the animals had been deceived; it turned out that Frederick was really less human than Pilkington, whom they had always supposed to be doddery and decadent. In fact, Snowball's relations had not been with Frederick but with Pilkington. For this reason Napoleon sold a pile of timber to Frederick, and at a much higher price than anyone had expected.

('When Hitler locked horns with France and England, Stalin increased his shipments of strategic materials to Germany. In 1938, for instance, Russia sold Germany 33,154 tons of oil: in 1940, 700,000 tons.'—Fischer.)

But Frederick was, after all, only human for he paid for the timber with forged cheques and then attacked the farm. However, the animals won a splendid victory under the glorious leadership of Napoleon.

There was no doubt about it, the pigs were beginning to live in a style and with a degree of luxury that had not been seen since the days of Jones. In their dim way the animals believed, for instance, that they were forbidden to drink alcohol but it was brought to their notice that the rubric only forbade them to drink it to excess. Then Squealer fell from a ladder under mysterious circumstances and was escorted back to the farmhouse by the dogs. This did not mean that there was any connection between alcohol and falling off a ladder, although Behjamin the donkey had a very knowing air about the whole affair. In general, the pigs and the dogs appeared to be leading a different kind of life from the rest of the animals.

('In the remote Soviet past, officers and soldiers in the Red Army wore uniforms of the same material and were equal except in their duties. Today, the officers are decked in epaulets, braids, fine clothing and all the accoutrements of a caste army, occupy the best apartments and impose strict discipline on shabby privates who no longer may mingle with officers. Officers have clubs, messes, and entertainment barracks to which soldiers have no access.'—Fischer.)

Writing about the new Soviet upper class in 1947, Orwell drew attention to the counter-revolutionary attempt to acquire a sense of superiority over the common people, expressed in a determination to have fine clothes and furniture, to own a gramophone, a wireless, to ride in 'soft' railways cars regularly used only by Government employees, to enjoy holidays in 'rest homes' restricted to their own use, to eat in restaurants operated for the special use of Soviet employees. Napoleon and his pigs undoubtedly had a good precedent.

Life for the common animal was hard, much harder than it was for the uncommon pig, but there were compensations—far more songs, speeches and processions than they had ever had before. Napoleon ordered a Spontaneous Demonstration to be held each week to celebrate the struggles and triumphs of Animal Farm. The animals enjoyed these demonstrations, especially the sheep, who could work themselves into a patriotic frenzy chanting 'Four legs good, two legs bad'. It was pleasant to be reminded so often that now they were their own masters and to forget for at least part of the time that they were hungry. Moses the raven, who used to preach about Sugarcandy Mountain where all good animals would one day rest from their labours, was allowed to return and he was even given an allowance of beer a day to lubricate his throat.

('In 1944 Stalin was eager to have the sympathy of Roman Catholics. He anticipated resistance in puppet Poland and thought popular support might be won by smiling on the Vatican. Stalin accordingly gave an audience to Father Orlewnanski, a Catholic parish priest of Polish origin from Springfield, Massachusetts, who, he vainly hoped, would sway Catholic opinion in Poland and Rome in favour of Russia. Stalin also wrote a conciliatory letter to the Pope.'—Fischer.)

An atrocious rumour was spread around the farm that faithful old Boxer had been taken away to the knacker's yard. Again Squealer had to explain that deviationists had been at work (undoubtedly Snowball) and he gave an affecting account of Boxer's last moments in a neighbouring hospital. Napoleon himself gave a short oration in Boxer's honour and commended him to them all as an example. The pigs held a memorial banquet and even managed to get enough money from somewhere to buy a case of whisky.

By now the farm population had grown and there was a new generation of animals who knew nothing of the Rebellion, except as a tradition. On the whole they were fine upstanding beasts, willing workers and good comrades, but very stupid. They believed everything they were told about the Rebellion and the principles of Animalism, but it was doubtful whether they understood much of it. The farm was much richer than it had been in the old days, though the animals themselves were no richer, except for the pigs and the dogs. This was partly because there were so many pigs and dogs, which didn't leave much over for the others. It must never be supposed that they did not work—they did, and very hard, but it was a different kind of work from farm work, something to do with 'files', 'reports', 'minutes' and 'memoranda'.

The Rebellion really reached its culmination, even if a late one, when the pigs began walking on two legs. Some of them were rather unsteady, but not Comrade Napoleon. He walked majestically upright, with his dogs gambolling around him, and he carried a whip in his trotter. The other animals were at first amazed, but the pigs, with their innate sense of rightness, suddenly set up a tremendous bleating of 'Four legs good, two legs better!' And then they discovered that the Seven Commandments had been replaced by one comprehensive Commandment which ran:

> ALL ANIMALS ARE EQUAL
> BUT SOME ANIMALS ARE MORE
> EQUAL THAN OTHERS

Next day all the pigs carried whips in their trotters and were busy buying wireless sets, installing telephones and taking out subscriptions to *John Bull*, *Tit-Bits* and the *Daily Mirror*.

('"These people think that Socialism requires equality, equality in the needs and personal life of the members of society", Stalin declared in 1934. "These are petty bourgeois views of our left-wing scatterbrains".'—Dallin.)

There had to be a celebration of this new twist in the theory of Animalism, naturally, and the pigs arranged a magnificent party to which they invited all the neighbours of Animal Farm —which they now gave its original name, Manor Farm. The animals could not restrain their curiosity and crept into the farmyard and peered through the dining-room window. They

heard Mr Pilkington make a speech in which he congratulated
the pigs on the low rations, the long working hours and the
general absence of pampering on Manor Farm. Napoleon
replied with great dignity and they all drank each other's
health. This was followed by a card game, which ended in
uproar, because both Napoleon and Pilkington had played an
ace of spades simultaneously. The bewildered animals glanced
from face to face, from man to pig and from pig to man, and
realised that it was quite impossible to say which was which.

Chapter XII

War Correspondent

A YEAR after he had finished writing *Animal Farm* Orwell became War Correspondent for the *Observer*. This was in the closing stages of the war and just after the collapse of Germany, and extended from February to June 1945. This period did not have any important formative influence on Orwell's political thought, which had matured by now, but I will summarise it briefly because it helps bridge the gap between his best book and his most ambitious book.

First of all he went to Paris. There he found a food shortage, a lack of coal and gas in the necessary quantity, no taxis, and the streets only half-lit. But Paris wore still a gay face: the girls were as carefully made up as ever and the hat shops and jewellery stores were full. Somehow, too, Paris had managed to escape bare feet and rags. Politically, he encountered the fact that every Englishman in France encounters, that the Frenchman has a far tougher attitude towards the Germans than the Englishman can understand. Many of the old 'progressive' trends in French politics seemed to have disappeared, swallowed up by the dominant anti-Germanism. Pacifism was only a memory and a militarily strong France was a universal demand. He felt that respect for democracy had probably weakened—not for the first time in modern France. The old conflict between Catholics and anti-clericals, which to Englishmen always sounds like a throwback to the Enlightenment, was in full vigour again. De Gaulle was trying to interest Frenchmen in the struggle in Indo-China, but the mention of imperialism does not rouse the emotions of the French, either one way or the other, as it does the English. In his reporting Orwell tended to concentrate on differences. In this way he managed to convey a sense of strangeness which is probably a good grounding for

political understanding. Without such a grounding far too
many people were prone to urge collective farms on the British
or the British party system on the French.

Next month he was in Cologne, where the destruction was
greater than any outsider could possibly imagine. The centre
of the city was 'simply a chaos of jagged walls, overturned
trams, shattered statues, and enormous piles of rubble out of
which iron girders thrust themselves like sticks of rhubarb'.
Again he looked for and found differences, this time between
Nazi propaganda and reality. The people were not the blond
giants of Goebbels's and Rosenberg's imagination but were
rather like the Belgians across the frontier except that they had
been better fed and were still better dressed. They seemed aloof
and hostile and he felt he saw in their eyes an expression of
shame—but merely for having lost the war.

When he considered the reconstruction of Germany he
adopted his familiar method of tabulating the reactions of
observers—presumably other newspaper men and the soldiers.
There were three things they were all saying. 'The people at
home have no conception of this.' 'It's a miracle that they've
gone on fighting.' 'Just think of the work of building this all up
again!' He took the opportunity to restate one of his convictions
about war, that bombing is not particularly inhumane and that
the bombing plane is a comparatively civilised weapon because
it is used to paralyse industry and transport rather than to kill
human beings. Moreover, bombs kill a cross-section of the
population rather than concentrating on healthy young men
as all previous weapons had done. The people of Britain, due
to the partial immunity from the worst consequences of war,
were feeling guilty about the wrong thing. It was not the loss of
life that was a danger to Germany and the world but the
frightful destruction which would ensure a long period of
impoverishment.

'To walk through the ruined cities of Germany is to feel an
actual doubt about the continuity of civilisation. For one has to
remember that it is not only Germany that has been blitzed. The
same desolation extends, at any rate in considerable patches, all
the way from Brussels to Stalingrad. And when there had been
ground fighting the destruction is even more thorough than where
there has merely been bombing. In the three hundred miles or so

between the Marne and the Rhine there is not, for instance, such a thing as a bridge or a viaduct that has not been blown up.' (8 April, 1945.)

After a brief return visit to Paris where he noted the obvious delight of the Displaced Persons at escaping from the Germans, he went on to Nuremberg. He watched German prisoners being brought in to a village, while gunfire could be heard from over a hillside. Apart from a little knot of elderly people the villagers paid less attention to the arrival of the American Army than they would have given to a passing circus. These people regarded the continuation of the war as lunacy and felt no sense of responsibility. Some civilians had even applied for protection against the vengeful D.P.s and for anti-aircraft guns for protection against German planes!

A week later he was in Stuttgart with the U.S. Third Army. Here again, watching German prisoners being rounded up, he noticed the gulf that existed between the Anglo-Saxon and the Continental European in their attitudes to treatment of the enemy. The French seemed to gain pleasure from the humiliation of Germans. The Germans themselves were consequently hoping that the greater part of Germany would be occupied by British and American troops, and as little as possible by French and Russian. They were shrewdly claiming that the various governments of the United Nations were not in 'substantial agreement'.

In May he returned to Paris where he noticed that the women's hats were more flamboyant than ever. Although he sensed a leftward swing, Paris was not behaving as though the war still continued. He was puzzled by the combination of apathy and revolutionary sentiment. The French were far more interested in internal affairs than in the war. France's principal act of war had been the Resistance, which involved only a minority, and the number of people directly engaged in the war effort was tiny compared with Britain. Everyone wanted France to reappear as a great power but there was little inclination to concern oneself with the necessary details. There were long cinema queues and a large proportion of the dwindled press was devoted to sport. He found the Victory celebrations impressive but the older people said they did not compare very well with 1918. (Of course, they never do.)

In Austria he noted the enormous number of military prisoners. The military government was very successful from a short-term viewpoint, i.e., restoring a wrecked city to order, but it was handicapped by having no long-term objectives. The Anglo-Saxon's pride in his political ignorance appeared to Orwell to be extremely dangerous in such a context. When you asked a military government official any question that touched on politics the stock answer was: 'I wouldn't know'. One such official 'wouldn't know' the difference between a Social Democrat and a Christian Socialist. The policy was considered admirably impartial but it was irritating to the people whose country was being administered and it could be insulting. He found considerable evidence to show that the average Austrian both feared and hated the Russians.

Orwell felt the chief political danger in Germany would be the division of control among the United Nations. Even before the fighting stopped the different powers were competing for the allegiance of the German people. The majority of Germans did not welcome Russian control but they knew the food situation might be difficult in the West. In his last dispatch from the continent he noticed some anomalies in the D.P. situation. At first they welcomed the liberators, but soon their enthusiasm began to decrease, especially when their rations were cut to feed the Germans. With characteristic fairness Orwell attacked the term 'slave labour'. Some of the D.P.s, he said, had volunteered and most were not ill-treated. A few, even including Frenchmen, did not wish to return. There were also large numbers of non-Germans serving in the Wehrmacht and Todt organisation (including Russians, Poles and Czechs). Some of these had changed their ideological grounds, some were adventurers and some were ignorant peasants. It is a useful reminder, however, that many people, perhaps a majority, have no firm political opinions and some of them are not even deeply influenced by national mythologies.

Chapter XIII

'Nineteen Eighty-Four'

ALL THE early work was really preparation for *1984*, although I do not mean by this that the *1984* he actually wrote was the inevitable product of the earlier development. I simply mean that in view of his growing absorption in the dominant aspects of the modern state it seemed natural that he should ultimately give a picture of the future state, the state towards which all others were tending. That the picture he did give us was almost devoid of hope was not entirely due to the existing situation; his now deteriorating health must have been an important factor. In his earlier work we can find hints in abundance of the malevolent superstate that might be building, but not until the end do we have the conviction that the worst must triumph. In fact, one of the weaknesses of this book lies in its utter surrender to a thoroughgoing spirit of rationalism. Criticism today tends to be too slavishly rational. The best criticism always allows for loopholes, and is partly based on the knowledge that rationalism is never the whole truth. *1984* is a completely rational demonstration of the victory of irrationalism in politics and human society. The corrective it needs is the irrational faith that rational behaviour will never be wholly abandoned.

The best analysis of the political basis of the society existing in 1984 is contained in the work of the system's chief enemy, Emmanuel Goldstein, and was to be found in his book, *The Theory and Practice of Oligarchical Collectivism*. It is doubtful if such a person as Goldstein ever existed, but he is as necessary to social discipline in the superstate of Oceania as Trotsky had been to Soviet Russia and Snowball to Animal Farm. Goldstein's analysis consisted of two parts, the War Situation and Party Control. It is possible to state his view of the War

237

Situation in a series of propositions. There is no doubt at all that Goldstein's analysis is accepted as a true one by Orwell. As Goldstein's book had been in all probability written by a member of the Inner Party of Oceania, it is also an official picture of the situation. It gives the truth that no one must know—no one, that is, except a few trusted leaders who will regard it as the basis of power and not of revolution.

The first proposition is that three great superstates exist and necessarily exist. None desires to defeat the other. Orwell discovered this conception of the political future in James Burnham's *The Managerial Revolution*. Although he was critical of much in this book he found it the most fruitful of all modern books of political speculation.

There is a state of permanent war but it is a contest of limited aims between combatants who cannot destroy each other. The war cannot be decisive. It is merely a struggle for possession of the equatorial quadrilateral and the northern ice-cap.

The disputed territories are reserves of cheap labour. The structure and process of world society would not be different without it.

The primary aim of the war is to use up the products of industry without raising the general standard of living. An all-round increase of wealth would threaten the destruction of hierarchical society. The masses could not be kept in poverty by the restriction of production because this always aroused opposition. Therefore the essential act of war was the destruction of the products of human labour. War accomplishes destruction in a psychologically acceptable way. All Party members believe passionately in the war.

The Party has two aims: to conquer the world and to extinguish the possibility of independent thought. The subject matter of scientific research has shrunk to methods of mass production and the detection of thought. As none of the states comes near conquering the others, however, the war deteriorates into a series of skirmishes. The protagonists store atomic bombs and the art of war remains stationary. No state risks defeat and frontiers are only crossed by missiles.

The conditions of life and the prevailing philosophies in the

three states are very similar. In the past, society had been kept
in touch with 'reality' (i.e., the fundamentals of living) by war.
When war becomes continuous it ceases to be dangerous, or at
least to appear dangerous. Efficiency is no longer necessary and
any perversion of thought may be practised—but by the rulers
only. The war is in fact an imposture. In each case it is a purely
internal affair. Each state is virtually a self-contained universe.

In Goldstein's book the analysis of the war situation comes
in its logical position, after the analysis of party control. Winston
Smith, however, reads them in reverse order, presumably
because for the English reader (not him, but us) a prevalent
war or near-war situation is closer to our present reality than
the organisation of a totalitarian state.

The first proposition in this section is that society had always
consisted of three classes, the High, the Middle and the Low,
and that it had always been the aim of the Middle to replace the
High by recruiting the support of the Low. During the twentieth century the Middle dropped the old concepts of liberty
and justice and planned to turn out the High and maintain its
position permanently by conscious strategy. By this time human
equality had become possible and so, to the new High, it was
no longer an ideal to be striven for but a danger to be averted.

One particular invention allowed the new aristocracy (scientists, trade union organisers and journalists) to maintain their
position more efficiently than had ever been done before. This
was the telescreen, transmitting and receiving simultaneously,
with its consequent power over opinion. The new High realised
that the secure basis for a modern oligarchy was collectivism.
By this means economic inequality could become permanent.

There were four ways of losing power: foreign conquest,
inefficiency leading to mass revolt, the existence of a strong and
discontented Middle, the loss of self-confidence. The first two
dangers were non-existent. The problem was how to mould the
consciousness of the directing and executive groups. This was
done by the institution of Big Brother, the organisation of the
Inner and Outer Parties, and the special part played by the
proles. All Party positions were adoptive; the hereditary principle had been abandoned. The proles were no longer to be
feared; they alone were granted intellectual liberty because

they had no intellect. The Party members underwent an elaborate mental training which left few loopholes for rebellion or the idea of rebellion, and the Thought Police kept watch. Every Party member was capable of *crimestop*, the ability to stop short, as by instinct, of a dangerous thought. *Blackwhite* was the ability to believe and *know* that black is white. One of the chief weapons in the hands of the Party was its constant alteration of the past so that every action and every policy change could be represented as completely consistent with whatever had gone before. The Party member (like the prole) must have no standards of comparison and the infallibility of the Party must be safeguarded. The political dogma of Oceania was known as Ingsoc and the mutability of the past was its central tenet. It was always necessary to *remember* (not merely to learn) that events had happened in the desired manner and to *forget* that records had been tampered with. In an earlier jargon, now known as Oldspeak, this had been called 'reality control', but in Newspeak it was called *doublethink*. This was the power of holding two contradictory beliefs simultaneously and accepting both of them. The great discovery of the Party was that to maintain permanent rule it was necessary to dislocate the sense of reality. Most of the expert *doublethinkers* and the chief war enthusiasts were the Inner Party, whose members were most successfully, both consciously and unconsciously, able to reconcile contradictions.

★

A reference to the 'overfulfilment' of the Ninth Three-Year Plan suggests that the regime of *1984* dated back to at least 1957. There are several references to purges in the early days, some of them in the 'fifties. We know that London was the capital of Airstrip One, which was the third most populous province of Oceanie. The second surprise for anyone fairly well versed in the literature of the future (the first is the early date at which the new regime is to assume control) is to discover that London was largely a city of rotting nineteenth-century houses. The graces of living had been outstripped by the pace of technical control. Instead of the glittering palaces of *The Sleeper Awakes* and *Brave New World* we have a tawdry conglomeration of buildings stamped with the yellow ochre depressiveness of an Army H.Q. A glimpse of the canteen in a Government building is sufficient to give the tone. 'a low-ceilinged, crowded room, its walls grimy from the contact of innumerable bodies; battered metal tables and chairs, placed so close together that you sat with elbows touching; bent spoons, dented trays, coarse white mugs; all surfaces greasy, grime in every crack; and a sourish composite smell of bad gin and bad coffee and metallic stew and dirty clothes'. The first reaction the reader has is that such squalor is unnecessary in such a technically advanced world, but on reflection he realises that there is a war on, the war effort dominates everything, and although these conditions are not technically necessary they are psychologically necessary. In 1984, no one must be seduced by comfort.

Society was controlled by four Ministries: the Ministry of Truth, which concerned itself with news, entertainment, education and the fine arts; the Ministry of Peace, which conducted the war; the Ministry of Love, which maintained law and order; and the Ministry of Plenty, which was responsible for economic affairs. Their names in Newspeak were Minitrue, Minipax, Miniluv and Miniplenty. The three slogans of the Party, which met your eye wherever you went and were the especial concern of the Ministry of Truth, were

WAR IS PEACE

FREEDOM IS SLAVERY

IGNORANCE IS STRENGTH

The new society expressed its freedom most perfectly by governing without laws, i.e., nothing was illegal. There were certain acts for which you might be severely punished but they were not, strictly speaking, illegal. Citizens were constantly reminded of their happy state by seeing the face of Emmanual Goldstein, the Enemy of the People, flashed on to the screen. He was the devil they didn't know and was correspondingly hated.

We can see the effect of the destruction of history on the mind of the individual when we consider Winston Smith, who was not particularly adept at *doublethink*. When there were no external records to refer to, even the outline of your own life lost its sharpness. Some of the events you remembered had probably

not happened and this dislocated large areas of private association. You found yourself remembering details of incidents
without being able to recapture their atmosphere, and there
were long blank periods to which you could assign nothing. We
are given a page from a child's history textbook, containing a
description of London before the Revolution. A normal man
with a pre-*doublethink* mind would know that the description
was entirely false. An expert *doublethinker* would know it was
false and also know it was true. A prole would believe it implicitly. But a misfit like Winston would know it was both true
and false for certain periods, and then simply know that it was
false at other periods. There were gaps in his *doublethinking* and
he was unable to control his private memories which spontaneously rose in rebellion against official records. But failure
in *doublethink* was the major treason. *Doublethink* was a more
powerful weapon than atomic power in the control of population, and it was of most value in the control of the past. 'Who
controls the past', ran the Party slogan, 'controls the future;
who controls the present controls the past.'

Alteration of the past as a political weapon had been one of
Orwell's subjects of study for some years past. In 'Notes on
Nationalism' (*Such, Such Were the Joys*) he had said that every
nationalist was haunted by the belief that the past can be
manipulated (1945). He spends much of his time in a fantasy
world in which, for example, the Spanish Armada had been a
success or the Russian Revolution was crushed in 1918. Orwell
gives examples of this manipulation of historical events in recent
times—how Chiang Kai-shek boiled hundreds of Communists
alive and then became the hero of the Left, how the Russo-
German Pact is already being omitted from Russian year-books
which table recent political events. The best example, of course,
is the minimisation of the part played by Trotsky in the Russian
Revolution. Even when quite important events are actually
happening it is often impossible to know the truth about them.
What do we know about the Warsaw rising of August 1944, for
instance, or the German gas ovens in Poland, or the facts of the
Bengal famine? Since nothing is ever quite proved or disproved,
the most unmistakable fact can be impudently denied. It is
often true to say that the average nationalist merely wants to

feel that his side is getting the better of the other side, and the accuracy of reports about a particular situation is quite unimportant in itself

In fact, many people today are already capable of *doublethink*: 'to know and not to know, to be conscious of complete truthfulness while telling carefully constructed lies, to hold simultaneously two opinions which cancelled out, knowing them to be contradictory and believing in both of them; to use logic against logic, to repudiate morality while laying claim to it, to believe that democracy was impossible and that the Party was the guardian of democracy; to forget whatever it was necessary to forget, then to draw it back into memory again at the moment when it was needed, and then promptly to forget it again: and above all, to apply the same process to the process itself. That was the ultimate subtlety: consciously to induce unconsciousness, and then, once again, to become unconscious of the act of hypnosis you had just performed. Even to understand the word *doublethink* involved the use of *doublethink*.'

Every member of the Party had to be capable of *doublethink* (with the proles it didn't matter, they weren't interested and their political memories, if existent, were short). But it was essential that the people actually responsible for the rectification of earlier reports—both those who took the decisions and those who executed them—should be experts. Winston himself has to rewrite a paragraph of a speech by Big Brother in such a way as to make him predict a military offensive by Eurasia which he had not only not foreseen but had stated would occur elsewhere. Three-Year Plan forecasts had to be written to make them agree with the actual output figures. This sort of thing is already happening. Orwell forecast that Spanish history books under Franco's rule would contain definite references to the Russian army which in fact never reached Spain. From my own knowledge I know that Egyptian history books idealised the family and government of Mehemet Ali, although they have probably followed the family into oblivion. But Orwell could also produce evidence of falsification from recent history. In 'As I Please' (*Tribune*, 17 November, 1944) he referred to an announcement in a London newspaper that Maurice Thorez, French Communist leader, was returning from Moscow where

he had been living in exile for the last six years. At the most the
period had been five years (as, said Orwell, the editor was well
aware). But this was not an unimportant mistake (in *1984*
'mistakes' are always due to misprinting or misquotation). It
was done to make it appear that Thorez deserted from the
French Army, if he did desert, a year *before* the war and not
after the fighting had started. In other words, an effort was
being made to whitewash the character of the Communists
during the period of the Russo-German pact. Orwell also
claimed, in the case of Mihailovich, that 'reputable British
newspapers connive at what amounted to forgery in order to
discredit a man whom they had been backing a few months
earlier'.

These examples are not very startling, and we all expect a
certain amount of falsification in the press. Orwell believed,
however, that it was becoming more frequent and more cynical,
i.e., writers and journalists in general felt far less compunction
about writing things they knew to be untrue or only half-true
than they had felt in, say, the days before the first World War.
In a sense, the society of *1984* already exists only it has not been
systematised. Or rather, it exists in patches and these patches
will spread like ink on blotting-paper until they embrace the
whole of mankind. There is very little doubt that manipulation
of statistics goes on to a very large extent today, particularly in
countries which indulge in large-scale economic planning and
where the fulfilment of the plan is a matter of social and international prestige. The Ministry of Plenty had estimated the
output of boots for one quarter at 145,000,000 pairs. The actual
output had been 62,000,000 and Winston was required to 'correct' the original forecast. When he did it he marked the figure
down to 57,000,000, allowing for the usual claim that the quota
had been overfulfilled. But in all probability 62,000,000 was no
nearer the true figure than 57,000,000 or 145,000,000. Very
likely no boots had been produced at all. The only question
that remains is why it was considered necessary to make any
alteration at all. There was no free, enquiring mind who would
ever check the figure or draw public attention to a discrepancy
between plan and performance. In fact, the manipulation of
statistics and the very existence of a Plan at all were probably

the relics of the transition period and would not be considered worth retaining after a few more years.

This new society was based on power-mania. In the past it had been correct to ask why men wanted power and there was always an answer. But now the appetite was for power itself. This was a characteristic of the twentieth century which Orwell had watched growing. He had analysed the novels of James Hadley Chase, noted how they gave their numerous readers of vicarious thrill of sadism. The sheer joy in power over other people, partly sexual, seemed to be capturing large sections of humanity, particularly in the 'advanced' countries. In *1984* we see the culmination of this trend. Winston has an illicit feeling for one of his co-workers. Love is banned. He would like to flog her to death with a rubber truncheon. He would like to tie her naked to a stake and shoot her full of arrows. He would like to ravish her and cut her throat at the moment of climax. These emotions are entangled with the Hate he has been trained to feel when the image of Goldstein is thrown upon the screen. Only members of the Inner Party are in a position to realise their power-mania. With the others it has to be sublimated and distorted. There are organisations, particularly for children, which canalise these emotions, which allow people to tyrannise over others in no matter how petty a way. The Youth League, the Spies and the Junior Anti-Sex League all give opportunities to those who must assert themselves—and they are now the great majority because the decent purposes of life have been blocked and forbidden. Winston's fantasies are of no value to the State and they are symbols of the malcoordination which led to his downfall. He is in the position of the Hadley Chase fan—he has lost the old decencies but he has been unsuccessful in replacing them with the new sanctions.

Once you have started the descent of the slippery path it is doubtful if anything can save you. The Thought Police are everywhere and you are bound to give yourself away by some apparently insignificant word or deed. For most of the day you are in the field of vision of the telescreen, simultaneously transmitting and receiving. You have no idea whether the Police have plugged in or not. Even at night you could give yourself away by a word muttered in sleep. The sensation of being watched or overheard without intermission will either conquer you entirely or bring any latent revolt into the open. And that is what the Inner Party want. They are not satisfied, as ancient tyrannies were, with unwilling obedience. Obedience had to be freely given or not at all. Big Brother was always watching you, actually and metaphorically. He looked knowingly down at you from the posters, you looked back at him on stamps and coins and book-jackets.

Winston believed that the only hope of salvation lay with the proles, but he knew at the same time (a kind of natural *double-think* that men have indulged in from the beginning of consciousness) that they were powerless. In his diary he wrote about them: 'Until they become conscious they will never rebel, and until after they have rebelled they cannot become conscious'. The Party naturally claimed to have liberated the proles from the capitalists, under whom they had suffered unspeakable agonies. At the same time, *doublethink* allowed the Party to think of the proles as natural inferiors, who had to be kept in subjection. No one knew much about the proles because it was not necessary to know much about them. They lived the conventional lives of all urban workers since the Industrial Revolution had established itself—they worked, married, had children, quarrelled with their neighbours, went to films and football matches, drank beer and gambled, and were not particularly concerned with any of life's delicacies or refinements. The Thought Police kept an eye on them but no attempt was made to indoctrinate them with Party ideology. All that was required of them was a primitive patriotism which could be appealed to when they were required to accept longer working hours or shorter rations. Sometimes they became discontented but they had no means of focussing their discontent. Very little attention was paid to their moral behaviour. It was only necessary to keep them at work and happy at an animal level.

The Government's method of controlling the minds, particularly the emotional responses, of the people might be defined as social indulgence masking a harsh dragooning. Fundamentally the whole population was at the mercy of the Government, but the Government cunningly persuaded the population that it was their servant. Just as law had been abandoned (the free state!), so there was no pretence of a social morality. Many of the activities which liberal bourgeois states had condemned in the capitalist nineteenth century were now revived, not because there had been a moral change but because the Government was prepared to indulge any criminal instinct if it strengthened the emotional tie between ruler and ruled. An example of this was the reintroduction of hanging as a public spectacle. It was especially popular with the children. The Government was not concerned with the debauchery of childish emotions; it was concerned with their manipulation for propagandist purposes.

The Government naturally had a much more positive attitude towards sex than any previous one. It countenanced free expression of the merely physical urge. What it could not allow was uninhibited love between individuals. It had to be especially careful in its treatment of children. If children indulged in sex they were liable to be carried away by their emotions and fall in love. Love simply meant a loyalty stolen from the state. Therefore children were enrolled in the Anti-Sex League to prevent their sexual instincts finding a sexual outlet. As they must find some outlet, however, they were sublimated into hate for the Party's enemies and the kind of sadistic impulses satisfied by a public hanging. The blocking of the sexual urge also had a positive value for the state as it induced hysteria, which could be transformed into war-fever and leader-worship. (After all, the great energy of seventeenth-century capitalism had been reinforced to a very great extent by a fierce sexual puritanism.) Julia saw this role of the sexual instinct very clearly:

'When you make love you're using up energy; and afterwards you feel happy and don't give a damn for anything. They can't bear you to feel like that. They want you to be bursting with energy all the time. All this marching up and down and cheering and waving flags is simply sex gone sour. If you're happy inside yourself, why should you get excited about Big Brother and the Three-Year Plans and the Two Minutes Hate and all the rest of their bloody rot?'

On the other hand, mere debauchery did not matter very much, so long as it was furtive and joyless, and only involved the women of a submerged and despised class. The unforgivable crime was promiscuity between Party members. The aim of the

Party was really to remove all pleasure from the sexual act. The only recognised purpose of marriage was to beget children for the service of the Party. The woman was taught to regard copulation as an unpleasant but necessary duty and a true Party man was compelled to agree with her.[1]

Julia is really a symbol of the particular weakness of love, its isolation. As an emotion love is stronger than anything else in the world but as a social force it suffers from a great disadvantage. It is purely individual in its action. There has never been, to my knowledge, a Lovers' Union, and I have never met anyone who had the slightest interest in organising one. The condition of love is isolation from the rest of the world. Although the new state had taken on a mighty opponent, it was at least able to pick off its antagonists one by one. Julia in fact thought any kind of organised revolt against the Party was stupid— because she was a lover through and through. Winston believed in organisation because he was only partly a lover, much more a politician. In fact, although his love was sincere, it was probably very much of a political weapon, the one which his instinct told him would work for him and not against him. Julia was satisfied to go into the country and make love. This was mere evasion from Winston's point of view. He wanted to challenge the Party with his love. He was already tinged with the fanaticism politicians are so prone to.[2]

Julia's attitude to the Party was much simpler than Winston's and maddeningly unethical. Winston, with his keen analytical mind, satisfied himself that he knew what was wrong and then immediately wished to create some kind of machinery that would put it right. Julia knew intuitively what was wrong and

1 Marriages between Party members had to be approved by a special committee and permission was always refused if the couple concerned gave the impression of being attracted to one another. Recently new courtship and marriage rules were laid down by the Burmese Communist Party. They ban the use of phrases such as 'You are beautiful' and 'I love you'. Approval has to be obtained from a party committee. Proposals must take the following form: 'I am deeply impressed by your qualities as a faithful and energetic member of the Party, and I wish to wage the Party struggle together with you'. (*Daily Express*, 9 June, 1953.)

2 Winston and Julia's love-making expeditions into the country are strongly reminiscent of Gordon and Rosemary's in *Keep the Aspidistra Flying*. In each case a couple (one in 1935 and the other in 1984), feeling victims of a social and political system, feel compelled to leave the capital and exchange intimacies in the depths of nature.

had no intention of attempting to put it right. She much preferred to cheat the Party. She believed that everyone would and did if they felt sure it was safe. In common with most of the young people, she was convinced the Party was invincible. It was madness to set yourself against it but you might be able to wriggle round it now and again.

The last section of the book is largely concerned with Winston's tortures, his confessions, conversations with O'Brien and his punishment. It is the world of violence and brutality which we all guessed must lie behind the façade of the society Orwell has protrayed for us, yet still it horrifies by its impact. Even this latest and most modern of all the societies must have its occasional human sacrifices. It is necessary that men should be outraged and broken, that now and again someone should die for the people. There is no question of reforming Winston. He knows that he has to be laid bare so that he becomes nothing, so that his bent body and empty mind can be displayed to the people as an instance of the Government's power when a man is so foolish as to set up in opposition. Winston is a kind of Wallace's head on London Bridge.

In 'A Footnote About *1984*' (*World Review*, June 1950) Aldous Huxley wrote that the hypnopaedic methods described in *Brave New World* are already in use today, to combat bed-wetting and childish fears and to teach foreign languages in a short time. Therefore, he felt, no intelligent dictator of the future would adopt the systematic brutality described in *1984* when he could condition his subjects into loving their servility. This may be true but it would not be true of the society of 1984. Orwell made it quite clear that the rulers of the new state actually hungered for power and power is not real unless it is given shape and expression. The type of person who dominated the world of 1984 would get no pleasure from seeing gentle slaves serving their masters with love and conviction. Only the infliction of physical punishment could bring a sense of fulfilled power. The rulers of 1984 are the direct heirs of Hitler and Stalin; *Brave New World*, it should be remembered, belongs to the seventh century after Ford. Hitler and Stalin tortured opponents, not to kill them (a bullet would have done that), but to assert power and to warn others. Like Big Brother, they

wanted to destroy all their enemies, not to lord it over conditioned cattle.

Big Brother, or O'Brien, or the junta in general, wanted to
hear Winston confess to the assassination of eminent Party
members, the distribution of seditious pamphlets, embezzle-
ment of public funds, sale of military secrets, sabotage. They
wanted him to confess that he had been a spy for many years
in the pay of the Eastasian government. They wanted to hear
him confess that he was a religious believer, an admirer of
capitalism and a sexual pervert; that he had murdered his wife,
though they knew she was still alive; that he had been in
personal touch with Goldstein, who almost certainly did not
exist. They wanted to hear him confess to all these things
although they knew they were untrue, because they wanted
him to touch rock bottom, to taste the dregs.

Winston's real failure was of *doublethink*. As O'Brien put it,
he suffered from a defective memory, he was mentally deranged.
He was unable to remember real events and he persuaded himself that he remembered other events that had never happened.
This sounds perfectly rational until we realise that the events
Winston remembered actually had happened but the Party
had expunged them not only from the records, not only from
human memory, but in effect from actual existence. But the
Party would not even accept the modifying 'in effect'. These
things had never happened. Reality was not whatever happened, it was what the Party said had happened. Only a disciplined mind could see reality, said O'Brien. Winston believed
that reality was something external, objective, existing in its
own right, that the nature of reality was self-evident. But
O'Brien maintained that reality existed in the human mind.
Thrasymachus in Plato's *Republic* had said that justice was the
will of the strong. O'Brien said that reality was the vision of the
strong, i.e., the Party. All along Winston had realised that the
Party had the power, not simply to claim that two and two
make five, but to establish as a working hypothesis that two and
two make five. That is why Winston had written in his diary:
'Freedom is the freedom to say that two plus two make four. If
that is granted, all else follows.'

It was the perfection of power that the Government desired,

power without blemish. It was intolerable that an erroneous thought should exist anywhere. It was no victory to martyrise men who maintained their defiance to the end. They only killed after they had won the victory, as a kind of celebration; earlier killings had been admissions of defeat. The mind had to be reshaped, made 'clean', before death—then it could be disposed of as so much rubbish. The command of the old despotisms had been 'Thou shalt not'; the command of the totalitarians had been 'Thou shalt'; the new command was 'Thou art'. The original man was annihilated, scooped hollow, his capacity for love, friendship, joy of living, laughter, curiosity, courage and integrity wholly removed. He was squeezed empty and the vacuum was filled with Party essence.

The Party sought power entirely for its own sake. It had even given up the pretence that it was interested in the good of others. Wealth, luxury, long life, happiness were forsaken aims. Power meant power over human beings, not over nature in the sentimental fashion of the nineteenth century. But this movement, based in its early stages on materialism, had swung to the opposite pole and acknowledged that power over humanity is power over mind. Control of matter was already absolute. It was only then that it was realised that this was not enough. An insatiable hunger had driven them to extend the area of appetite. The old reformers had been stupid hedonists, in their view. They demanded a 'world of fear and treachery and torment, a world of trampling and being trampled upon, a world which will grow not less but *more* merciless as it refines itself'. Progress would be progress towards more pain. Like many other psychological trends, this had been a long time growing. For centuries various men, including many ruling groups, had manifested a desire to inhibit pleasure. In 'Urban Foible?' ('I Write as I Please', *Shooting an Elephant*) Orwell had commented on the number of important people who would prevent us enjoying simple pleasures if they could, not from any defined philosophy but from a budding urge to assert their power over the activities and emotional responses of others. This urge gathers strength secretly, and then suddenly and unexpectedly it leaps to power and finds a host of allies where least expected.

O'Brien said, 'If you want a picture of the future, imagine a boot stamping on a human face—for ever'.

He told Winston not to give up hope. 'Everyone is cured sooner or later. In the end we shall shoot you.'

But even in the midst of annihilation Winston saw his real hope. 'To die hating them, that was freedom.' If at the last moment he could retain a grain of heresy he would have defeated them. His mind would have remained free.

*

Why did Orwell date this horrible world so early? He mentions somewhere that intellectuals tend to be correct in their forecasts of the future but usually get the tempo of change wrong. This is in general true, although Wells was an outstanding example of the opposite—he postdated the first World War, the military aeroplane and the discovery of atomic power. Many critics have expressed surprise that the society depicted in *1984*, although a credible one if you apply merely rational criteria, should have been placed only three decades on. There is little doubt that Orwell was aware of this particular improbability, and it seems likely that it was part of his propagandist purpose. He wished to rouse people to the dangers inherent in existing political tendencies. He did not believe that the individual was altogether powerless, although this is probably the majority feeling in the Western world today. He knew that many of his readers would still be living in 1984 and he hoped that this book would act as a stimulus, cause them to take first warning and then action to avert it.

1984 is one of those books that overpower you as you read but which do not leave any strong conviction in the mind. After you have read it you find yourself discovering faults in retrospect. The imaginative effort which impresses the reader at first turns out to be not imagination at all but a painstaking pursuit of existing tendencies to what appear to be logical conclusions.[1] There is no tension in the story, which weakens its appeal as art. We know, and Orwell always maintained, that totalitarianism can only be challenged by individual values. This Winston Smith was quite incapable of doing. He was a weak creature

[1] He accuses both Wells and Burnham of this same fault.

who was born to be victimised. There is truth in this but no
drama, and great fiction requires drama. Walter Allen refers to
the book's 'sheer intellectual power', but this is not enough.
Herbert Read calls it mythology for the future but it is a
modern fallacy to believe that a work admired by a cultural
élite only can ever be raised to the level of myth. The novel is
internally consistent, except in one passage which jars on the
alert reader. This is where an announcement is made that
Oceania is not after all at war with Eurasia but with Eastasia.
Eurasia was an ally. We know that such switches were common
and we can believe in them. It is not easy to believe, however,
in the automatic way in which the crowd receives and accepts
the news. We know that they are mentally servile but this is
more than servility, it is sheer mechanism. Orwell has not
persuaded us that the citizens of Airstrip One have become quite
so inhuman. We know that the possibility exists, but generations
of indoctrination and probably drug injection are necessary
before possibility could become actuality. In fact, for a few
pages Orwell slides from his prevalent realism to satire, which
is completely out of place. This passage would read well in a
novel by Rex Warner, who would introduce it deliberately to
emphasise the idiocy. But Orwell is not concerned with extrava-
gant emphasis. All his emphases (with this exception) are based
on probability.

My advice to old ladies is not to be too frightened by this
book. Apart from the soothing syrup of 'It may never happen',
even an aware and informed mind finds it hard to accept the
world of *1984* after a little reflection. It is the kind of world
many of us have feared but we have not had the skill to portray
it. Now Orwell has done it for us and we immediately see (or
rather sense) its flaws. At first we think that Orwell has expressed our own fears, but a little later we realise that he has
spotlighted their improbabilities. I think our chief hope lies in
the evident inefficiency of large-scale bureaucracy that we see
all over the world. Neither bureaucracy nor its inefficiency is a
product of socialism or collectivism, as is so often asserted.
Bureaucracy is a condition of large-scale enterprise, whether
public or private. Administration in large-scale enterprise is
always more inefficient and wasteful than in small-scale

enterprise, and it always provides more loopholes for speculation, intrigue and even rebellion. It is possible that a foolproof
bureaucratic system may be devised but I see no signs of it at
present. Under modern conditions it is inconceivable that any
Government could control, even with the most advanced technical resources available, a population so completely as is done
in *1984*. So far the highly efficient totalitarian systems have
been much less successful in their search for security and longe-
vity than the blundering, old-fashioned liberal systems. There
is one exception, and periodically that pot appears to come near
boiling over. The most thoroughgoing of all the modern dic-
tatorships and the most contemptuous of the effete liberal
democracies was to have lasted a thousand years, and collapsed
in ruins after twelve.

1984 was very much a product of Orwell's last pain-wracked
years. Before then he had always recognised the dangers latent
in totalitarian development but he had never lost hope. The
best expression of his doubts about the future is to be found in a
review of N. de Basily's *Russia Under Soviet Rule* ('The Russian
Regime', *New English Weekly*, 12 January, 1939):

> 'The terrifying thing about the modern dictatorships is that
> they are something entirely unprecedented. Their end cannot be
> foreseen. In the past every tyranny was sooner or later overthrown,
> or at least resisted, because of "human nature", which as a matter
> of course desired liberty. But we cannot be at all certain that
> "human nature" is constant. It may be just as possible to produce
> a breed of men who do not wish for liberty as to produce a breed
> of hornless cows. The Inquisition failed, but then the Inquisition
> had not the resources of the modern state. The radio, press-
> censorship, standardised education and the secret police have
> altered everything. Mass-suggestion is a science of the last twenty
> years and we do not yet know how successful it will be.'

I do not quote this for comfort, for it is surely nothing of the
kind. But it does state the vagueness of the present situation. As
we look into the future we see even less than our ancestors were
able to see. There are certain influences at work in the world
which we cannot evaluate through any previous experience. We
can be fairly certain that the Empire of Notting Hill will not be
established in the year 1984 A.D., but we can have no certainty
that Big Brother will smile down at us from the hoardings.

Chapter XV

The Way to the Truth

IN MOST of Orwell's earliest work appearing in the *Adelphi* there was a rather bumptious lack of maturity such as we often get from the pen of a young man who is feeling his way. The bumptiousness was later modified and became a blend of plausibility and knowingness, often charming but occasionally irritating. One gets the impression that he is a little awed by writing for an 'advanced' magazine and is trying rapidly to get his literary personality in order. He is particularly concerned with the neat classification of literature into classical and romantic—labels that don't matter a damn but which most of us are guilty of at the beginning of our careers. Young men write in the shade of professors who use such terms with assurance and sometimes with an air of significance. It took Orwell a few years to discover his true literary self, and when he did discover it he promptly ceased to be Eric Blair to his readers. In the March-May issue of the *New Adelphi* he reviewed Lewis Mumford's *Herman Melville* and reproached the author for trying to interpret the poetry. This is of course exactly what the later Orwell always insisted on doing (as when he reviewed Yeats and Eliot), but even in those early days he had a turn of phrase which later made his more mature criticism a pleasure to read. 'One can only "interpret" a poem', he wrote, 'by reducing it to an allegory—which is like eating an apple for the pips.' It is difficult to understand what this means, if it means anything, but it is an arresting phrase. He goes on to say it would have been much better if Mumford had discoursed simply on the form, which is the 'stuff of poetry', and left the meaning alone. This alone indicates the great gap between Blair and Orwell.

In the June-August issue he wrote that 'it is possible, and

perhaps necessary, to divide all art into classical and romantic'. The irresponsible 'perhaps' was something he never abandoned —we find him using it many years later when he claimed that George Gissing was 'perhaps' the greatest of English novelists. Classicism was a 'trim formal garden' and romanticism a 'jungle, full of stupendous beauty, and also of morasses and sickly weeds'. These are brave words, but any young man with a taste for language could deliver them, and they have no felt meaning. Orwell (or Blair) was still trying to persuade himself that he was a fit contributor to an 'advanced' periodical. He probably felt he was being watched. The schoolboy was not far behind, either. 'This is the reply churlish to all romantic poetry', he said of a book by Sherard Vines.

Two years later he claims that spirituality is part of the modern Englishman's mental equipment. Spirituality is an odd term and means nothing much, but he opposes it to the earthiness of the eighteenth century. He also says that a modern English writer is deliberately throwing away a part of his mind if he attempts to be classical. This is very interesting, for it marks a phase in the transmutation of Blair into Orwell. I have already shown how Orwell insisted that a writer must write from his actual experience and world-view and not attempt to create a new and necessarily artificial corpus of experience. Apparently he held this view throughout his literary life, but in later years he denounced spirituality vehemently. It is presumably fair to deduce from this that in later life he no longer believed that religion was an integral part of the modern Englishman's experience. In fact, he appeared to regard it as a propagandist weapon used on behalf of the ruling classes.

Again, he criticised Priestley's *Angel Pavement* because 'a novelist is not required to have good intentions but to convey beauty'. This is utterly opposed to the spirit of the man who wrote *1984* and who said that the chief motive of his work was the defence of democratic socialism against Fascism (totalitarianism would have been a truer description).

But there is no need to spend too long examining the opinions of the early Eric Blair. The characteristic views of George Orwell, despite the obsession with classicism and romanticism and the priority of style over meaning, begin to appear fairly

early. For instance, in a review of Edith Sitwell's *Alexander Pope*
he reprimands her for saying that

> 'Twas more the time when Phoebus yields to Night,
> And rising Cynthia casts her silver light,
> Wide o'er the world in solemn pomp she drew
> Her airy chariot, hung with pearly dew.

'has "an exquisite lightness", not noticing, apparently, that it
has also an insufferable staleness and obviousness'. This may be
because it is 'classical' but, whatever the motive, it is certainly
a judgment which the later Orwell would have accepted. In
December 1933 he declared that 'most modern literary criticism
is literary and nothing else—that is, it concentrates on an
author's style and thinks it rather vulgar to notice his subject
matter'. This is a complete *volte face* from the view he held only
three years earlier. But in the last contribution by Eric Blair
(November 1934) there are still occasional gaucheries, as when
he wrote 'I could a tale unfold' when there was no particular
reason to be funny—if it is funny. Yet the very act of changing
his name seems to have spurred him into literary maturity. We
find nothing like this above the name of Orwell.

In my opinion (not shared by everyone) most of the writing
in his first book, *Down and Out*, is excellent. He is attempting to
make us see, feel and smell and I think he succeeds to a very
great extent. There is amateurishness here and there, but it is
in the presentation rather than the expression. He finds it
necessary now and again to tell us why he is writing the book,
but I doubt if anyone who reads it needs to be told. He says he
is telling us about his life in Paris because the slum he lived in
was first an object-lesson in poverty and then the background
of his own experiences. Both of these are obvious and need not
be stated. Later he says he describes Charlie just to show us what
diverse characters could be found in the Coq d'Or quarter.
Actually, the description of a single person does not give any
idea of diversity at all. Orwell had not yet realised that a writer
writes because he has to and not for an overt reason—or it
would probably be more true to say that he did realise it but
did not realise it was safe to leave the reader unappeased. At
school one writes essays for very palpable reasons.

Much of the conversation is stilted—exact, grammatical and

without colloquial abbreviations. (In this it resembles that other classic of the underworld, Davies's *Autobiography of a Super-Tramp*.) In view of Orwell's love of exact description this may be surprising, until it is remembered that literary conversation is a knack and requires practice before it can be successfully captured. But in other ways he exhibits that plodding vein of exactness that runs through most of his descriptive work (though not to the same degree through his opinionative work), as when he counted the number of times he was called *maquereau* during one day, and found it was thirty-nine. His justly famous literary integrity expressed itself in this book in his refusal to compromise with the tastes of the public. Such 'refusal' is not uncommon today—in fact, it has become fashionable and some writers have strained themselves to the utmost to shock their readers. But here lies the difference between true and false 'refusal'—Orwell gives the impression of writing down exactly what he saw without exaggeration. He did not compromise but nor did he distort. We appreciated Orwell because he had found a very delicate point of balance which few writers attain and fewer maintain. The following passage is typical of the writing in this book, especially in its texture. It is irritating to have to write by metaphor, but I want a word that will describe the arrangement of the words and their fall on the ear.

'In the kitchen the dirt was worse. It is not a figure of speech, it is a mere statement of fact to say that a French cook will spit in the soup—that is, if he is not going to drink it himself. He is an artist, but his art is not cleanliness. To a certain extent he is even dirty because he is an artist, for food, to look smart, needs dirty treatment. When a steak, for instance, is brought up for the head cook's inspection, he does not handle it with a fork. He picks it up in his fingers and slaps it down, runs his thumb round the dish and licks it to taste the gravy, runs it round and licks it again, then steps back and contemplates the piece of meat like an artist judging a picture, then presses it lovingly into place with his fat, pink fingers, every one of which he had licked a hundred times that morning. When he is satisfied he takes a cloth and wipes his fingerprints from the dish, and hands it to the waiter. And the waiter, of course, dips *his* fingers into the gravy—his nasty, greasy fingers which he is for ever running through his brilliantined hair. Whenever one pays more than, say, ten francs for a dish of meat in Paris (1933), one may be certain that it has been fingered in this manner. In every cheap restaurant it is different; there, the same trouble is not taken over the food, and it is just forked out of the pan and flung on to a plate, without handling. Roughly speaking, the more one pays for food, the more sweat and spittle one is obliged to eat with it.'

By any standard I think this would be called a vivid description. You can see it clearly, and you can feel it emotionally as well. (Contemporary jargon would call it 'powerful writing'.) Part of it might very well be quoted in a review (as I have quoted it here) to give an idea of the writer's 'quality'. But it demonstrates something more than 'vividness' or 'power', which are trite and question-begging terms respectively. I wish to draw attention to two points, both small, but close inspection of a writer always leads to a consideration of the microscopic, which usually turns out to be more rewarding than broad generalities. Note how Orwell describes the finger-licking. To him finger-licking is sufficiently repulsive in itself. Imagine this passage as it would have been written by some authors who shall be nameless, though the temptation is great. Finger-licking would be much too trivial for them to dwell on. It would have acted merely as an aperitif for the disgusting orgy to follow. The cook would have scratched his armpit, probably his crutch, he would have come straight from the lavatory without washing his hands, he would have sneezed over the steak. We would have been revolted or disbelieving. We believe Orwell because of his restraint. This may be art, but it is more likely to be fidelity to fact—we are urged to believe this because there are numerous instances of his essential honesty in other parts of his work. Think of the brilliantined hands of the waiter—we accept them because we know how disgusting Orwell could have made his cook if he had wished. And finally, the family word 'nasty' clinches the effect of truth. Orwell uses it as my mother does. Orwell is not sitting over his work with a smug grin, laughing at your discomfiture and insisting that although he is only a writer he is nevertheless unsqueamish. He *is* squeamish, and there would be no point in writing these things if he didn't think them horrible.

Honesty was his chief literary virtue. There were few fire-works in his style, though he could turn a phrase very neatly. Recognising honesty is largely an intuitive matter and it is normally impossible to give any proof. When we can offer proof it is usually circumstantial, while literary honesty is a reflection of psychological integrity. Sometimes he tells us things that hardly any other writer would tell us because it might reflect on his honesty. In *The Road to Wigan Pier* Orwell said that *nearly* all the incidents described in *Down and Out* actually happened! There have been few writers under sixty who would have dared admit that. I could imagine Roy Campbell inviting us to slit his throat if he told a lie!

There was a coolness and nonchalance about Orwell that made a respect for truth natural to him. It is rather trite to call his attitude scientific but I think it is the term that comes nearest. (It is also rather insulting to people who are not scientists but it is late in the day to snipe at scientific prestige.) Part of this aspect of Orwell's literary personality derives from his tendency to under-statement. 'The whole experience of being hit by a bullet is very interesting and I think it is worth describing in detail.' (*Homage to Catalonia.*)

Yet fidelity to fact can be a literary vice as well as a virtue. We like to feel that our author is describing things truthfully, but we soon get tired of an excess of fact. One reason why Orwell's novels are not successful is because he cannot resist the temptation to put in all he knows or feels about a particular person or situation. *Coming Up For Air*, the most popular of his novels, is a particularly bad offender in this respect. We never stop hearing new things about Tubby Bowling, and he is not the kind of character one likes to have detailed knowledge of. On the first page he gets into his bath and starts soaping his arms—and then we are told in parenthesis that 'I've got those kind of pudgy arms that are freckled up to the elbow'. Throughout his novel Orwell demonstrated a failure to select the significant. He was attempting to portray a society bathed in mediocrity but he did it at the expense of his readers' patience. This trait was particularly noticeable in any reference to food. Tubby cannot eat without his creator placing his menu before us ('haddock, grilled kidneys, toast and marmalade and a pot of coffee', again in parenthesis). If Tubby had revelled in his meals we might have revelled with him, but they are largely on a level with visits to Joe's Snack Bar. We know that Orwell was greatly impressed by Dickens's particularity about food—in fact, he ascribes the success of one passage that he quotes to the statement that dinner consisted of 'baked shoulder of mutton and potatoes under it'. And the difference between the two writers probably does exist in that undefinable connection between feeling and style, which we sense but cannot analyse.

There are innumerable little ways in which Orwell's honesty expressed itself—unconsciously, you might say. Take this passage from 'Charles Dickens': 'According to Aldous Huxley, D. H. Lawrence once said that Balzac was a "gigantic dwarf".' Most other writers would have omitted any reference to Huxley, allowing it to be supposed that they were much better read than they were. I say this because it is quite obvious to anyone who has read reviews consistently for some years that nearly all reviewers claim to have read far more than is physically possible. I once conducted a correspondence with a writer in which we confessed the important books, even authors (all of them *musts*) which we had not read, until we gave up in shame. In his review of *The Development of William Butler Yeats* Orwell admitted that he had never read *A Vision*. Many reviewers would have referred to *A Vision* knowingly, implying that they were quite familiar with it; of the remainder, the majority would have kept quiet. It is an occupational disease, the refusal to admit ignorance. This may be a small matter but it is also significant. There was a compulsion in Orwell to tell the truth, even when it was not necessary and on occasion when it reduced the artistic effect, just as the political argument in *Homage to Catalonia* spoiled the aesthetic effect created by the descriptive sections. There was no external need for Orwell, when listing his books in 'Books v. Cigarettes' (*Shooting an Elephant*), to admit that ten were borrowed and not returned, but he had to do it. We can only judge by such minor pieces of evidence, which support the overwhelming impression derived from a sympathetic reading of his opinions and arguments. The total impact is one of extreme fairmindedness. Cyril Connolly (who, it should be remembered, had the advantage of knowing him personally and well), when listing the best qualities of the realist writers of his generation for the guidance of the young, referred to 'the honesty of Orwell'.

If Orwell's honesty was so integral as to be unconscious, he was also fully convinced that sincerity and arristic integrity were of the greatest importance for a writer. He even went so far as to say that a half-lunatic belief was of more value to a writer, if sincerely held, than a commonsense one that was not deeply felt. He distinguished between sincerity and artistic integrity, placing the second higher than the first, though without defining his terms very closely. It is difficult to see how one can exist without the other. But it is clear that a sincerely held view may not be true in an objective sense, yet will produce a higher literary value than a merely acquired truth, however strong the evidence for it. A sincerely believed falsehood is more creative than a truth that is not inherent in the personality. This is parallel to his other conviction that a world-view must be rooted in a person's own experience, not grafted on at a later date. It was along these lines that he attacked the Marxist claim that at the present time all good literature must derive from Marxist theory.

> '. . . a belief which was appropriate several centuries ago might be inappropriate and therefore stultifying now. But this does not get one much farther, because it assumes that in any age there will be *one* body of belief which is the current approximation to truth, and that the best literature of the time will be more or less in harmony with it. Actually no such uniformity has ever existed.'
> ('Inside the Whale', *Such, Such Were the Joys.*)

His example of a good writer holding an almost lunatic world-view was Poe. If Poe had enjoyed a commonsense outlook he would no longer be read. 'It seems therefore that for a creative writer possession of the "truth" is less important than emotional sincerity. . . . There are occasions when an "untrue" belief is more likely to be sincerely held than a "true" one.' He cited Hardy and Baudelaire as writers who were absurd as well as demoralising—but they could create poetry simply because they believed sincerely in the absurdities.

One question that arises is Orwell's own place in relation to these statements. 'Commonsense' is one of the words most frequently used about his views on life. I think there are two things we must bear in mind which clarify his position. First, he was writing about creative writers and he was largely a

critical one. But as there is a creative element in the best criticism we must look for something else in his literary character
that will reconcile two apparent opposites. It is that with
Orwell commonsense was a passion and stimulated his mind in
the way that love or beauty have stimulated poets. Orwell
resembled Balzac whose creativity arose out of a passionate consideration of money, and Defoe whose creativity arose out of a
passionate consideration of economic facts. It is the passion that
matters, not its object.

I would never claim that Orwell was incapable of dishonesty,
for that would be to make an idol of him. Inconsistency is
common enough in any writer and is by no means the same
thing as dishonesty. At one period of his life, the frustrated war
period, Orwell became a victim of his own plausibility and all-
knowingness, and minor dishonesties began to appear in his
work. The really remarkable thing is that he was able to check
this degeneration and even to produce his best work afterwards.
In *Partisan Review* (November-December 1941) he admitted
that Hitler's invasion of Russia took everyone very much by
surprise. Later he was to claim that all thinking people realised
that the arrival of Hess was incontrovertible evidence that
Hitler was about to attack Russia and wished to make things
up with Britain. Here we have a direct conflict of opinion, not
merely an inconsistency, and he must have known that at the
time he was either surprised or not surprised. But his innate
honesty finally came to his assistance and gave him strength to
make sure that the same thing could not happen again. Dishonesty is often the penalty of becoming a pundit. If you have a
reputation for being always right you are tempted to make
sure that you always will be right—in the eyes of the world. But
Orwell cared more for his own opinion of himself than for other
people's. I believe this sense of internal deterioration precipi-
tated his retreat to the Hebrides.

I am not even being unkind when I accuse him of deterioration at this time. He was fully aware of it himself. In his Notebook (17 June, 1940) he wrote:

'Nowadays, when I write a review, I sit down at the typewriter
and type it straight out. Till recently, indeed till six months ago,
I never did this and would have said that I could not do it.

Virtually all that I wrote was written at least twice, and my books
as a whole three times—individual passages as many as five or
ten times. It is not really that I have gained in facility, merely
that I have ceased to care, so long as the work will pass inspection
and bring in a little money. It is a deterioration directly due to the
war.'

He could be careless. Carelessness in journalism is forgivable.
It is really a matter of degree. Some kinds of carelessness are
criminal but Orwell was never guilty of them. He was guilty of
peccadilloes, such as claiming that 'thirty years ago any bittern
that dared to show its beak in this country would have been
shot and stuffed immediately'. ('As I Please', *Tribune*, 16
February, 1945.) Some years less than thirty before that date
I heard the bittern continually in the Norfolk Broads area. But
there was nothing to be gained from such a statement (it was
not equivalent to saying that the Spanish Armada had succeeded or that the Russian Revolution had been crushed in
1918); it was a mistake by a weekly columnist who had not been
able to check his facts and took the risk of making an inaccurate
statement to support some other point. It was similar to his
claim that *In Good King Charles's Golden Days* 'sticks close to
history' (*Time and Tide*, 18 May, 1940). No one criticised
journalists more severely than Orwell for their inaccuracies. He
himself demonstrated how impossible it is to avoid them. With
the best will in the world a journalist will write falsehoods or
nonsense, simply because he is a journalist and has to send in his
copy by a deadline.

Sometimes he appeared rather naive. He was capable of
speaking to you like a schoolmaster to a bright boy and you
tended to be irritated by his careful explanation of what any
informed person knows. Perhaps he had just discovered something for himself and wished to share it. He once explained to
me that a name means a lot to a person (he was thinking of
changing his own name by deed poll). Primitive people, especially, he said, regarded their names as indivisible parts of their
personalities—they were even loth to lose their nail-parings.
But he was not really being arrogant or undervaluing you. He
wanted to make sure that you were both starting from scratch
together, that the background for discussion was completely
mutual, that it would never be possible for any one at a later

stage to say, 'I didn't know that. . . .' It is, after all, a method popularised by scientific writers, this establishment of all data on which subsequent discussion is to be based.

He was inclined to lecture, to lay down the law. 'Spleen, of course, is the exact word for Carlyle's peculiar temper', he wrote in a review. The 'of course' plays the same role as the 'perhaps' in a statement referred to earlier. This view of Carlyle is sprung upon us, it may or may not be true, but Orwell wished to establish it and to establish it without argument before he went any further. In conjunction with the word 'exact' it is a considerable statement, one which not everyone might be inclined to accept without a little thought. But the reader has little opportunity to think when he reads a review. No one would call Orwell a psychological bully, but he tended to take some of his basic judgments for granted. Perhaps it is necessary for a writer to do this.

His belief in a literary message became so strong, quite early in his career, that it inhibited his skill as a novelist. He felt compelled to impart his ideas by direct tuition as well as by the glancing technique of fiction. His attack on private schools in *A Clergyman's Daughter* reminds us of Dickens's attack on the Yorkshire schools. (One feels constantly that Dickens was Orwell's most admired literary model, and that this admiration many times served as an obstacle to the freeing of his own talents.) Unlike Dickens, he could not be content with a fictional account of what happened at such schools but had to follow it up with an analytical criticism—thus saying many things twice, each time antagonising one section of his readers, according to the treatment they preferred. (As they had set out to read a novel it is likely that the majority found the criticism irksome.) The same characteristics marred *Keep the Aspidistra Flying*—at least, from the orthodox point of view. (I should confess at this point that I personally don't object to non-fictional sections in novels—to the contrary, I believe a novel can be enriched by them. But Orwell's fiction was too mediocre to be benefited in this way.) The last sentence of chapter VI in this novel is enough to exasperate a purist. See here:

'They had nowhere to go, except the open air. There are so many pairs of lovers in London with "nowhere to go"; only the streets and the parks, where there is no privacy and it is always cold. It is not easy to make love in a cold climate when you have no money. *The "never the time and the place" motif is not made enough of in novels." '*

My italics, as they say.

I doubt if even his best friends would have called him a novelist. Mrs Leavis became quite vehement about the time he had wasted in attempting to write novels. Then why' did he attempt it? The answer emphasises one of the oddities of the English literary situation: it is almost a law that no English writer shall be treated seriously until he has first attained a measure of success as a novelist, no matter what his capacity. There is nothing sacred about writing fiction, but it is regarded in the literary field with a kind of sacred awe. Too many young writers have had to torture their talents for criticism or description or poetic evocation or humour into a fictional mould until at last, often quite late in life, they are released by fiat (though who issues fiats in the literary field it is never easy to know) to write in the manner for which nature has fitted them. By this time they are frequently semi-exhausted and in any case have picked up tricks in the service of fiction which they would be better without. Orwell managed to escape the ill-effects of writing turgid books like *A Clergyman's Daughter*, just as he managed to resist the personal deterioration of the war years. But he was exceptionally tough. It is not just that a non-literary virtue such as toughness should be required for a writer to give us the best he has got.

There are individual parts of the novels which are extremely well done, but usually they are good outside the fictional canon. The Trafalgar Square episode in *A Clergyman's Daughter*, for instance, is a vignette which would be better by itself, preferably making its first appearance in a literary magazine. *Down and Out* masqueraded as fiction—Orwell had to cheat the public to get it published, presumably, or at least to find readers. But viewed as fiction they contain most of the available faults. (*Burmese Days* is the best, and every year scores of novels just as good appear, many of them by unknown writers.) They do not move, the atmosphere is as depressive as a fog, the characters go on repeating themselves, and there is a lack of ease in transition. A novelist needs a quality which I can best call fluidity—the power to persuade the reader that time is actually moving at its accustomed pace, not progressing in leaps and bounds, now jumping like a kangaroo, now hopping like a flea. Orwell did not possess this gift. One of the most unconvincing chapters he ever wrote is the second chapter of *A Clergyman's Daughter*. Dorothy has left her village and finds herself straying in London, suffering from loss of memory. Orwell is faced with the problem of describing the first return to consciousness of a person who has had a mental black-out. Although this is not a state most of us know by experience, we have enough instinctive konwledge of human behaviour to feel the truth or untruth of a description. Orwell does not live this experience, he thrusts himself into it by an effort of will. It jerks like a fourth-form exercise. Dorothy meets some rough youths and a girl who realise they can make use of her. They are not alive, they are tired memories of types. Here is an opportunity for Orwell to make use of his acquaintance with low language. He does so, abruptly and naively. Perhaps the abruptness is necessary, but the characters are not speaking from themselves, they are speaking to their creator's dictation. Dorothy is unbelievably slow in grasping their meaning. She is a sheltered girl from a country vicarage, but she would have shown more facility in understanding another language when she had to. People usually do. Then we move on to the hop-picking episodes which are not organically one with the rest of the narrative but are hauled in by the scruff of the neck. In short, this novel is a ragbag into which go episodes which Orwell had not used in *Down and Out*.

There is more of this psychological falsity in *Burmese Days*. The lowest point is reached in chapter XI. Flory has already made a great blunder in taking Elizabeth, the little English miss, to the native *pwe* dancing. She had hated it, and Flory knew it. He was falling in love with her, not because she was particularly lovable to him but because she was a single female and he was lonely. He was also reasonably intelligent. It is inconceivable that after this flop he would have risked repeating it by taking her to the Burmese bazaar, yet Orwell tells us he did. He constantly praises Burmese civilisation, although he

knows how much it irritates her. We should not expect him to
surrender his opinions but we could reasonably expect him to
change his methods. Having seen that the direct approach failed,
he might have tried some subtlety. Why did he throw away her
friendship, when he needed her so much, by antagonising her?
Many a man has been irritated by the attitudes and opinions of
the woman he loves, and it is part of the thrill of love to attempt
to find reconciliation. But Flory lectures Elizabeth: 'They're
highly civilised', he says to her of the Burmese; 'more civilised
than we are, in my opinion. Beauty's all a matter of taste. There
are a people in this country called the Palaungs who admire
long necks in women. The girls wear broad brass rings to
stretch their necks, and they put on more and more of them
until in the end they have necks like giraffes. It's no queerer
than bustles or crinolines.' Flory is quite right—but meanwhile
Elizabeth's suburban little soul is writhing and he wants her.

   In all Orwell's fiction there is one attractive character. I do
not mean by this that there is only one person whom we can
like but only one whom we can feel interest in. This is not an
ethical judgment, it is a question of literary vitality. Rosemary
in *Keep the Aspidistra Flying* is the only person we might be
tempted to follow beyond the last page of the book. She is a cut
above the normal ineffectual, conventional Orwell female. He
intended her to be conventional (he was mainly interested in the
ordinary, rarely in the extraordinary) and she *is* conventional,
but she can surprise us as even the most conventional person
can. (It is a mistake, and Orwell makes it, to imagine that conventionally is ever absolute.) Rosemary possesses sufficient
understanding and sympathy to rise occasionally above her
class and to enter into the processes of a deliberate failure like
Gordon. She is really more mature than Gordon, who flaunts a
kind of *fin-de-siècle* maturity which is largely literary, because she
is not the slave of an obsession. Like most women, she is more
willing than he to surrender a point for the sake of peace. She
probably understands his pigheadedness better than most
women would. With better chances Rosemary might have been
a delightfully fulfilled character, but her loyalty to Gordon
makes this impossible. She is the only character in Orwell whom
we can feel developing.

His literary models were chiefly Victorian. We know this not only from his own confession but also from his method of writing a novel. He plods, and chronology is sacred. There is an unnatural correctness about the conversations which is characteristic of Victorian fiction. His admiration for Dickens even goes so far in *Burmese Days* as to sum up the subsequent histories of the leading characters in the last chapter, very much in the manner of *David Copperfield*. There is nothing essentially wrong in this, but it is a convention that has fallen out of use and cannot be revived creatively except for a humorous purpose. I doubt if he had sufficient patience to be a novelist. He had a curious habit of ending a conversational outburst with the words 'etc., etc.' Perhaps the etceteras were not worth giving in full but by this device the author intrudes himself and destroys the illusion. When a novelist arises who will not pretend he does not exist this will be allowable, but there was nothing *avant-garde* about Orwell. Very often, instead of finding the exact word, he uses an inexact word in inverted commas, leaving the reader to discover what he really intended. One page in *Keep the Aspidistra Flying* has five examples of this usage. He tries to give specialised meanings to words like 'education' and 'manage' without attempting to define the quality he is searching for.

He was a fluent writer but in his fiction could not always control his fluency. Sometimes this led to an *embarras de richesses* which really did embarrass. Take this passage from *Coming Up For Air*:

> 'When you lift the bonnet and look at the engine it reminds you of the old Austrian Empire, all tied together with bits of string but somehow keeps plugging along. You wouldn't believe any machine could vibrate in so many directions at once. It's like the motion of the earth, which has twenty-two different kinds of wobble, or so I remember reading. If you look at her from behind when she's running in neutral it's for all the world like watching one of those Hawaiian girls dancing the hula-hula.'

The engine is compared to three different things, which is a surfeit. The whole novel is spoiled by repetition and, rather unexpectedly, overstatement. Orwell often obtained a good effect by understatement, but that was usually in an account of his own feelings. It was in his imagery that he sometimes tended to say too much. Nothing in this passage adds to our knowledge of Bowling, except perhaps that he was a remarkably well-informed insurance agent. Imagine how Hemingway would have dealt with the car. He would have been content with the first sentence and a half of the paragraph of which this is part. They read:

> 'I switched the engine off and got out. I never like leaving the old car running in neutral. . . .'

In a review of *The Lion and the Unicorn* (*Partisan Review*, March-April, 1942) Dwight Macdonald listed some of the virtues and defects of Orwell as a political writer. Some of these are the ones we have noticed in his fiction, but they do not coincide absolutely. For instance, Macdonald stresses the *human* quality of Orwell's political writing—and it is the human quality that is largely lacking in the novels. He is always conscious of his characters as class types with typical class reactions and phobias. Perhaps it was his obstinacy. When he turned to politics he brought into play human sympathies which we do not normally find in left-wing writing but expect to find in fiction. Macdonald says you feel politics 'engages him as a moral and cultural whole, not merely as a specialist'. His values are rarely inhuman, however muddled they seem at times. But he has the defects of the amateur; his scope is broad but none too deep; he describes where he should analyse and poses questions so impressionistically that his answers get nowhere; 'he uses terms in a shockingly vague way; he makes sweeping generalisations with the confidence of ignorance; his innocence of scientific criteria is appalling'. It is astonishing how his literary values varied from one sphere of writing to another. I have referred to his exactness, but this can only be found in his descriptive writing (particularly in *Down and Out* and *Homage to Catalonia*). In his novels he used terms fluffily, as I have already said, and he did the same in his political writing—and Macdonald gave some good examples, e.g., 'No real revolutionist has ever been an internationalist'. If we are sympathetic we have to realise that Orwell gave different meanings to the same word at different times. But outside England the modern political temper has not much time for that.

His literary criticism also suffered from the same disease,

although some of it, like the essay on Dickens, is among his very best work. Normally the prose is lucid and well-balanced, but sometimes we come across passages like this:

> 'How complete or truthful a picture has Kipling left us of the long-service, mercenary army of the late nineteenth century? One must say of this, as of what Kipling wrote about nineteenth-century Anglo-India, that it is not only the best but almost the only literary picture we have.' ('Rudyard Kipling', *Critical Essays*.)

It is the second sentence I object to. It is both slipshod and undefined. What does he mean by 'the only literary picture'? Presumably the only well-written picture—so that he might just as well have written that Kipling wrote 'not only the best but almost the only best picture we have'. He meant something else but he doesn't help us to discover it. This was partly because he did not like jargon and always preferred to use common speech. Jargon is irritating and, in the wrong mouths, meaningless but when it is used technically it can be in the service of clarity. One of the attractions of Orwell's style was its unpretentiousness but sometimes it is at the expense of exactness. It is only because we respect his unassuming honesty that we accept it; if we had even a slight tendency to hostility we would accuse him of vagueness and imprecision.

Orwell was very interested in the connection between 'tendency' and literary style, although he was baffled by it. Some critics have traced a connection between his own stylistic simplicity and his love of freedom, and claimed that the enemies of freedom usually write in a staccato manner suggestive of mechanism. Orwell himself remarked that although Marxist critics could explain the subject-matter and imagery of a book in sociological terms they had not yet managed to put style or 'texture' on a sociological basis. We know so little about the inner life of style that it is not even easy to explain what we mean by style in concrete terms—we only know it by its emotional impact and are quite incapable of discovering a foolproof link between the impact and the word. Orwell explains what is meant expressionistically when he says that we know that no Socialist would ever write like G. K. Chesterton and no Tory imperialist would ever write like Bernard Shaw. Then he confesses that how we know this is beyond him—or anyone else to date.

In the early days of his literary career he said he liked 'a florid style'. The style which won him his reputation was anything but florid, nor was even his earliest writing—although he was sometimes tempted to put down a rather magnificent phrase which didn't really convey what he wanted to say. At first sight this may sound inconsistent, but it is probably an example of a writer voicing his admiration for something of which he himself was incapable. How many people have confessed to a liking of the many styles in which *Ulysses* was written, and how many people could emulate them? It is not uncommon for a writer to admire most of all the kind of writing which is quite outside his compass. Presumably T. S. Eliot enjoys Kipling and I have heard de la Mare admire Dylan Thomas. 'If your motto is "Cut out the adjectives",' wrote Orwell, 'why not go a bit further and revert to a system of grunts and squeals, like the animals?' (*New English Weekly*, 23 July, 1936.) But time is an enemy of the adjective and as he grew older Orwell began to pare them away. In *The English People* (1947) he said there were no reliable rules for writing English, 'only the general principle that concrete words are better than abstract ones, and that the shortest way of saying anything is always the best'. Whoever writes English is involved in a constant struggle against vagueness, obscurity and 'the lure of the decorative adjective'.

One of the easiest ways to literary fame in England is *via* the paradox. Chesterton wallowed in it and Shaw mastered it. Orwell is not generally thought of as a paradoxical writer but there is a subtle paradox at the heart of all his best writing. Chesterton's method was perfectly simple: invert the usually accepted judgment, and then project it to the most lunatic conclusions. Orwell was an intellectual writing for intellectuals. His form of inversion was to back the common man's judgment, which is rarely the same as the intellectual's, with intellectual arguments. It was the reason why Orwell's earlier criticism seemed so fresh—it said so many things we believed in but it said them in a highly respectable manner which left no grounds for shame or feelings of inadequacy. Later, when Orwell became too conscious of his intuition's usage as a 'method' it became degraded and sometimes led him astray. The best example is to be found in the attack on General Wavell which appeared in *Horizon*, December 1940. Things were not going too well in North Africa and Wavell had just been put in command. There was the usual press chorus of Wavell's magnificent qualities which was no doubt partly responsible for Orwell's almost automatic assumption that Wavell must therefore be no good. But in any case, it had become Orwell's role to oppose the experts and their publicists with closely reasoned argument. But in this case he threw caution aside and made a frontal attack. His argument is worth reproducing in some detail:

'One test one might apply is: Can one imagine Allenby,[1] or anyone like him, making much of a showing in the present war? No. Yet it is obvious that our present commanders are of the same type as we had in the last war, and to a large extent actually the same men. Meanwhile war has changed its character and we are fighting against people who are above all else intellectuals, people whose strategy, tactics and propaganda are all part of a coherent plan which is ultimately governed by a Weltanschauung. At such a time a poet or philosopher who does not even how how to handle a .303 rifle, but who does at least know something about the nature of Fascism, is a better guied to grand strategy than an elderly soldier who has given his life to the study of war but who, politically and philosophically, has learnt nothing since 1918. The history of the past five years, the Spanish civil war for instance, proves this beyond a doubt.

'Perhaps General Wavell's claims are justified and Allenby was the best of a bad lot. But we are certainly lost if we cannot produce something better this time. Since Waterloo England's wars have been won either by sea power and overwhelming resources or, as in the Indian Mutiny, by brilliant individuals who were out of reach of the central authorities, or by letting loose the native talents which it is the normal job of the governing classes to bottle down. This happened to some extent in the Great War. The thick-necked cavalry generals remained at the top, but the lower middle classes and the colonies came to the rescue. The thing is happening again, and probably upon a much larger scale, but it is happening with desperate slowness.

"History to the defeated
May say Alas! but cannot alter or pardon."

'Moreover, this time we need a different kind of rescuer. If we are saved it is not likely to be anyone whom General Wavell would admire.'

1 Orwell was reviewing *Allenby, a Study in Greatness*, by General Sir Archibald Wavell, K.C.B., C.M.G., M.C.

This is the voice of the frustrated middle-class intellectual, whose plight Orwell wrote about in strong terms in *The Lion and the Unicorn*. It is safe to assume that Wavell himself is the target. Allenby was the best of a bad lot, but not good enough, and Wavell had modelled himself upon him. I am certain that Orwell read the book from cover to cover but he could have written this review without opening it. It is based upon a general class theory, a theory that is acceptable *in general*, but will not give the clue to any individual. It is not the theory that is at fault but Orwell's critical method. Note once again that it was written during his 'bad period', as he himself might have called it. The review brought forth a number of protests after Wavell had started rolling the Germans back—as I recall, almost immediately after publication. In his Notebook Orwell commented: 'So the laugh is on me—though, God knows, I am glad enough to have been wrong.'

I have called this method paradoxical. It involved the plausible presentation of unpopular views—usually commonplace views, but unpopular because Orwell was normally writing for people who detested commonplace views.[1] I once had a theory that Chesterton, whose name springs to mind whenever paradox is mentioned, had been a favourite of Orwell's when he was a young man. Whenever we discussed writers and Chesterton's name cropped up (as it did now and again, because I enjoyed his exuberance) Orwell used to hedge. I got the impression that he had been perhaps immoderately keen on Chesterton and wanted to forget it. It is a familiar trend these days to enjoy Chesterton when young and uncritical and romantic and to be ashamed of it in later life when one's physiological processes are getting sluggish and one becomes over-conscious of reality, especially the reality of reality. Orwell himself once wrote, for instance, that 'one major objective of young English Catholic writers is not to resemble Chesterton'. (*The New Yorker*, 17 July, 1948.) But there are a considerable number of references to Chesterton in his early writing. Flory used to read his articles in the *London News*. Orwell's well-known

---

1 The instance I have quoted is not typical because in it Orwell writes more like an intellectual than a common man. It is the best example, however, of the method going wrong.

phrase, 'good bad book', was an invention of Chesterton's. In an early review we are told that it is impossible not to like Chesterton. He is praised for his championship of the poor, which is more than could be said for many left-wingers. Chesterton in his criticism used to concern himself with what the book was about, not merely its manner of saying it. And it may be more than an astonishing coincidence that *The Napoleon of Notting Hill* begins its story in the year 1984. That date may have stuck in Orwell's mind as a year to look forward to long after he had forgotten what it signified. It is possible that as a boy or a young man he was fascinated by the paradoxes of Chesterton and later made his own use of the device, though greatly refined.

Another quality in Orwell's work was what George Woodcock called his 'complete lack of aesthetic affectation . . . he never sought to make any distinction between his literary work and the social criticism towards which he always felt impelled'. ('Orwell and Conscience', *World Review*, April 1950.) For this reason Herbert Read compared him with Daniel Defoe. 'Defoe was the first writer to raise journalism to a literary art; Orwell perhaps the last.' (Revaluation of *1984*, *World Review*, June 1950.) Orwell could not differentiate between journalism and literature because for him the two had merged. We sometimes use the term 'journalism' to denote hurried, superficial writing, but Orwell could not accept this. Journalism was 'daily writing' and there was no reason at all why it should be inferior in quality to fiction or criticism because they also were becoming aspects of 'daily writing'. No worthwhile fiction or criticism could ignore contemporary events. 'Contemporary reality' had become so pervasive it dominated every written word and expressed thought. He was impatient of any contemporary writing which ignored the universally significant events that engulfed all of us. He objected to a book like *Midnight* by Julian Green on these grounds.

> 'Ours is not an age for mysterious romances about lunatics in ruined chateaux because it is not an age in which one can be unaware of contemporary reality. You can't ignore Hitler, Mussolini, unemployment, aeroplanes and the radio; you can only pretend to do so, which means lopping off a large chunk of your consciousness.' (*New English Weekly*, 12 November, 1936.)

Like Defoe, he found the ordinary events of everyday life too overwhelming to allow subsidiary matters to concern him. He could not relax when he was writing, which probably explains why the dry humour of which he was capable in conversation never found its way into his writing. And now I must quote his solitary joke, as promised earlier. It occurred in the *New English Weekly* of 26 September, 1935, and never again did he allow such a note of flippancy to intrude. Complaining of the Lancashire dialect in a novel, he wrote:

> 'I rather object to it. I feel sure that there is quite enough north-country dialect in real life without letting it get into novels.'

There is the evidence for those people who say he had no humour. Such a statement could not be an accident. It is an example of glorious irresponsibility. It would have been better if he had released it more often.

Sometimes this immersion in the present produced curious results. It led him to drag in all kinds of extraneous considerations which did not illuminate his argument at all. Reviewing a novel about the Saxon period, he makes a reference to the Battle of Hastings. The mechanism clicked and he commented solemnly, '1066, lest there should have been another Battle of Hastings before this is printed'. ('History Books', *New Statesman*, 21 September, 1940.) He told us that after a certain date all his work was devoted to the defence of democratic socialism against Fascism, and this determination caused every event, wherever and whenever it occurred, to be related in his mind to the contemporary struggle. He believed that this was true of any worthwhile writer, that the majority of good novels, for instance, were written 'with a purpose'. In his article 'Why I Write' he admitted that a book is often the result of vanity but when it lacked political purpose it was lifeless. During Orwell's lifetime any purpose had become political because the organisation of life had become totalitarian. This had nothing to do with the principles or desires of the government. Circumstances had related every single act of every single individual inextricably and it was useless pretending that one could live outside the network. It was this belief and the practice that followed from it that made *1984* and also *Coming Up For Air*, another product of his maturity, such unsatisfactory novels. Both were much too slow-moving to be good fiction. In each his main purpose had been the diagnosis of society or a section of society and the fictional values had been thrown overboard. The chief motive of *1984* was the publication of Goldstein's analysis in such a way that it would reach the largest possible public.

He was not oblivious of the fact, however, that indulgence in politics may destroy the literary values and performance of a writer. V. S. Pritchett said Orwell was an excellent argument against a writer going in for politics. Either the writer retained his values and lost the confidence of the politicians, or he became a hack. Orwell knew this and he also knew that it was a thankless task trying to keep your political principles un-sullied. He discussed this problem in 'Writers and Leviathan' (*Such, Such Were the Joys*). But the solution was not to keep out of politics—in fact, it was impossible for any thinking person to insulate himself from politics. He tried to find a compromise:

'I only suggest that we should draw a sharper distinction between our political and our literary loyalties, and should recognise that a willingness to *do* certain distasteful but necessary things does not carry with it any obligation to swallow the beliefs that usually go with them. When a writer engages in politics he should do so as a citizen, as a human being, but not *as a writer*. I do not think that he has the right, merely on the score of his sensibilities, to shirk the ordinary dirty work of politics. Just as much as anyone else, he should be prepared to deliver lectures in draughty halls, to chalk pavements, to canvass voters, to distribute leaflets, even to fight in civil wars if it seems necessary. But what-ever else he does in the service of his party, he should never write for it. He should make it clear that his writing is a thing apart. And he should be able to act co-operatively while, if he chooses, completely rejecting the official ideology. He should never turn back from a train of thought because it may lead to a heresy, and he should not mind very much if his unorthodoxy is smelt out, as it probably will be. Perhaps it is even a bad sign in a writer if he is not suspected of reactionary tendencies today, just as it was a bad sign if he was not suspected of Communist sympathies twenty years ago.

'But does all this mean that a writer should not only refuse to be dictated to by political bosses, but also that he should refrain from writing *about* politics? Once again, certainly not! There is no reason why he should not write in the most crudely political way, if he wishes to. Only he should do so as an individual, an outsider at the most an unwelcome guerrilla on the flank of a regular army. This attitude is quite compatible with ordinary political usefulness. It is reasonable, for example, to be willing to fight in a war because one thinks the war ought to be won, and at the same time to refuse to write war propaganda. Sometimes, if a writer is honest, his writings and his political activities may actually contradict one another. There are occasions when that is plainly undesirable: but then the remedy is not to falsify one's impulses, but to remain silent.'

The penultimate sentence gives as persuasive a defence and explanation of inconsistency as we are likely to find. All honest writers are aware that inconsistency is inevitable. If a writer boasts of his consistency you can be sure he is leaving certain things out of account. Even the subtlest mind cannot always see the distant implications of everything he writes. Orwell joins Emerson and Aldous Huxley in decrying the 'hobgoblin of consistency', but his reasons are different from theirs. The general and the particular frequently have to be opposed in their values; attempts to reconcile them may lead to nullity and inaction.

Orwell is the most outstanding example of common sense in modern English literature. It is not so remarkable as it seems that his common sense sometimes led him to what appear to be extreme and even crankish conclusions. This may have been because we have lost sight of common sense in our social and political lives and are astonished by common sense when we meet with it. Like most of the apostles of common sense, he thought in terms of psychological types and wished to legislate for blank faces rather than for organic men and women. This again helps to explain the weakness of his fiction. He knew much less about what human beings were like than about what they ought to be like. This did not mean he had a saintly conception of humanity—indeed, it was quite the reverse. He was rather too eager to assume that human beings never were saints, or rather than one who became a saint had in some way contracted out of humanity. There was a perversity in this, an insistence that *all* people ought to prefer beer and baccy to champagne and cigars and that *no one* really had the right to behave outrageously about something they believed in. Perhaps they shouldn't, but they do in large numbers. Sir Richard Rees has drawn attention to the extreme academicism to which his outlook could push Orwell.

'There were areas of his mind where a rather wintry bleakness reigned. He lacked psychological insight, and it is possible to regret that he never criticised his own rather rough and ready conception of common sense. Having dismissed, to his own satisfaction and in the manner of Dr Johnson kicking the stone, all the speculations of philosophers and the assertions of saints and mystics, he would present you with some grotesque dilemma such as this: Suppose the earth had cooled to such a point that it would soon become uninhabitable, would you prefer to stay here and make a last stand as a human being, or would you join an expedition to some other planet where life might be possible but where for all we know conditions would gradually change us into something unrecognisably different from human beings?' (Scots Chronicle, 1951.)

He was interested in the fate of humanity in a million years' time as well as now. He often misjudged the abnormal human being (of whom there are large numbers) but he was fairly accurate in his understanding of the normal. There is a tendency among Europeans to believe that abnormality (by European standards) is running riot in America. It is our pride that we are remaining relatively sane while the Americans are running relatively mad. But Orwell saw through this. He realised that Americans are, broadly speaking, as sane as we are but they are under a different set of social pressures which causes them to react in a way that seems alien to us. If we were subject to the same pressures we would respond in the same way. He alone, so far as I know, was not amused by the panic caused in America by Orson Welles's broadcast based on Wells's *The War of the Worlds*. He pointed out that apart from the opening announcement and a piece of dialogue at the end the play was produced in the form of news bulletins. People who switched on after the beginning heard what purported to be actual reports. But in addition to this they believed that news bulletins, in general, are truthful. This is true not only of Americans but also of Englishmen. We have now passed the stage where everyone believes that what is written in the newspapers must be true, but we are only at the beginning of the stage where people believe that the wireless does not lie. This has been confirmed by opinion-finding bodies and Orwell was aware of the fact.

This was his strength. He knew that ordinary people tend to believe the wireless, much more readily than intellectuals, for instance, believe it. The common sense of the ordinary man is tangled up with all kinds of naiveties, and Orwell possessed the one alongside an awareness of the second. Similarly he had the ordinary man's scepticism about supernatural or paranormal phenomena, a conviction that there is no knowledge that is not perceived through the senses. The ordinary man gives lip-service to spiritual phenomena—he has to if he confesses to religion—but at this point Orwell's ordinariness stopped short and he dismissed them as a box of tricks. He flatly states in a review of Jean Burton's *Heyday of a Wizard*, 'It is clear that things of this kind cannot actually have happened'. (*Observer*, 6 June, 1948.) His only interest in the subject is the one we would expect: how can people be induced to believe in such nonsense? This is an excellent example of how perverse common sense can be, for the evidence supporting paranormal activities would be considered overwhelming in any of the physical sciences. Again, reviewing Sacheverell Sitwell's *Poltergeists* he writes: 'As with spiritualistic phenomena, three explanations are possible. One is "spirits", one is hypnotism and hallucination, and another is vulgar fraud. Few sensible people would accept the first. . . .' (*Horizon*, September 1940.) In each of these examples one cannot help remarking on the poverty of Orwell's reasons for disbelief. In fact, there are no reasons, only denials which in another context he would have called bigotry.

Perhaps the basis of this bigotry is to be found where we should most expect to find it, in Orwell's political opinions. In his essay on Yeats he notes a connection between occultism and Fascism. Even if this does put the cart before the horse, so far as convincing argument is concerned, it was sufficient to rouse Orwell's hostility. Of the type of occultism that believes in recurring cycles, he said it implied that progress was impossible. A year before the war he counted thirty-eight occult advertisements in one copy of *Gringoire*, the French Fascist weekly. The concept of occultism involved the idea that knowledge is secret and is limited to a small circle of initiates, and the same idea is integral to Fascism. In addition, both Fascism and magic are hostile to the Christian ethical code. It is easy to see why Orwell never gave occultism a fair chance. If he had applied the same reasoning to the truth or falsity of biology or musical theory he could have reached the same conclusions. There are some beliefs that must be shared, by Fascists and democrats alike.

Chapter XV

The People's Reading

ANYTHING THAT 'the people' did was of interest to Orwell, with one strange exception. He never showed the normal Englishman's enthusiasm for sport, nor did he show any curiosity about this new industry-cum-entertainment. Being a writer, however, he did show a very marked interest in what people read.

In *Coming Up For Air* we are given a brief history of Tubby Bowling's reading. With the addition of a few highbrow titles (the ones Bowling specifically denied acquaintance with—it was rather strange that he should have heard of them and even considered them readable) the list is probably a fairly accurate description of Orwell's own early reading. No one had ever urged him to read highbrow books, only 'good' books, and it is likely that until he left Burma his reading was very much the same as any other young man's of his age and class. We get corroboration of this from his criticism, which is nearly always of popular writers. It is only later in life that he tackles Eliot and Yeats and even then he extracts their message (the most 'popular' aspect of their work, if we can use the term) and tends to ignore the rest. Bowling classed himself as a typical Boots' Library subscriber who later joined the Left Book Club. This might also be a description of Orwell at the beginning; later his innate sense of criticism caused him to see through the insincerities of popular writing, whether fictional or political, and led him to those books which antagonise most readers because they do not shrink from the unpleasant or the difficult.

From eleven to sixteen Bowling read the boys' penny weeklies —'little thin papers with vile print and an illustration in three colours on the cover'—and then he graduated to books: *Sherlock Holmes, Dracula, Raffles*. He was pushed through *Quentin Durward* at school, but there were no books in his home. (This was almost certainly not true of Orwell's home and at school there was a library which he used. Most of the literature was improving, no doubt—we know he was frowned upon for reading *Sinister Street.* Despite his opportunities I feel convinced, from the case of his mind, that he was at base a popular reader, but also that his mind was capable of great development. If we may equate him with Flory, in a discussion of reading tastes, it seems likely that he was dissatisfied with the books that were available but was unable to replace them with anything better, although he knew they existed, until he liberated himself by leaving Burma.) During his teens *Chums* became Bowling's literary standby. When he was eighteen he suddenly turned highbrow (he had passed through a 'hot' phase with Maupassant and Paul de Kock) and started reading Marie Corelli and Hall Caine and Anthony Hope.

Bowling educated himself through reading when, late in the war, he became officer-in-charge of a backwater called Twelve-Mile Dump. Up till then a 'good' book was one you had no intention of reading. Now he came across books, left by one of his predecessors, which were obviously 'good' and also readable. One was *Mr Polly*, another was Conrad's *Victory*, and *Sinister Street* is also mentioned. This encouraged him to take out sub-scriptions at two libraries and during the next year or so he wallowed in books: Kipling, W. W. Jacobs, Compton Mac-kenzie, Stephen McKenna, Elinor Glyn and Silas Hocking among others. There is no doubt in my mind that these are more than names taken from a catalogue; they are the authors whom Orwell read and, to varying degrees, enjoyed when he was a young man. In his later work he often referred to many of them in respectful terms. He wrote essays on Kipling, he ad-mired Wells until he became bored by him, he saw through Galsworthy while admitting his good points, he had some kind words to say about Jacobs. Later Bowling learned to distinguish between good work and tripe (Orwell always called it tripe) and summed up as follows:

'I got hold of Lawrence's *Sons and Lovers* and sort of half-enjoyed it, and I got a lot of kick out of Oscar Wilde's *Dorian Gray* and Stevenson's *New Arabian Knights*. Wells was the author who made the biggest impression on me. I read George Moore's *Esther Waters*

and liked it, and I tried several of Hardy's novels and always got
stuck about half-way through. I even had a go at Ibsen, who left
me with a vague impression that in Norway it's always raining.'

From the evidence of his later writing one would suppose that
Kipling was the author who had made the greatest impression
on Orwell—Dickens always excepted. He does not mention
Chesterton, whose work he knew fairly well (he made frequent
references to it). This strengthens my impression that Chesterton
was one of those authors he was deliberately trying to put aside.
He can ruin a young writer as effectively as James Joyce.

By this time Bowling had passed out of his lower middle-class
milieu intellectually and was hovering in the sub-intellectual
air. Elizabeth in *Burmese Days* was irrevocably lowbrow. 'In a
general way Michael Arlen was her favourite author, but she
was inclined to prefer William J. Locke when she wanted
something serious.' Before Flory's affair with a native girl was
known to her, she knew he was not to be trusted because he was
a highbrow ('her deadliest word'), to be classed with Lenin,
A. J. Cook and 'the dirty little poets in the Montparnasse cafés'.
Hatred of highbrows was the dominant intellectual characteristic of the lower middle class and it controlled their reading
tastes rigidly.

Apart from what he himself tells us and what we can guess
from his novels, we have a little information about Orwell's
personal tastes from his friend, Sir Richard Rees. He liked
obscure, partly forgotten authors such as Gissing, Leonard
Merrick and Arthur Morrison—writers of 'good bad books',
says Rees, although Orwell would probably not have considered
this a true description of Gissing. He was curious about the
seedy, the shabby and the queer, which helps explain this predilection and his admiration of Dickens. Rees agrees that his
tastes were largely orthodox, although they were exerted on
several different levels. Even when he admired highbrow
writers he chose those whom other highbrows of the period
admired—Eliot and Hopkins, for instance. He considered *Felix
Randal* one of the best short poems in the language.

He believed that the lower middle class had an actual dis-
taste for reading. It encouraged preciosity and false attitudes,
i.e., an insufficiently realistic attitude to life or money. When

Dorothy in *A Clergyman's Daughter* fetched a novel from the public library her headmistress was shocked. Dorothy was paid to work, not to waste time in self-indulgence. Mrs Creevy, said Orwell, had never read a book in her life and was proud of it. But not everyone had her strength of character. There were many people who could not resist reading just as others cannot resist smoking, and they were catered for by what Orwell called 'mushroom libraries'. Gordon Comstock (*Keep the Aspidistra Flying*) worked in one.

> 'In libraries like these there is not a single book that is ever mentioned in the reviews or that any civilised person has ever heard of. The books are published by special low-class firms and turned out by wretched hacks at the rate of four a year, as mechanically as sausages and with much less skill. In effect they are merely fourpenny novelettes disguised as novels, and they only cost the library proprietor one-and-eightpence a volume.'

The subscribers to this type of library probably merged with the working class. Even Elizabeth would have regarded them as trash, not because they were any worse than what she read but because she enjoyed the comfort of a 'name' on the title-page. She didn't want to be considered highbrow, but there was a certain cachet about mentioning Locke or Arlen in company and being understood.

Orwell's reference to the manufacture of sausages was more significant than it may have seemed at the time. Later, in 'The Prevention of Literature' (*Shooting an Elephant*) he drew attention to the danger that literature may in time become a mechanical product. Popular songs were turned out by a versificator in the world of 1984. What helps this trend enormously is the fact that the mass of people in industrialised countries feel no need of any kind of literature. They refuse to spend money on books and without sales literature must perish. If literature survives at all it may be in the form of low-grade sensational fiction, produced by a conveyor-belt process that will reduce human initiative to a minimum. He points out that the Disney films are produced by a factory process, that radio features are chopped into shape by producers and censors, that government pamphlets and cheap fiction are produced to a mechanical formula. Literary schools offer ready-made plots, opening and closing sentences of each chapter, algebraical formulae or packs of cards marked with characters and situations which only have to be shuffled to produce stories automatically. Imagination would be eliminated from such 'writing'. And the literature of the past would have to be suppressed or rewritten. (The latter is already being done.) This would be the price of totalitarianism, for a centralised system in the modern world must suppress thought and any independence or strangeness of outlook.

In an article entitled 'Vessel of Wrath' in the *Observer* (21 May, 1944) Orwell made his most outspoken attack on the mechanical method of compiling a book. In this case he was not concerned with 'tripe' but with an ostensibly serious book on world politics. But the same argument applies. Books can be written and are being written without any creative stimulus behind them. Just as the young man with his Plotto chops up situations, climaxes and denouements, so a journalist can paste together bits of speeches and newspaper articles, and imagine he is producing something of value.

'The chief difficulty of writing a book nowadays', wrote Orwell with unusually heavy sarcasm, 'is that pots of paste are usually sold without brushes. But if you can get hold of a brush (sometimes procurable at Woolworth's) and a pair of scissors and a good-sized blank book, you have everything you need. It is not necessary to do any actual writing. Any collection of scraps—reprinted newspaper articles, private letters, fragments of diaries, even "radio discussions" ground out by wretched hacks to be broadcast by celebrities—can be sold to the amusement-starved public.'

The occasion of this attack was H. G. Wells's *42' to '44!*

Something in society was producing this new trend but Orwell did not seem quite clear what it was. In 1942 he said that Fascism killed good prose though not necessarily poetry; 'Conservatism of the half-hearted modern kind' was deadly to both. ('Points of View—T. S. Eliot', *Poetry London*, October-November 1942.) Early in the following year he claims that although the best writers of our time have been reactionary they can expect nothing from Fascism which does not really offer a return to the past. ('W. B. Yeats', *Critical Essays*.) Orwell probably believed that any form of conservatism killed literature eventually, but Fascism did it more brutally and cold-bloodedly than conservatism of the mild, gentlemanly English type, which merely induced death by paralysis of the spirit. But if the 'best' writers are reactionary, are they not somehow conservative? And who are they? Wyndham Lewis and Eliot, presumably, but among the runners-up is there any clearly marked qualitative distinction between 'reactionaries' and 'progressives'? The true answer, and one which Orwell hinted at elsewhere, is that no creative writer can wear such labels. He knows that art and literature do not respond to such criteria and that the most progressive writer may also be the most reactionary. Totalitarians hate them all and will find offences against the canon in the work of all of them.

But Orwell's main interest in current literature was sociological and it was towards the second- and third-rate writers that he directed his attention. These *can* be dubbed, in fact, they usually wish to be dubbed because they believe that literature is a branch of some other study or an expression of some overt point of view. Prominent among these was the 'country house' novel with which this land has been blessed so abundantly—novels which mourn the passing of 'all this', an evocative phrase which is concerned with such eternal verities as tea on the lawn and nectarines from your own glasshouse. Literary values are not aimed at, only squads of nostalgia. Orwell reviewed some by Angela Thirkell, Mary Lutyens and Susan Gillespie in the *New Statesmen*, 16 November, 1940.

> 'When one looks at novels of this kind, so spiritually flaccid, so lacking in any kind of purpose, artistic or political, one sees that they can only be produced because large pockets of the pre-war mind are still in existence. It seems almost incredible, after the bombs. However, fear not, times are changing, taxes are rising, and within a year from now, even if the submarines have not forced us to do all our writing on brick tablets, the novel about people with pale, sensitive faces in lovely old country houses will have gone to join the dodo and the plesiosaurus.'

It is always the low-grade fiction writers who give themselves away the most. He refers to Professor Whitehead's remark that every philosophy is coloured by a secret imaginative background, and notes how true this is of fiction. Every novelist writes out of a personal fantasy, but the best novelists are those who manage to obscure the fantasy and therefore carry

conviction to other people, even people who indulge in a different
or opposed fantasy. It is easy to guess, for instance, that Stendhal
had a fantasy life in which he pictured himself as a duke, but he
was too much aware of his own snobbishness to let it get on to
paper undisguised. In his novels the snob motif is either turned
upside down (*Le Rouge et le Noir*) or it reappears as a vision of
spiritual aristocracy (*La Chartreuse de Parme*). But lesser writers
(he cites E. F. Benson, Saki and Michael Arlen) simply put their
narcissism on to paper with no notion of what they are doing.
While they are inferior as novelists they are reliable guides to
the popular fantasies of their time.

There is a strong desire among ordinary people, even if
unconscious, that literature should be unreal. Literature is
really expected to act as a pander, bringing pleasant dreams
to the patient's bed. Somteimes the revered great disappoint.
It is part of our national code, for instance, to revere Shakespeare. It may be possible to go through life without reading
him, which leaves his reputation unsullied. But one is sometimes
brought up against Shakespeare in the most unexpected way
and then it is necessary to decide whether the idol has not, after
all, erred. The erring is usually moral. When Dorothy introduced her class of girls to *Macbeth* she unsuspectingly brought
on a crisis of this kind (*A Clergyman's Daughter*). The parents
were horrified to hear that

> 'Macduff was from his mother's womb
> Untimely ripped.'

A meeting was called and Mr Poynder put the parents' point
of view.

> 'To my mind it's a disgrace that school-books can be printed
> with such words in them. I'm sure if any of us had ever known that
> Shakespeare was that kind of stuff we'd have put our foot down
> at the start. It surprises me, I must say. Only the other morning
> I was reading a piece in my *News Chronicle* about Shakespeare
> being the father of English Literature; well, if that's Literature
> let's have a bit less Literature, say I !'

The idea that the reading public demands the indulgence of
private fantasy has become so strong it is difficult to publish a
novel today without making such a concession. Even a serious
novelist such as Graham Greene appears to find it necessary to

play continuously on the theme of sex guilt, one of the most exciting of contemporary fantasies. If you cannot imagine yourself enjoying the felicities of 'all this' then you can fall back on the forbidden joys of sexual misconduct, with a background of religion to give you the sensation of being pitted romantically against the Fates. One of Orwell's greatest achievements was to write a book which did not pander to any popular fantasy, and get away with it—at least, *1984* had a large sale. As Herbert Read has said, it has no charm, it makes no concession to sentiment and it has only a few traces of eroticism—and those few create a sensation of acute discomfort. He thought it possible that its success may have been explained by the element of sado-masochism in the public. Yet there is no evidence that it helped turn the tide against the totalitarian state any more than Foxe's *Book of Martyrs* produced a mood of tolerance in its readers.

Apart from their sophistication, Orwell came to the conclusion that four-fifths of 'the things that pass as novels nowadays' were not essentially different from the serials to be found in *Peg's Paper*. The main difference is that the novels are paragraphed differently and usually have a smart title ('this is done by choosing a title that ought to have a "the" in it and then leaving out the "the" '). Very often they are worse than the serials because while being just as infantile and vulgar they have much less vitality. The market for such novels consists mainly of women and Orwell had a very low opinion of feminine literary taste. He said that one of the surest signs of Conrad's genius is that women dislike his books. The same might be said of Ford Madox Ford.

He believed that the novels that were being published during the early years of the war were on a level lower than any in living memory. He added that it was poor consolation to reflect that the ones being published in Germany were probably worse. In a London Letter to *Partisan Review* written at about the same time he said that nothing of consequence was being written, except in fragmentary form such as diaries and short sketches. The best novels he had read were either American or translations of foreign books written several years earlier. Reviewing Greene's *The Heart of the Matter* in *The New Yorker* he said it was a remarkable feat for a novelist to write a novel at all in post-war England. (Presumably he meant above the level of sex-crime, unadorned fantasy or 'prolefeed' as in *1984*.) The only good word he had to say about the general run of fiction concerned political thrillers. But this was simply because the modern political world, with its underground parties, tortures, pass-words, denunciations, forged passports and cipher messages was a gift to the light novelist. Fiction had not drawn closer to life, life had drawn closer to fiction, or at least the fiction writer's dream. This at least was an advance, for the average thriller had been socially and politically more out of date than the *Daily Telegraph* correspondence column or the jokes in *Punch*.

Orwell's literary enthusiasm was most easily roused by the social novels of the nineteenth century. These at least appeared to attempt reality without conceding too much to fantasy. Throughout his work there are references, often in superlatives, to this branch of fiction. *Mark Rutherford's Deliverance*, for instance, 'is one of the best novels in English'. Gissing is 'perhaps the best novelist England has produced'. He admitted that many other novelists were superior to him in natural talent, but he was one of the few who had no temptation to burlesque. Nearly all the characteristic English novelists, from Smollett to Joyce, wish to be 'like life' and yet at the same time want to get a laugh as often as possible. 'Very few English novelists exist throughout on the same plane of probability.' ('Not Enough Money', *Tribune*, 2 April, 1943.) Gissing lacked the high spirits, the instinct to play the fool, which made Dickens, for instance, as unable to pass a joke as some people are to pass a pub. In fact, Orwell traced the excellence of many novelists to a quality which they lacked rather than one they possessed. George Moore's great advantage as a novelist, for instance, lay in not having an over-developed sense of pity; he could resist the temptation to make his characters more sensitive than they would be in real life. The real value of Henry Miller's early work, Orwell believed, lay in his refusal to idealise sex as nearly every other writer before him had done. Orwell's strength as a literary critic lay to a very large extent in his flair for noticing what was absent—this is noticeable in the essay on Dickens. He seemed to see literature as a parade of faculties which frequently obscured the truth; the truth shone through in flashes when a writer had the power to put off this blanket of virtuosity. Too many writers had misled their readers with their stupendous weaknesses.

The real reason why Orwell admired the social writers of the past was because they had felt at home in the world they lived in. They not only wrote about life but they shared the life they wrote about. A modern writer is almost hopelessly isolated. Specialisation makes it difficult for him to live at more than one level at once; if he is to be a writer, he must specialise at the craft. The amateur is disappearing, in writing as in sport, and also in every other type of activity. Although some of the nineteenth-century novelists earned a lot of money from their writing, they retained the characteristic attitudes of the amateur. They were able to make forays into other sectors of society without suffering from a sense of slumming. But today it is more and more difficult for a novelist to merge with non-novelists; if he does he runs the risk of ceasing to be a novelist. As a man can only write about things he knows from first-hand experience, the modern novel tends to be about a novelist or a novelist thinly disguised as a normal citizen. Orwell points out that when Joyce spent a decade planning and writing his story of a 'common man' he turned out to be a slightly highbrow Jew. In addition to this disability of the modern writer his raw material, society, is intrinsically less manageable than the societies of the past, in Orwell's view. The adjectives he used to describe modern society as compared with, say, Tolstoy's are 'very much meaner, less comely and less carefree'. ('As I Please', *Tribune*, 10 March, 1944.) Some people have been repelled by the characters in Joyce's *Dubliners*, but he would have been falsifying the facts if he had made them different. In the long run this sets up a tension between writer and reader which does not make his task easier. Taken together, these trends mean that the contemporary novelist often has no choice between writing intellectual novels for intellectuals or escape-fantasies for people who cannot face facts. Orwell admired Henry Miller because he was one of the few who could write about the majority-life that lay between these poles.

'The interest of *Tropic of Cancer* was that it cast a kind of bridge across the frightful gulf which exists, in fiction, between the intellectual and the man-in-the-street. English fiction on its higher levels is for the most part written by literary gents about literary gents for literary gents; on its lower levels it is generally the most putrid "escape" stuff—old maids' fantasies about Ian Hay male virgins, or fat little men's visions of themselves as Chicago gangsters. Books about ordinary people behaving in an ordinary manner are extremely rare, because they can only be written by someone who is capable of standing both inside and outside the ordinary man, as Joyce for instance stands inside and outside Bloom; but this involves admitting that you yourself *are* an ordinary person for nine-tenths of the time, which is exactly what no intellectual ever wants to do.' (*New English Weekly*, 24 September, 1936.)

There was once a mistaken notion in Left-wing circles that the advent of Socialism would raise the standard of current literature. This was because the leaders of Socialist thought are intellectuals and they believed that Socialism was intellectually more advanced than the reactionary political systems. In fact, said Orwell, the Left is no more friendly towards highbrows (i.e., any writer or artist who makes experiments in technique) than the Right. 'Not only is "highbrow" almost as much a word of abuse in the *Daily Worker* as in *Punch*, but it is exactly those writers whose work shows both originality and the power to endure that Marxist doctrinaires single out for attack.' ('Literature and the Left', *Tribune*, 4 June, 1943.)

But the attacks of the Marxists are really only symbolic of all criticism. Despite the discussion of values and standards Orwell believed that nearly all literary criticism was fraudulent. Marxist doctrinaires attacked original writers not for literary reasons but because they refused to follow the Party Line. Nearly all critical attacks are of the same nature—the author is not following the 'line' favoured by the critic. There is not and cannot be any *external* reference by which one can dub a book 'good' or 'bad': 'every literary judgment consists in trumping up a set of rules to justify an instinctive preference'. Literary criticism in the main is a facade and the really outstanding thing about it is that it is rarely literary. Apart from poetry, literature is rarely appreciated for literary reasons.

'One's real reaction to a book, when one has a reaction at all,

is usually "I like this book" or "I don't like it", and what follows
is a rationalisation. But "I like this book" is not, I think, a non-
literary reaction; the non-literary reaction is "This book is on my
side, and therefore I must discover merits in it". Of course, when
one praises a book for political reasons one may be emotionally
sincere, in the sense that one does feel strong approval of it, but
also it often happens that party solidarity demands a plain lie.
Anyone used to reviewing books for political periodicals is well
aware of this. In general, if you are writing for a paper that you
are in agreement with, you sin by commission, and for a paper of
the opposite stamp, by omission. At any rate, innumerable
controversial books—books for or against Soviet Russia, for or
against Zionism, for or against the Catholic Church, etc.—are
judged before they are read, and in effect before they are written.
One knows in advance what reception they will get in what
papers. And yet, with a dishonesty that sometimes is not even
quarter-conscious, the pretence is kept up that genuinely literary
standards are being applied.' ('Writers and Leviathan', *Such,
Such Were the Joys*.)

Orwell's argument is not really so good as it sounds; he had
an immense aura of plausibility about him and his work. The
type of book he is referring to in the above passage does not
invite the application of literary criteria. They are books of
information or exegesis. But the method of valuation he describes is true and for that matter he is justified in calling most
criticism fraudulent. Literary criticism proper is also subject to
the same abuses, but these are not normally the product of, say,
political opinions. It is true that a Marxist will attack a book
by Winston Churchill but he will not even consider it as a piece
of literature—he is only concerned with its political meaning
and judges it on that level. I am aware that the word 'literature'
or 'literary' is bandied about to an alarming extent, but I doubt
if we have the right to allow it to alarm us. The same Marxist
may, in his enthusiasm, describe a volume of Stalin's speech-
porridges as 'literature', but there is no compulsion for us to
lower our own standards by taking the trouble to refute him.
He is probably as ignorant of the real nature of literature as an
illiterate, and we shouldn't trouble to quarrel with the latter.
I think Orwell was making vigorous passes at ghosts in this
matter. He should have confined discussion of literary matters
to those few who understood the meaning of literature.

Orwell approached the question of literary value again in

'Lear, Tolstoy and the Fool' (*Shooting an Elephant*). When Tolstoy says Shakespeare is a bad writer we feel affronted. But a little consideration will show us that Tolstoy had as much foundation for his opinion as we have for ours. None of us can *prove* that Shakespeare is good any more than we can prove that Warwick Deeping is bad. Ultimately there is no test of literary merit except survival, which is itself an index to majority opinion. Tolstoy's type of criticism is useless because it starts out with arbitrary assumptions and depends on vague terms such as 'sincere' and 'important' which can be interpreted in any way you choose. Survival of literature is something that is very difficult to understand, for although it implies a majority test it is usually a majority that appears several years after publication. It is a classic example of the democratic dictum that a minority must have the opportunity to become a majority. One might well ask, what is the value of criticism? The answer is, Very little—if the critic or reviewer believes that his opinion is final. He only demonstrates his arrogance, which is not an interesting characteristic. The true aim of criticism is elucidation and appraisal, never judgment.[1]

I have of course entered on dangerous ground in any consideration of Orwell's own judgments. Neither he nor I would suggest that the right of literary judgment is denied us. In fact, we insist on it—but we must not pretend we are exercising a critical faculty. We are merely expressing a personal preference. I can best express our rights in the matter by an actual example. Logically, those with the best literary judgment should be people who have devoted their lives to the training of this faculty, i.e., Professors of Literature. In fact, when dealing with contemporary writers literary dons often find themselves in difficulties. Orwell quoted a blurb to Ian Hay's *A Safety Match*. It was a message from Professor Saintsbury and it read, 'Let me congratulate you on *A Safety Match*. I have read nothing so good for a long time.' Orwell's comment: 'This shows you what happens to Professors of Literature when they are so unwise as to write about contemporary books.' (*New English Weekly*, 24

---

[1] When I said this at greater length in my book on Hemingway many reviewers professed to be shocked. As susual, however, they gave no indication of why they were shocked.

September, 1936.) Now according to our lights neither Orwell
nor I can show that *A Safety Match* is a bad book. A large number of people read it when it first appeared and there were
subsequent editions. But fewer people are reading it now and it
is fairly certain that soon no one will be reading it. Some people
have the ability to foresee the kind of books that are likely to be
read in the future. Orwell was one and altogether they are
fairly numerous. But Saintsbury wrote with tremendous authority and, in the eyes of some people, canonised Hay's 'tripe' with
his blurb. Now if Saintsbury were really a literary critic he
should have been sacked. But he was not a literary critic, there
being no such animal, merely an extremely widely-read man
with little knowledge of people. (If you question that last statement you will find corroboration from Orwell himself in *The
Road to Wigan Pier*.

In general Orwell had little respect for academic critics.
They had a regrettable tendency to praise just those contemporary literary products that he knew, with his keener nose,
could not survive. 'Not to be made to think—and therefore, if
possible, to prevent literature from developing—is often the aim
of the academic critic.' ('Wandering Star', *Observer*, 19 December, 1943.) The critics had for years praised the poetry of
W. H. Davies. giving the impression that it was a collection of
dreamy and wishy-washy pastorals. When Orwell read the
Collected Works he found that they *were* good, but in quite a
different way from that suggested by the critics. Davies's poetry
had a masculine character and it had clearly marked affinities
with the traditional body of English poetry. (The critics had
given the impression that it sprang self-created from a plough-
boy's lips.) C. E. Montague was another example. Knowing
people liked to call him 'deliciously witty', but Orwell looked
behind the wit and realised it was 'all sparkle and no taste, like
soda-water'. (*New English Weekly*, 24 September, 1936.) The
academic critics sometimes made a 'corner' in a particular
writer, partly to prove their own breadth of outlook and partly
to use as a stick with which to beat other writers. Orwell felt
that Rabelais was used in this way. We are always being told
that while pornography is reprehensible (Swinburne, George
Moore, D. H. Lawrence, Henry Miller), 'hearty Rabelaisian,

humour' is quite all right. This attitude is an easy one to maintain. Hardly anyone reads Rabelais these days. Orwell considered Rabelais 'an exceptionally perverse, morbid writer, a
case for psycho-analysis', and was particularly annoyed to think
that he should be held up as an example for writers such as
Lawrence. (One can imagine the treatment Lawrence would
have received if he had attempted to be realistically funny about
sex or W.C.s.)

The state of contemporary literature was extremely low,
according to Orwell. It was being subjected to too many
pressures to allow much optimism: the totalitarian outlook, the
spiritual vacuum of conservatism, doctrinaire criteria, the
academic fear of the intellect. A creative writer was a liberal
and liberalism was dying. Only the passive attitude was possible; nothing was left but quietism. Writers were struggling
back into 'the whale', the large, comfortable womb required by
an adult. They were giving themselves over to the world-pro-
cess, enduring it and recording it. Anything positive and con-
structive, anything that was not emotionally spurious, was
difficult to imagine. But Orwell regarded the situation as a
challenge and in 1936 published a plan for the revival of the
novel. The real solution was political and social, the liberalisa-
tion of society, which was beyond his powers. But there were
certain practical steps that could be taken to hold up the
general deterioration until politicians or sociologists could
engineer a society which would make creative literature possible
again.

He began by stating that the prestige of the novel was
extremely low ('In Defence of the Novel', *New English Weekly*,
13 and 19 November, 1936). 'There are still a few contemporary
or roughly contemporary novelists whom the intelligentsia consider it permissible to read; but the point is that the ordinary
good-bad novel is habitually ignored while the ordinary good-
bad book of verse or criticism is still taken seriously.' The novel
was being shouted out of existence by the blurb-reviewers. (He
quoted the *Sunday Times*: 'If you can read this book and not
shriek with delight your soul is dead.') When *all* novels are
acclaimed as works of genius it is natural to assume they are all
'tripe'. But there are commercial reasons for this acclamation.

Z writes a book, Y publishes it and X reviews it in the *Weekly W*. If the review is adverse Y removes his advertisement. Therefore X has to announce an 'unforgettable masterpiece' or lose his job. He goes on to say that there can be no good novel-writing so long as it is assumed that every novel is worth reviewing. Our friend X receives a dozen books, eleven of which fail to arouse the faintest spark of interest. He has to manufacture 300 words about a book which means nothing to him at all. He gives a resume of the book but he also has to say whether it is good or bad. He probably has high standards (he was attracted to the ill-paid role of reviewer because he had enjoyed Stendhal, Jane Austen or Dostoievski) but it is impossible to measure the review-book against them. He can't say monotonously, "This is tripe", and leave it at that. And so you get the familiar picture of contemporary reviewing. Ethel M. Dell's *Way of an Eagle* is a fairly good book, which makes *The Constant Nymph* a superb book and *The Man of Property* 'a palpitating tale of passion, a terrific, soul-shattering masterpiece, an unforgettable epic which will last as long as the English language'.

Orwell said it would be a good thing if novels were not reviewed at all, but this would never happen. Intelligent publishers might like to see an end of the blurb review, but it is like disarmament—no one will start. The next best thing is to disregard blurb-reviewing, but this will only happen when there is a periodical which makes a speciality of novel-reviewing and disregards 'tripe'. The highbrow magazines review a few novels intelligently but only as side-lines. About five thousand novels were being published a year at the time. Ralph Straus says he read 'em all (or would if he could). *Criterion* noticed a dozen. These are the two extremes. There may have been two or even three hundred which had genuine merit. The solution Orwell suggested was to grade novels. Books that are worth mentioning belong to different categories. '*Raffles* is a good book and so is *The Island of Dr Moreau* and so is *La Chartreuse de Parme* and so is *Macbeth*; but they are good at very different levels. Similarly *If Winter Comes* and *The Well-Beloved* and *An Unsocial Socialist* and *Sir Lancelot Greaves* are all bad books, but at different levels of "badness". This is the fact that the hack-reviewer has made it his special business to obscure.' Orwell's plan was to grade novels A, B, C and so forth, so that you would know how seriously to take a reviewer. The reviewers would have to be people interested in the art of the novel and in discerning what a book is *about*. A serious amateur would be better than a bored professional. Such a paper would be obscure but would probably raise the standard of reviewing simply by providing contrast. As it is, many intelligent people avoid novels almost instinctively, established novelists go to pieces and beginners turn to other forms. The novel will not disappear, but if an attempt is not made to rescue it it may survive only at the level of the fourpenny novelette (i.e., at 1936 prices).

I don't think such a scheme would have the smallest effect on the standard of the novel, nor do I think Orwell would have subscribed to it ten years later. He himself did use an embryonic system of grading: some novels were 'tripe', others were 'pernicious tripe'. Cyril Connolly was the only novel-reviewer in England who did not make him sick. But if his views on the salvation of the novel changed, his opinion of English reviewing did not. In his 'Confessions of a Book Reviewer' ('I Write As I Please', *Shooting an Elephant*) he again said that the great majority of books should not be reviewed at all. The few that mattered should be reviewed at length—1,000 words was a minimum. Before the war honest reviewing had been technically impossible. The literary pages of several well-known papers had been practically owned by a handful of publishers, who had quislings planted in important jobs. A book from a big publisher, who habitually spent large sums on ads., might get fifty or seventy reviews. One from a small publisher would get only twenty.

'Even reputable literary papers could not afford to disregard their advertisers altogether. It was quite usual to send a book to a reviewer with some such formula as, "Review this book if it seems any good. If not, send it back. We don't think it's worth while to print simply damning reviews."

'Naturally a person to whom the guinea or so that he gets for the review means next week's rent is not going to send the book back. He can be counted on to find something to praise, whatever his private opinion of the book may be.

'In America even the pretence that hack-reviewers read the books they are paid to criticise has been partially abandoned.

Publishers, or some publishers, send out with review copies a short synopsis telling the reviewer what to say. Once, in the case of a novel of my own, they misspelt the name of one of the characters. The same misspelling turned up in review after review. The so-called critics had not even glanced into the book—which, nevertheless, most of them were boosting to the skies.' ('As I Please', *Tribune*, 9 June, 1944.)

In the following year his article on Dali was accepted by the *Saturday Book*. The book was in print when the publishers decided it must be suppressed on grounds of obscenity. It was accordingly cut from every copy, but for technical reasons it was impossible to remove its title from the table of contents. Yet in all the press cuttings he received his name was given as a contributor.

There was little hope for the sincere writer in the large-circulation newspapers and periodicals. Unfortunately the literary reviews were scarcely more promising, though for different reasons. Their literary values were too often those of a coterie and a writer could not gate-crash the coterie by merit alone. In *Keep the Aspidistra Flying* he referred to the *Primrose Quarterly*, 'one of those poisonous literary papers in which the fashionable Nancy Boy and the professional Roman Catholic walk bras dessus, bras dessus'. He adds that it was also by a long way the most influential literary paper in England. In 1946 he writes in a London Letter that 'the kind of streamlined, high-powered, slickly got-up, semi-intellectual magazine which you are familiar with in the U.S.A.' is beginning to appear in England. It was only possible to get a large circulation for a magazine in which the letterpress existed round the edges of photographs and which gave the average reader the feeling of being 'advanced' without actually having to think. So much of the British periodical press was hopelessly antiquated that the American-style magazine would not have much difficulty in conquering the market.

This discussion of reviews and periodicals has led me away from the main subject under discussion: what makes a good book? Orwell was convinced that all art was propaganda but a superior kind of propaganda. It was not until the latter part of the nineteenth century that anyone had any other view of art.

The two major 'apologists' for poetry, Sydney and Shelley, could not imagine an art which did not set out to do something —actually, to perfect something. 'Art for art's sake' had a short run as a serious artistic principle, but it has long shadows which reach into the present. Orwell was a fervent believer in what he called 'tendency'.

> 'On the last occasion when *Punch* produced a genuinely funny joke, which was only six or seven years ago, it was a picture of an intolerable youth telling his aunt that when he came down from the University he intended to "write". "And what are you going to write about, dear?" his aunt enquires. "My dear aunt", the youth replies crushingly, "one doesn't write *about* anything, one just *writes*." This was a perfectly justified criticism of current literary cant. At that time, even more than now, art for art's sake was going strong, though the phrase itself had been discarded as ninetyish; "art has nothing to do with morality" was the favourite slogan. The artist was conceived as leaping to and fro in a moral political and economic void, usually in pursuit of something called "Beauty", which was always one jump ahead. . . . To admit that you liked or disliked a book because of its moral or religious tendency, even to admit noticing that it *had* a tendency, was too vulgar for words.' ('Propagandist Critics', *New English Weekly*, 31 December, 1936.)

This sounds very reasonable, but there is a trap for the unwary. If we go to the other extreme we will find ourselves praising a book for its 'tendency', which is another form of appreciation which Orwell rejected, as I have already shown. But when the two methods become mixed you find a critic praising a book for one quality but privately liking it for another. Communists and Catholics in particular say a book is good only if it preaches the right sermon, but they will not admit that this is the reason. 'Few people have the guts to say outright', says Orwell, 'that art and propaganda are the same thing.' He notes how the *Church Times* gnashes its teeth at modern poetry but makes an exception of Eliot. Communists are contemptuous of Proust, Joyce, Wyndham Lewis (bourgeois), attack Lawrence (prole turned bourgeois), but respect Hemingway (toying with Communism), bow to Barbusse and praise fulsomely *Daughters of Albion*, a mediocre 'proletarian' novel by Alec Brown, though he himself is a member of the middle class.

But there is a perfectly reasonable middle way between these

two extremes, and Orwell found it. If his work is to possess conviction the writer must have a message or 'tendency'. What the
message is does not matter, so long as it is not 'blazingly silly'.
The real test is conviction and it should be possible for a
Catholic to admire and even enjoy a book by a Communist and
vice versa. Some people say that a book cannot be 'good' if it
expresses a palpably false view of life. We are told today that
any book possessing genuine literary merit will also be more or
less 'progressive' in tendency. This ignores the fact that a
similar struggle between progress and reaction has raged
throughout history and that the books we deem 'good' have
been produced by both sides. Orwell says that today it is
possible for a good book to be written by a Catholic, a Communist, a Fascist, a pacifist, an anarchist, perhaps by an old-
style Liberal or an ordinary Conservative, because each of these
stands for a conceivable way of life. But no one could imagine
a good book being written by a spiritualist, a Buchmanite or a
member of the Ku-Klux-Klan because their views do not provide a basis for a possible way of life.

Yet Orwell himself was aware (without the awareness perhaps ever becoming fully conscious) that 'good' books could be
written without a purpose. In 'Lear, Tolstoy and the Fool' he
remarks that Shakespeare was not a systematic thinker and that
'we do not know to what extent he wrote with a "purpose" '.
If this is true it is a grave rift in his view that art is propaganda,
for Orwell ranked Shakespeare as highly as the majority of
Englishmen, informed and uninformed. In 'Politics vs. Literature' he says that *if* there is such a thing as good or bad art,
then the goodness or badness must reside in the work of art
itself—not independently of the observer but independently of
the mood of the observer. Most of the time he claimed that the
goodness and badness could only be released by the writer's
urge to persuade—until he came face to face with the oddity
that many others had noticed before him, that Shakespeare
appeared to have little urge to persuade. But this contradiction
never became obtrusive enough in Orwell's mind for him to
attempt to explain it, or explain it away.

Whether a writer, good or bad, intends his work to be
propagandist or not, there is no doubt that its effect on the

public is that of propaganda. Even the purest 'art for art's sake' tries to urge a particular view of beauty upon the recipient— sometimes succeeding and just as frequently setting up contrary motions. Orwell believed that most people are influenced far more than they care to admit by novels, serials and films. (It is an axiom in the commercial world that advertising breaks down even the toughest resistance.) From this point of view the worst books are the most important because they are read earliest in life, during the most impressionable years. 'It is probable that many people who would consider themselves extremely sophisticated and "advanced" are actually carrying through life an imaginative background which they acquired in childhood from (for instance) Sapper and Ian Hay.' ('Boys' Weeklies'.) From this kind of literature people absorb a set of beliefs that would be regarded as hopelessly out of date by the Central Office of the Conservative Party. These beliefs include the conviction that the major problems of our time do not exist, that there is nothing wrong with *laissez-faire* capitalism, that foreigners are unimportant comics and that the British Empire is a sort of charity concern that will last for ever. The beliefs may have changed during the few years since Orwell wrote this essay (1939), but they have only been replaced by others correspondingly out of date. Orwell believed that it was senseless merely to bemoan this situation. It could be capitalised. There is no fundamental reason why a boys' paper as thrilling and lively as *Hotspur* but with a Left-wing bias could not exist, nor a woman's paper at the same level as *Oracle* but taking more account of the realities of working-class life.

While low-grade fiction has remained as popular as ever, poetry seems to have lost its appeal completely. Yet Orwell thought it was necessary to qualify such a statement. There is still a large amount of folk poetry that is widely known, a few ancient songs and ballads which have never gone out of favour, and a considerable amount of enthusiasm for 'good bad' poetry, usually of a patriotic or sentimental kind. To a serious student of poetry this may seem beside the point, but the ordinary man sees in 'good bad' poetry all the characteristics of highbrow poetry: it is in verse, it rhymes, it deals in lofty sentiments and unusual language—all these things to an often marked degree.

(Bad poetry is more 'poetical' than good poetry.) His conclusion
was that the public was only hostile to poetry but not to verse.
'Poetry is disliked because it is associated with unintelligibility,
intellectual pretentiousness and a general feeling of Sunday-on-
a-weekday. Its name creates in advance the same sort of bad
impression as the word "God" or a parson's dog-collar.'
('Poetry and the Microphone', *Such, Such Were the Joys*.)

This trait in the English public had led to the production of
a vast amount of good bad poetry, all of it subsequent, he
thought, to 1790. (The odd, unexplained date is extremely
Orwellian.) He cited 'The Bridge of Sighs', 'When All the
World is Young, Lad', 'The Charge of the Light Brigade', Bret
Harte's 'Dickens in Camp', 'The Burial of Sir John Moore',
'Jenny Kissed Me', 'Keith of Ravelston', 'Casabianca'. They
all reek of sentimentality yet were capable of giving pleasure to
many people who knew what was wrong with them. 'Good'
poetry can only be the cult of a few people in an age like our
own. It is sometimes acceptable when disguised as something
else, such as nursery rhymes and the songs invented by soldiers.
But good bad poetry can get across to the most unpromising
audiences if the right atmosphere has been worked up beforehand. He cites the success of Churchill's quotation of Clough's
'Endeavour' in one of his wartime speeches.[1]

Yet he believed that radio had brought back the possibility
of an audience for true poetry. However many millions may be

---

1 Orwell was not really a poetry critic. More attention must be paid to form in
poetry criticism than in prose criticism, because it is distinguished by its form.
But Orwell concentrated on meaning. When he ventured to discuss technique
he fell back on automatic criteria. In his essay on Yeats he quotes
> The sedentary soul
> In toils of measurement
> Beyond eagle or mole,
> Beyond hearing or seeing,
> Or Archimede's guess,
> To raise into being
> That loveliness?

Orwell's comment was that 'loveliness' was a 'squashy, vulgar word', although
it did not seriously spoil the passage. He said this because one of his rules was to
keep an eye open for the 'poetical'. 'Loveliness' is a poetical word. This is merely
automatic criticism. The use of the word in this place in fact heightens the whole
passage by its unexpectedness, one of the essential qualities of poetry. 'Loveliness' is only a vulgar word when used loosely and colloquially. Here it is given
precision by the foregoing, particularly the words it is linked with most closely,
'Archimedes' guess'. See de la Mare for the successful use of 'poetical' words.

listening, each person is an audience of *one*, or at most is one of a small group of usually like-minded people. The audience can switch off if it doesn't like what it is hearing and in any case has no power over the speaker. On a platform the speaker must take his tone from the audience. Also the enjoyment of each member of an audience is affected by his neighbours, as anyone who has tried to listen to 'modern' music in the company of people who dislike it will realise.

'That grisly thing, a "poetry reading", is what it is because there will always be some among the audience who are bored or all-but frankly hostile and who can't remove themselves by the simple act of turning a knob. And it is at bottom the same difficulty—the fact that a theatre audience is not a selected one—that makes it impossible to get a decent performance of Shakespeare in England. On the air these conditions do not exist. The poet *feels* that he is addressing people to whom poetry means something, and it is a fact that poets who are used to broadcasting can read into the microphone with a virtuosity they would not equal if they had a visible audience in front of them.'

('Poetry and the Microphone', *Such, Such Were the Joys*.)

But the poet would also have to do something. He must not rely on technique alone. Verbal fireworks would create a following for a period but it would not last. Only meaning has staying power. Orwell said that any poem that was any good had a prose-meaning which the poet urgently wished to express.

Finally, the short story. Orwell was as little impressed by the contemporary short story as he was by the contemporary novel. In the *New Statesman* of 25 January, 1941, he picked out what he thought to be the distinguishing marks of the English short story that was not a thriller. First there was a sort of flatness and greyness, something he could best describe as *low pressure*. One would expect a story to be more lyrical and highly-coloured than a novel, but in fact most modern stories avoided emotional high-lights and were written in a deliberately unsophisticated, over-simplified style, what he called the 'and then he went on and came to another place' manner of writing. Another peculiarity of the modern story was that nothing ever happened. There was no vulgar plot, no denouement, no surprise at the end. The formula was nearly always the same: a pointless little sketch about fundamentally uninteresting people, written in

short flat sentences and ending in a vague query. 'There seems
to be a sort of cult of pointlessness and indefiniteness.' He attributed the blight to the spirit of Katherine Mansfield. He then
gives a list of his 'best' short stories, as follows:

'The Premature Burial' (Poe).
'A Little Dinner at Timmins's' (Thackeray).
'The Man that Corrupted Hadleyburgh' (Twain).
'Baa, Baa, Black Sheep' (Kipling).
'The End of the Tether' (Conrad).
'A Slip Under the Microscope' (Wells).
'The Dead' (Joyce).
'England, my England' (Lawrence).
'The Fox' (Lawrence).
'Rain' (Maugham).

He adds that two of these are wild burlesque, one is a shocker,
one is a hair-raiser and two are tear-jerkers. Most of them have
a plot, some are long, some ramble, but all are written with
gusto. They were written by men who were either sure of their
subject or took financial failure for granted. He concluded that
the short story 'is a form suited to more spacious times, when
spirits are higher, money more plentiful, magazines fatter and
leisured readers more numerous'. He returned to the charge in
Tribune three years later, adding that it had become impossible
to publish stories of any length and that most of the great
stories of the past were fairly long.

One of the short story's practitioners, V. S. Pritchett, rushed
to its defence in the next issue of the *New Statesman*. He said he
had read Mr Orwell's remarks with astonishment. He could
not understand what was meant by 'plot', for one of the stories
attacked by Orwell (by H. E. Bates) was bursting with it.
Among the writers he singled out for commendation, Lawrence
and Joyce were flagrant examples of that poetic evocation of
'atmosphere' and 'character' that Orwell believed to be the
bane of the modern story. An indignation meeting was evidently going on in Orwell's mind, but it was hard to know what
the indignation was about. Perhaps Orwell was only saying that
he personally liked action stories. 'When he says a story must
"plot" does he mean "situation", and when he says "story"
does he mean "narrative"? Surely character and atmosphere,
the isolation of moments, are especially suited to the short-story

writer, and in emancipating himself from the mechanical tricks and formulae to which so short a form inevitably lends itself, the modern writer has been both refreshing and original.'

Orwell replied to this in the next issue. He said something must *happen* in a story. There must be some event, and sufficient element of surprise for the reader to be unable, if not to foresee the end, at least to foresee how it will come. He thought *The Dead* would have been a good story even if written by Agatha Christie.

'If one asks that every story should contain an incident, one is not necessarily asking for a rape, a murder or even a sock on the jaw. It can be a very tiny happening, provided that the author feels it to be significant and can make it seem so. But there the question of talent and sincerity comes in. Katherine Mansfield, who presumably derived from Chekov, specialised in the kind of story that is no more than a small-scale psychological adventure. On the whole her work has not worn well, but one feels only that her taste is at fault and not that she is faking her own emotions. She was writing in the week-ending period of literature, when in spite of the war the outer world had not butted its way into the novelist's rose-grown cottage, and the tiny misfortunes of over-sensitised people could fill her horizon. That H. E. Bates and others should carry on that type of story *now*, when an incendiary bomb in a baby's perambulator seems a commonplace, is a different matter.'

This controversy showed Orwell's critical method at its worst. He was not really a literary critic but a literary sociologist. All his best criticism was sociological, e.g., the essays on Dickens and Boys' Weeklies. Where he could not focus his critical skill upon some social problem he showed considerable psychological immaturity, even a lack of interest in individual psychology. He gave the impression that people ought not to have individual minds, that they ought to be cells in a collective psyche and fully conscious of it. Society blotted the individual out of his range of vision. This is, of course, contradicted by *1984*. But it was only towards the end of his life that Orwell fully realised the implications of group-consciousness and collective responsibility. He could only see things 'happening' and the things that didn't 'happen' but which were apparently there were the unimportant twitchings of over-sensitised souls. It was a shrewd remark of Pritchett's, to say that he only liked action stories. At bottom Raffles and Sherlock Holmes were still his heroes. But he could not admit this if he was to be accepted as a writer so he had to rationalise his interest in them. Another remark of Pritchett's, less kind, was that Orwell must have been confused by his readings of *The Gem* and *The Magnet*. Yet there is truth in it. He only turned away from the literature of his youth because it carried the wrong political implications. If only Kipling had been a member of the Labour Party!

As soon as Orwell turned away from literature with a political or sociological message he was lost. If one wasn't there he would give the illusion of one. The faintest shadow of a message could be magnified into a thunder-cloud. His views on the short story could not fall back on sociology in the main, so he hedged and twittered until finally he was reduced to claiming that one kind of story was good for peace and another for war. As usual, he cannot define his terms. There must be a 'plot' and something must *happen*. He tried desperately to make inverted commas and italics work for him but they only illuminated his unsociological writhings. When he finally clutches at society to save him from Katherine Mansfield and H. E. Bates, it fails him. He excuses Mansfield's delicacies because the war had not kicked her in the pants, or not hard enough. Bates should have known better, or been hurt more. But the writers he praised had for the most part been as sheltered as Mansfield, so apparently the war had nothing to do with the kind of stories they wrote. If Kipling could write a good story without benefit of Passchendaele, ought Bates to have written a better story because of the Battle of Britain? Orwell did not realise that art is not born in that way. He gave no cogent reasons to support the view that Kipling wrote better than Bates, he merely said he preferred reading Kipling to reading Bates—and automatically dragged in the war. At other times it was unemployment or the class system. The real reason for his preference was chronological— he read Kipling when he was a boy.

Chapter XVI

The Power of Words

ONE THING that marked Orwell out as a genuine writer and not a mere journalist was his intense interest in words. This is evident in his first book, *Down and Out*, where he devotes a chapter to the vocabulary of tramps. Some of the theorising in this chapter is rather naive compared with the much more convincing passages on language and its use that he wrote in later life. Words are the tools of the writer; this is unbearably trite, but it is not so trite to point out that the writer should be more careful and exact in his approach to words than to anything else. Alongside the close observation in this first book there is much that is slapdash and inaccurate. In later life Orwell spent more care and hard thinking on the English language and its possible developments than on any other single subject. In *Down and Out* he had not yet acquired this discipline. One outstanding example is his statement that the London working classes have abandoned the word 'bloody', though novelists still represent them as using it. This is so flagrantly untrue it is difficult to understand how Orwell came to make the claim. Only the lowest strata of the London working class have abandoned the word, even today, believing it to be rather 'cissyish', but Orwell did not qualify his statement at all. In fact, he is contradicted by himself. In *A Clergyman's Daughter* Flo and other women, both 'on the beach' and hop-picking, use the word continually. But Orwell's ear is less efficient than his powers of deduction. He could study language, both written and spoken, and get a shrewd idea of what was happening to it, how its usage was changing, how it was affecting thought and how thought was affecting it. But in his comments on the use of particular words he was far less reliable. As I have said before, his reproduction of conversation, particularly in the earlier novels, was not very convincing. Even in *Coming Up For Air* (1939) he allows his insurance agent to call working men 'proles'. This destroys the credibility of Tubby Bowling as efficiently as if he had been allowed to wear a monocle. 'Prole' is a self-conscious word used by Left-wingers with a tinge of Bloomsbury.

But if he was weak at noticing the kinds of words that certain types of people used he was very good at noticing the immense differences of meaning that a slight syllabic change might involve. The English language is rich (or perhaps the word should be 'prolific') in verbs whose character is completely metamorphosed by the conjunction of certain insignificant-looking prepositions. Expressions such as 'set to' and 'come to' baffle the foreigner, who expects some kind of relationship with the meaning of the basic verb. In *Burmese Days* Orwell noted the enormous difference between the phrases 'sticking by' and 'sticking to'. During the war the civilians in Burma had avoided military service by 'sticking by' their jobs. If anyone had accused them of 'sticking to' them they would have been genuinely upset.

Such words and expressions tend to exist in pairs, representing either reality or fantasy. One group of words are euphemisms, pretending things are not what they seem; the other group consists of harsh and bitter words, allowing no concessions. But there are other categories. There are the class words, for instance. Both 'luncheon' and 'dinner' are respectable words, providing they are used at the right time. The Rev. Hare was disgusted to hear his daughter, who was spending too much time with the parishioners, confusing the two as they did: 'an abominable lower-class habit'. Even when you got to the table you weren't quite sure whether you were faced with a 'serviette' or a 'napkin' and it was difficult to know whether to 'commence' or 'begin'. But with the democratisation of English society these class expressions are slowly being superseded—or so Orwell claimed in *The English People*—and it is being done by way of America. American slang is acceptable to all classes. No one objects to the words 'stooge' and 'stool-pigeon' while their English equivalents, 'nark' and 'split', are considered unbearably vulgar by large sections of the population. 'Even a very snobbish English person would probably not mind calling

a policeman a "cop", which is American, but he would object
to calling him a "copper", which is working-class English.'
English people of all classes will use the American slang phrase
'sez you', and will almost certainly claim that there is no
English equivalent, forgetting a whole string of them: 'not
half', 'I don't think', 'come off it', 'less of it', 'and then you
woke up' or simply 'garn'.

Disraeli spoke of two nations but in language there are more,
corresponding to the very subtle class divisions which Orwell
loved to enumerate. Yet a number of pressures were forcing
these languages into one universal amalgam, among them the
needs of propaganda, the influence of America, the national
press and the political drive towards uniformity. Orwell's later
work on language was largely concerned with the new comprehensive language that was being forged for the nation as a
whole, ultimately a classless nation, though not a casteless
nation. The press, for instance, had to devise a universal language, one that would appeal to and be understood by public
schoolboys and miners, if it were to gain a national readership.
The press succeeded. Although *The Times* is read by one only
type of person, the *Daily Express* is read by all types in every
class. Words were becoming associative counters. The com-
munalisation of life was making this easy. The director of a
public opinion organisation once told me that the word *book*
has three separate meanings, each of which is dominant in a
particular class or group. To the educated it means what you
are reading now. To the working class it means a magazine.
To the sporting crowd it is what a bookmaker 'runs'. As society
becomes more homogeneous these three meanings will either
be shared or one will oust the others. The word will be the same
for all men. The press can print a word and the effect is as
automatic as if it had pressed a button. In *Coming Up For Air*
Bowling sees a newsboy with a poster flapping against his
knees: LEGS. FRESH DISCOVERIES. This sounds arcane or immensely scientific, but it was perfectly clear to the public of
that day. A woman's legs, wrapped in brown paper, had been
found in a railway waiting-room. Everyone knew what 'legs'
meant. There were only two legs in the whole country worthy
of the name.

This careful manipulation of words, even leading to a brand
new science which enjoyed the name 'semantics', could be and
would be of immense value in propaganda. And in the twentieth-century propaganda meant political propaganda. Words
were as important as bullets to the modern ruler. They were in
fact more efficient. Everyone knew that bullets were unjust,
but everyone used words and most people believed that words
were essentially democratic. My word is as good as yours,
which implies that yours is as good as mine. Publicists, politicians and propagandists were learning how to use words to
compel people to act against their own interests—only the beauty
of words was that it was not widely realised that they could be
the instruments of compulsion. People believed they were
persuaded by words, that the process was entirely logical and
fair-minded. They might be persuaded against their wills and
desires but they made up their own minds. Orwell watched this
word-management closely and in *1984* language became the
major weapon of tyranny. But as language became disciplined
for this one social and political purpose, so it was losing its
power in other fields. In simple terms, it was becoming less
poetic. In the past language had reached its height in the
description of beauty and the expression of love. Now it had
become impoverished for these purposes, as Winston and Julia
discovered. While their masters could say exactly what they
wanted to say in Newspeak the lovers fumbled awkwardly in
their attempts to explore each other's personalities. But much
earlier Flory had discovered the inadequacy of words in a
similar situation. Struggling to describe his feelings for Elizabeth
he said to her, 'It's useless trying to tell you what you mean to
me'. The latter phrase struck him with its feebleness. These
blunted phrases! They lacked all significance. Meaning had
been rubbed away by the usage of generations and modern
man had not the imaginative vitality to invent a rich new substitute.

Imagery and freshness of phrase served the emotions. The
new world was trying to weaken, eventually destroy, the
emotions. The new language was to be bare, devoid of stimulation. Repetition was one of its methods. Repetition kills
emotion. In the early, amateur days of political strategy

attempts had been made to enlist the emotional support of the people—they were urged to demand justice, liberty, equality, concepts on an emotional level with love and beauty. But the new men realised the dangers of this. Once people started demanding these things they might get a genuine taste for them and then they would be uncontrollable. Ordinary people look forward to an uncontrolled future. Their leaders, of whatever political complexion, cannot see beyond control. It is best not to arouse these unruly emotions, to win people's support through the inculcation of habit which may eventually become so like instinct as to be indistinguishable. So the new appeals will be made in unexciting language, repeated over and over again, until they become part of the popular tradition. Today we are midway. The totalitarian slogans are often inflammatory but they are repeated so often that they lose their rational significance and become tribal calls or pavlovian stimuli. This is the hypnopaedic method, by which the mind is drummed into acceptance.

His first serious examination of the interaction between language and political method was published soon after the second World War. It had now become obvious to him that the new political systems that were threatening to master the world found more and more of their strength in the management and direction of opinion. This led him to study, not so much methods of propaganda (others had been doing that for some time and it was typical of Orwell that he always adopted a different approach from other people), as the way in which daily, unofficial speech was reacting to the impact of the new political situation and the thought processes that it encouraged. He begins his essay 'Politics and the English Language' (*Shooting an Elephant*) with these words: 'Most people who bother with the matter at all would admit that the English language is in a bad way, but it is generally assumed that we cannot by conscious action do anything about it'. He did not agree that nothing could be done. At first sight the decline of the language moved in a circular direction. The language is becoming ugly and inaccurate because our thoughts are foolish, but the slovenliness of our language makes it easier to have foolish thoughts. But this process is reversible. Modern English is full of bad habits but they can be eliminated if one is willing to take the necessary trouble.

Towards the end of his life Orwell came to believe that the best way of saying a thing was always the shortest and simplest. This was probably the only point in which he was in whole-hearted sympathy with another leading Socialist propagandist, Bernard Shaw. When Basic English was being canvassed as a possible international language Orwell gave the idea his sympathy. He felt it might act as a corrective to the oratory of statesmen and publicists. Basic English deflated high-sounding phrases without mercy. He tells us in *Tribune* (18 August, 1944) how he presented to a Basic expert the sentence, 'He little knew the fate that lay in store for him'. In Basic this would become, 'He was far from certain what was going to happen.' He was told that in Basic it is impossible to make a meaningless statement without its being apparent that it is meaningless—'which is quite enough to explain why so many schoolmasters, editors, politicians and literary critics object to it'. But it would be possible to purify the language without resorting to Basic. It was purity and simplification that he desired, rather than any attempt to restore the old imaginative vigour of the language. There were in fact four modes of writing English, two of them good and two bad. Some of the finest language of the past had been rich in imagery. We no longer seemed capable of it. This kind of language had been debased into cliché and floweriness, much used in contemporary propaganda and publicity. This was the mode he fought against, because it was dead and failed to stimulate. In its place he wished to put a pure and unadorned language which would at least express itself cleanly. It existed in our literary tradition, though not so strongly as the poetic mode, in the work of Bunyan, Addison and Defoe. Finally there was the debased development of this, where the language was pared away to the bone, where synonyms or near-synonyms did not exist, and where a minimum vocabulary was used. This stage has not yet been reached but the ground is being prepared for it. Such a language destroys the possibility of subtlety. It cannot produce new ideas. It is the language of 1984.

Orwell's campaign was therefore for a language that should be both pure and subtle, flexible and simple. He fought enemies on two fronts. Perhaps the reason why his sympathy with Basic English never developed into overt support was because he feared that Basic might be the forerunner of the manipulative language that he illustrated in *1984*. Apart from *doublethink* (which is quite another matter) he wanted a language in which it would be possible to think critically. But it was becoming more and more difficult to think critically in the language as it existed in 1944 or 1954, which brought him up against the other enemy: cliché, sloppiness, vagueness, meaninglessness. Large numbers of words which once had precision are becoming impossible to use accurately because however you may intend to use them other people, your readers and your audience, have lost sight of any clarity of outline. Words such as 'peace', 'democracy', 'freedom' and 'equality' no longer have exact meaning. 'Peace' is a state where armed powers hurl threats at each other. 'Democracy' is a system of government where popular aspirations are monopolised by a single party. And so on. Words of this type are of immense value in 1984 just because of their ambiguity, while the rest of the language becomes speciously precise. In *Tribune* (24 March, 1944) Orwell discusses the much-used word 'Fascism'. What does it mean? To begin with, the major Fascist states differed considerably in their structure and ideology. It is usually assumed that Fascism is inherently warlike. This ignored the existence of Fascist states such as Portugal and those of South America. Anti-Semitism is usually considered to be a characteristic, yet not all Fascist movements have been anti-Semitic. Mussolini only adopted it under pressure from Hitler. Orwell then listed the various groups to whom the term has been applied in internal politics.

(*a*) Conservatives. British rule in India is cited. Certain patriotic organisations have been labelled crypto-Fascist: Boy Scouts, Metropolitan Police, M.I.5, British Legion.

(*b*) Socialists. Defenders of old-style capitalism, such as Sir Ernest Benn, claim that Socialism and Fascism are indistinguishable. The same charge is made by the Catholics, the Communists and the Anarchists.

(*c*) Communists. They have been identified with the Fascists by Rauschning, Drucker, Burnham and Voigt. The claim was maintained by the pre-war *Times*, the Anarchists and Trotskyists.

(*d*) Trotskyists. The Communists claimed that Trotsky was in Nazi pay.

(*e*) Catholics. 'Outside its own ranks the Catholic Church is almost universally regarded as pro-Fascist, both objectively and subjectively.'

(*f*) War-resisters. They made things easier for the Axis and became tinged with pro-Fascist feeling.

(*g*) War-supporters. British Imperialism is worse than Nazism. The People's Convention practically claimed that willingness to resist a Nazi invasion was a sign of Fascist sympathy.

(*h*) Nationalists. All nationalisms were held to be inherently Fascist if the speaker disapproved of them.

> 'It will be seen that, as used, the word "Fascism" is almost entirely meaningless. In conversation, of course, it is used even more wildly than in print. I have heard it applied to farmers, shopkeepers, Social Credit, corporal punishment, foxhunting, bullfighting, the 1922 Committee, the 1941 Committee, Kipling, Gandhi, Chiang-Kai-shek, homosexuality, Priestley's broadcasts, Youth Hostels, astrology, women, dogs, and I do not know what else.
>
> 'Yet underneath all this mess there does lie a kind of buried meaning. To begin with, it is clear that there are very great differences, some of them easy to point out and not easy to explain away, between the régimes called Fascist and those called democratic. Secondly, if "Fascist" means "in sympathy with Hitler" some of the accusations I have listed above are obviously very much more justified than others. Thirdly, even the people who recklessly fling the word "Fascist" in every direction attach at any rate an emotional significance to it. By "Fascism" they mean, roughly speaking, something cruel, unscrupulous, arrogant, obscurantist, anti-liberal and anti-working-class. Except for the relatively small number of English sympathisers, almost any English person would accept "bully" as a synonym for "Fascist". That is about as near to a definition as this much-abused word has come.'

Vagueness and sheer incompetence, said Orwell, are the most marked characteristics of modern English prose, particularly political writing. As soon as certain topics are raised the concrete melts into the abstract. Prose consists less and less of *words* chosen for the sake of their meaning, and more and more of *phrases* tacked together 'like the sections of a prefabricated hen-house'. There are four main tricks by which the work of prose-construction is habitually dodged. One of these, the use of meaningless words, is particularly common in art and literary criticism, where we are always coming across *romantic, plastic, values, human, dead, sentimental,* used without meaning, in the sense that they not only do not point to any discoverable object but are hardly ever expected to do so by the reader. In political writing, in addition to the words I have already mentioned, there are *socialism, realistic, class, science, reactionary* and *bourgeois.* Words of this kind are used in a consciously dishonest way, i.e., the person who uses them has his own private definition, but allows his hearer to think he means something quite different. Statements like *Marshal Pétain was a true patriot, The Soviet press is the freest in the world, The Catholic Church is opposed to persecution,* are almost always made with intent to deceive.

Another trick he referred to as the use of operators or verbal false limbs. 'These save the trouble of picking out appropriate verbs and nouns, and at the same time pad each sentence with extra syllables which give it an appearance of symmetry.' There is an example in this sentence of Orwell's I have just quoted— the use of 'picking out' instead of 'choosing'. Examples he gives include *render inoperative, be subjected to, have the effect of, take effect,* etc. Simple verbs are eliminated and replaced by phrases. (I think it is fair to say, however, that in some cases the only simple verbs available are Latin in origin, and Orwell abhorred their use.) The passive voice is used wherever possible in preference to the active and noun constructions are used instead of gerunds (*by examination of* instead of *by examining*). Simple conjunctions and prepositions are replaced by such phrases as *with respect to, the fact that, in view of, on the hypothesis that;* the ends of sentences are saved from anticlimax by such resounding commonplaces as *greatly to be desired, a development to be expected in the near future, brought to a satisfactory conclusion.*

Thirdly there is pretentious diction. Words like *phenomenon, objective, virtual, promote, exploit* and *liquidate* are used to dress up simple statements and give an air of scientific impartiality to biased judgments. Adjectives like *epoch-making, unforgettable* and *inevitable* 'are used to dignify the sordid processes of international politics, while writing that aims at glorifying war usually takes on an archaic colour', characteristic words being *realm, mailed fist, shield,* and *jackboot.* It is here that he deplores the use of foreign words and expressions such as *cul de sac, mutatis mutandis* and *weltanschauung,* which are supposed to give an air of culture and elegance. He said there was no need for any of the hundreds of foreign phrases now current in English, except for the useful abbreviations i.e., e.g. and etc. In his earlier days, particularly while reviewing for the *New English Weekly,* Orwell had been frequently guilty of this offence himself. But by the time he wrote *The Road to Wigan Pier* he had become a well-known enemy of Latinised English—to such an extent that when Victor Gollancz in his 'Foreword' used the phrase *in propria persona* he hastily corrected it to 'in his own person' out of deference to Orwell. He also included in this classification borrowings which are commonly misunderstood, e.g., the expression 'barking up the wrong tree', the origin or true meaning of which he found few people understood. He admitted that there were occasions when it might be necessary to take over a foreign word, but in these cases we should anglicise the pronunciation as our ancestors used to do. If we really need the word *café* (though in his opinion *coffee house* was perfectly adequate) we ought to spell it *caffay* or pronounce it *cayfe. Garage* should be pronounced *garridge,* he thought.

As a result of these usages the whole tendency of modern prose is away from concreteness of expression. He believed that English was peculiarly subject to jargon. Doctors, scientists, business men, officials, sportsmen, economists and political theorists all have their characteristic perversion of the language, all leading to increased imprecision. (It is interesting to note, though Orwell does not do so, that the original purpose of jargon is to give *more* precision, just as cliché usually derives from a striking piece of imagery. But language blunts as easily as steel and as soon as it is used without thought it loses its conscious meaning.) Orwell thought that the deadliest jargon of all was to be found in what is called 'standard English', the language of leading articles, White Papers, political speeches and the B.B.C. news bulletins. It was dangerous because it was spreading, far more quickly and widely than the specialised jargons could ever hope to do. He admits that anyone preparing a broadcast or writing a letter to *The Times* adopts this kind of language almost instinctively. People are too ready to *take the earliest opportunity* and to *take up the cudgels* or declare that *the answer is in the affirmative*. They even find it *easier* to say *In my opinion it is a not unjustifiable assumption* instead of *I think* because it is a ready-made phrase and slips off the tongue without resistance. When they use the word *think* they may actually be driven to think. Quite ordinary men are using these phrases today, men who instinctively turn in horror from Marxist jargon, for instance, but do not realise that they are making use of one just as bad.

There is one other usage that Orwell held responsible for the decay of English language. This is the use of dying metaphors. 'A newly invented metaphor assists thought by evoking a visual image, while on the other hand a metaphor which is technically "dead" (e.g., *iron resolution*) has in effect reverted to being an ordinary word and can generally be used without loss of vividness.' But in between these two classes is a huge dump of worn-out metaphors which have lost all evocative power and are only used now because people cannot take the trouble to invent fresh phrases. Examples: *ring the changes on, ride roughshod over, no axe to grind, on the order of the day, hotbed.* Many of these are used without knowledge of their meaning, and incompatible metaphors are frequently mixed, a sure sign that the writer is not interested in what he is saying. By using stale metaphors, similes and idioms, you save much mental effort, at the cost of leaving your meaning vague, not only for your reader but for yourself. This is the significance of mixed metaphors. The sole aim of a metaphor is to call up a visual image. When these images clash—as in *The Fascist octopus has sung its swan song, The jackboot is thrown into the melting pot*—it can be taken as certain that the writer is not seeing a mental image of the objects he is naming; in other words, he is not really thinking. Orwell kept a close watch on current press and literature for examples of this type of looseness, and found Professor Lancelot Hogben playing ducks and drakes with a battery and the daily press stating that 'bombs were falling like manna'. It was not only English that suffered from these abuses. There were signs that the malady was international. In *Tribune* (17 March, 1944) he quoted from an address delivered by the citizens of Pantelleria to the liberating Allied army, there were references to a 'megalomaniac and satanic régime' which 'sucked like a monstrous octopus' and men who, 'plotting together with the German pirates, hatch the lowest egoism and blackest treatment', etc.

'This filthy stew of words is presumably a translation from the Italian, but the point is that no one would recognise it as such. It might be a translation from any other European language, or it might come straight out of the *Daily Worker*, so truly international is this style of writing. Its characteristic is the endless use of ready-made metaphors. In the same spirit, when Italian submarines were sinking the ships that took arms to Republican Spain, the *Daily Worker* urged the British Admiralty to "sweep the mad dogs from the seas". Clearly, people capable of using such phrases have ceased to remember that words have meanings.'

It is at this point, says Orwell, that the special connection between politics and the debasement of language becomes clear. Ready-made phrases construct your sentences for you, even think your thoughts for you, to a certain extent. They also partially conceal your meaning, if you have one. Today it is broadly true that political writing is bad writing. Where it is not true it will generally be found that the writer is some kind of rebel, expressing private opinions (which have to be thought out) and not a party line. Orthodoxy, of whatever colour, demands a lifeless, imitative style. A speaker who uses this kind of phraseology has already started turning himself into a machine. If the speech he makes is one he is accustomed to make over and over again he may become almost unconscious of what he is saying, as when one utters the responses in church. And this reduced state of consciousness is favourable to political conformity.

'In our time, political speech and writing are largely the defence of the indefensible. Things like the continuance of British rule in India, the Russian purges and deportations, the dropping of the atom bombs on Japan, can indeed be defended, but only by arguments which are too brutal for most people to face, and which do not square with the professed aims of political parties. Thus political language has to consist largely of euphemism, question-begging and sheer cloudy vagueness. Defenceless villages are bombarded from the air, the inhabitants driven out into the countryside, the cattle machine-gunned, the huts set on fire with incendiary bullets: this is called *pacification*. Millions of peasants are robbed of their farms and sent trudging along the roads with no more than they can carry: this is called *transfer of population* or *rectification of frontiers*. People are imprisoned for years without trial, or shot in the back of the neck or sent to die of scurvy in Arctic lumber camps: this is called *elimination of unreliable elements*. Such phraseology is needed if one wants to name things without calling up mental pictures of them. Consider for instance some comfortable English professor defending Russian totalitarianism. He cannot say outright, "I believe in killing off your opponents when you can get good results by doing so". Probably, therefore, he will say something like this:

'"While freely conceding that the Soviet régime exhibits certain features which the humanitarian may be inclined to deplore, we must, I think, agree that a certain curtailment of the right to political opposition is an unavoidable concomitant of transitional periods, and that the rigours which the Russian people have been called upon to undergo have been amply justified in the sphere of concrete achievement." ' ('Politics and the English Language.')

But if thought corrupts language, language can also corrupt thought. The debased language Orwell describes is a continuous temptation—he likens it to a packet of aspirins always at your elbow. Yet the decadence is curable, though it requires an act of will. It is true that the state of a language reflects prevailing social conditions and that therefore not much can be done by tinkering with it. But this is only true in general, not in detail. Silly words and expressions have disappeared in the past and those two old favourites of public speakers, *explore every avenue* and *leave no stone unturned*, have been laughed out of existence. There are other flyblown metaphors which could be eliminated if enough people would take the trouble. Orwell said the *not un-* formation could be abolished if enough people would memorise this sentence: A not unblack dog was chasing a not unsmall rabbit across a not ungreen field. In *Tribune* (9 February, 1945) he proposed to start the campaign with attacks on the following literary diehards: *cross swords with, ring the changes on* and *take up the cudgels for*. Finally, he suggested a few rules which writers might keep in reserve for occasions when instinct failed them.

(*i*) Never use a metaphor, simile or other figure of speech which you are used to seeing in print.

(*ii*) Never use a long word where a short one will do.

(*iii*) If it is possible to cut a word out, always cut it out.

(*iv*) Never use the passive where you can use the active.

(*v*) Never use a foreign phrase, a scientific word or a jargon word if you can think of an everyday English equivalent.

(*vi*) Break any of these rules sooner than say anything outright barbarous.

While the general tendency of the English language is degenerative there are certain ways in which it is still enriching itself. Among these Orwell included borrowings from other languages, which is surprising in view of the attacks he sometimes made on such words. In *The English People* he listed such words as *garage, alibi, role* and *rendezvous* which he thought were of value, although native synonyms existed for some of them. But synonyms enrich a language. Newspeak would have none of them. During the war Orwell noticed how the German word *blitz* was adopted, first as a noun and then as a verb, which it never was in German. This could not have happened in 1984. The word censor, whose appointment Cyril Connolly lightheartedly proposed during the war, existed. Syme was working on the Eleventh Edition of the Newspeak Dictionary with the enthusiasm of one who really believed in what he was doing.

'It's a beautiful thing, the destruction of words', he says. 'Of course, the great wastage is in the verbs and adjectives, but there are hundreds of nouns that can be got rid of as well. It isn't only the synonyms; there are also the antonyms. After all, what justification is there for a word which is simply the opposite of some other word? A word contains its opposite in itself. Take "good", for instance. If you have a word like "good", what need is there for a word like "bad"? "Ungood" will do just as well— better, because it's an exact opposite, which the other is not. Or again, if you want a stronger version of "good", what sense is there in having a whole string of vague useless words like "excellent" and "splendid" and all the rest of them? "Plusgood" covers the meaning; or "doubleplusgood" if you want something stronger still.'

Syme goes on to explain the aim of Newspeak, the narrowing of the range of thought. *Thoughtcrime* will eventually become impossible because there will be no words in which to express it. 'The Revolution will be complete when the language is perfect.'

1984 ends with an appendix on 'The Principles of Newspeak', the language of the future. It was designed to provide a medium of expression for the world-view and mental habits proper to the devotees of Ingsoc, but to make all other modes of thought impossible. (Ingsoc was English Socialism.) Words were stripped of secondary meanings. For example, the word *free* was still in use but only in such a sentence as *This dog is free from lice*. Newspeak was designed to diminish the range of thought. It contained three vocabularies. The A vocabulary consisted of words needed for the business of everyday life. All ambiguities and shades of meaning had been purged out of them. This vocabulary could not have been used for literary purposes or political or philosophical discussion. The B vocabulary consisted of words which had been deliberately constructed for political purposes. Each word had a political implication and was intended to impose a desirable mental attitude upon the person using it. The C vocabulary was supplementary and consisted entirely of scientific and technical terms. In this language it was practically impossible to express unorthodox opinions.

Orwell writes somewhere of the queer sensation that sometimes overcame him at public meetings. As the ready-made phrases dropped from the speaker's lips Orwell would feel that he was not really a human being at all but a talking machine. Then, as the speaker moved his head and the light caught his glasses and momentarily blotted his eyes from sight behind shining opaque circles, the impression would be strengthened: it was just a mouth and it was unsupported by vision. Winston Smith in *1984* sometimes felt the same sensation as he watched and listened to some of his colleagues in the Ministry of Truth. 'As he watched the eyeless face with the jaw moving rapidly up and down, Winston had a curious feeling that this was not a real human being but some kind of dummy. It was not the man's brain that was speaking, it was his larynx. The stuff that was coming out of him consisted of words, but it was not speech in the true sense: it was a noise uttered in unconsciousness, like the quacking of a duck.' And *duckspeak* was the word for it. Like various other words in the B vocabulary, it was ambivalent in meaning. Provided that the opinions that were quacked out were orthodox ones, it implied nothing but praise. If a Party orator was called a *doubleplusgood duckspeaker* he was receiving a warm and valued compliment.

Chapter XVII

Left-Wing Patriot

WHEN ORWELL returned to England from Paris after his work in the hotels a couple of Roumanians asked him questions about the country and he told them 'some startling lies'. England, he said, seemed a 'sort of Paradise' after being hard up for months in a foreign city. But it wasn't only because he had been hard up and absent; England was really his first love and it was a kind of self-torture to find fault with her—not that he didn't enjoy it now and again. There are so many things in England that make you glad to get home: bathrooms, armchairs, mint sauce, new potatoes properly cooked, brown bread, marmalade, beer made with hops—all splendid things if you can pay for them. He was looking forward to not being poor, and the thought of not being poor made him very patriotic. For the benefit of the Roumanians he praised English climate, scenery, art, literature, laws, architecture. 'Then the boat drew alongside Tilbury Pier. The first building we saw on the waterside was one of those huge hotels, all stucco and pinnacles, which stare from the English coast like idiots staring over an asylum wall.' The Roumanians looked uncomfortable. Orwell assured them it was built by French architects. A few weeks later he was 'down and out' and finding England not so wonderful. He even found that it cost money to sit down.

No writer of his generation criticised his own country and fellow-countrymen more severely than Orwell, but there is no doubt at all that the criticism came out of love. His desire to record all the good things about England was a genuine one, and all through his work, after the warnings and the denunciations, he always returns to his conviction that, everything else notwithstanding, England was the best place in the world. Her faults hurt him because they spoilt her excellence. Whenever he returned to England from abroad he felt he was coming into a refuge, where the storms and disturbances that plagued the rest of the world would not be felt. His attitude to this was mixed. It was good to be able to find security in such a country, but could it last? Would the English always be able to insulate themselves from their neighbours? And wasn't it perhaps immoral for a whole people to bury themselves in this way? It was this last point that troubled him more than anything else. He was afraid, it is true, that one day England would be unpleasantly awakened, but morality always appealed to him more than expediency. The last paragraph in *Homage to Catalonia* describes his return to England after the dangers and inconveniences of Spain. There might be earthquakes in Japan, famines in China and revolutions in Mexico, but the milk would always be on the doorstep in England next morning and the *New Statesman* would come out on Friday. (This was symptomatic of Orwell's patriotism. A conventional patriot would have referred to *The Times*, but Orwell always insisted that Socialism and the Left-wing movement were as important a part of English tradition as bishops and tea on the lawn.) As he passed through southern England ('the sleekest landscape in the world') in the train he basked in its quiet beauty—the industrial towns were far away, a smudge of smoke and misery hidden by the curve of the earth's surface.

> 'Down here it was still the England I had known in my child-hood: the railway cuttings smothered in wild flowers, the deep meadows where the great shining horses browse and meditate, the slow-moving streams bordered by willows, the green bosoms of the elms, the larkspurs in the cottage gardens; and then the huge peaceful wilderness of outer London, the barges on the miry river, the familiar streets, the posters telling of cricket matches and Royal weddings, the men in bowler hats, the pigeons in Trafalgar Square, the red buses, the blue policeman—all sleeping the deep, deep sleep of England, from which I sometimes fear that we shall never wake till we are jerked out of it by the roar of bombs.'

Several years later he must have been often reminded of this passage or at least of the belief that lay behind it. England was at war and numerous prophets had foretold disaster. No one really knew how destructive a modern war might be—few Englishmen had had first-hand experience of foreign wars. People who did take the trouble to think about it were afraid of a fearful holocaust—Havelock Ellis had stated quite confidently

in one of his books that a couple of aeroplanes would probably
flatten out the whole of London in a few hours. Ellis was no
expert, it is true, but he was fairly representative of thinking
people. Only most English people did not think, or did not think
about such things. Even in May 1940 they were still in their
deep sleep, quite unimpressed by the gloomy forecasts of
'experts' and the minority who thought about the future. In his
Notebook Orwell tells us how he tried to overhear comments
on the war but failed. (At the time I was working with Mass-
Observation. It was part of my job to overhear comments on
the war and I know how very difficult it was to gather anything. A couple of comments in a day's work was not a bad
bag.) Orwell used to go to a pub to hear the nine o'clock news
and had to ask to have it switched on. Neither the barmaid nor
anyone else would have turned it on. As it was, no one listened
to it. The bombs were not yet falling. It would certainly need
them to wake the people up, unless it made their sleep eternal.

One night he heard the news between acts at a highbrow
play at the Torch Theatre. He found the audience listened
much more attentively than they did in the pubs. This was
typical of England. The intellectuals were sharply divided from
the rest of the population. Even a war, which one might expect
to unite the nation, did not bring them together. But it was not,
for once, the intellectuals who were being peculiar or awkward.
In any other country there would have been universal recognition that a war was important. The English sleepwalkers
took it in their stride, along with railway accidents and Test
defeats. This division persisted and was actually emphasised in
the England of *1984*, where the intellectuals of the Inner Party
were the only people who seriously concerned themselves with
the military situation. There was still no evidence of public
interest in the war even when the B.E.F. were falling back on
Dunkirk. The national belief that the nation would somehow
muddle through was far too strong to be eradicated by a distant
alarm—for anything outside England was distant. By-elections
and the response to appeals for men proved that the English
realised they had a duty to perform, but they put their duty in
a separate mental compartment, isolated from their traditional
daily lives. The newspapers were forecasting an attempted

invasion within a few days but this was not enough to move the English working man. He would wait for the invasion to start; then would be the time to think about it. 'They will grasp nothing until the bombs are dropping', Orwell wrote (30 May, 1940). Connolly thought they would then panic, but Orwell knew better. On the following Sunday the usual crowds were drifting about—perambulators, cycling clubs, people exercising dogs, knots of young men loitering at street corners, 'with not an indication on any face or in anything that one can overhear that these people grasp that they are likely to be invaded within a few weeks, though today all the Sunday papers are telling them so'. People were being urged to evacuate their children from London but the response was very poor. He added that they would behave bravely enough when the time came if they were only told what to do.

Five years later, after the bombs had fallen and the worst had happened, Orwell was still making the same point, this time in one of his London Letters to *Partisan Review*. He had just returned from the continent and he said that the thing that had struck him most about the behaviour of the British people during the war was their *lack* of reaction of any kind. 'In the face of terrifying dangers and golden political opportunities, people just keep on keeping on, in a sort of twilight sleep in which they are conscious of nothing except the daily round of work, family life, darts at the pub, exercising the dog, mowing the lawn, bringing home the supper beer, etc., etc.' He wasn't sure whether this semi-anaesthesia, as he called it, in which the British people contrived to live was a sign of decadence (as so many foreigners and British intellectuals believe) or a kind of instinctive wisdom. 'It may well be that it is the best attitude when you live among endless horrors and calamities which you are powerless to prevent. Possibly we shall all have to develop it if war becomes continuous, which seems to me a likely development in the fairly near future.' Which means that the British, despite certain unfavourable characteristics, possessed one quality to a high degree which fitted them for the society of *1984*. Whenever he discussed the English people there was a conflict in Orwell's mind between the traditional Englishman and the intellectual. The latter tried hard to be reproving but

the natural Englishman in him was considerably impressed by
the unconscious strength (or doltish obstinacy, depending on
your point of view) that veined the English character.

Excitement finally overtook the English people during the
war when the French surrendered. Animation appeared in
public places. People could be heard discussing the news
spontaneously. But the usual reaction was typically English:
'Thank God we've got a Navy!' Actual danger was still something alien or worse, un-English. Orwell even heard a drunken
Scottish private making a patriotic speech on the Underground, which was well received. (The English are very
patriotic but they don't usually like to talk about it.) And then
a little later the bombs did come, and there was confusion and
mal-co-ordination but no panic. People began to talk to
strangers and the streets were filled with people evacuated from
their houses because of delayed-action bombs, wandering
around aimlessly and not always knowing exactly where they
were. In the daytime Orwell noticed that most of them seemed
quite happy. It was nonsense to talk about the pattern of
people's lives being destroyed, they just weren't going to allow
it to happen. Orwell likened them to animals who are unable
to foresee the future so long as they have a bit of food and a
place in the sun. They accommodated themselves to the new
situation by refusing to dwell upon the probable events of the
coming night.

I have dwelt upon this dourness (phlegm to the French) of
the English people because although Orwell scarcely mentioned
it in his book on them it is a characteristic that he frequently
refers to in the rest of his work. He regarded it as one of the
most important factors in English *political* life. It was a force as
real as the struggle for markets but it was usually ignored by
political commentators, especially Marxists, because it was not
universal and had no apparent connection with economic conditions. It can probably be traced to the historical security that
England has enjoyed for so many centuries—the Navy again!
And along with the dourness goes a certain primness which is
abhorred by the 'advanced' and mocked by foreigners, and
produces jokes about the Englishman and the Frenchman. We
cannot be proud of the primness, but if we regard the dourness

as a good thing we must accept the primness as a by-product. The Englishman spends a good deal of time stuffing back his emotions; he has even invented a peculiar phrase for it, 'keeping a stiff upper lip'. He does not embrace other men like foreigners, he thinks love is something that dogs youth, he regards emotion as a kind of disease. His refusal to panic has had valuable political results; its social corollary is a rejection of feeling which tends to make English society turgid and immature.

The Englishman's immense respect for law is part of the same complex. It makes for stability and placidity at the expense of the excitements and fluidity that characterise some other societies. Orwell says that the Spanish or Italian peasant believes that the law is simply a racket and should be evaded where possible. The Englishman has so much confidence in the law that he will sometimes allow tampering that would not be tolerated elsewhere. On the other hand it also causes some ugly situations to end peacefully. Orwell recalls how during the London blitz the authorities tried to prevent the public from using the Tube stations as shelters. In some countries this would have caused riots and the gates of the Underground would have been stormed. But the Londoners simply bought three-halfpenny tickets and thus had legal status as passengers. Orwell noticed this trait as early as 1932, when he was still writing as Eric Blair. Standing on the steps of an English bank in Marseilles he watched a procession of working people carrying banners inscribed 'Sauvons Sacco et Vanzetti'. The thought crossed his mind that while such a scene might have occurred in the England of the eighteen-forties it could never have occurred in the nineteen-twenties. A century of strong government had developed what O. Henry called 'the stern and rugged fear of the police' to a point where any public protest seemed an indecency. A few years later the unemployed in England resorted to parades and demonstrations, but in general the Englishman regards such activities as 'public emotion' and as such tabu.

Orwell returned to this characteristic in *The Lion and the Unicorn*, where he made his first objective study of the English people as a whole. He said that concepts such as justice, liberty and truth are still believed in, and from this comes the convic-

tion that 'the law' is above both the State and individual, and
though it may sometimes be cruel and studid it is always incorruptible. If you want proof of this you only have to look about
you.

'Where are the rubber truncheons, where is the castor oil?
The sword is still in the scabbard, and while it stays there corruption cannot go beyond a certain point. The English electoral
system, for instance, is an all-but open fraud. In a dozen obvious
ways it is gerrymandered in the interest of the moneyed class.
But until some deep change has occurred in the public mind, it
cannot become *completely* corrupt. You do not arrive at the polling
booth to find men with revolvers telling you which way to vote,
nor are the votes miscounted, nor is there any direct bribery. Even
hypocrisy is a powerful safeguard. The hanging judge, that evil
old man in scarlet robe and horsehair wig, whom nothing short
of dynamite will ever teach what century he is living in, but who
will at any rate interpret the law according to the books and will
in no circumstances take a money bribe, is one of the symbolic
figures of England. He is a symbol of the strange mixture of
reality and illusion, democracy and privilege, humbug and
decency, the subtle network of compromises, by which the nation
keeps itself in its familiar shape.'

When writing about England it was impossible for Orwell to
keep away from the subject of class distinctions for long.
Although they have become less exaggerated during the last
thirty years, newcomers to England are still astonished and
sometimes horrified by the blatant differences between class and
class. The great majority of people can still be 'placed' in an
instant by their manners, clothes and general appearance. The
physical type differs considerably but the most striking difference is in language and accent. Orwell quotes Wyndham Lewis,
who says the English working class are 'branded on the tongue'.
But he also warns us not to ignore the emotional unity of
English society, the tendency of nearly all its inhabitants to feel
alike and to act together in moments of supreme crisis. England
is the only great country in Europe that is not obliged to drive
hundreds of thousands of its nationals into exile or the concentration camp. (This seems a little far-fetched but it is true in
tendency.) And then he gives us a new image of England,
remote from either the jewelled isle of Shakespeare or the
inferno of Dr Goebbels.

'More than either it resembles a family, a rather stuffy Victorian family, with not many black sheep in it but with all its cupboards bursting with skeletons. It has rich relations who have to be kow-towed to and poor relations who are horribly sat upon, and there is a deep conspiracy of silence about the source of the family income. It is a family in which the young are generally thwarted and most of the power is in the hands of irresponsible uncles and bedridden aunts. Still, it is a family. It has its private language and its common memories, and at the approach of an enemy it closes its ranks. A family with the wrong members in control—that, perhaps, is as near as one can come to describing England in a phrase.' (*The Lion and the Unicorn*.)

The practical effect of this is that in England national solidarity is stronger than class antagonism, a fact that Marxist commentators, whose thinking is surprisingly wishful in view of the claims of objectivity made for it, always miss. When Orwell asked whether 'national cultures' really exist his reply was that all the arguments are on one side and instinctive knowledge on the other. It is not easy to discover the connecting thread that runs through English history from the sixteenth century onwards but all English people who bother about such subjects feel that it exists. They feel they understand the institutions that have come to them out of the past with an inherited knowledge impossible to a foreigner. There is a national myth which may be quite false but which is believed in implicitly and which therefore influences conduct. These myths set up a type, or 'persona', which the average person will do his best to resemble. English stolidity under bombing was largely due to the power of the national 'persona', an immovable John Bull. 'Traditionally the Englishman is phlegmatic, unimaginative, not easily rattled: and since that is what he thinks he ought to be, that is what he tends to become.' (*The English People*.)

Orwell said that a completely uninformed visitor to England might conclude, after observation, that the abiding features of the English character are a profound, almost unconscious patriotism and an inability to think logically. If English people had thought logically in 1940 they would have clamoured for a negotiated peace. But pride in the national 'persona' would not allow them to. In June of that year Orwell was puzzled by the importance that people still attached to long-term contracts, stocks and shares and insurance policies. The sensible thing to do, he thought, would have been to borrow money right and left and to buy solid goods. He found that sewing-machines were still being offered for sale on hire-purchase terms with agreements stretching over two and a half years. Elsewhere such an attitude would have been regarded as economic suicide, but in England it would have amounted to admission of defeat. And defeat was impossible. It had never happened in the past and it required much too great an effort of the imagination to envisage it happening at any time in the future.

The ingredients of English patriotism were therefore a historical past of shared security, the emergence of a national myth and 'persona' which influenced conduct, an inability to think logically and also a distrust of any point of view that appeared to derive from emotion except the universal emotion of 'Englishness'. As a group the intellectuals did not share these attitudes but they had their apostates. Orwell was one himself. In the last resort his patriotism was always stronger than his intellectual convictions. He illustrated the process from the career of Malcolm Muggeridge, who began life as a Left-winger. When the war came Muggeridge discovered he was a thoroughgoing patriot.

'It is all very well to be "advanced" and "enlightened"', wrote Orwell, "to snigger at Colonel Blimp and proclaim your emancipation from all traditional loyalties, but a time comes when the sand of the desert is sodden red and what have I done for thee, my England? As I was brought up in this tradition myself I can recognise it under strange disguises, and also sympathise with it, for even at its stupidest and most sentimental it is a comelier thing than the shallow self-righteousness of the left-wing intelligentsia.' ('The Limit to Pessimism', *New English Weekly*, 25 April, 1940.)

The intelligentsia had rid themselves of patriotism and had gone on to proclaim that it no longer existed. Yet the whole of contemporary history contradicted them. Most men, he felt, would 'die for their country' more readily than they would go on strike for higher wages. Failure to understand that most middle-class English people and the better-off working class (together, a majority of the nation) were patriotic to the middle of their bones, and would always fight in defence of their country although they usually had no knowledge of foreign politics and the events leading to war, was one of the reasons why Left-wing political parties were seldom able to produce an acceptable foreign policy.

The outward side of English patriotism is expressed by xenophobia—milder now than it was, but up to the first World War quite virulent. Orwell noticed how this basic attitude to foreigners cropped up continually in the boys' weeklies he studied. The politics of *Gem* and *Magnet* were more than Conservative, they were pre-1914. The two basic assumptions were that nothing ever changes and that all foreigners are funny. Frenchmen were Froggies and Italians Dagoes. Mossoo, the French master at Greyfriars, wore a pointed beard and pegtop trousers. Inky, the Indian boy, was the comic *babu* of *Punch*. Fisher T. Fish was a stage Yankee, introducing most of his remarks with 'Waal, I guess'. Wun Lung, the Chinese, wore a saucer-shaped hat and pigtail and spoke pidgin English. It was assumed that foreigners of any one race were all alike and would conform to the following patterns:

> *Frenchman:* Excitable. Wears beard, gesticulates wildly.
> *Spaniard, Mexican,* etc.: Sinister, treacherous.
> *Arab, Afghan,* etc.: Sinister, treacherous.
> *Chinese:* Sinister, treacherous. Wears pigtail.
> *Italian:* Excitable. Grinds barrel organ or carries stiletto.
> *Swede, Dane,* etc.: Kind-hearted, stupid.
> *Negro:* Comic, very faithful.

Millions of English boys must have picked up these ideas before they ever met a foreigner. The majority never met more than one or two, if any, of some of the nationalities listed above. Until very recently English children were brought up to despise the southern European races, and history as taught in the schools was mainly a tale of battles won by England. Meanwhile the English were building up their legend of themselves as 'sturdy islanders' and 'stubborn hearts of oak' (the national 'persona') and were accepting it as almost a scientific fact that one Englishman was the equal of three foreigners. Even America was not exempt, particularly among the 'cultured' classes. Up till 1930, Orwell said, they loathed the U.S.A. which they regarded as the vulgariser of England and Europe. In a London Letter (March-April 1942) he said he knew people who automatically switched off the radio as soon as any

American news came on, and the most banal English film would always get middle-class support because 'it's such a relief to get away from those American voices'. Americans were supposed to be boastful, bad-mannered and worshippers of money, and were also suspected of plotting to inherit the British Empire. He said the working-class attitude was different. They nearly always disliked Americans when they came in contact with them, but this was not the result of preconceived cultural hostility.

There is a very interesting passage in *The Road to Wigan Pier* about the English conviction that northern races are superior to southern.

'When nationalism first became a religion, the English looked at the map and, noticing thàt their island lay very high in the Northern Hemisphere, evolved the pleasing theory that the further north you live the more virtuous you become. The histories I was given when I was a little boy generally started off by explaining in the naivest way that a cold climate made people energetic while a hot one made them lazy, and hence the defeat of the Spanish Armada. This nonsense about the superior energy of the English (actually the laziest people in Europe) has been current for at least a hundred years. "Better is it for us", writes a Quarterly Reviewer of 1827, "to be condemned to labour for our country's good than to luxuriate among olives, vines and vices." "Olives, vines and vices" sums up the normal English attitude towards the Latin races. In the mythology of Carlyle, Creasey, etc., the Northerner ("Teutonic", later "Nordic") is pictured as a hefty, vigorous chap with blond moustaches and pure morals, while the Southerner is sly, cowardly and licentious. This theory was never pushed to its logical end, which would have meant assuming that the finest people in the world were the Eskimos, but it did involve admitting that the people that lived to the North of us were superior to ourselves.'

This in turn led to the North-South antithesis in the British Isles themselves. There exists in England a cult of Northern snobbishness. A Yorkshireman in the South will always take care to let you know that he regards you as an inferior. If you ask him why hc will say that it is only in the North that life and work are 'real'. Northerners are 'real' people, Southerners are rentiers and parasites. The Northerner has 'grit', he is grim, 'dour', plucky, warm-hearted and democratic. The Southerner is snobbish, effeminate and lazy.

Orwell said that insularity and xenophobia are much stronger in the working class than among the bourgeoisie. In all countries the poor are more nationalist than the rich, but the English working class are outstanding for their abhorrence of foreign habits—of which they know next to nothing. Even when they are obliged to live abroad for several years they often refuse to accustom themselves to foreign food or to learn a foreign language. (I once travelled in Germany with an Englishman who preferred to go hungry when he couldn't get an English breakfast.) Nearly every Englishman of working-class origin considers it effeminate to pronounce a foreign word correctly. (I know a man who pours scorn on a mutual acquaintance because he insists on pronouncing Khartoum as the Sudanese pronounce it.) When the English people were brought into closer contact with Europeans during the war of 1914-18 than they had ever been before, the sole result was a hatred of all Europeans except the Germans, whose courage they admired. In four years on French soil they did not even gain a liking for wine. At bottom, he said, this dislike of foreigners is the same quality in the English character that repels the tourist and keeps out the invader.

The English intellectual tries to make good this deficiency, yet it is a fact, as Orwell pointed out in a broadcast to India ('The Re-Discovery of Europe', published in *Talking to India*, edited by Orwell), that many of the best English writers, despite wide differences, have a common denominator in their complete unawareness of anything outside the contemporary English scene. This is true of Bernard Shaw and A. E. Housman, Thomas Hardy and H. G. Wells, even Bennett and Galsworthy, despite their superficial debt to French and Russian models. It may help to explain the actual popularity of some writers, e.g., P. G. Wodehouse, whom the reader may feel to be a thoroughly representative Englishman. In his defence of P. G. Wodehouse (*Critical Essays*) Orwell stressed his political innocence and claimed that it was typical of English political innocence in general. Wodehouse simply did not realise that there was anything even vaguely treasonable in broadcasting for the Nazis. Wodehouse was neither better informed nor more interested in politics than the general run of his readers.

Thanks to the sheltered conditions of English life the majority
of Englishmen imagined for ten years that Hitler was merely a
figure out of comic opera, not worth taking seriously.[1] The
Left Book Club was at bottom a product of Scotland Yard just
as the Peace Pledge Union was a product of the Navy. The best
political writers were all foreigners, and they were also men
who had seen totalitarianism at close quarters and knew the
meaning of exile and persecution. Only in England was it
possible to believe right up to the outbreak of the war that Hitler
was an unimportant lunatic and the German tanks were made
of cardboard. English patriotism was partly a habit of mind
that had grown up over the centuries but it was also reinforced
by the ignorance about foreign countires which in turn helped
to produce contempt for foreigners. As with most of these group
thought and behaviour patterns, a circle was established and the
pattern became more and more rigid until finally it would take
a catastrophe to break it. Orwell thought the catastrophe had
come in 1940 but it wasn't catastrophic enough. Yet it seems
likely to have weakened the pattern.

The other 'abiding characteristic' of the English that a new-
comer would notice is the inability to think logically. Orwell
always linked this with their lack of artistic gifts, which on the
face of it seems to be a contradictory quality. It is best to let him
speak in his own words.

'Here are a couple of generalisation about England that would
be accepted by almost all observers. One is that the English are
not gifted artistically. They are not as musical as the Germans and
Italians, painting and sculpture have never flourished in England
as they have in France. Another is that, as Europeans go, the
English are not intellectual. They have a horror of abstract
thought, they feel no need for any philosophy or systematic
"world-view". Nor is this because they are "practical". as they
are so fond of claiming for themselves. One has only to look at
their methods of town-planning and water-supply, their obstinate
clinging to everything that is out of date and a nuisance, a
spelling system that defies analysis and a system of weights and
measures that is intelligible only to the compilers of arithmetic
books, to see how little they care about mere efficiency. But they

1 Michael Arlen, writing about the world of 1987 in *Man's Mortality* (1933),
dismissed Hitler as 'part of a tradition of abject "leadership" to which the world
had grown accustomed'. Stalin and Mussolini, on the other hand, were 'intelligent autocrats' who were never overthrown.

have a certain power of acting without taking thought. Their world-famed hypocrisy—their double-faced attitude towards the Empire, for instance—is bound up with this. Also, in moments of supreme crisis the whole nation can suddenly draw together and act upon a species of instinct, really a code of conduct which is understood by almost everyone, though never formulated. The phrase that Hitler coined for the Germans, "a sleep-walking people", would have been better applied to the English.' (*The Lion and the Unicorn.*)

He then draws attention to their love of flowers (which he claims has nothing to do with aesthetic feeling) and their addiction to hobbies. English life is intensely *private*—even their communal activities (pubs, football, the fireside) are not official. This is coming to an end but the English impulse is against co-ordination. It may well be asked, considering how many qualities the English are supposed to lack, what qualities they can possibly possess. They are not artistic, they distrust emotion, and yet they are not logical. Although he never used the word, Orwell appeared to agree with many other commentators that English thought and action derive from an empirical attitude, guided by instinct. Their hatred of formalism leads them to proceed by trial and error until they find a satisfactory *modus vivendi*. When that is done they are not worried by untied ends or a lack of co-ordination that in their view is purely superficial and unimportant. Again, it may seem strange that a people that distrusts emotion so strongly in its daily life should have produced so much first-rate poetry. But I think the production of poetry is compensation for the social inhibition. The formal approach necessary to art is only partly emotive. In fact, the major difference between 'art' and 'poetry', in my view, is that the formal element is dominant in the one and the emotive in the other. The English do not possess a formalising instinct to any high degree but are necessarily as emotionally-centred as any other race. It is the repression of emotion in everyday life that has led to its canalisation into poetry. The English are not proud of their poets but perhaps instinctively realise that they perform a necessary service.

Distrust of the emotions and dislike of poetry are both expressions of the English rejection of the exceptional. They have been called a middle-class people, 'a nation of shopkeepers', and they have made a cult of the ordinary. A mythical 'man-in-the street' has been enthroned and made the arbiter of taste and morals. The Englishman has an instinctive horror of 'line-shooting', 'flannel' and 'bullshit', all synonyms for boasting or display. (This used to be relaxed when the Englishman considered himself in relation to 'lesser breeds', which was part of his national myth, but even this attitude has been weakened in recent years.) But once again this is a quality which has had valuable political results. The Englishman does not like to hear anyone express himself in exceptional language and at the same time he is repelled by flamboyant behaviour. Consequently he has never fallen victim to the superman who will realise the national aspirations in his own person. England's one dictator was a monument of stolidity in his relations with the public, whatever unusual qualities he hid behind the exterior. In *The English People* Orwell noted that one of the basic folk-tales of the English-speaking peoples is Jack the Giant-killer—the little man against the big man. The English took Mickey Mouse, Popeye the Sailorman and Charlie Chaplin to their hearts. Chaplin's films were banned in Germany as soon as Hitler came to power, he was attacked by Fascist writers in England, and he has now lost the allegiance of the American people. But there is a tendency in England, not merely to attack the bully, but also to support the weaker side merely because it is weaker. Hence the admiration for a 'good loser' and the easy forgiveness of failures, either in sport, politics or war. (The English have an almost sentimental loyalty to their heavyweight boxers. Bruce Woodcock once threw away an important fight because he didn't have the heart to go in and 'kill' in the approved American style.) The campaign in Greece during the last war was typical. Before it was undertaken everyone knew it would fail and was militarily futile, but the gesture was supported by all.

But Orwell thought he could detect a change in the traditional English attitude towards power. He traced it in the growing popularity of a certain type of crime and thriller story and examined this trend in 'Raffles and Miss Blandish' (*Critical Essays*). The old novel of this type, the Sherlock Holmes, John Thorndyke and Max Carrados stories, for instance, had a gentlemanly tone about them that is completely lacking in the

new kind. The main impression they left behind was one of
boyishness. They belonged to a time when people had standards,
though they were often foolish standards. They were set in a
civilised society, where even the worst acknowledged certain
tabus and prohibitions. The key-phrase was 'not done'. Neither
the bully, nor the power of the bully, won any admiration. It is
very significant that the Raffles stories, written from the angle
of the criminal, were much less anti-social than most modern
stories written from the angle of the detective. There is an
entirely new attitude to crime. Orwell says that in James Hadley Chase's *He Won't Need It Now* the distinction between crime
and crime-prevention practically disappears. This is a new
departure for it used to be widely accepted as a literary convention that crime doesn't pay and that virtue always triumphs in
the last chapter. This is part of the American legacy. Apart
from its dilution of the traditional English attitude towards
crime, brute force and the law, Orwell believed it had a wider
significance as an indication of the growing acceptance of
power-worship. In the *New English Weekly* for 23 April, 1936,
he quoted from an American novel (an exuberant account of a
beating-up) and then commented:

'This kind of disgusting rubbish (hailed as "genius" when it
comes in a slightly more refined form from Hemingway) is growing
commoner and commoner. Some of the threepenny "Yank Mags"
which you buy at Woolworth's now consist of nothing else.
Please notice the sinister change that has come over an important
sub-department of English fiction. There was, God knows,
enough physical brutality in the novels of Fielding, Meredith,
Charles Reade, etc., but

'our masters then
Were still, at least, our countrymen.'

'In the old-style English novel you knocked your man down
and then chivalrously waited for him to get up before knocking
him down again; in the modern American version he is no sooner
down than you take the opportunity of jumping on his face.'

The convention is American, but it was gaining popularity in
England and there were already some very successful and skilful
British imitators.

Orwell does not claim that admiration for power was completely absent from the English make-up before the American
pulp invasion. He refers to Edgar Wallace, for instance, in

whom he detects 'a fearful intellectual sadism'. But Wallace's bully-worship found expression in his admiration of the police —reprehensible, perhaps (particularly in the case of Wallace's police, who behave much more brutally than British police do in real life), but at least it is on the side of the law. Moreover his sadism is unconscious and is not overtly sexual—he doesn't lick his lips over dismemberment and rape. 'The British public tolerates a harsh criminal law', Orwell writes, 'and gets a kick out of monstrously unfair murder trials: but still that is better, on any account, than tolerating or admiring crime.' The difference between Wallace and Raffles on the one hand and Hadley Chase on the other is that the former are still governed by the concept of 'not done' while the latter will admit anything so long as it leads to power. 'Chase is a worse symptom than Wallace, to the extent that all-in wrestling is worse than boxing, or Fascism is worse than capitalist democracy.'

The net effect is that the basic Western myth is being changed from Jack the Giant-killer to Jack the Dwarf-killer. This attitude had been inherent in Carlyle and is today endemic in those intellectuals who bow down to Soviet Russia. Orwell said it was correct to label a book such as *No Orchids For Miss Blandish* as 'pure Fascism' although it had no obvious connection with politics or social and economic problems, because it translated the horrors of totalitarian methods into a simple story about individuals. People who could accept characters like Slim and Fenner would find no difficulty in coming to terms with a Gestapo or G.P.U. People worship power in the form in which they are able to understand it. A twelve-year-old boy worships Jack Dempsey. An adolescent in the Glasgow slums worships Al Capone. An aspiring pupil at a business college worships Lord Nuffield. A *New Statesman* reader worships Stalin. (This essay was written in 1944.) There is a difference in intellectual maturity but none in moral outlook.

All the same, it is only a minority who have been affected in this way, although there is always the possibility that a minority may become a majority—and in this case the trend is not encouraging. But when Orwell wrote *The English People* (1947) he could still say that the English common people had lagged behind their century in their attitude to power. They had failed to catch up with power politics, 'realism', *sacro egoismo* and the doctrine that the end justifies the means. The English are not good haters, their memory is very short, their patriotism is largely unconscious, they have no love of military glory and not much admiration for great men. 'They have the virtues and the vices of an old-fashioned people.'

Let us now turn to another subject, the famed Puritanism of the English. I think it can be connected with their distrust of artists and poets and their lack of power-worship through their dislike of flamboyance and arrogance. Puritanism is partly the art of reducing life to a dead level. It rejects passion (except when it becomes a passion in itself) and it imposes a moral code which makes natural sensual enjoyment furtive and inhibits the free play of certain healthy emotions. Orwell in fact believed that Puritanism had been foisted on to the British working class. There is considerable evidence for this. I have read a report written by a mediaeval papal nuncio complaining about the levity and rather coarse high spirits of the English people. 'Merrie England' was apparently not a myth. Yet if this is true it is an example of one of the most remarkable changes in 'human nature' enforced from the outside to be found in history. Orwell says that it is universally agreed that the working classes are far more moral than the upper classes but the idea that sexuality is wicked in itself has no popular basis. Music-hall jokes, comic postcards and soldiers' songs are sufficient evidence to the contrary. The practical disappearance of drunkenness is due less to temperance reform than to the rivalry of other forms of amusement. Most forms of gambling are illegal according to the letter of the law, but they all happen on an enormous scale. 'The motto of the English people might be the chorus of Marie Lloyd's song, "A little of what you fancy does you good". They are not vicious, not even lazy, but they will have their bit of fun, whatever the higher-ups may say.' So perhaps 'human nature' has changed less than appears. Emotionally the English have lived under siege conditions for the last three hundred years, with occasional sallies beyond the ramparts.

Yet there is the pronounced English primness which I have already referred to, a quality that has been seared into the English soul over the generations. One of its manifestations really brought it home to Orwell that he was back in England after he had left the Paris hotels. He went into a coffee shop on Tower Hill, a little stuffy room with high-backed pews, the day's menu written on a mirror with a piece of soap and a girl of fourteen handling the dishes.

> 'On the wall beside my pew was a notice saying "Pocketing the sugar not allowed", and beneath it some poetic customer had written:
>   "He that takes away the sugar,
>   Shall be called a dirty ———",
> but someone else had been at pains to scratch out the last word. This was England.'

It is difficult to reconcile the genuine political freedom that England enjoys with the petty prohibitions that hem in normal movements and enjoyments. The explanation is that political freedom has very little to do with pleasure. Pleasure is a vice, judging by a host of official enactments and bye-laws, the spirit of which is so acceptable to many English people that they reinforce them with their own little regulations. Orwell pointed out that England *ought* to be able to attract tourists: it has much beautiful scenery, an equable climate, innumerable attractive villages and mediaeval churches, good beer and foodstuffs of excellent natural taste. If you could walk where you chose instead of being fenced in by barbed wire and 'Trespassers will be prosecuted' boards, if speculative builders had not been allowed to ruin every pleasant view within ten miles of a big town, if you could get a drink when you wanted it at a normal price, if an eatable meal at a country inn were a normal experience, and if Sunday were not artificially made into a day of misery, foreign visitors might be expected to come. But if these things were true England would no longer be England and it would probably be necessary to find some other way of acquiring foreign currency more in accord with the national character. But propaganda may be able to persuade the foreigner to accept the national hardships in a truly British manner—it can manage most things.

The English rejection of hatred and illegality has helped to produce a civilisation that, for all its puritanical and killjoy elements, is attractively gentle. Compared with other societies

it is remarkably stable: marriage is still considered to be indis-
soluble (despite the growing ease of divorce procedure) and
family loyalty is taken for granted (totalitarian societies always
put the weakening of family loyalty in the front line of their
policies). Its literature is still free of what Orwell called the
'concentration camp' element. The special world created by
secret police forces, censorship of opinion, torture and frame-
up trials, is known about and disapproved of but has made
little emotional impact. Here we see insularity and native
mildness working together. It seems scarcely worth mentioning
(because so generally true) that most Englishmen believe a
Communist and an Anarchist aɩe the same—until we recognise
that in most of Europe the distinction is universally known and
understood. This seemed to exasperate Orwell, though it is
perfectly easy to understand. But on the whole opinion is less
important in England than style. It doesn't matter much whether
a man is a Tory or a Socialist, but the way in which he conducts
himself in his political career is held to be of the utmost importance. This may help to explain the often slight differences
between the major parties, despite their apparently opposed
labels and policies. Everyone likes Mr Eden because he does
everything in style. Mr Churchill is rarely happier than when
he can share a joke with Mr Morrison, and from time to time
the two men shyly compliment each other. The headline differences between nationalisation and private enterprise tend to
lose their sharpness and voters tend to support a man for what
he is and the way he behaves rather than for what he believes.

Orwell made very few references to the English love of sport,
but in 'Raffles and Miss Blandish' he did explain the importance
of cricket in English society. Again, it is a matter of style.
Raffles was a particularly good cricketer, wore the I Zingari
blazer (like Dennis Tripod) and was as cunning a slow bowler
as he was a burglar. Orwell comments:

> 'Cricket is not in reality a very popular game in England—it is
> nowhere so popular as football, for instance—but it gives expres-
> sion to a well-marked trait in the English character, the tendency
> to value "form" or "style" more highly than success. In the eyes
> of any true cricket-lover it is possible for an innings of ten runs
> to be "better" (i.e., more elegant) than an innings of a hundred
> runs: cricket is also one of the very few games in which the

amateur can excel the professional. It is a game full of forlorn hopes and sudden dramatic changes of fortune, and its rules are so defined that their interpretation is partly an ethical business. When Larwood, for instance, practised body-line bowling in Australia he was not actually breaking any rule: he was merely doing something that was "not cricket". Since cricket takes up a lot of time and is rather an expensive game to play, it is predominantly an upper-class game, but for the whole nation it is bound up with such concepts as "good form", "playing the game", etc., and it has declined in popularity just as the tradition of "don't hit a man when he's down" has declined. It is not a twentieth-century game and nearly all modern-minded people dislike it. The Nazis, for instance, were at pains to discourage cricket, which had gained a certain footing in Germany before and after the last war.'

Orwell believed that even the English class system, which he deprecated so severely, contained a kind of idealism, a feeling that style and tradition are more important than money. Not even the snobbishness could be completely divorced from the idealism. The tendency to give the upper classes more than their due is mixed up with a respect for good manners and something vaguely describable as culture. In the South of England he thought it unquestionable that most working-class people wished to resemble the upper classes in manners and habits as much as possible. Snobbishness about local accent is dying out in the South and there is a growing tendency to preserve all aitches intact—although there was a time when, if left to its natural development, the English language would probably have discarded its aitches as the French did long since. The repression of emotion, the emphasis on style and the native mildness that is the product of security and strong (but not oppressive) government have combined to produce the special contribution of the English to human society: their habit of *not killing one another*. Once a state of war exists the English will kill other people gladly, but they have been averse to killing each other for many generations. That is why Orwell believed that if only they would take the trouble to make their own democracy work they could become the political leaders of Western Europe and probably of some other parts of the world as well. They would provide the much-needed alternative to Russian authoritarianism on the one hand and American materialism on the other.

After all the criticism, Orwell's dominant feeling about his country was that it was a good place to live in. The rest of this chapter will largely be in praise of England, as seen through Orwell's writings. Flory used to think nostalgically of England as the land of the free, for in Burma the Englishman was as much a prisoner as the Burmese. In England one was not condemned for ever to dance the *danse du pukka sahib* for the edification of the lower races—though there was the *danse du bourgeois* as an alternative. In Spain Orwell could not get used to the idea that he might be arrested, for he was not conscious of having done anything wrong. 'I had the ineradicable English belief that "they" cannot arrest you unless you have broken the law.' England was certainly undemocratic in its social structure but it was democratic in its free speech.

> 'If democracy means popular rule, it is absurd to call Britain democratic. It is a plutocracy haunted by the ghost of a caste system. But if democracy means a society in which you can safely go into the nearest pub and utter your true opinion of the government, then Britain is democratic. In any country two things are of fundamental importance, its economic structure and its history.' ('Tapping the Wheels', *Observer*, 16 January, 1944.)

And although England would not be able to resist change he was convinced she would keep her peculiar characteristics. He believed that the war would wipe out class privilege, and he was wrong. Not even the second World War was strong enough to break the tradition. The new red brick cities of Greater London horrified traditionalists, but Orwell called them merely the rash that accompanied change. The intellectuals who hoped to see England Russianised or Germanised would be disappointed, and in this he was right. The gentleness, the hypocrisy, the thoughtlessness and the reverence for law and the hatred of uniforms would remain, along with the suet puddings and the misty skies. Only a great disaster, such as prolonged subjugation by a foreign enemy, can destroy a national culture. 'The Stock Exchange will be pulled down, the horse plough will give way to the tractor, the country houses will be turned into children's holiday camps, the Eton and Harrow match will be forgotten, but England will still be England, an everlasting animal stretching into the future and the past, and, like all

living things, having the power to change out of all recognition
and yet remain the same.' (*The Lion and the Unicorn.*)

He was not blind to things on the other side of the account,
for instance, what he called the physical degeneracy of the
English. Standing in Trafalgar Square while George V's body
passed through London on its way to Westminster, he was
appalled by the appearance of the people around him. They
were not working-class people for the most part but the shop-
keeper-commercial-traveller type with a sprinkling of the well-
to-do. Everywhere he saw puny limbs and sickly faces, hardly a
well-built man or a decent-looking woman, and not a fresh
complexion anywhere. When the men took off their hats a
friend remarked to him, 'The only touch of colour anywhere
was the bald heads'. The war had done its work in selecting the
best specimens for slaughter, but the real agent had been
industrialism—not so much the living in towns but the modern
industrial technique which provided cheap substitutes for
everything of value. The English palate had learnt to reject
good food automatically. Several pages in *Coming Up For Air* are
devoted to the defilement of England: fish pools drained of their
water and filled up with tin cans, fake Tudor houses with curly
roofs and buttresses that buttress nothing, rock-gardens with
concrete bird-baths and red plaster elves, all existing smugly
behind sentimental names like Pixy Glen and Mon Repos.

Sir Richard Rees said that Orwell's hatred of imperialism
came out of a permanent and real love of England, not out of
a sentimentalising and transitory infatuation for India. His
Englishness was demonstrated in his first book, *Down and Out
in Paris and London*, which should be read and not read about.
It has the harsh bite of actual experience and it illuminates his
innate English qualities. The most celebrated part of the book
is the Paris section, but this is largely because of the cultured
English reader's predilection for all things French—they are
more chic, more stylish, more significant in a rather mystical
way. (Koestler ranked it as a disease which he called French
'flu.) This section is keenly felt and admirably described, yet the
sweat and smells of the Parisian hotel kitchens are not quite as
sensuously realised as the squalor and ugliness of the English
spikes. Orwell had spent most of his adult life out of England

yet his Englishness could immediately apprehend and trans-
cribe the English atmosphere. Paris was known and known
intimately, yet it still remained alien. And it is possible to draw
a parallel with his attitude to imperialism, which derived from
what he knew and felt (and the shame that came out of it) and
not from the glamorisation of a culture he could only know
from the outside.

The name he chose for the chief character of *1984*, Winston
Smith, combines the two elements which he felt characterised
the English people: the common decency of the common man
and the stolid traditionalism of an exceptional man whom
Orwell, I am convinced, came to admire more and more, despite differences of opinion, simply because he was so representative. Churchill is admired by most Englishmen because he
refuses to give up, and because he has the simple patriotic virtue
of putting his country before himself or even his class. And this
was exactly the virtue that Orwell admired and which he himself possessed to a high degree. It was all the more surprising to
find this quality in a Left-wing intellectual. It explains his
occasional outbursts of bad temper during the war when writing
about pacifists—for once, he flung his reason and his tolerance
to the winds because he was dealing with people who actually
proposed to surrender England to the enemy. In his reply to
Obadiah Hornbooke ('As One Non-Combatant to Another')
he pointed out that while it needed courage to 'object' in 1917
it was almost expected in certain circles in 1940.

> 'At times it's almost a more dangerous deed
> *Not* to object; I know, for I've been bitten.
> I wrote in nineteen-forty that at need
> I'd fight to keep the Nazis out of Britain;
> And Christ! how shocked the pinks were! Two years later
> I hadn't lived it down; one had the effrontery
> To write three pages calling me a "traitor",
> So black a crime it is to love one's country.
> Yet where's the pink that would have thought it odd of me
> To write a shelf of books in praise of sodomy?'

Orwell will probably be remembered as a Patriot of the Left,
an unfamiliar animal in these days though one with a noble
tradition. In the eighteenth century the patriots were the progressives, the men who wished to work for their country and

not for a privileged group. Orwell was another of these, but at a time when the word 'patriot' usually indicated a flag-wagging blockhead who thought the 'lower orders' should be kept in their places. Orwell believed in ordinary people and he also believed that the true traditions of the country were in their keeping and not in that of the rich. He was also prepared to trust the common people, which few others, of whatever political persuasion, were willing to do. The last sentence of *The Lion and the Unicorn* reads, 'I believe in England, and I believe that we shall go forward'.

BOOKS BY GEORGE ORWELL

(C.E. means Collected Edition. These volumes are easy to obtain but the others require hunting. Some of then are even difficult to obtain through libraries.)

Down and Out in Paris and London, 1933. Autobiography, C.E. Orwell samples low life for the first time.

Burmese Days, 1934. Novel, C.E. The early stages in a changing society in Imperial Burma.

A Clergyman's Daughter, 1935. Novel. Low life again, plus loss of faith.

Keep the Aspidistra Flying, 1936. Novel. The power of money.

The Road to Wigan Pier, 1937. An examination of poverty, developing into an attack on the intelligentsia.

Homage to Catalonia, 1938. C.E. Orwell goes to the Spanish War and leaves it, a wanted man.

Coming Up For Air, 1939. Novel, C.E. An ordinary man makes mental preparation for the coming war.

Inside the Whale, 1940. Essays, all reprinted later in other collections.

The Lion and the Unicorn, 1941. Orwell's first diagnosis of English society and people.

Animal Farm, 1945. C.E. The famous parody of the Russian Revolution and its developments.

Critical Essays, 1946. C.E. Contains 'Charles Dickens', 'Boys' Weeklies' and 'Raffles and Miss Blandish'.

The English People, 1947. Orwell's second excursus into the Sociology of the English. (Britain in Pictures edition.)

Nineteen-Eighty Four, 1949. Novel, C.E. Vision of the future.

Shooting an Elephant, 1950. Essays, C.E. Contains 'Politics *v.* Literature', 'Politics and the English Language' and 'The Prevention of Literature'.

Such, Such Were the Joys, 1953. The title essay is about Orwell's schooldays. Also includes 'Why I Write', 'Writers and Leviathan', 'Notes on Nationalism'. Published in England, 1953, as *England, your England.*

M